Special Issues
in Women's Health

The American College of
Obstetricians and Gynecologists

Women's Health Care Physicians

409 12th Street, SW
PO Box 96920
Washington, DC 20090-6920

The information in *Special Issues in Women's Health* should not be viewed as a body of rigid rules. The guidelines are general and are intended to be adapted to many different situations, taking into account the needs and resources particular to the locality, the institution, or the type of practice. Variations and innovations that improve the quality of patient care are to be encouraged rather than restricted.

Current Procedural Terminology (CPT) is copyright 2004 American Medical Association. All Rights Reserved. No fees schedules, basic units, relative values, or related listings are included in CPT. The AMA assumes no liability for the data contained herein. Applicable FARS/DFARS restrictions apply to government use. CPT® is a trademark of the American Medical Association.

Library of Congress Cataloging-in-Publication Data

Special issues in women's health.
        p. ; cm.
    Includes bibliographical references and index.
    ISBN 1-932328-06-8
    1. Women—Health and hygiene. 2. Women's health services.
    [DNLM: 1. Women's Health. 2. Women's Health Services. WA 309 S741 2005] I.
American College of Obstetricians and Gynecologists.

    RA564.85.S75 2005
    362.1'082—dc22

                           2005002111

    Copies of *Special Issues in Women's Health* can be ordered through the ACOG Distribution Center by calling toll free 800-762-2264. Orders also can be placed from the ACOG web site at www.acog.org or sales.acog.org.

12345/98765

Contents

Preface

The American College of Obstetricians and Gynecologists (ACOG) has a strong commitment to addressing the issues of health care for underserved women. ACOG policy calls
for quality health care appropriate to every woman's needs throughout her life and for
ensuring that a full array of clinical services are available to women without costly delays
or the imposition of geographic, financial, attitudinal, or legal barriers (see Appendix A).
Special Issues in Women's Health highlights ways to improve health care for all women,
while focusing on specific populations and issues. Underserved women, including incarcerated women, women with disabilities, lesbians and bisexual women, and transgendered individuals, lack access to quality health care by virtue of barriers created by
poverty, cultural differences, race and ethnicity, geography, and other factors contributing
to health care disparities. Lack of adequate health insurance, psychosocial factors,
providers' lack of familiarity with specific health issues, bias or prejudice, and patients'
inability to navigate the health care system all can impede access to appropriate services.

Certain health issues, such as domestic violence, sexual assault, and substance abuse,
do not receive the attention they merit. Often, physicians are inadequately trained, have
insufficient support, are constrained for time, fear offending the client, or feel powerless
in addressing these problems. This lack of attention also may result from a lack of
research about these issues as they affect women. When data are lacking, neither patients
nor health care providers will understand the significance or prevalence of these issues
that greatly affect the lives of women.

The College and its membership are committed to improving the health status of
women, particularly those whose health care needs are not fully met by the health care
system or health care providers. For several decades, ACOG has conducted organized
activities in the area of health care for underserved women and produced policy
statements, committee opinions, educational bulletins, and other reports on issues
of particular importance to this population.

This book is designed to equip Fellows and engage a greater number of them in
expanding and extending those services to patients in need. It contains new information
on patient communication, health care for women with mental disabilities, primary care
for lesbians and bisexual women, health care for transgendered individuals, and health
care for incarcerated women. It also includes documents previously issued by the ACOG
Committee on Health Care for Underserved Women as of December 31, 2002, which have

been updated or expanded to reflect more recent data and findings. These materials have been compiled into one volume for ease of use and reference.

Previous separate Technical Bulletins (TB), Educational Bulletins (EB), and Committee Opinions (CO) encompassed in this volume are listed as follows:

Access to Health Care for Women with Physical Disabilities (CO No. 202, June 1998)

Adolescent Victims of Sexual Assault (EB 252, October 1998)

Adult Manifestations of Childhood Sexual Abuse (EB 259, July 2000)

Cultural Competency in Health Care (CO No. 201, March 1998)

Domestic Violence (EB 257, December 1999)

Mandatory Reporting of Domestic Violence (CO No. 200, March 1998)

Pediatric Gynecologic Disorders (TB 201, January 1995)

Sexual Assault (EB 242, November 2000)

Smoking and Women's Health (EB 240, September 2000)

Substance Abuse (TB 194, July 1994)

ACOG Committee on Health Care for Underserved Women

Acknowledgments

Special Issues in Women's Health was developed by the American College of Obstetricians and Gynecologists (ACOG) Committee on Health Care for Underserved Women. Past and present committee members who have contributed to the development of this document include: Francisco Arredondo, MD, MPH; Kurt Barnhart, MD, MSCE; Gene Burkett, MD; Ronald A. Chez, MD; Raymond L. Cox Jr, MD; Bruce B. Ettinger, MD, MPH; Regina D. Gomez, MD; Elwyn Grimes, MD; William H.J. Haffner, MD; Richard Hollis, MD; Iffath A. Hoskins, MD; Douglas H. Kirkpatrick, MD; Ann M. Koontz, DrPH, CNM; Kelli M. Miller, MD; Nawal M. Nour, MD, MPH; John T. Queenan, MD; Carol W. Saffold, MD; Deborah Smith, MD; Kirsten M. Smith, MD; JoAnn M. Thierry, MS, MSW; Josephine Von Herzen, MD; Gael Wager, MD, MBA; Heather Watts, MD; and Alan Waxman, MD, MPH.

Special thanks are given to the following contributors to specific sections:

Patient Communication
Carol Saffold, MD

Cultural Competency, Sensitivity, and Awareness in the Delivery of Health Care
Francisco Arredondo, MD, MPH
Bruce Ettinger, MD, MPH

General Management of Pediatric Gynecology Patients
Past members of the ACOG Committee on Adolescent Health Care, especially Abbey B. Berenson, MD; Ann J. Davis, MD; and S. Paige Hertweck, MD

Access to Reproductive Health Care for Women With Disabilities
Melvin Bayly, Jr, MD
Carol Gill, PhD
Cassing Hammond, MD
Kristi Kirschner, MD
Ellen Murphy, MD
Elisabeth H. Quint, MD
Judy Panko Reis, MA, MS
JoAnn Thierry, PhD

Primary Care of Lesbians and Bisexual Women in Obstetric and Gynecologic Practice
Katherine A. O'Hanlan, MD
Gael P. Wager, MD, MBA

Health Care for Transgendered Individuals
Bruce Ettinger, MD, MPH
Marshall Forstein, MD
Katherine A. O'Hanlan, MD

Health and Health Care of Incarcerated Adult and Adolescent Females
Linda Bresolin, PhD
Ronald Chez, MD
Kimberly Switlick

Substance Use: Obstetric and Gynecologic Implications
Gene Burkett, MD
Joanne A. Byars
Cynthia Chazotte, MD
Kimberly Frost-Pineda, MPH
Mark S. Gold, MD
Amanda E. Pusey

Smoking and Women's Health
Carol W. Saffold, MD

Intimate Partner Violence and Domestic Violence
Bruce Ettinger, MD, MPH

Sexual Assault
Deborah Smith, MD

The ACOG Committee on Health Care for Underserved Women is grateful for the contribution and guidance provided by Lisa Smith Goldstein, MS, Director, Health Care for Underserved Women, without whose research, writing, and editing, the development of this document would not have been possible. Finally, the Committee on Health Care for Underserved Women wishes to thank the following current or former members of ACOG staff: Luella Klein, MD; Janet Chapin, RN, MPH; Deborah Horan, MSW; Jeanne Mahoney; Wendy Root, MPH; and interns Noriko Cruz, Samata Kodolikar, Elyse Pegler, and Erum Siddiqui.

For additional information about the Committee on Health Care for Underserved Women, please contact Lisa Smith Goldstein, MS, Director, Health Care for Underserved Women, ACOG, PO Box 96920, Washington, DC 20090-6920; Tel: (202) 863-2497; e-mail: underserved@acog.org.

Improving Access to Quality Health Care for Women

Patient Communication

Key Points

- In medicine, the quality of information transfer, understanding, and the development of rapport are critical in an effective physician–patient relationship and ongoing patient health and psychosocial status.

- Effective communication between physicians and their patients facilitates a more complete understanding of health and illness and ultimately affects the outcome of disease and patient encounters. Furthermore, a partnership model significantly decreases the likelihood of medical liability litigation.

- Communication with patients that indicates sensitivity and empathy is particularly important in obstetrics and gynecology, where patients may be more reluctant to discuss problems related to sexuality and intimacy.

- Patients with special issues or risk factors often do not have their needs addressed because of communication barriers.

- A physician who encourages open communication often will obtain more complete information that enables an accurate diagnosis and appropriate counseling.

- Many reviews of physician communication show a striking absence of efforts to engage in discussions of treatment options. These reviews also reveal both a failure to consider differing cultural backgrounds and minimal attempts to communicate at the level of the patient's knowledge.

- The following four qualities can be important in "caring communication skills": 1) comfort, 2) acceptance, 3) responsiveness, and 4) empathy. Often practitioners are not aware that their own cultural and social backgrounds affect the way they communicate. Regardless of the discordance between a patient's and practitioner's backgrounds and cultural beliefs, increased sensitivity by providers to patients' behaviors, feelings, and attitudes can result in increased patient and provider satisfaction.

Responsiveness and empathy refer to the quality of reacting to indirect messages expressed by a patient.

- Perhaps the greatest contemporary challenge in implementing the principles of effective communication lies in the current environment that demands increasing physician productivity and less time with each patient. Improving communication in the physician–patient relationship will help, as will using more nonphysician health care providers and computer-based interactive health communication.

The importance of effective communication is recognized universally in all human relationships. Difficulty with expression of ideas and emotions often results in functional problems in families and friendships, in government, and corporations. In medicine, the quality of information transfer, understanding, and the development of rapport are critical in an effective physician–patient relationship and ongoing patient health and psychosocial status. As such, the Accreditation Council for Graduate Medical Education identified interpersonal and communication skills as one of the six areas in which physicians need to demonstrate competence (1).

The benefits of skilled, successful communication in medicine are many. First, a physician who encourages open communication often will obtain more complete information, which enables an accurate diagnosis and appropriate counseling. Combining this diagnosis with an understanding of the patient's concerns, level of education, and culture allows for the development of an individualized treatment plan. This, in turn, leads to improved patient adherence and enhancement of long-term health (2) (Box 1). In addition, patients show greater satisfaction with their care. Many studies have demonstrated that this "partnership" model significantly decreases the likelihood of medical liability litigation (3).

Communication with patients that indicates sensitivity and empathy is particularly important in obstetrics and gynecology, where patients may be more reluctant to discuss problems related to sexuality and intimacy. Survivors of sexual abuse and sexual assault may be particularly difficult to assess and examine, and provision of their care may require special skills (see chapters on "Sexual Assault" and "Adult Manifestations of Childhood Sexual Abuse"). Regardless of their own and their patients' cultural backgrounds, sexual orientation, or lifestyles, practitioners must focus objectively on the medical or health promotion and maintenance issues presented by their patients (4, 5).

Box 1   Partnership Model of Health Care Communication

Understanding and appreciation of patient's beliefs, concerns, and level of education → development of an individualized treatment plan → improved adherence → better long-term health

---

Defining Communication: What Are the Issues?

Women patients often express emotional concerns related to relationships, gender roles, and interactions. A study of primary care encounters with women has shown that medical practitioners often marginalize social, cultural, and psychologic issues of great concern to patients (6). Interruptions of patient dialogue with forced return to technical issues interfere with complete expression.

Many reviews of physician communication show a striking absence of efforts to engage in discussion of treatment options. These reviews also reveal both a failure to consider differing cultural backgrounds (7) and minimal attempts to communicate at the level of the patient's knowledge. Also absent are expressions of empathy and understanding.

A review of communication patterns in underserved populations shows significant contextual barriers to physician–patient interaction (8). Physicians commonly hold stereotypes about poor and minority patients that may undermine constructive communication. A meta-analysis illustrated that indigent and minority patients receive less information about their conditions; less positive, reinforcing talk; and less communication overall than do patients of higher socioeconomic status (9).

In addition, patients with special issues or risk factors often do not have their needs addressed because of communication barriers. In a study of adolescents, most individuals surveyed report not receiving information on sex and risk prevention from their physicians (10). This lack of information and interaction may be attributed to health care providers' reluctance to discuss such matters with their patients. Similarly, women approaching menopause express dissatisfaction about discussions of sexuality issues.

Developing Effective Communication

The following four qualities can be important in "caring communication skills:" 1) comfort, 2) acceptance, 3) responsiveness, and 4) empathy (3). Examples of clinical situations in which these qualities are applied are in Table 1. Comfort refers to, in this case, the physician's ability to deal with difficult topics without

Table 1. Examples of Competent Communication

Clinical Presentation	Competent Communication Example
A physician enters the examination room and greets a long-term patient, noticing that she appears tearful. On further questioning, she states, "I'm just having a bad day." The physician completes the routine history and examination without further discussion of her affect.	The physician shakes the patient's hand, stating, "I'm sorry you're having a hard time; perhaps it will help to talk about it." Open-ended questions follow, including assessment of energy level, sleeping behavior, appetite, and mood. The provider is thus able to detect multiple signs of depression and to offer or refer her for treatment.
An adolescent girl comes to you for a new patient appointment, accompanied by her mother. Most of the history information is delivered by the parent, who states that the 14-year-old has "discharge and bad cramps." The mother insists on remaining in the examination room, stating that her daughter is "shy" and afraid of being examined. After a tense and suboptimal examination, both patient and mother leave the office visibly upset.	Following an extended general history from both mother and daughter, the physician requests that the mother allow private time for discussion with her daughter. The physician explains the importance of confidentiality in adolescent health care and reassures the mother that the nurse will be present to help calm her daughter if a pelvic examination is necessary. After explaining to the girl that all staff in the office will protect the privacy of the physician–patient relationship, she reveals that she has been sexually active for several months with limited protection. The physician explains what to expect in the examination and provides written information on sexuality, sexually transmitted diseases (STDs), and contraception. The nurse then counsels the patient on STD protection and contraception and schedules a follow-up visit in a few days for examination, testing, and further counseling.
A 58-year old woman, widowed for many years, presents with vaginal discomfort. The patient provides limited information on her symptoms. Following an examination, demonstrating atrophic changes, the physician prescribes a local treatment.	After hearing the vague history, the physician states, "I know this can be difficult to talk about, but it is important to explore more details in order to help you feel better." After asking further questions related to the general medical history and the specific vulvovaginal symptom, the physician asks, "Have you developed a new relationship since your husband passed away?" The patient then reveals that she has attempted to resume sexual activity, unsuccessfully, because she is tense and afraid of pain. The physician is then able to explain how her body has changed in the decade since she was last sexually active and to suggest treatment options. A follow-up visit for further discussion is scheduled in several weeks.
A 50-year-old woman presents with a 6-month history of amenorrhea and hot flashes, which interfere with her sleep at night. Following an examination, which includes breasts, abdomen, and pelvis with Pap test, the physician advises her to schedule a mammogram. In addition, after a discussion of the balance of dis-ease risk and benefits, she is advised to begin short-term hormone therapy for symptom relief. She is advised to return	The physician probes beyond the presenting symptom to develop a more complete understanding of the patient's concerns about menopause by asking several open-ended questions such as: ■ "Are you taking any nonprescription drugs or using dietary supplements to treat your symptoms?" ■ "What have you learned about hormone therapy from reading, over the Internet, or from friends or relatives? Does this information agree with the information I have given you?" ■ "What steps have you taken in developing a personal wellness program?"

(continued)

Table 1. Examples of Competent Communication *(continued)*

Clinical Presentation	Competent Communication Example
in 6 months for follow-up and to call the office with any questions. The patient leaves the office feeling that her presenting symptoms were addressed but that her other concerns were not.	■ "Do you have other concerns about menopause that we have not yet covered?" The physician then answers questions that are raised and addresses diet, exercise, and role, if any, for dietary supplements for this patient. Also addressed are the importance of an overall health maintenance program, including recommended immunizations; medical risk screening, including hypertension, diabetes, thyroid dysfunction, and obesity; and cigarette smoking cessation, as appropriate. If time does not permit a thorough discussion at this visit, a point is made that these issues will be discussed further at a follow-up visit in 2–3 months.
A 68-year-old woman who is a long-standing patient fails to keep her appointment for her annual examination. The office nurse sends her a reminder to which the patient responds by telephone stating that she stopped taking hormone therapy last year because she does not need it any longer, she is too old for these examinations anyway, and has read that since her husband died 6 months ago she does not need a Pap test.	The physician contacts the patient directly and inquires about her health status in general and any gynecologic symptoms in particular. The physician acknowledges the patient's current status and then proceeds to explain that even considering all of these factors, her continued gynecologic evaluations are important in addressing her long-term health status. When she is further advised that these visits include counseling about steps that can be taken to encourage muscle strength and balance, skeletal bone health, cardiovascular fitness, cancer screening and risk reduction, and urinary and genital tract issues, including comfort with coitus, she expresses an understanding that there really is much more to her gynecologic visits than a Pap test. An appointment is made with the physician to establish a long-term, mutually agreed-upon gynecologic care and health maintenance plan.

displaying uneasiness. Specific skills include maintaining eye contact (when culturally appropriate), using appropriate wording, remaining nonjudgmental, and accepting the feelings and attitudes a patient brings to the interview without showing irritation or intolerance. Practitioners must always demonstrate patient respect. It is important to take the time to explore a patient's life and past relationships to discover the background for current behaviors and beliefs. It has been noted that "self-awareness is at the heart of professional competence" (3). Often practitioners are not aware that their own cultural and social backgrounds affect the way they communicate. Regardless of the discordance between a patient's and health care provider's background and cultural beliefs, increased sensitivity by health care providers to patients' behaviors, feelings, and attitudes can result in increased patient and health care provider satisfaction.

Responsiveness and empathy refer to the quality of reacting to indirect messages expressed by a patient. Recognizing when emotions are present but not directly expressed is important and can lead to an exploration of the patient's feelings. Empathy involves both cognitive and behavioral processes and responses. An accurate understanding is gained and then followed by effective communication of that understanding to the patient (11). Simple acknowledgement of a patient's emotions and needs facilitates open communication. A technique that encourages dialogue and helps to avoid misunderstanding is to restate a patient's concerns.

In a detailed study of patterns of speech in the medical interview, communication events were identified that enhance or prevent dialogue between physicians and patients (11). Particularly obstructive to effective communication is an "empathetic opportunity terminator." These are behaviors or statements by the practitioner that direct the interview away from emotion expressed by the patient. Physicians were observed to often allow emotions to pass without acknowledgement and focus instead on diagnostic assessment. It is, therefore, important for practitioners to identify and avoid behaviors and language that unknowingly limit personal expression.

In studies examining the influence of physician gender on communication techniques (6, 12–15), female physicians were observed to make greater use of participation, such as smiles, head-nods, and other forms of nonverbal encouragement. Regardless of the physician's gender, however, expression of empathy, demonstrating more warmth and attentiveness, using verbal facilitators, and making "partnership" statements enhance the physician–patient relationship. The integration of these behaviors, which have been shown to improve patient communication, into routine care is important (Box 2).

To enhance communication, physicians can show a positive, empathetic response to feelings expressed by patients. It is important to invite exploration and direct expression of attitudes and feelings. Use of open-ended questions, active listening, repetition of patient's statements, and positive nonverbal facilitators (smiling, head-nods, gesturing) may all assist in enhancing communication. In addition, consideration of the patient's level of education and medical knowledge, as well as her beliefs, is helpful when communicating and developing a treatment plan. Medical information should be presented in a fashion that is easily understood and tailored to the individual patient. It is helpful to request that patients repeat their understanding of key issues and to allow ample time for questions and discussion. A collaborative relationship, which involves patients as partners in the ongoing process of health maintenance, will foster greater adherance and patient satisfaction (16).

Perhaps the greatest contemporary challenge in implementing the principles of effective communication lies in the current environment that demands increasing physician productivity and less time with each patient. How can a physician expand the time spent with each patient and encourage individual expression while at the same time produce a greater volume of patient visits? The first answer to this challenge rests on improving communication in the physician–patient relationship. In addition, many practices have solved this dilemma by using more nonphysician health care providers and computer-based interactive health communication. If a strong physician–patient relationship is built, specific details of patient education may be communicated through other staff, written materials, and interactive computer programs.

References

1. Accreditation Council for Graduate Medical Education. General competencies. Chicago (IL): ACGME; 1999. Available at: http://www.acgme.org/outcome/comp/compFull.asp. Retrieved September 10, 2004.

2. Mechanic D. Public trust and initiatives for new health care partnerships. Milbank Q 1998;76:281–302.

3. Myerscough PR, Ford MJ. Talking with patients: keys to good communication. 3rd ed. Oxford: Oxford University Press; 1996.

4. Kripke CC, Vaias L. The importance of taking a sensitive sexual history. JAMA 1994;271:713.

5. Newman J. Managing cultural diversity: the art of communication. Radiol Technol 1998;69:231–42; quiz 243–6, 249.

6. Borges S, Waitzkin H. Women's narratives in primary care medical encounters. Women Health 1995;23:29–56.

7. Parrott R, Huff T, Kilgore M, Williams M. Peer discussion on training physicians to be competent communicators: support for a multiple discourse approach. South Med J 1997;90: 709–19.

8. Ventres W, Gordon P. Communication strategies in caring for the underserved. J Health Care Poor Underserved 1990;1:305–14.

9. Hall JA, Roter DL, Katz NR. Meta-analysis of correlates of provider behavior in medical encounters. Med Care 1988;26:657–75.

10. Schuster MA, Bell RM, Petersen LP, Kanouse DE. Communication between adolescents and physicians about sexual behavior and risk prevention. Arch Pediatr Adolesc Med 1996;150:906–13.

<hr />

Box 2   Components of Effective Physician Communication

- Accept patient's perspective
- Respond to patient's concerns
- Include both verbal and nonverbal communication (eg, head nodding, smiling)
- Be nonjudgmental
- Engage patient in discussion of treatment options
- Convey comfort in discussing sensitive topics
- Abandon stereotypes

11. Suchman AL, Markakis K, Beckman HB, Frankel R. A model of empathic communication in the medical interview. JAMA 1997;277:678–82.

12. Hall T, Lloyd C. Non-verbal communication in a health care setting. Br J Occup Ther 1990;53:383–6.

13. Roter D, Hall JA. Doctors talking with patients/patients talking with doctors: improving communication in medical visits. Westport (CT): Auburn House; 1992.

14. Hall JA, Roter DL. Patient gender and communication with physicians: results of a community-based study. Womens Health 1995;1:77–95.

15. van den Brink-Muinen A, Bensing JM, Kerssens JJ. Gender and communication style in general practice. Differences between women's health care and regular health care. Med Care 1998; 36:100–6.

16. Joos SK, Hickam DH, Gordon GH, Baker LH. Effects of a physician communication intervention on patient care outcomes. J Gen Intern Med 1996;11:147–55.

Resources

ACOG Resources

American College of Obstetricians and Gynecologists. Confidentiality in adolescent health care. In: Health care for adolescents. ACOG: Washington, DC; 2003. p. 25–35.

American College of Obstetricians and Gynecologists. Talking with teens. In: Tool kit for teen care. ACOG: Washington, DC; 2003.

Other Resources

The resources listed as follows are for information purposes only. Referral to these sources and web sites does not imply the endorsement of ACOG. This list is not meant to be comprehensive. The exclusion of a source or web site does not reflect the quality of that source or web site. Please note that web sites are subject to change without notice.

American Academy on Physician and Patient
1000 Executive Parkway, Suite 220
St. Louis, MO 63141
Tel: (314) 576-5333
Fax: (314) 576-7989
Web: www.physicianpatient.org

The American Academy on Physician and Patient explores how patient–physician communication functions as a diagnostic and treatment tool. The academy offers courses that use real and simulated patients.

Bayer Institute For Health Care Communication, Inc.
400 Morgan Lane
West Haven, CT 06516
Tel: 800-800-5907
Fax: (203) 812-5951
E-mail: bayer.institute@bayer.com
Web: www.bayerinstitute.org/index.htm

The mission of the Bayer Institute For Health Care Communication is to enhance the quality of health care by improving the communication between clinician and patient through three major activities: education, research, and advocacy. The institute stresses the concept that effective communication between clinician and patient is a necessity, not an option.

The Center for Health Care Strategies
PO Box 3469
Princeton, NJ 08543-3469
Tel: (609) 895-8101
Fax: (609) 895-9648
Web: www.chcs.org

Since 1995, the Center for Health Care Strategies has strived to continuously improve the quality of health and health related services for beneficiaries of publicly funded health care. It works with state officials, health plan leaders, and consumer organizations across the country to improve health services for low-income families and for people with severe illnesses and disabilities whose needs cross over from the routine to the highly specialized. It has developed a packet of fact sheets on health literacy for providers who are designing materials for consumers.

Center for Primary Care Research
Agency for Healthcare Research and Quality
6010 Executive Boulevard, Suite 201
Rockville, MD 20852
Tel: (301) 594-1357
E-mail: HBurstin@ahrq.gov
Web: www.ahcpr.gov/about/cpcr/

The Center for Primary Care Research (CPCR) has as its broadest vision to support and conduct research that will improve the access, effectiveness, and quality of primary health care services in the United States. Designated by Congress as "the principal source of funding for primary care practice research in the Department of Health and Human Services," CPCR also is a major source of information on primary care practice and is recognized internationally for the research they support and conduct.

The Foundation for Medical Excellence
Northwest Center for Physician–Patient Communication
One SW Columbia Street, Suite 800
Portland, OR 97258
Tel: (503) 636-2234
Fax: (503) 796-0699
E-mail: info@TFME.org

The Northwest Center for Physician–Patient Communication is dedicated to improving health care quality in the Pacific Northwest through education and research on physician–patient communication. It offers onsite educational programs.

Internet Healthcare Coalition
PO Box 286
Newtown, PA 18940
Tel: (215) 504-4164
Fax: (215) 504-5739
Web: www.ihealthcoalition.org

The Internet Healthcare Coalition is dedicated to educating health care consumers, health care professionals, health care educators, health care marketers, both health care and mainstream media, and public policy makers on the full range of uses of the Internet—current and potential—to deliver high-quality health care information and services.

National Committee for Quality Assurance
2000 L Street, NW
Suite 500
Washington, DC 20036
Tel: (202) 955-3500
Fax: (202) 955-3599
Web: www.ncqa.org

The National Committee for Quality Assurance is an independent, 501(c)(3) nonprofit organization whose mission is to improve health care quality everywhere. It provides information that can be used to help make more informed decisions about health care.

Cultural Competency, Sensitivity, and Awareness in the Delivery of Health Care

Key Points

- Culture is not limited to race or ethnicity; it also includes age, gender, faith, class, activity, profession, sexual orientation, tastes, or any other group characteristic that individuals share.

- When an individual's culture is at odds with that of the prevailing medical establishment, the patient's culture generally will prevail, often straining physician–patient relationships. Physicians can minimize such situations by increasing their understanding and awareness of the cultures they serve or by being open-minded regarding those that they do not know.

- To bridge differences between the culture of medicine and a patient's culture, more credence can be given to such cultural factors as the role of the extended family in treatment decisions, the role of spiritual or religious beliefs in health care decisions, and the role of traditional remedies for cures and relief from symptoms.

- To become culturally proficient, health care systems and providers not only need to acknowledge and respect but also to incorporate (not just tolerate) the relevant elements of the patient's set of values. Culturally proficient health care providers create and tailor new preventive, diagnostic, and therapeutic approaches incorporating characteristics of their patient's particular cultural backgrounds.

> *... culture is the dynamic and multidimensional context of many aspects of the life of an individual.*

- Cultural sensitivity and awareness is particularly relevant to maternity care. The challenge for obstetrician–gynecologists and other prenatal health care providers is to incorporate those individual family traditions that will strengthen family ties and provide a support system for the woman and her neonate into a medically safe birth experience.

- Communication barriers for those who do not speak English can be addressed by having available appropriately trained interpreters and written translations of forms and patient education materials.

- Health education programs jointly sponsored with community organizations and health care providers can help to clarify the health care system and familiarize women with preventive health care measures in a nonthreatening environment.

The racial and ethnic composition of the population of the United States has changed significantly during the past decade. Between 1990 and 2000, there was a 74% increase in the Asian population, a 58% increase in individuals of Hispanic or Latino origin, a 92% increase in American Indians and Alaskan Natives, and a 21% increase in the African-American population. The white non-Hispanic population, however, increased by only 5%. According to the U.S. Census 2000, there are more than 281 million inhabitants in the United States. Asians represented 3.6% of the population; Hispanics (of any race) represented 12.5%; African Americans represented 12.3%; and American Indians, Alaskan Natives, Native Hawaiians, and other Pacific Islanders represented 1% of the total U.S. population (1). Minority individuals outnumber whites in some communities in the United States.

Behind these figures are countless cultural differences that define and distinguish an increasingly diverse populace. Culture is a broad term encompassing ideas, concepts, beliefs, and common goals and can include ethnicity. Hofstede defines culture as, "the collective programming of the human mind that distinguishes the members of one human group from those of another. Culture is a system of collectively held values" (2). Culture is not static. It is newly defined as the shared experiences and commonalities that evolve under changing social and political environments. This is especially evident when groups are compared with the dominant culture or society. Therefore, culture is not limited to race or ethnicity, and includes age, gender, faith, class, activity, profession, sexual orientation, tastes, or any other group characteristic that individuals share.

Culture is the dynamic and multidimensional context of many aspects of the life of an individual (3). Individuals from similar racial and ethnic groups, countries of origin, and socioeconomic levels all may have distinct cultures. Similarly, each age group, such as adolescents or baby boomers, also has a separate and distinct culture. Culture encompasses rural versus urban identities as well. The shared systems and values of a given culture serve to facilitate interactions among its members. Conversely, interactions between members of differing cultures can be complicated by a lack of cultural awareness.

Culture and Health Care

During every health care encounter, the culture of the patient, the culture of the health care provider, and the culture of medicine as seen in medical facilities and institutions converge and may affect patterns of health care utilization, adherence with recommended interventions, and, eventually, health outcomes. Often, health care providers may not appreciate the effect of culture on their own lives, their professional conduct, and the lives of their patients (4). When an individual's culture is at odds with that of the prevailing medical establishment, the patient's culture generally will prevail, often straining physician–patient relationships (5). Physicians can minimize such situations by increasing their understanding and awareness of the cultures they serve or by being open-minded regarding those that they do not know. Although it is impossible for a health care provider to be familiar with all customs and beliefs, it is always helpful to be respectful and mindful that differences do exist. In these circumstances, recommendations can be presented to patients as ranked opinions rather than as absolutes. Increased cultural sensitivity and awareness may facilitate positive interactions with the health care delivery system, optimize health outcomes, and increase patient and health care provider satisfaction. Failure to do so can result in conflict, which can negatively affect the physician–patient relationship and increase direct and indirect costs to the health care system (3).

The Culture of Medicine

Medicine has a culture of its own, with traditional codes of conduct that have been passed on from generation to generation. This culture is pervasive within the medical profession, and it often supersedes the individual culture of the health care provider (5). Medical practice is a system designed to offer diagnosis and treatment options to an individual patient, who in turn, is expected to make decisions and follow through on treatments. Furthermore, it is underpinned by the assumption that those seeking care will understand how the system works and are able and willing to comply with its stipulations.

This system and the values that shape it, however, may compromise access to care for patients from other cultures. Efforts can be made to value appropriately the effect of the quality of interpersonal relationships between patients and health care providers rather than an exclusive focus on adherence and health care outcomes. More credence can be given to such cultural factors as the role of the extended family in treatment decisions, the role of spiritual or religious beliefs in health care decisions, or the role of traditional remedies for cures and relief from symptoms (6). In some cultures, health and healing cannot be separated from religious beliefs. In fact, many women seek help from a religious-based practitioner before seeing a physician. Patients may seek traditional practices from their home country or try traditional remedies before or along with the treatments prescribed by their physicians. These remedies may augment, interfere, or have no interaction with the physician's management plan.

The physical structure of the health care system also can be improved to reduce unintended cultural barriers for patients and their families. Hospitals, for example, often have detailed and complex requirements surrounding admissions, visiting hours, and meal times that may not have to be so rigid. Additionally, the size of many hospitals and outpatient complexes, the volume of paperwork, and the constant use of professional jargon can intimidate new immigrants, minorities, and those with little exposure to the health care system (7).

Cultural Competency, Sensitivity, and Awareness

As the health care system changes and increasingly focuses on primary care and prevention, it is critical that health care providers develop ongoing and trusting relationships with their patients. To provide appropriate care to an increasingly diverse patient population, health care providers are encouraged to develop what has come to be known as cultural competency. This refers to "the knowledge and interpersonal skills that allow health care providers to understand, appreciate, and work with individuals from cultures other than their own. It involves an awareness and acceptance of cultural differences, self awareness, knowledge of a patient's culture, and adaptation of skills" (8). A culturally competent health care system values diversity, has the capacity for cultural self-assessment, is conscious of the dynamics inherent in any multicultural encounter, and has developed the necessary adaptations to service delivery that reflect an understanding and appreciation of cultural diversity (9). Achieving cultural competency may be difficult given wide exposure to multiple cultures. However, it may be easier and more practical for health care providers at the individual, group, and institutional levels to achieve a level of cultural proficiency that includes awareness of differences and sensitivity to

the needs of patients whom they may not totally understand. The first step in this process is to develop an understanding of the cultures represented in the communities served.

For health care providers to be culturally aware, an objective and nonjudgmental view is needed toward actions, practices, and lifestyles that are broad in scope and responsive to the local, national, and international dynamics of people and societies. This is underscored by a recent survey conducted by the American Social Health Association that found that 20% of the women surveyed avoided gynecologic care because of language and cultural differences (10). Cultural discord pertaining to certain practices and lifestyles may exist between health care providers and patients. By increasing their understanding of their own and other cultures, physicians will be better able to separate their attitudes toward the cultural practice or lifestyle in general from the way they interact with individual patients of that culture. This will allow health care providers to address the patient in a nurturing, nonjudgmental manner and maximize the rapport and trust between their patients and themselves.

To become culturally proficient, health care systems and providers not only need to acknowledge and respect but also incorporate (not just tolerate) the relevant elements of the patient's set of values. The culturally proficient health care provider creates and tailors new preventive, diagnostic, and therapeutic approaches incorporating characteristics of his or her patient's particular cultural background (3).

Cultural sensitivity and awareness is particularly relevant to maternity care. The birth of a child initiates another generation into a family and affords a new opportunity for cultural traditions to be solidified, thus strengthening the bond between parents and child and serving to unify family members. As such, pregnancy and childbirth often are entangled in complex cultural beliefs and traditions that may be less obvious in other settings. Additionally, the perinatal period often may be an immigrant family's first significant contact with the health care system. The sensitivity and understanding with which a pregnant woman and her family are treated can have a long-term effect on the family's future patterns of health care utilization.

The challenge for obstetrician–gynecologists and other prenatal care providers is to incorporate those individual family traditions that will strengthen family ties and provide a support system for the woman and her neonate into a medically safe birth experience.

Families from nonwestern cultures may perceive technology-centered hospital births as leaving little room for the inclusion of individual family traditions and values. One way that prenatal health care providers can accommodate a pregnant woman's cultural preferences into her experience of pregnancy is through the use of a "birth plan." In a birth plan, a woman outlines the activities she would like to have take place at her child's birth, such as the individuals she would like to be present, her desires about clothing for the infant, or her decision regarding the circumcision of a male infant. Every effort then is made to accommodate her wishes, as long as they fall within the guidelines of safe maternity practice. If an activity falls outside the usual guidelines of safe practice, discussion with the patient and her family often can lead to a safe substitution or compromise. The same level of sensitivity and awareness can be performed in any situation in a daily clinical practice (Table 2).

Learning From the Community

In addition to valuing diversity, physicians should be sensitive to the unique needs of women in the communities they serve. Communication barriers should be examined and addressed (11). For those who do not

Table 2. Cultural Competency In Practice

Old Paradigm	Cross-Cultural Competence
An Amish woman undergoes a cesarean delivery in a hospital. After surgery, the woman and her husband are interviewed by a social worker who was routinely called to see them by a nurse who noted that they had no health insurance. The social worker immediately begins to tell them how to enroll in Medicaid. They are visibly upset.	The social worker notices on rounds that the Amish couple have no health insurance and she wonders how the couple will pay their hospital bill. Before she approaches the couple, she learns from the couple's physician that the Amish do not believe in or accept what they consider to be welfare. When she meets with the couple, she helps them plan transportation home because they do not have a car, and she assists them with reaching other members of their Amish community who, by tradition, provide financial and other assistance to their own people.
A physician addresses a 50-year-old African-American woman by her first name.	Using first names for patients, especially for minority patients, may be perceived as disrespectful. Every patient can be asked an open-ended question about how she would like to be addressed (Miss, Ms., or Mrs.) by the health care provider. The name by which she wishes to be addressed may vary by many factors, including whether the patient resides in a rural or urban setting, knows the health care provider or is a stranger, is a new patient or a long-standing patient, and the patient's age. This same patient is addressed by all health care workers using Mrs. and her last name.
A nurse insists that a young Hispanic mother sign a consent form for a cesarean delivery.	The entire staff involves the woman's husband and family in a discussion of the need to undergo a cesarean birth. Among many women of Hispanic heritage, it is customary to involve family members in medical and personal decisions.
A woman misses her appointment for colposcopy. The nurses in the clinic make many attempts to reach her by telephone without success.	The hospital asks a peer health counselor to locate the patient and explain to her the reason why the colposcopy is necessary. When the peer counselor locates the patient, she discovers that the woman's phone has been disconnected because of lack of money to pay the phone bill. The woman's 5-year-old son had a high fever and diarrhea on the day of the colposcopy appointment. She had just enough money and time to get him to a pediatrician. Her son was hospitalized.

(continued)

Table 2. Cultural Competency In Practice *(continued)*

Old Paradigm	Cross-Cultural Competence
An elderly Chinese woman is asked by her physician to go to the laboratory to have blood drawn for tests. She takes the laboratory slip but does not get the tests as ordered.	The primary care physician notes the woman's hesitation and asks her why she is worried. She tells him that she believes that blood taken from her body will never be replenished, and she is weak already. The physician spends time explaining how blood is replaced.
A woman sees a gynecologist for the first time. He is sensitive to her needs but keeps insisting that she consider using birth control. She had filled in a form saying she was sexually active. She is "not married." The woman is upset and refuses to see this gynecologist again.	The physician takes his time in asking about the patient's sexual history. One question asked very openly is: "Do you have sex with men, women, or both?" He then learns that she is a lesbian in a long-term committed relationship.
A couple is newly arrived in the United States from Afghanistan. The wife is obviously in pain. They do not speak English well, so an interpreter is found. The interpreter appears to be having some difficulty interpreting the woman's symptoms. The physician is rushed. He cannot find any abnormalities on physical examination so he sends the patient home. She returns later with a ruptured ectopic pregnancy and is immediately admitted to the operating room.	The physician notices that the interpreter is not able to communicate well with the couple. He takes the time to discover the problem: the interpreter speaks Farsi whereas the couple speaks to each other in Dari; as a result, much historical information is lost. The physician admits the patient for appropriate tests and an unruptured ectopic pregnancy is diagnosed.
A young woman has recently moved to a city from a farm. She has four small children and is 4 months pregnant. She is always late for her appointments and is made to wait until everyone else is seen before she is seen.	The staff show concern and inquire about her difficulties. She has no one to take care of her children, so she must bring them to the prenatal clinic for her appointments. She needs to take two buses to get to the clinic, and she does not read. A peer counselor arranges for help with learning the bus route and planning her trips. She also is referred to a literacy program for help. One of her first triumphs is learning to recognize the signs on the buses. Over the course of her pregnancy, she learns to read the bus route map and schedule.

Modified with permission from Leppert, PC. Cultural competency. In: Leppert PC, Howard FM, editors. Primary care for women. Philadelphia (PA): Lippincott-Raven; 1997. p. 939–42. © Lippincott Williams & Wilkins

speak English, efforts should be made to provide assistance, such as appropriately trained interpreters and written translations of forms and patient education materials (12). In some circumstances, federal and state laws and regulations impose responsibilities on health care providers to accommodate individuals with "limited English proficiency."* Appropriate measures for overcoming communication barriers will depend on the circumstances of the individual practice and patient population. Various options may be available, including hiring interpreters as office staff, using appropriate community resources, or using translation telephone services.

*See, for example, Department of Health and Human Services, Title VI of the Civil Rights Act of 1964; Policy Guidance on the Prohibition Against National Origin Discrimination as it Affects Persons with Limited English Proficiency, 65 Fed. Reg. 52762-74 (Aug. 30, 2000).

Physicians or their staff should consider meeting with representatives from the community to discuss how the delivery of services can be modified. Health education programs jointly sponsored with community organizations and located at appropriate sites can help to demystify the health care system and familiarize women with preventive health care measures in a nonthreatening environment. Because patients interact with many individuals in the office and hospital, it is important for staff to receive training in cultural awareness and sensitivity (preferably provided by a member of the community being served) or appropriate resources for self-education (see "Resources").

Every health care encounter provides an opportunity to have a positive effect on patient health. Health care providers can maximize this potential by learning more about their patients' cultures. The examples in Table 2 illustrate some of the many benefits that can be gained by learning about patients' cultures and investing in cultural sensitivity training.

References

1. US Census Bureau. Statistical abstract of the United States: 2001. 121st ed. Washington, DC: USCB; 2001.

2. Hofstede G. Cultures and organizations software of the mind. New York: McGraw-Hill; 1997.

3. Wells MI. Beyond cultural competence: a model for individual and institutional cultural development. J Community Health Nurs 2000;17:189–99.

4. Cross Cultural Health Care Program. Voices of the communities: a survey of health care experiences of 22 medically underserved communities in the Seattle area. Seattle (WA): CCHCP; 1995.

5. Leppert PC, Washington K, Partner SF. Teaching sensitivity to cultural issues in women's health care in a community hospital setting. Am J Prev Med 1996;12:69–70.

6. Kohn S. Dismantling sociocultural barriers to care. Health Forum 1995;38(3):30–3.

7. Chapman TW. Opening doors for your patients. Trustee 1995;48(3):16–20.

8. Davis BJ, Voegtle KH. Culturally competent health care for adolescents: a guide for primary care providers. Chicago (IL): American Medical Association; 1994.

9. Goode TD. Getting started. . . planning, implementing and evaluating culturally competent service delivery systems for children with special health needs and their families. Washington, DC: National Center for Cultural Competence; 2002. Available at http://www.georgetown.edu/research/gucdc/nccc/nccc9.html. Retrieved November 26, 2002.

10. American Social Health Association. National survey reveals women avoid gynecologic care. Available at http://www.ashastd.org/news/gynsurvey.html. Retrieved November 26, 2002.

11. Augustyn M, Maiman LA. Psychological and sociological barriers to prenatal care. Womens Health Issues 1994;4:20–8.

12. U.S. Department of Health and Human Services. Office of Minority Health. National standards for culturally and linguistically appropriate services in health care. Final report. Washington, DC: DHHS; 2001.

Resources

ACOG Resources

The following patient education materials are available in Spanish at: http://sales.acog.org.

American College of Obstetricians and Gynecologists. Birth control. ACOG Patient Education Pamphlet AP005. Washington, DC: ACOG; 2003.

American College of Obstetricians and Gynecologists. Cesarean birth. ACOG Patient Education Pamphlet AP006. Washington, DC: ACOG; 1999.

American College of Obstetricians and Gynecologists. Diabetes in pregnancy. ACOG Patient Education Pamphlet AP051. Washington, DC: ACOG; 2000.

American College of Obstetricians and Gynecologists. Domestic violence. ACOG Patient Education Pamphlet AP083. Washington, DC: ACOG; 2002.

American College of Obstetricians and Gynecologists. HIV testing and pregnancy. ACOG Patient Education Pamphlet AP113. Washington, DC: ACOG; 2000.

American College of Obstetricians and Gynecologists. How to prevent sexually transmitted diseases. ACOG Patient Education Pamphlet AP009. Washington, DC: ACOG; 1999.

American College of Obstetricians and Gynecologists. How to tell when labor begins. ACOG Patient Education Pamphlet AP004. Washington, DC: ACOG; 1999.

American College of Obstetricians and Gynecologists. Mammography. ACOG Patient Education Pamphlet AP076. Washington, DC: ACOG; 2004.

American College of Obstetricians and Gynecologists. Maternal serum screening for birth defects. ACOG Patient Education Pamphlet AP089. Washington, DC: ACOG; 2000.

American College of Obstetricians and Gynecologists. The menopause years. ACOG Patient Education Pamphlet AP047. Washington, DC: ACOG; 2003.

American College of Obstetricians and Gynecologists. Nutrition during pregnancy. ACOG Patient Education Pamphlet AP001. Washington, DC: ACOG; 2002.

American College of Obstetricians and Gynecologists. Osteoporosis. ACOG Patient Education Pamphlet AP048. Washington, DC: ACOG; 2003.

American College of Obstetricians and Gynecologists. Planning Your Pregnancy and Birth. 3rd ed. Washington, DC: ACOG; 2001.

American College of Obstetricians and Gynecologists. Staying healthy: for women of all ages. ACOG Patient Education Booklet AB006. Washington, DC: ACOG; 2001.

American College of Obstetricians and Gynecologists. Understanding hysterectomy. ACOG Patient Education Pamphlet AP008. Washington, DC: ACOG; 1999.

American College of Obstetricians and Gynecologists. Vaginal birth after cesarean delivery. ACOG Patient Education Pamphlet AP070. Washington, DC: ACOG; 1999.

American College of Obstetricians and Gynecologists. You and your baby: prenatal care, labor and delivery, and postpartum care. ACOG Patient Education Booklet AB005. Washington, DC: ACOG; 1998.

Limited quantities of the following materials, which are available in Spanish, can be obtained for free by e-mailing violence@acog.org.

American College of Obstetricians and Gynecologists. Domestic violence cards: no matter how you say it, it's all abuse. Washington, DC; ACOG.

Other Resources

The resources listed as follows are for information purposes only. Referral to these sources and web sites does not imply the endorsement of ACOG. The list is not meant to be comprehensive. The exclusion of a source or web site does not reflect the quality of that source or web site. Please note that web sites are subject to change without notice.

The Access Project
30 Winter Street, Suite 930
Boston, MA 02108
Tel: (617) 654-9911
Fax: (617) 654-9922
Web: www.accessproject.org

The Access Project works to strengthen community action, promote social change, and improve health, especially for those who are most vulnerable. By supporting local initiatives and community leaders, The Access Project is dedicated to strengthening the voice of underserved communities in the public and private policy discussions that directly affect them. To that end, it published *Language Services Action Kit: Interpreter Services in Health Care Settings for People with Limited English Proficiency* with the National Health Law Program. The kit includes materials that explain the federal laws and policies that require health care providers to ensure access to services for people with limited English proficiency and lists resources for additional information about language services. It also published *Immigrant Access to Health Benefits*, which is a primer on health access for immigrants. It details and explains basic eligibility requirements for key programs and identifies barriers to health care for immigrants and their families.

American Academy of Family Physicians
11400 Tomahawk Creek Parkway
Leawood, KS 66211-2672
Tel: 800-274-2237; (913) 906-6000
Web: www.aafp.org

The American Academy of Family Physicians works to increase cultural sensitivity through activities such as Quality Care for Diverse Populations, which is a training program developed to assist physicians and other health care professionals in becoming more culturally proficient in the provision of care to their patients.

American Institute for Research
1000 Thomas Jefferson Street, NW
Washington, DC 20007-3835
Tel: (202) 403-5000
Fax: (202) 403-5001
Web: www.air.org

The American Institutes for Research (AIR) is a not-for-profit corporation that performs basic and applied research, provides technical support, and conducts analyses based on methods of the behavioral and social sciences. Their program areas focus on education, health, individual and organizational performance, and quality of life. In addition, AIR is working with the U.S. Department of Health and Human Services Office of Minority Health to develop national standards for health care language services, as well as to develop and disseminate a set of self-instructional modules to promote culturally competent care among providers.

American Medical Association
515 N State Street
Chicago, IL 60610
Tel: 800-621-8335
Web: www.ama-assn.org/ama/pub/category/6759.html

The American Medical Association (AMA) has products that specifically cover issues regarding the delivery of culturally effective health care. For example, the AMA published a document, *Delivering Culturally Effective Health Care to Adolescents*, to offer recommendations for enhancing communication with young people and their families. It also published *Cultural Competence Compendium*, which is a resource for physicians in identifying issues surrounding different populations. In addition, the AMA has a major health literacy program, which includes a train-the-trainer component.

American Medical Student Association
1902 Association Drive
Reston, VA 20191
Tel: (703) 620-6600
Fax: (703) 620-5873
E-mail: amsa@www.amsa.org
Web: www.amsa.org/programs/gpit/cultural.cfm

The American Medical Student Association is an independent association of physicians-in-training in the United States. This organization is committed to improving health care and health care delivery to all people; promoting active improvement in medical education; involving its members in the social, moral, and ethical obligations of the profession of medicine; assisting in the improvement and understanding of world health problems; contributing to the welfare of medical students, interns, residents, and post-MD/DO trainees; and advancing the profession of medicine. Their web site provides various resources on cultural competency, including assessment questions for patients, guidelines for how to use an interpreter, tips for improving the care-giver/patient relationship across cultures, and case studies.

Bureau of Primary Health Care
U.S. Department of Health and Human Services
East West Towers
4350 East West Highway
Bethesda, MD 20814
Web: www.bphc.hrsa.gov/quality/cultural.htm

The Bureau of Primary Health Care (BPHC) works to provide cultural-ly and linguistically appropriate, high quality, comprehensive, coordi-nated primary and preventive care at the community level. To that end, the BPHC has published a Cultural Competence Monograph Series. Four new collaborative volumes have been added to this series, including one on American Indians and Alaskan Natives.

The Center for Cross-Cultural Health
PO Box 8184
St. Paul, MN 55108
Tel: (651) 209-8999
E-mail: ccch@crosshealth.com
Web: www.crosshealth.com

The mission of the Center for Cross-Cultural Health is to integrate the role of culture in improving health. Its vision is increased health and well-being for all through cross-cultural understanding. To achieve this goal, the center is actively involved in the education and training of health and human service providers and organiza-tions in the state of Minnesota and beyond. The center also is a research and information resource. Through information sharing, training, organizational assessments, and research, the center works to develop culturally competent individuals, organizations, systems, and societies.

Center for Substance Abuse Treatment
Substance Abuse and Mental Health Services Administration
U.S. Department of Health and Human Services
Web: http://csat.samhsa.gov/

The Center for Substance Abuse Treatment (CSAT) of the Substance Abuse and Mental Health Services Administration, U.S. Department of Health and Human Services, was created in October 1992 with a congressional mandate to expand the availability of effective treat-ment and recovery services for alcohol and drug problems. Cur-rently, CSAT is developing a publication to provide ways to improve cultural competence in substance abuse treatment.

Cross Cultural Health Care Program
270 South Hanford Street, Suite 100
Seattle, WA 98134
Tel: (206) 860-0329; (206) 860-0331
Fax: (206) 860-0334
Web: www.xculture.org

Since 1992, the Cross Cultural Health Care Program (CCHCP) has been addressing broad cultural issues that affect the health of indi-viduals and families in ethnic minority communities in Seattle and nationwide. Through a combination of cultural competency train-ings, interpreter trainings, research projects, community coalition building, and other services, the CCHCP works with communities and health care institutions to ensure full access to quality health care that is culturally and linguistically appropriate.

CEO Services
914 Ironwood Road
Alameda, CA 94502
Web: www.culturalcompetence2.com

CEO Services provides consulting, educational, and organizational development services for those committed to the transformation of work and organization environments toward multicultural, cultural-ly competent organizations for today's diverse society.

EthnoMed
Web: www.ethnomed.org

The EthnoMed web site contains information about cultural beliefs, medical issues, and other related issues pertinent to the health care of recent immigrants to Seattle and the United States, in general. Information specific to certain cultures is available on this web site.

Health Resources and Services Administration
U.S. Department of Health and Human Services
Parklawn Building
5600 Fishers Lane
Rockville, MD 20857
Web: www.hrsa.gov

The Health Resources and Services Administration's mission is to improve and expand access to quality health care for all. To that end, it published *Cultural Competence Works: Using Cultural Competence to Improve the Quality of Health Care for Diverse Populations and Add Value to Managed Care Arrangements*, which can be accessed at http://www.hrsa.gov/financeMC/ftp/cultural-competence.pdf.

Indian Health Service
The Reyes Building
801 Thompson Avenue, Suite 400
Rockville, MD 20852-1627
Web: www.ihs.gov

The Indian Health Service is the agency of the U.S. Department of Health and Human Services that provides health services to American Indians and Alaskan Natives. Its goal is to ensure that comprehensive, culturally acceptable personal and public health services are available and accessible to American Indian and Alaskan Native people.

Henry J. Kaiser Family Foundation
2400 Sand Hill Road
Menlo Park, CA 94025
Tel: (650) 854-9400
Fax: (650) 854-4800
Web: www.kff.org

The Henry J. Kaiser Family Foundation is a nonprofit, private operating foundation focusing on the major health care issues facing the nation. It published a *Compendium of Cultural Competence Initiatives in Health Care*, which describes public and private sector activities that seek to reduce cultural and communi-cation barriers to health care. This resource also includes brief definitions for the major terms regarding cultural competence, organizational descriptions of initiatives, and a list of experts in the field.

Kaiser Permanente
National Diversity Department
One Kaiser Plaza, 22 Lakeside
Oakland, CA 94612
Tel: (501) 271-6663

The Kaiser Permanente National Diversity Department developed monographs to provide a comprehensive overview of health care for populations, including those who are African American; Asian and Pacific Islander; Latino; lesbian, gay, bisexual, and transgendered; and individuals with disabilities. The books contain sections on demographics; health beliefs; risk factors; major diseases; infectious diseases; and special areas of clinical focus including obstetrics and gynecology, childhood and adolescent health, and mental health. The monographs also contain a list of web-based resources and an extensive bibliography.

Let Everyone Participate—Access for People with Limited English Proficiency
Web: www.lep.gov

LEP.gov was designed to promote a positive and cooperative understanding of the importance of language access to federal programs and federally assisted programs. This web site provides information on implementation of various regulations regarding language access. This web site also acts as a clearinghouse, providing and linking to information, tools, and technical assistance regarding limited English proficiency and language services for federal agencies, recipients of federal funds, users of federal programs and federally assisted programs, and other stakeholders. This web site is maintained by the U.S. Department of Justice.

Medtronic Foundation
710 Medtronic Parkway
Minneapolis, MN 55432-5604
Tel: (763) 514-4000
Fax: (763) 514-4879
Web: www.medtronic.com

The Medtronic Foundation is committed to empowering all people to live healthy, productive lives. It published *Getting the Word Out*, which is designed to help patient support organizations make their information, referral, support, and advocacy services more accessible to people from a variety of cultural communities.

National Alliance for Hispanic Health
1501 Sixteenth Street, NW
Washington, DC 20036
Tel: (202) 387-5000
E-mail: alliance@hispanichealth.org
Web: www.hispanichealth.org/

The National Alliance for Hispanic Health is the nation's oldest and largest network of Hispanic health and human services providers. The programs of the Alliance inform and mobilize consumers; support providers in the delivery of quality care; promote appropriate use of technology; improve the science base for accurate decision-making; and promote philanthropy. The Alliance published a training manual, *A Primer for Cultural Proficiency: Towards Quality Health Services for Hispanics*. This primer consists of eight chapters discussing culture, working in diverse cultures, language, history of Hispanics and Hispanic data, and the role of community-based organizations.

National Asian Women's Health Organization
250 Montgomery Street, Suite 1500
San Francisco, CA 94104
Tel: (415) 989-9747
Fax: (415) 989-9758
Web: www.nawho.org

The National Asian Women's Health Organization is a nonprofit organization providing research, education, and public advocacy to improve the health status of Asian women and their families.

National Black Women's Health Imperative
600 Pennsylvania Avenue, SE
Suite 310
Washington, DC 20003
Tel: (202) 548-4000
Fax: (202) 543-9743
Web: www.blackwomenshealth.org

The National Black Women's Health Imperative is a nonprofit organization working to improve the health of black women through wellness education and services, health information, and advocacy.

The National Center for Cultural Competence
Web: http://data.georgetown.edu/research/gucchd/nccc/index.html

The mission of the National Center for Cultural Competence is to increase the capacity of health and mental health programs to design, implement, and evaluate culturally and linguistically competent service delivery systems. Its resources include conference calls and various full-text publications, including *A Guide to Planning and Implementing Cultural Competence Organizational Self-Assessment*.

National Health Law Program
1101 14th Street, NW, Suite 405
Washington, DC 20005
Tel: (202) 289-7661
Fax: (202) 289-7724
E-mail: nhelpdc@healthlaw.org
Web: www.healthlaw.org

The National Health Law Program (NHeLP) is a national public interest law firm that seeks to improve health care for America's working and unemployed poor, minorities, the elderly, and people with disabilities. It published the *Language Services Action Kit: Interpreter Services in Health Care Settings for People with Limited English Proficiency* with The Access Project. The kit includes materials that explain the federal laws and policies that require health care providers to ensure access to services for people with limited English proficiency and lists resources for additional information about language services. It also published *Immigrant Access to Health Benefits*, which is a primer on health access for immigrants. It details and explains basic eligibility requirements for key programs and identifies barriers to health care for immigrants and their families. In 2003, NHeLP published a revision of their 1998 manual, *Ensuring Linguistic Access in Health Care Settings: Legal Rights and Responsibilities*. This manual details how providers can overcome language barriers to obtain appropriate medical care for their patients.

National Medical Association
1012 Tenth Street, NW
Washington, DC 20001
Tel: (202) 347-1895
Fax: (202) 898-2510
Web: www.nmanet.org

The National Medical Association promotes the collective interests of physicians and patients of African descent. It advocates for parity in medicine, elimination of health disparities, and promotion of optimal health.

National Multicultural Institute
3000 Connecticut Avenue NW, Suite 438
Washington, DC 20008-2556
Tel: (202) 483-0700
Fax: (202) 483-5233
E-mail: nmci@nmci.org
Web: www.nmci.org

The National Multicultural Institute initiatives have focused on organizational training and consulting; twice-annual conferences that offer opportunities for in-depth diversity training and skills-building; publications and resource materials that include trainer manuals, books on cross-cultural mental health, and videos; and projects that promote the creation of a professional association for diversity practitioners and partnerships with government and private organizations.

Office of Minority Health
U.S. Department of Health and Human Services
Tel: 800-444-6472
Web: www.omhrc.gov

The Office of Minority Health provides a list of state offices on minority health and a list of regional consultants on minority health. It developed recommendations for national standards for culturally and linguistically appropriate health services, which are available at http://www.omhrc.gov/wwwroot/clas/.

Resources for Cross Cultural Health Care
8915 Sudbury Road
Silver Spring, MD 20901
Tel: (301) 588-6051
Web: www.DiversityRx.org

Resources for Cross Cultural Health Care is a national network of individuals and organizations working to increase access to health care for linguistically and culturally diverse populations. Particular areas of expertise among members, staff, and consultants include medical interpretation program design and training; cross cultural assessment and training; and development of linguistically and culturally competent health care programs, policies, and laws. Services include program design, policy development and analysis, research, and community advocacy. Resources for Cross Cultural Health Care currently is engaged in facilitation of the Diversity Rx web site (www.DiversityRx.org), which is a comprehensive clearinghouse of information on model programs, policies, and legal issues related to cross cultural health, in collaboration with the National Conference of State Legislatures and the Kaiser Family Foundation.

University of California–San Francisco
Web: medicine.ucsf.edu/resources/guidelines/culture.html

The University of California–San Francisco developed a web site to provide a listing of multilingual resources, curricula, articles, and organizations that address cultural competency.

Special Populations

General Management of Pediatric Gynecology Patients

Key Points

- A variety of gynecologic problems commonly occur in young girls. With patience, gentleness, and flexibility, the gynecologist can examine and treat most disorders that occur in this age group in the office setting.

- Evaluation of breast and external genitalia should be performed before the newborn is discharged from the hospital.

- The genital examination in prepubertal girls requires a gentle, patient approach to minimize fear or embarrassment. Forcible restraint is never indicated and sedation is rarely necessary.

- A speculum examination is not indicated in the office examination of prepubertal children.

- Vulvovaginitis is the most common etiology of gynecologic-based conditions in prepubertal children. Symptoms involve the vulva more than the vagina in prepubertal girls, the opposite of what typically is seen in females of reproductive age.

- Pediatric-aged patients with symptoms of vulvovaginitis who visit gynecologists often have had a previous evaluation and failed treatment. They deserve a thorough evaluation with cultures and testing.

- Obstetrician–gynecologists should be familiar with childhood hormonal patterns and psychologic and physical developmental stages. This will assist in the identification of precocious puberty.

- Sexual abuse should be considered in the course of an evaluation for vaginitis or trauma. Findings suspicious of abuse include lacerations of the vulva, posterior fourchette or anus, or transactions of the hymen; however, most sexually abused children will have normal findings on examination.

A thorough review of the child's history and a physical examination provide the basis for diagnosis in most instances.

- There are an increasing number of immigrants and refugees who circumcise their daughters before their arrival in the United States. Consequently, seeing the immediate complications of female circumcision may become more frequent. It is crucial to remember that this practice often is performed out of a strong sense of tradition. Sensitivity toward both the parents and child is paramount.

Female children are referred to obstetrician–gynecologists for a variety of reasons, including evaluation of vaginal discharge or bleeding, vulvar disorders, or suspected sexual abuse. Referrals also are made for abnormalities of pubertal development or congenital anomalies. Assessment usually can be accomplished in the office setting. A thorough review of the child's history and a physical examination provide the basis for diagnosis in most instances.

Evaluation

Neonates

Evaluation of breasts and external genitalia should be performed before the newborn is discharged from the hospital. A general examination should note any abnormal findings, such as a webbed neck, abdominal mass, or inguinal hernia that could be associated with a gynecologic problem.

During inspection of the breasts, a small amount of breast tissue may be palpable, and discharge may be expressed from the nipples as a result of exposure to maternal estrogen in utero. These effects usually resolve spontaneously within 6–8 weeks (1).

The external genitalia may be visualized by placing the infant in the supine position with thighs flexed against the abdomen. Estrogenic effects that may be apparent include thickened and bulbous labia majora and a white vaginal discharge. The labia minora and hymen may protrude slightly from the vestibule. A small amount of withdrawal bleeding also may be observed. If bleeding is excessive or persists beyond 10 days of life, additional evaluation is required (1).

The clitoris may appear large in proportion to the other genital structures. If it appears enlarged, the clitoral index (glans length × width in mm^2) should be measured. Values greater than 5 mm^2 indicate a need for further evaluation in a newborn. The mean adult size is 18.5 mm^2 (2). If clitoromegaly is suspected, the infant should be evaluated immediately for congenital adrenal hyperplasia. A delayed diagnosis may lead to dehydration and death of the neonate. A referral to a specialist may be required.

Visualization of the vaginal orifice using labial separation may be difficult because of the redundancy of the hymenal tissue resulting from exposure to maternal estrogen. Gentle traction on the labia majora usually allows for complete visualization of the hymen and vaginal orifice (Fig. 1) (3). The hymenal entrance may be positioned very anteriorly.

Hymenal polyps may be seen in newborns and almost always will resolve without therapy. Hymenal variations do not require treatment during the neonatal period. However, their presence should be noted and followed-up on at a later time. If an imperforate hymen is present, a mucocolpos rarely may occur from the accumulation of cervical secretions behind the blocked outflow tract. Experts recommend correction in the neonatal period if urinary obstruction occurs.

In the neonate, the ovaries are less than 1 cm in diameter. Small, simple ovarian cysts secondary to maternal hormonal stimulation may be noted on antenatal or postnatal abdominopelvic ultrasound and may or may not be palpable on an abdominal examination. These cysts may persist for 4–6 months postnatally. Large cysts (greater than 5 cm) or those of a complex nature may signify neonatal ovarian torsion, hemorrhage into the cyst or, quite uncommonly, ovarian disease (4). Because the ovaries in the neonate are located intraabdominally, ovarian enlargement may present as a palpable abdominal mass. Expert consultation should be sought in the very rare situations of a nonresolving or enlarging neonatal ovarian cyst.

When an infant is born with ambiguous genitalia, the immediate concerns of the obstetrician are to prevent dehydration of the newborn and to counsel the parents. Congenital adrenal hyperplasia is the most common cause of ambiguous genitalia (accounting for more than 90% of cases), and salt-wasting forms may lead to rapid dehydration and fluid and electrolyte imbalance. Therefore, fluid intake and output, serum electrolytes, and glucose concentration should be monitored carefully.

The parents should be informed that the infant's genitalia are "incompletely formed" and that further evaluation is warranted. Intensive investigation and a multidisciplinary approach are helpful in making treatment decisions. Rectal examination, selected imaging studies, and evaluation of laboratory test results are necessary. The initial laboratory tests include determination of the blood 17-hydroxyprogesterone, dehydroepiandrosterone sulfate, testosterone, and dihydrotestosterone levels and a karyotype. Although knowledge of the karyotype assists with the diagnosis of the patient's condition, sex assignment is based on additional criteria. Other equally important criteria include the potential for an unambiguous genital

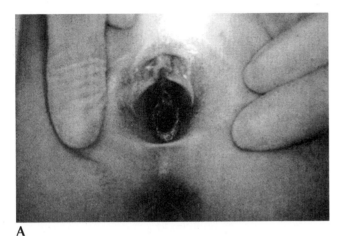

A

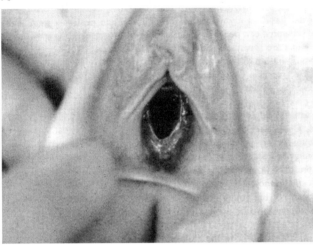

B

Fig. 1. Examination of the vulva, hymen, and anterior vagina by gentle lateral retraction **(A)** and gentle gripping of the labia and pulling anteriorly **(B).** (Reprinted with permission from Emans SJ, Laufer MR, Goldstein DP, editors. Pediatric and adolescent gynecology. 5th ed. Philadelphia [PA]: © Lippincott Williams & Wilkins; 2005. p. 7.)

appearance and the potential for normal sexual functioning and fertility. Gender identity is a complex issue. Recent advances in psychosexual development point to the multifactorial nature of gender identity and emphasize the need for a multidisciplinary approach to the surgical and psychosocial management of these special patients (5).

Pediatric Patients

When the maternal estrogen effect subsides, the genitalia appear different during the prepubertal years than in the neonatal period. The labia begin to flatten out. The hymenal membrane loses its redundancy and becomes translucent. Normal configurations of the

hymen include an annular hymen (hymenal membrane tissue extends completely around the circumference of the entire vaginal orifice) and a crescentic hymen (hymen with attachments at approximately the 11 o'clock and one o'clock positions without tissue being present between the two attachments). Nonobstructive hymenal variations, such as a microperforate, septate, or cribriform hymen, also may be detected (Fig. 2) (3). A microperforate hymen has a small, ventrally displaced orifice. In the septate hymen, a band of hymenal tissue bisects the hymenal orifice creating two or more orifices. A cribriform hymen has multiple small openings. The hymen is of urogenital origin in contrast to the uterus and vagina, which are of müllerian origin. The concomitant renal malformations seen with müllerian anomalies are not associated with hymenal anomalies.

The hypoestrogenic prepubertal vaginal epithelium is thin, red, and sensitive to the touch. The vaginal mucosa of young children has longitudinal ridges running along the axis of the vagina (3), rather than the circumferential rugae seen in the adult female. During infancy, the uterus regresses in size and does not return to its birth size until the fifth or sixth year. The cervix to fundus ratio is 2:1, although the cervix often is difficult to visualize because it is flush with the vaginal vault.

Between ages 5 and 10 years, the child experiences increasing endocrine activity of the ovaries, adrenal gland, and pituitary gland. The labia majora begin to fill out and the labia minora thicken as a result of increased estrogen levels. The hymen thickens and becomes more redundant. Physiologic secretions may be present. Between ages 10 and 13 years, the cervix to uterus ratio reverses, with the uterus twice the size of the cervix.

The genital examination in prepubertal girls requires a gentle, patient approach to minimize fear or embarrassment. For the older prepubertal patient, the physician may wish to discuss with the patient whether she wishes to have a family member present during the examination. If she does not, the option to have a chaperone during the examination to provide reassurance to the patient about the professional context and content of the examination should be offered. Even in the presence of the caregiver, the examiner should speak directly to the child, explaining that the caregiver has given permission for the examination. To improve communication, it is sometimes helpful to inquire about the name the child uses for her genitalia and use those terms during the examination. This is an opportunity to explain to the child about the privacy of body parts. Before each step

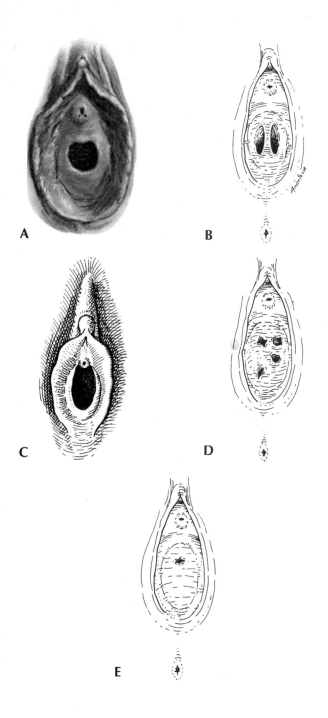

Fig. 2. Commonly observed hymenal types **(A)** annular, circular, lunar; **(B)** septate; **(C)** crescentic; **(D)** cribriform, fenestrated; **(E)** microperforate. (Drawings of septate; cribriform, fenestrated; and microperforate hymen reprinted with permission from Emans SJ, Laufer MR, Goldstein DP, editors. Pediatric and adolescent gynecology. 5th ed. Philadelphia [PA]: Lippincott Williams & Wilkins; 2005. p. 10. Drawing of annular, circular, lunar hymen: Copyright 1989. Icon Learning Systems, LLC, a subsidiary of MediMedia USA Inc. Reprinted with permission from ICON Learning Systems, LLC, illustrated by Frank H. Netter, MD. All rights reserved. Drawing of crescentic hymen reprinted with permission from Smout CF, Jacoby F. The anatomy of the female pelvis. Baltimore [MD]: Williams and Wilkins; 1943. © Lippincott Williams & Wilkins)

of the examination, it is helpful for the physician to explain what will occur. It may be helpful to allow the patient to see and hold or touch each instrument before it is used. Forcible restraint is never indicated and sedation is rarely necessary.

A variety of different techniques may be used to visualize the genitalia of prepubertal females. Children younger than 4 years can be placed on the mother's lap with the child's legs straddling the mother's thighs. If the child permits, she may be positioned on the table in the supine position with the hips fully abducted and the feet together in the "frog-leg" position. Children near the age of 4 years may prefer to use stirrups. To view the vaginal introitus, it is necessary to grasp the labia along the inferior portion between the thumb and index finger and gently pull outward and downward (labial traction). Alternatively, the child may be placed in the knee-chest position with elevation of the buttocks and hips (Fig. 3). This position provides excellent exposure of the inferior portion of the hymen, where breaks are most commonly observed in children who have been sexually abused (6); the lower vagina; and usually the upper vagina and cervix. This may be assisted by using an otoscope for light and magnification without inserting it into the vagina (3). A speculum examination is not indicated in the office examination of prepubertal children. A gentle digital rectal examination can be done, if necessary given the patient's symptoms, because it allows for assessment of the cervix, uterus, solid foreign bodies, or other masses.

Examination of the genitalia of children should be documented adequately in the medical record. Documentation of the examination of prepubertal females is different than that for adult females. Each structure visualized should be noted (eg, clitoris, labia majora, labia minora, urethra, vestibule, and rectum) as should the configuration of the hymen (eg, annular, crescentic). Future examiners will rely on this documentation as a database with which they compare their findings and note any variances. A sketch may be helpful. Changes should be noted in any follow-up examinations.

Pediatric Gynecologic Problems

Vulvovaginitis

Vulvovaginitis is the most common etiology of gynecologic-based conditions in prepubertal children. It may be associated with genital discomfort or pruritis, ery-

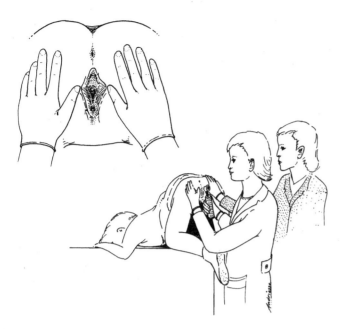

Fig. 3. Examination of the prepubertal child in the knee-chest position. (Emans SJ, Laufer MR, Goldstein DP, editors. Pediatric and adolescent gynecology. 5th ed. Philadelphia [PA]: © Lippincott Williams & Wilkins; 2005. p. 13.)

thema, evidence of excoriation, and, in approximately 50% of the cases, a vaginal discharge (7). Symptoms involve the vulva more than the vagina in prepubertal girls; the opposite of what is seen typically in females of reproductive age.

Vulvovaginitis often is divided into two groups based on etiology: 1) nonspecific vulvovaginitis and 2) specific infectious vulvovaginitis. Nonspecific vulvovaginitis is more common than specific infectious vulvovaginitis. Children are especially prone to nonspecific vulvovaginitis for a variety of reasons, including their nonestrogenized state; proximity of the anus to the vagina, which is without geographic barriers given the flattened labia and lack of pubic hair; and poor perianal hygiene.

Diagnosis of Nonspecific Versus Specific Vulvovaginitis

Evaluation of the child presenting with symptoms consistent with vulvovaginitis includes a history and inspection of the vulva and vagina, which may or may not appear normal, or erythematous. Symptoms for nonspecific vulvovaginitis are indistinguishable from those in patients with specific infectious vulvovaginitis, although patients with specific causes tend to present more acutely. Nonspecific causes of vulvovaginitis include chemicals (shampoos, creams, perfumes, soap, or bubble

bath), tight-fitting or nylon clothing, suboptimal hygiene with the normal rectal flora (particularly *Escherichia coli*) irritating the mucosa, or allergens.

Infectious vulvovaginitis, where a specific pathogen is isolated as the cause of symptoms, may be caused by respiratory pathogens, such as *Streptococcus pyogenes*, *Staphylococcus aureus*, and *Haemophilus influenzae*. These organisms may be transmitted manually by the child from the nasopharynx to the vagina. *Neisseria gonorrhoeae* or *Chlamydia trachomatis* also are causes of specific infectious vulvovaginitis, the presence of which strongly suggests sexual abuse (see "Sexual Abuse" section). Other causes of specific infectious vulvovaginitis include Shigella (often presents with a blood-tinged purulent discharge) and Yersinia. Although *Trichomonas vaginalis* can be transmitted vertically and can be seen in the newborn, it is an uncommon cause of specific infectious vulvovaginitis in the unestrogenized prepubertal female (3). Mycotic infections (yeast), although commonly a cause of diaper rash, are rarely the cause of inflammation in vulva or vagina. The alkaline pH of the vagina does not support fungal infections. Exceptions may occur in immunocompromised children or those children on prolonged antibiotics.

Pinworm infection, another specific etiology of vulvovaginitis, is the most common helminthic infestation in the United States, with the highest rates in school-aged and preschool children. Itching may lead to excoriation and, rarely, bleeding. Vulvar and perianal erythema often is present. If pinworms are suspected, transparent adhesive tape or an anal swab should be applied to the anal region in the morning before defecation or bathing and then placed on a slide. Eggs seen on microscopic examination confirm the diagnosis. Several samples may be required to detect the eggs, and false negative results still may occur. In symptomatic girls with negative tape or swab test results, a therapeutic trial of an antihelminthic medication is reasonable.

Clinicians seeing a child with no prior history of vulvovaginitis, no purulent discharge, and no historical findings suspicious of sexual abuse may opt to treat the patient for nonspecific vulvovaginitis, avoiding the cost of cultures. Cultures and further testing may be reserved for nonresponsive patients. However, pediatric-aged patients with symtoms of vulvovaginitis visiting gynecologists often have had a previous evaluation and failed treatment. They deserve a thorough evaluation with cultures and testing, such as an aerobic vaginal culture and gonorrhea and chlamydia testing. Polymerase chain reaction (PCR), ligase chain reaction, and DNA probe testing are not appropriate for use in prepubertal patients because of theoretic risk of false-positive results. Genital cultures and testing will differentiate nonspecific vulvovaginitis from specific vaginitis. Cultures to test for specific pathogens may be obtained with urethral swabs moistened with nonbacteriostatic saline. Use of a swab can cause mild discomfort or, rarely, minimal bleeding.

Treatment

The treatment of specific vulvovaginitis should be directed at the specific organism causing the symptoms, such as *H influenzae* or pinworms (Table 3). Treatment of nonspecific vulvovaginitis includes sitz baths and avoidance of irritating or harsh soaps and chemicals and tight clothing that abrades the perineum. External application of barrier creams containing zinc oxide, such as over-the-counter diaper rash medications, may be helpful. Proper perineal hygiene is critical for long-term cure. Children should be advised to wipe from front to back and wear 100% cotton undergarments.

Vaginal cultures from children with nonspecific vulvovaginitis often grow normal rectal flora, including *E coli*. Temporary use of broad-spectrum antibiotics may alleviate symptoms in these children, but these should be used only when other initial responses have failed or when symptoms are so acute that the daily life of the patient is affected, such as school attendance. The vagina will recolonize with the normal rectal flora and symptoms will return unless hygienic practices are being used. Low-dose steroids, such as topical 0.5% hydrocortisone, may be helpful to reduce the itch–scratch cycle in cases of nonspecific vulvovaginitis that are unresponsive to hygienic changes and sitz baths.

Vulvar Disorders

Vulvar disorders in children may be infectious (eg, candidiasis, molluscum contagiosum, condyloma, or herpes) or noninfectious (eg, labial agglutination, lichen sclerosis, psoriasis, atopic dermatitis, contact dermatitis, or seborrheic dermatitis). Each is discussed as follows.

Infectious Vulvar Disorders

Candidiasis. The most common infectious cause of vulvitis in children who wear diapers is *Candida albi-*

cans. Most cases present as mild erythema and edema accompanied by pruritus. Severe cases may result in intense, red, weeping, eczematoid dermatitis with satellite pustules. Diagnosis is confirmed by KOH smear or culture, using selective media for yeasts. Topical antifungal agents usually are effective. Because *C albicans* is enhanced in an estrogenic environment, infection is rare inside the vagina in prepubertal females unless other risk factors are present, such as diabetes mellitus, immunosuppression, or recent antibiotic usage (8). The prepubertal vagina is alkaline and does not support candida species.

Molluscum Contagiosum. Molluscum contagiosum is characterized by 1- to 5-mm discrete, skin-colored, dome-shaped, smooth papules with a central cheesy plug, sometimes referred to as "umbilicated lesions." The area surrounding the lesions may be erythematous or pruritic. It is common in school-aged children, especially among those who live in overcrowded areas or have poor hygiene. Diagnosis usually is made by visual inspection. A warmed KOH smear under 10% magnification will reveal ballooned keratinocytes. If not treated, the average outbreak lasts 6–9 months, although lesions may last for years. Because the disease generally is self-limited and the lesions sometimes resolve spontaneously, treatment may not be necessary. If treatment is indicated, however, it should not be excessive or overly aggressive, especially in young children (9). Treatment choices in children may include cryosurgery, curettage after EMLA cream anesthesia, and topical silver nitrate (9). Oral cimetidine may be a safe, painless, and effective alternative treatment for extensive molluscum contagiosum in children younger than 10 years (10), but cimetidine has not been approved for use in this population* (11). Recent successful use of topical 5% imiquimod cream has been reported (12).

Condyloma. Condyloma accuminata, or warts, result from perinatal transmission of the human papillomavirus (HPV) or close sexual or nonsexual contact with an infected individual or object. Perinatal transmission is less likely to be the cause if the child has a new onset after age 3 years. It is impossible to define

---

*Cimetidine is not recommended for use in children younger than 16 years, unless the physician judges anticipated benefits outweigh the potential risks.

Table 3. Treatment of Specific Vulvovaginal Infections in the Prepubertal Child

Etiology	Treatment
Streptococcus pyogenes	Penicillin V potassium, 250 mg orally two to three times daily for 10 days
Haemophilus influenzae	Amoxicillin, 40 mg/kg/d for 7 days
	Alternate: amoxicillin/clavulanate, cefuroxime axetil, trimethoprim-sulfamethoxazole, erythromycin-sulfamethoxazole
Staphylococcus aureus	Cephalexin, 25–50 mg/kg/d orally for 7–10 days
	Dicloxacillin, 25 mg/kg/d orally for 7–10 days
	Amoxicillin-clavulanate, 20–40 mg/kg/d (of the amoxicillin) orally for 7–10 days
	Cefuroxime axetil suspension 30 mg/kg/d divided twice daily (maximum 1 g) for 10 days (tablets: 250 mg twice daily)
Streptococcus pneumoniae	Penicillin, amoxicillin, erythromycin, trimethoprim-sulfamethoxazole, clarithromycin
Shigella	Trimethoprim/sulfamethoxazole or ampicillin for 5 days
	For resistant organisms: ceftriaxone
Chlamydia trachomatis	Children ≤45 kg: erythromycin base or ethylsuccinate, 50 mg/kg/d orally divided into four doses daily for 14 days
	Children ≥45 kg but <8 years: azithromycin, 1 g orally in a single dose
	Children ≥8 years: azithromycin, 1 g orally in a single dose *or* doxycycline, 100 mg orally twice a day for 7 days
Neisseria gonorrhoeae	Children <45 kg: ceftriaxone, 125 mg intramuscularly in a single dose (alternate: spectinomycin 40 mg/kg (maximum 2 g) intramuscularly once PLUS if chlamydial infection not ruled out prescribe for chlamydia as above.
	Children ≥45 kg: treat with adult regimen of cefixime, 400 mg orally in a single dose, or ceftriaxone, 125 mg intramuscularly in a single dose, or ciprofloxacin, 500 mg orally in a single dose*, or ofloxacin, 400 mg orally in a single dose*, or levofloxacin, 250 mg orally in a single dose*, plus, if chlamydial infection is not ruled out azithromycin, 1 g orally in a single dose or doxycycline, 100 mg orally twice a day for 7 days.
	Children with bacteremia or arthritis: ceftriaxone, 50 mg/kg (maximum dose for children who weigh <45 kg: 1 g) intramuscularly or intravenously in a single dose daily for 7 days
Candida	Topical nystatin, miconazole, clotrimazole, or terconazole cream; oral fluconazole
Trichomonas	Metronidazole, 15 mg/kg/d given three times dailly (maximum 250 mg three times daily) for 7 days
Pinworms (*Enterobius vermicularis*)	Mebendazole (Vermox), one chewable 100 mg tablet, repeated in 2 weeks

*Quinolones should not be used for infections acquired in Asia or the Pacific, including Hawaii. In addition, use of quinolones is probably inadvisable for treating infections acquired in California and in other areas with increased prevalence of quinolone resistance.
Modified from Emans SJ, Laufer MR, Goldstein DP, editors. Pediatric and adolescent gynecology. 5th ed. Philadelphia (PA): © Lippincott Williams & Wilkins; 2005. p. 98. Data from Sexually transmitted diseases treatment guidelines 2002. MMWR Recomm Rep 2002;51(RR-6):1–78.

the longest latency period between virus infection at the time of delivery and the development of clinical disease. The average latency period appears to be approximately 3 months, but intervals of up to 20 or more months are plausible. In addition, a child examined at age 2 years with condylomata may have had a disease that could have been discovered months earlier on close inspection (13). Diagnosis usually is made by visual inspection. Biopsy has a limited place in management and should be reserved for those cases in which the diagnosis is in question or operative treatment is planned. DNA typing generally is not helpful.

Nonintervention is a reasonable approach in asymptomatic children because lesions may resolve spontaneously or decrease in size over time (13, 14). A variety of treatment options are available for symptomatic children, although none is uniformly effective (15), and the recurrence risk is high with all modalities. Treatment options may include trichloroacetic acid applied topically or cryosurgery. Children may experience burning with therapy, and multiple treatments often are required. Pretreatment use of long-acting, local, topical anesthetics, such as prilocaine, may be helpful to numb the pain. Liquid nitrogen should be applied with a cotton-tipped swab and the warts frozen until a circle of ice is visible around the outer edges. One option is to then refreeze the lesions with the same end point after allowing them to thaw (16). The therapeutic use of this is limited by pain and discomfort.

Experimental treatments, including cimetidine, imiquimod, and cidofovir, have shown some efficacy (15, 17), but have not been approved by the FDA* (11). Although interferon alpha has been approved for use in genital warts in adults, it is expensive, relatively difficult to use, associated with systemic side effects, and somewhat slow acting (18). Laser excision requires anesthesia and, although the long-term cure rate is no better than that of conservative methods, it has the advantage of removing multiple lesions at one time. Referral to a specialist should be considered for children in need of extensive treatment. Because condylomata accuminata frequently are sexually transmitted, the possibility of sexual abuse should be addressed (see "Sexual Abuse" section).

Herpes Simplex. The herpes simplex virus (HSV) can spread by autoinoculation or close nonsexual or sexual contact. Beyond the neonatal period, the presence of HSV indicates the need for a sexual abuse evaluation. Both type 1 and type 2 may involve the genitalia. The condition begins as clusters of painful vesicles on an erythematous base that may be accompanied by malaise, fever, and myalgia. Rupture results in ulcerations covered with a hemorrhagic yellowish-gray crust. Culture has been the criterion standard by which to diagnose HSV; a PCR technique has become available recently.

Children older than 2 years may be treated with acyclovir orally for 5–10 days for the first infection (40–80 mg/kg/d given in three to four divided doses not to exceed 1 g/d) (19). The safety and effectiveness of acyclovir for those younger than 2 years has not been studied adequately (11). Prolonged low-dose administration of acyclovir should be limited to children with five or more outbreaks per year to minimize the emergence of drug-resistant HSV and varicella zoster virus. Famciclovir and valacyclovir hydrochloride can be administered twice per day but currently are not approved by the FDA† (11).

Noninfectious Vulvar Disorders

Labial Agglutination. Labial agglutination occurs when the adjacent edges of the labia adhere. It may occur anywhere along the vestibule, but most commonly occurs posteriorly. Extensive agglutination is found in 5% of prepubertal girls and in up to 10% of infants younger than 12 months (20). Although usually there are no symptoms, the condition may cause urinary dribbling or be associated with vulvitis, urinary tract infection, or urethritis. This condition does not require treatment if the patient is asymptomatic because spontaneous resolution will occur before or at puberty in most cases.

If the patient has symptoms, estrogen cream may be applied twice per day for 2–6 weeks directly on the line of adhesions. The parent should be instructed how to apply the cream, taking care to apply only a small amount to the gray line of adhesions while applying gentle labial traction. The use of traction may be a very important part of the efficacy of the treatment. Use of estrogen must be discontinued if breast budding occurs. To avoid pain, anesthesia should be used if mechanical separation of the adhesions is attempted. If indicated, adhesions can be lysed easily with a cotton swab under general anesthesia. Recurrences are frequent, especially after surgical correction. To decrease the risk of recurrence and to prevent reagglutination of raw opposing skin surfaces, an emollient should be applied nightly for at least 1 month.

Lichen Sclerosus. Approximately 10–15% of cases of lichen sclerosus occur in prepubertal children. This skin condition can affect the vulvar, perianal, or perineal skin, producing a sclerotic, atrophic, parchmentlike plaque with an hourglass or keyhole appearance, similar to that noted in older women with this condition. The affected area breaks down easily; thus, children may

---

*Cimetidine is not recommended for use in children younger than 16 years, unless the physician judges anticipated benefits outweigh the potential risks. Safety and efficacy of imiquimod for use in children younger than 18 years, and of cidofovir for use in children have not been established.

†Safety and efficacy of famciclovir for use in children younger than 18 years have not been established. Valacyclovir hydrochloride has not been tested for use in children.

present with vulvar bleeding. Accompanying subepithelial hemorrhages may be misinterpreted as sexual abuse or trauma. Alternatively, the patient may experience perineal itching, soreness, or dysuria. The vulva may become infected secondarily. Chronic cases may result in atrophy of the labia majora or clitoris, constriction of vaginal introitus or urethral meatus, anal stenosis, or anal fissures.

Treatment includes: 1) avoidance of trauma by having the patient avoid irritation to the vulvar areas; 2) use of emollients; and 3) moderate-to-high potency topical corticosteroids for 1–3 months, which effectively treat the symptoms in most children but are not curative. Testosterone cream has been proved to be no more effective for treatment than petroleum jelly and is not indicated (21). Classically, it has been taught that affected girls often experience improvement or partial clearing of lesions at menarche. However, some experts report little change in the course of the disease at that time (22).

Psoriasis. Psoriasis is an inherited disorder that can occur at any age and usually is associated with other extragenital findings. The classic extragenital psoriatic lesions are red plaques with well-demarcated silvery scales that are intensely pruritic. Vulvar psoriatic lesions may not exhibit this classic appearance. Genital psoriasis is seen more commonly as poorly demarcated areas of erythematous plaques. The typical scales may be absent on the mons pubis. Scratching may cause excoriation, eczematization, crusting, and secondary infection. Symmetrical fissures may be evident between the labia minora and labia majora extending to the periclitoral area. Diagnosis may be confirmed by locating other affected areas on the body, such as crusting behind the ears, on the scalp, or in nasolabial folds. Vulvar lesions may be treated topically with a moderate- to high-potency fluorinated corticosteroid preparation (3).

Atopic Dermatitis. Atopic dermatitis, an inflammatory skin disease that begins in infancy and usually occurs between ages 1 and 5 years, affects 2–8% of children. It characteristically affects the face, neck, chest, and extremities. Chronic cases may result in crusty, weepy lesions that are accompanied by intense pruritus and erythema. Scratching often results in excoriation of the lesions and secondary bacterial or candidal infection. Serum immunoglobulin E levels are elevated in 80% of patients and may aid in diagnosis. Children with this condition should avoid common irritants and use topical fluorinated corticosteroids for flare-ups. If dry skin is present, lotion or bath oil can be used to seal in moisture of hydrated skin.

Contact Dermatitis. Contact dermatitis is associated with exposure to an irritant, such as perfumed soaps, bubble bath, talcum powder, or lotions. Erythematous, edematous, or weepy vulvar vesicles or pustules may result. The localized nature distinguishes it from atopic dermatitis, but symptoms and treatment are the same.

Seborrheic Dermatitis. Seborrheic dermatitis presents with erythematous, oily, circumscribed patches on the face, scalp, chest, and intertriginous areas of the body. The condition may affect the outer labia minora, the labia majora, and the genitocrural folds. The etiology is unknown. It can produce symmetrical fissures from the labia to the level of the clitoris or to the midline of the perineum. The patient may be asymptomatic or may experience bleeding, pain, tenderness, pruritus, or dysuria. Secondary infections are common. This disorder can be treated with 1% hydrocortisone cream applied topically two to five times per day for 3–4 weeks.

Vaginal Bleeding

Vaginal bleeding in the prepubertal child requires careful assessment. The most common cause in the neonate occurs in the first week of life as a response to the withdrawal of maternal estrogen. Vaginal bleeding in prepubertal girls can be the result of a foreign body, vaginitis, urethral prolapse, neoplasms, trauma, or precocious puberty (3). Other causes include lichen sclerosis, genital warts (HPV), blood dyscrasias, hemangiomas, and endocrinologic causes (Box 3) (3). The most common causes are described in this section. In rare situations, prepubertal vaginal bleeding can be a possible clue to leukemia and immune thrombocytopenic purpura. It may, therefore, be important to ask about and examine the patient for any other unusual bleeding or easy bruising.

Foreign Body

A foul-smelling, bloody discharge suggests a foreign body in the vagina, although foreign objects may be present with vaginal bleeding without a discharge. Toilet paper is the most common foreign body identi-

---

Box 3   Differential Diagnosis of Vaginal Bleeding in the Prepubertal Girl

Trauma
- Accidental
- Sexual abuse

Vulvovaginitis
- Irritation, pinworms
- Nonspecific vulvovaginitis
- *Streptococcus pyogenes*, Shigella

Endocrine abnormalities
- Newborn bleeding caused by maternal estrogen withdrawal
- Isosexual precocious puberty
- Pseudoprecocious puberty
- Precocious menarche
- Exogenous hormone preparations
- Hypothyroidism

Dermatoses
- Lichen sclerosus
- Condyloma accuminata (human papillamavirus)

Foreign body

Urethral prolapse

Blood dyscrasia

Hemangioma

Tumor
- Benign
- Malignant

Emans SJ, Laufer MR, Goldstein DP, editors. Pediatric and adolescent gynecology. 5th ed. Philadelphia (PA): © Lippincott Williams & Wilkins; 2005. p. 106.

---

fied in young children, although any small object may be the cause (23). Because most foreign objects usually are not radio-opaque, a KUB film is rarely helpful. It may be possible to remove foreign bodies, like toilet paper, by irrigating the vagina with water using a soft rubber catheter, such as an IUI catheter or small plastic angiocath. Small objects, such as coins or plastic marker caps, left in the vagina may be difficult to remove without anesthesia because they often are imbedded in the tissue. If a foreign body is suspected but not visible on inspection of the genitalia or if a foreign body is visualized but cannot be removed, a vaginoscopy under anesthesia is indicated.

Vaginitis

Streptococcus pyogenes (group A β-hemolytic streptococci) is primarily a respiratory pathogen affecting the oropharynx that commonly can infect the prepubertal vagina. The vulva and perianal areas often have a distinctive bright red appearance with an introitus that is friable and bleeds easily.

Shigella infection also can result in a mucopurulent and bloody vaginal discharge. Although shigella commonly is thought to be an etiology for diarrhea, only 25% cases of shigella vaginitis are associated with diarrhea (24).

Urethral Prolapse

Urethral prolapse is the result of eversion of the urethral mucosa through the external meatus. Children may be asymptomatic or present with vaginal bleeding. Dysuria, urinary retention, or urinary frequency are infrequent. Upon visual inspection, a cherry-red, doughnut-shaped tissue or a mass 2–3 cm in diameter is apparent. Although the lesion extends from the urethra, it may, when large, appear to arise from the vagina (23). When in doubt of the etiology, examination in the knee-chest position may be helpful to clarify the origin of the mass by allowing better visualization of the vagina. If this is unsuccessful, topical application of lidocaine to the mass and gentle probing with a moistened swab or small catheter through the lesion may be done. Urine will pass through the catheter if the mass extends from the urethra.

Symptoms usually resolve with sitz baths. Some clinicians also have used estrogen creams and antibiotic ointments, although the effectiveness of these therapies has not been proved. Urethral redundancy may persist for months to years. If necrotic tissue is present and unresponsive to medical management, surgical removal may be indicated.

Neoplasms

Patients with rhabdomyosarcoma, the most common malignant tumor seen in the pediatric vagina, usually present with vaginal bleeding. These tumors characteristically arise from the anterior wall of the vagina and then expand to fill the vagina and create a visible mass (25). Definitive diagnosis requires biopsy under general anesthesia. Rarely, bleeding may be secondary to leukemia or a hemangioma.

Trauma

Genital trauma may be the result of an accidental injury or sexual abuse. Straddle-type injuries, which often result in only minor lacerations or abrasions of the labia, account for most accidental genital injuries in children (26, 27). These are most often hymen-sparing injuries. Although in most cases of sexual abuse there are no abnormal anatomic findings, suspicion of abuse is raised when a transectional injury to the hymen is present.

If a vulvar hematoma results, conservative management (bed rest, ice packs) is recommended unless the hematoma is actively expanding. Broad-spectrum antibiotics to prevent secondary infection may be indicated. Penetrating trauma to the vagina can cause serious injury to the retroperitoneal area and requires examination under anesthesia and possibly exploration of the abdomen with laparotomy or laparoscopy. Because cases of penetrating vaginal trauma may be the result of sexual abuse, forensic evidence should be collected at the time of the evaluation (see "Sexual Abuse" section).

Precocious Puberty

Precocious puberty may occur with early development of pubic hair or the breasts. Vaginal bleeding may be a symptom. When a patient presents with vaginal bleeding at an early age with associated pubertal development, suspicion of an ovarian or central tumor is elevated and referral to a specialist is indicated (see "Precocious Puberty" section).

Ovarian Masses

Ovarian cysts present beyond the neonatal period may cause pain or be found in conjunction with other signs of hormonal stimulation. In a retrospective chart review of 5 years of ultrasonographic experience, ovarian cysts in prepubertal girls were seen as an incidental finding in 2–5% of ultrasound assessments. Most of these were less than 1 cm in diameter and not pathologic. In older children with early pubertal

changes, it is quite common to see multiple small cysts signifying follicular activity. Large cysts (greater than 5 cm), those with complex characteristics, or any ovarian cyst in premenarchal girls with associated signs or symptoms of hormonal stimulation deserve prompt evaluation (28). The differential diagnosis for a pathologic ovarian cyst formation includes benign and malignant tumors and ovarian torsion. Ovarian cysts may develop in the presence of severe primary hypothyroidism, possibly caused by cross-reaction of high levels of thyroid-stimulating hormone with ovarian follicle-stimulating hormone receptors. In children with delayed bone age, this possibility should be strongly considered (29).

Children with an ovarian mass may present with abdominal pain that may be accompanied by nausea, vomiting, or urinary frequency or retention. In some cases, no symptoms are present and the mass is detected on routine examination. Only 10% of ovarian masses in children are malignant, of which two thirds are germ cell tumors (30). Evaluation includes a careful history and physical and ultrasound examinations. Serum assay for tumor markers and additional imaging should be performed when indicated (30).

Surgical therapy with tissue biopsy is indicated for persistent cysts, solid or complex masses, or if tumor markers are positive. If malignancy is found or suspected, consultation with a gynecologic oncologist is recommended.

Precocious Puberty

Obstetrician–gynecologists should be familiar with childhood hormonal patterns and psychologic and physical developmental stages. This will assist in the identification of precocious puberty. Precocious puberty was defined previously as sexual development in girls younger than 8 years. A recent study conducted by the Pediatric Research in Office Settings Network on more than 17,000 girls between ages 3 and 12 years demonstrated that Tanner stage 2 pubic hair and breast development is reached approximately 1 year earlier in Caucasian girls and 2 years earlier in African-American girls residing in the United States than documented in previous studies conducted in other countries (31). Based on these data, the Lawson Wilkins Pediatric Endocrine Society recommended new guidelines for the evaluation of premature development. These guidelines state that pubic hair or breast development requires evaluation only when it occurs before age 7 years in non-African-American girls and before age 6 years in African-American girls. These guidelines are reasonable only in the absence of symptoms such as rapid growth in height, new central nervous system-related findings, or behavior-based factors (32). A recent review of girls aged 6–8 years with breast development and pubic hair determined that 12% had an endocrinologic diagnosis (33). In this age population, therefore, if there is any uncertainty, an evaluation should be done and referrals made as appropriate.

The most common cause of precocious puberty is idiopathic activation of the hypothalamic–pituitary–ovarian axis. However, other serious etiologies must be excluded. Central nervous system (CNS) lesions that can activate gonadotropin-releasing hormone include vascular lesions and infiltrative lesions of the hypothalamus, such as sarcoid and other granulomatous diseases. Steroid-producing ovarian and adrenal tumors also can cause precocious puberty. A rare cause of precocious puberty is McCune Albright syndrome, which is described classically as the triad of sexual precocity, polyostotic fibrous dysplasia, and cutaneous pigmentation in the form of café au lait lesions of the skin. Premature onset of a single secondary sex characteristic, such as breast budding or growth of pubic hair, may be caused by end-organ sensitivity to low circulating levels of sex steroids. When this is observed, the child should be monitored closely, and her growth should be plotted on a growth chart. A thorough examination and precocious puberty workup is warranted in the presence of accelerated growth and evidence of multi-site organ stimulation. In the absence of these symptoms, therapy may not be required. A bone age assessment may be helpful in making this diagnosis.

Evaluation of the child presenting with symptoms of precocious puberty should include CNS imaging (magnetic resonance imaging or computed tomography) and ultrasonography of the ovaries and, as appropriate, the adrenal gland. Estradiol levels may be helpful because levels higher than 250 pg/mL are almost certainly associated with ovarian steroid-producing tumors. Patients with precocious puberty generally need to be referred to an endocrinologist for definitive diagnosis and consultation regarding the treatment of precocious puberty. This consultation should include a discussion of the many controversies surrounding appropriate treatment before the initiation of treatment. Once treatment is initiated, careful follow-up should be done as necessary. If a tumor is found, the patient should undergo definitive treatment, which often is surgical.

Sexual Abuse

Sexual abuse should be considered in the course of an evaluation for vaginitis or trauma. Findings suspicious of abuse include lacerations of the vulva, posterior fourchette or anus, or transections of the hymen. However, most sexually abused children will have a normal examination. Therefore, a physical examination should not be used to determine which children require an interview. Although most physicians are not skilled in techniques for interviewing a child about sexual abuse, using nondirective questions to elicit spontaneous responses can help in obtaining details regarding the assault. It is helpful if these details include the name or description of the perpetrator, the location and time of the assault, and the exact type of sexual acts. Precise documentation of the interview and examination is critical; responses should be recorded verbatim (34).

A physical examination should be performed as soon as possible if the alleged sexual abuse occurred within the past 72 hours or if the child presents with bleeding or acute injury (35). The focus of this examination is on forensic evidence collection. It is critical to pursue vigorously the collection of clothing and linens. In one study of children evaluated for sexual abuse in the emergency room, most of the forensic evidence (64%) was obtained from clothing and linens. However, only slightly more than one third of the children had clothing or linens evaluated for evidence. Almost all of the forensic evidence collected 24 or more hours after the assault was obtained from clothing and linens (36). If more than 72 hours has passed since the last episode of abuse, the examination may be scheduled at the earliest convenient time. Referrals to a health care facility specializing in child sexual abuse may be appropriate.

The objectives of the physical examination are to identify for legal purposes any signs of sexual contact; to identify and treat adverse consequences of assault, such as sexually transmitted diseases (STDs) or injuries; and to reassure the child and caregiver about the child's physical well-being. The external genitalia should be inspected and photographed when possible. A colposcope with a camera attachment or hand-held camera with a macro lens may be used. A speculum examination should rarely be performed in a prepubertal patient (35).

The decision to test for human immunodeficiency virus/acquired immunodeficiency syndrome (HIV/AIDS) and other STDs is made on an individual basis. Strong indications for testing include: 1) if the suspected offender is known to have an STD, including HIV/AIDS or is at high risk for STDs; 2) if the prevalence of STDs in the community is high or if other members of the household have an STD; 3) if the child has signs or symptoms of an STD, such as a vaginal discharge; or 4) if there is a history of genital or oral penetration or ejaculation.

Chlamydia and gonorrhea present in children as vaginitis, not cervicitis. Cultures for chlamydia and gonorrhea should be obtained from the lower vagina and not the cervix. Only tests with high specificities (ie, cultures) should be used to avoid obtaining a false-positive result (37); thus DNA probes are not recommended. Follow-up cultures should be collected 2 weeks after the most recent sexual exposure. Prophylactic treatment for STDs is not recommended unless exposure to STDs is suspected (37). Every clinician who examines the genitals of children should know their state-mandated protocols and standards for diagnosis as well as requirements for reporting suspected child sexual abuse (35). Each state has its own protocol, but diagnosis of sexual abuse is strongly supported if findings reveal semen, sperm, or direct DNA evidence; a positive culture for gonorrhea; a positive serologic test for syphilis or HIV; or a positive culture for chlamydia in children older than 2 years.

Female Circumcision

Because significant numbers of females continue to emigrate from countries where female circumcision is practiced, the population of females in the United States who have undergone or are at risk for this practice is increasing (38). Consequently, seeing the immediate complications of female circumcision may become more frequent. It is crucial to remember that this practice often is performed out of a strong sense of tradition. Sensitivity toward both the parents and child is paramount (39).

Physicians should review the child protection or child abuse statutes in their state and comply with the reporting requirements as they apply to parents or guardians who perform female circumcision or allow female circumcision to be performed in the United States. It is illegal under U.S. federal law to perform female circumcision on any female younger than 18 years. Parents should be encouraged to bring their daughters who are experiencing complications associated with female circumcision, including acute infections, urinary retention, dysmenorrhea, and vaginitis, to an emergency room or a physician's office (39).

Although the cohort of circumcised girls in this country is relatively new and there are no documented cases of minors requesting confidential deinfibulation, it is possible that this may occur. As with other requests by minors for surgical procedures, state laws regarding confidentiality and consent should be consulted. The patient should be encouraged to discuss the matter with her parents, and the physician should offer to facilitate this discussion, if necessary (39).

References

1. Gidwani GP. Approach to evaluation of premenarchal child with a gynecologic problem. Clin Obstet Gynecol 1987;30:643–52.
2. Sane K, Pescovitz OH. The clitoral index: a determination of clitoral size in normal girls and in girls with abnormal sexual development. J Pediatr 1992;120:264–6.
3. Emans SJ, Laufer MR, Goldstein DP, editors. Pediatric and adolescent gynecology. 5th ed. Philadelphia (PA): Lippincott Williams & Wilkins; 2005.
4. Luzzatto C, Midrio P, Toffolutti T, Suma V. Neonatal ovarian cysts: management and follow-up. Pediatr Surg Int 2000;16:56–9.
5. Zucker KJ. Intersexuality and gender identity differentiation. Annu Rev Sex Res 1999;10:1–69.
6. Kerns DL, Ritter ML, Thomas RG. Concave hymenal variations in suspected child sexual abuse victims. Pediatrics 1992;90:265–72.
7. Paradise JE, Campos JM, Friedman HM, Frishmuth G. Vulvovaginitis in premenarcheal girls: clinical features and diagnostic evaluation. Pediatrics 1982;70:193–8.
8. Fivozinsky KB, Laufer MR. Vulvar disorders in prepubertal girls. A literature review. J Reprod Med 1998;43:763–73.
9. Janniger CK, Schwartz RA. Molluscum contagiosum in children. Cutis 1993;52:194–6.
10. Dohil M, Prendiville JS. Treatment of molluscum contagiosum with oral cimetidine: clinical experience in 13 patients. Pediatr Dermatol 1996;13:310–2.
11. Physicians' Desk Reference. 57th ed. Montvale (NJ): Medical Economics Company; 2003.

12. Liota E, Smith KJ, Buckley R, Menon P, Skelton H. Imiquimod therapy for molluscum contagiosum. J Cutan Med Surg 2000;4:76–82.

13. Davis AJ, Emans SJ. Human papilloma virus infection in the pediatric and adolescent patient. J Pediatr 1989;115:1–9.

14. Allen AL, Siegfried EC. The natural history of condyloma in children. J Am Acad Dermatol 1998;39:951–5.

15. Siegfried EC, Frasier LD. Anogenital warts in children. Adv Dermatol 1997;12:141–66; discussion 167.

16. Bourke JF, Berth-Jones J, Hutchinson PE. Cryotherapy of common viral warts at intervals of 1, 2 and 3 weeks. Br J Dermatol 1995;132:433–6.

17. Trizna Z, Tyring SK. Antiviral treatment of diseases in pediatric dermatology. Dermatol Clin 1998;16:539–52.

18. Baker GE, Tyring SK. Therapeutic approaches to papillomavirus infections. Dermatol Clin 1997;15:331–40.

19. Antiviral drugs for non-human immunodeficiency virus infections. In: American Academy of Pediatrics. Red book 2000: report of the Committee on Infectious Diseases. 25th ed. Elk Grove Village (IL): AAP; 2000. p. 675–7.

20. Berenson AB, Heger AH, Hayes JM, Bailey RK, Emans SJ. Appearance of the hymen in prepubertal girls. Pediatrics 1992;89:387–94.

21. Sideri M, Origoni M, Spinaci L, Ferrari A. Topical testosterone in the treatment of vulvar lichen sclerosus. Int J Gynaecol Obstet 1994;46:53–6.

22. Redmond CA, Cowell CA, Krafchik BR. Genital lichen sclerosus in prepubertal girls. Adolesc Pediatr Gynecol 1988;1:177–80.

23. Baldwin DD, Landa HM. Common problems in pediatric gynecology. Urol Clin North Am 1995;22:161–76.

24. Murphy TV, Nelson JD. Shigella vaginitis: report of 38 patients and review of the literature. Pediatrics 1979;63:511–6.

25. Sanfilippo JS. Pediatric and adolescent gynecology. In: Copeland LJ, editor. Textbook of gynecology. 2nd ed. Philadelphia: WB Saunders; 2000. p. 571–602.

26. Jones LW, Bass DH. Perineal injuries in children. Br J Surg 1991;78:1105–7.

27. Bond GR, Dowd MD, Landsman I, Rimsza M. Unintentional perineal injury in prepubescent girls: a multicenter, prospective report of 56 girls. Pediatrics 1995;95:628–31.

28. Millar DM, Blake JM, Stringer DA, Hara H, Babiak C. Prepubertal ovarian cyst formation: 5 years' experience. Obstet Gynecol 1993;81:434–8.

29. Gordon CM, Austin DJ, Radovick S, Laufer MR. Primary hypothyroidism presenting as severe vaginal bleeding in a prepubertal girl. J Pediatr Adolesc Gynecol 1997;10:35–8.

30. Lazar EL, Stolar CJ. Evaluation and management of pediatric solid ovarian tumors. Semin Pediatr Surg 1998;7:29–34.

31. Herman-Giddens ME, Slora EJ, Wasserman RC, Bourdony CJ, Bhapkar MV, Koch GG, et al. Secondary sexual characteristics and menses in young girls seen in office practice: a study from the Pediatric Research in Office Settings network. Pediatrics 1997;99:505–12.

32. Kaplowitz PB, Oberfield SE. Reexamination of the age limit for defining when puberty is precocious in girls in the United States: implications for evaluation and treatment. Drug and Therapeutics and Executive Committees of the Lawson Wilkins Pediatric Endocrine Society. Pediatrics 1999;104:936–41.

33. Midyett LK, Moore WV, Jacobson JD. Are pubertal changes in girls before age 8 benign? Pediatrics 2003;111:47–51.

34. Muram D. Child sexual abuse. In: Sanfilippo JS, Muram D, Dewhurst J, Lee PA, editors. Pediatric and adolescent gynecology. 2nd ed. Philadelphia: WB Saunders; 2001. p. 399–414.

35. Guidelines for the evaluation of sexual abuse of children: subject review. American Academy of Pediatrics Committee on Child Abuse and Neglect. Pediatrics 1999;103:186–91.

36. Christian CW, Lavelle JM, De Jong AR, Loiselle J, Brenner L, Joffe M. Forensic evidence findings in prepubertal victims of sexual assault. Pediatrics 2000;106:100–4.

37. Sexually transmitted diseases treatment guidelines 2002. Centers for Disease Control and Prevention. MMWR Recomm Rep 2002;51(RR–6):1–78.

38. Toubia N. Female genital mutilation: a call for global action. New York (NY): Women, Ink.; 1993.

39. American College of Obstetricians and Gynecologists. Female circumcision/female genital mutilation: clinical management of circumcised women. Washington, DC: ACOG; 1999.

Resources

ACOG Resources

American College of Obstetricians and Gynecologists. Precis: an update in obstetrics and gynecology: gynecology. 2nd ed. Washington, DC: ACOG; 2001.

American College of Obstetricians and Gynecologists. Precis: an update in obstetrics and gynecology: reproductive endocrinology. 2nd ed. Washington, DC: ACOG; 2002.

Nonsurgical diagnosis and management of vaginal agenesis. Committee Opinion No. 274. American College of Obstetricians and Gynecologists. Obstet Gynecol 2002;100:213–216.

Other Resources

The resources listed as follows are for information purposes only. Referral to these sources and web sites does not imply the endorsement of ACOG. This list is not meant to be comprehensive. The exclusion of a source or web site does not reflect the quality of that source or web site. Please note that web sites are subject to change without notice.

American Academy of Family Physicians
11400 Tomahawk Creek Parkway
Leawood, KS 66211-2672
Tel: 800-274-2237
Web: www.aafp.org

The American Academy of Family Physicians is the national association of family doctors. The academy was founded in 1947 to promote and maintain high-quality standards for family doctors who are providing continuing comprehensive health care to the public.

The American Academy of Pediatrics
141 Northwest Point Boulevard
Elk Grove Village, IL 60007-1098
Tel: (847) 434-4000
Fax: (847) 434-8000
Web: www.aap.org

The American Academy of Pediatrics (AAP) and its member pediatricians dedicate their efforts and resources to the health, safety and well-being of infants, children, adolescents and young adults. The AAP established a section on endocrinology, which is committed to improving the care of infants, children, and adolescents with endocrinological disorders. The section holds educational programs directed to the practicing pediatrician on topics such as precocious puberty. The AAP also has a Committee on Child Abuse and Neglect that has issued statements on topics such as gonorrhea in prepubertal children.

American Medical Association
515 N State Street
Chicago, IL 60610
Tel: (312) 464-5000
Web: www.ama-assn.org

The American Medical Association's (AMA's) work includes the development and promotion of standards in medical practice, research, and education; strong advocacy agenda on behalf of patients and physicians; and the commitment to providing timely information on matters important to the health of America. Among other documents relating to pediatric issues, the AMA publishes *Archives of Pediatrics & Adolescent Medicine*.

North American Society for Pediatric and Adolescent Gynecology
PO Box 791
Hockessin, DE 19707
Tel: (302) 234-4047
Fax: (302) 234-0865
Web: www.naspag.org

The North American Society for Pediatric and Adolescent Gynecology (NASPAG) is dedicated to conducting and encouraging programs of medical education in the field of pediatric and adolescent gynecology. The practice of pediatric and adolescent gynecology requires the expertise of multiple disciplines, including pediatrics and gynecology, as well as related subspecialties and disciplines in the medical, surgical, and psychosocial areas. Therefore, NASPAG's goals include developing educational programs for adolescents and their parents and serving as advocates for infants, children, and adolescents and their families in the areas of gynecology and sexuality.

Teaching Hospitals With Expertise in Pediatric Gynecology

Allegheny General Hospital
320 East North Avenue
Pittsburgh, PA 15212
Tel: (412) 359-6890
Fax: (412) 359-5133

Boston Children's Hospital
300 Longwood Avenue
Boston, MA 02115
Tel: (617) 355-5785
Fax: (617) 566-2971

Cincinnati Children's Hospital Medical Center
3333 Burnet Avenue
Cincinnati, OH 45229-3039
Tel: (513) 636-2911
Fax: (513) 636 –7844

St. Louis Children's Hospital Pediatric Center
Program in Pediatric and Adolescent Gynecology
Tel: (314) 747-1454
Web: www.obgyn.wustl.edu/Divisions/pediatric.html

University of Louisville School of Medicine
550 South Jackson Street
Louisville, KY 40202
Tel: (502) 852-1371

Access to Reproductive Health Care for Women With Disabilities

Key Points

- Women with disabilities have unique obstetric and gynecologic needs requiring health care provider awareness, sensitivity, and skill.

- The gynecologic health care of women with disabilities should be comprehensive, affirm the patient's dignity, maximize the patient's interests, and avoid harm.

- Women with disabilities often undergo screening for cervical cancer and breast cancer less frequently than recommended. If possible, screening for cancer should be performed according to standard recommendations of the American College of Obstetricians and Gynecologists (ACOG).

- Physical limitations and communication difficulties that might hinder routine examinations can be overcome by alternative positioning, technology, sensitivity, and patience.

- Sexuality issues facing women with disabilities need to be addressed, including desire and ability for consensual sexual relationships and childbearing.

- Numerous safe, effective, and easy to use contraceptive methods are available for women with disabilities. Of particular value are methods that are not administered daily or have a relatively long duration.

- Women with developmental disabilities may have unidentified sexual activity and need to be routinely screened for sexually transmitted diseases (STDs).

The more insidious barriers to health care for women with disabilities involve the ignorance, social prejudice, and pervasive negative attitudes about life with disabilities.

Physical, developmental, sensory, cognitive, and psychiatric impairments may affect both the quality and availability of health care services for women. Current estimates are that approximately 12.5% or 17 million civilian noninstitutionalized women and girls older than 5 years in the United States are living with disabilities (1) (Table 4).

Women with disabilities report significant difficulties in meeting their reproductive health needs (2). Most individuals with disabilities—both male and female—have experienced physical, financial, attitudinal, communication, and knowledge barriers to obtaining quality medical care.

The more insidious barriers to health care for women with disabilities involve the ignorance, social prejudice, and pervasive negative attitudes about life with disabilities. Not infrequently, women with disabilities report feeling degendered by their experiences in health care settings—viewed as asexual and unlikely to be lovers, wives, and mothers (3). During the twentieth century, forced sterilization programs affected a large number of women in the United States—particularly those with cognitive disabilities. Even today, involuntary abortions are still known to occur (4). Whereas obstetricians and gynecologists who are knowledgeable and sensitive to these issues can directly affect the health status of women with disabilities, additional indirect benefits to these patients also may result with regard to self-esteem and gender identity. As for all women, the optimal gynecologic health care of women with disabilities is comprehensive, affirms the patient's dignity, maximizes the patient's interests, and avoids harm (4). (See Box 4 for sugested office practice systems.) With all disabilities, consideration of the history of the disability, the number and severity of limitations, and its expected progression is critical in meeting the health care needs and concerns of women.

Definitions and Demographics of Disability

Disability, as defined by the Americans with Disabilities Act of 1990 (ADA), is a "physical or mental impairment that substantially limits one or more of the major life activities of an individual, a record of such impairment, or being regarded as having such an impairment"(5). It is important to recognize that some women may have multiple disabilities that include

Table 4. Selected Types of Disabilities for the Civilian Noninstitutionalized Population of Women Aged 5 Years and Older: 2000

Population	Number	Percentage
Total number of women in population	132,530,700	100
With a sensory, physical, mental, or self-care disability	16,857,190	12.5
With a self-care disability	3,999,815	3
No self-care disability	12,857,375	9.7
With a sensory, physical, or mental disability	16,588,995	12.5
All three disabilities	1,123,710	0.8
With two disabilities: sensory and physical	1,332,530	1
With two disabilities: sensory and mental	299,535	0.2
With two disabilities: physical and mental	2,292,305	1.7
With sensory disability only	1,741,460	1.3
With physical disability only	7,281,240	5.5
With mental disability only	2,518,215	1.9

Disability status of the civilian noninstitutionalized population by sex and selected characteristics for the United States and Puerto Rico: 2000 (PHC-T-32). Washington, DC: U.S. Census Bureau, 2004. Available at: www.census.gov/population/www/cen2000/phc-t32.html. Retrieved September 21, 2004.

physical, cognitive, sensory, and psychiatric impairments. Disabilities may be congenital or acquired from trauma or chronic illness. Similarly, they may be static or progressive. A woman's health care provider must have a general understanding of the particular disability of the patient in order not to exacerbate the disability (6) and can obtain this by asking the woman herself, through the woman's primary care provider (after patient consent is obtained), or disability resources (see "Resources").

The leading causes of physical disability include orthopedic disorders, such as arthritis or amputation, motor dysfunction from brain injuries (eg, strokes, cerebral palsy, traumatic brain injury), mental retardation, central nervous system and spinal cord lesions (eg, trauma, multiple sclerosis, spina bifida), neuropathies and muscular dystrophies (eg, genetic, diabetic), and cerebrovascular disease (7).

Individuals with developmental disabilities are those with a cognitive or psychologic disability or impairment beginning in infancy or childhood that may be expected to continue indefinitely. Such conditions include pervasive developmental disorders (eg,

Box 4　Suggestions for Office Practice for Women With Disabilities

Before scheduling an appointment for the patient:

- Become familiar with provider responsibilities stipulated in the Americans with Disabilities Act. Assess the medical practice environment and make appropriate modifications in layout, equipment, and staff training. If possible, include women with disabilities in the assessment and development of service delivery plans.

- Identify a point person within the practice to research local disability resources and be responsible for assuring the development and documentation of a plan of care for each woman with disabilities.

Scheduling an appointment for the patient:

- Ask about the special needs of the patient, including extra time, access considerations, and communication requirements, when scheduling appointments.

- Determine at the time the appointment is made whether or not the patient usually gives consent for examination or treatment. If the patient is not able, the legal guardian or authorized (documented) caregiver is asked to accompany the patient to the appointment.

- Contact, with consent, the primary care physician to ascertain medical history and gain advice or direction concerning:

    1. Psychosocial factors, such as living arrangements and reliability of patient and caretakers to follow through with advice and medical treatment; the most effective methods of health education and community resources available to the patient.

    2. Physical factors, such as patient's ability to use a standard examination table, method of transfer (for patients with physical disabilities), best position for examination, person to best accompany patient during examination, the extent of examination available without sedation, history of examination under sedation or anesthesia.

- Determine the patient's mode of transportation to the office and, if dependent on a public disability transport system, allow for some time flexibility.

- Scan the office or clinic to determine the accessibility of the reception areas, restroom, examination room, consultation room, X-ray and laboratory area, and other equipment for this patient.

- Determine the need for assistants to aid in transferring, positioning, and supporting the woman.

- Determine the need to arrange for an interpreter (sign language or other).

- Determine the patient's desire to have a chaperone present during the examination, and schedule the examination to accommodate this need.

- Schedule, if possible, the patient's appointment at a time of light patient volume and maximum staffing.

Before or at the time of the appointment:

- Discuss patient's appointment with office staff before the appointment and designate a point person for facilitation.

- Allow the patient to determine who, if anyone, is to accompany her during the examination.

- Allow time before the examination for the patient to become familiar with the examination room and the health care provider.

- Be alert to cold or hard instruments and loud noises because the patient may be extremely sensitive to tactile and auditory stimulation.

- Become alert to signs of physical and sexual abuse, such as statements by the patient, or physical signs of abuse, including the presence of sexually transmitted diseases and bruising or swelling of the genitals. Reporting requirements on abuse differ with each state.

Giving health education:

- Stock office with health education resources and materials available for women with physical and developmental disabilities.

- Patients living in a group situation may have multiple caregivers. For these women, all printed health education, instruction, and treatment information is best delivered in lower literacy English (other language as indicated) as well as orally to the accompanying attendant. Consider using visiting nurses to ensure instructions or treatment regimens are understood and followed.

women who have difficulty with thinking and reason-
ing, social interaction, or psychologic growth and
development), autism, and mental retardation (8).
Autism is defined as a developmental disorder that
affects the brain areas controlling language, social
interaction, and abstract thought (8). According to the
National Institutes of Health and the American
Association on Mental Retardation, mental retardation
is defined as a disability characterized by significant
limitations both in intellectual functioning and in
adaptive behavior as expressed in conceptual, social,
and practical adaptive skills (9).

Sensory disabilities may vary in severity from mild
to profound. Although sensory disabilities are present
in all ages, they become more predominant with
aging. Refractive errors are the most common visual
disorder in adolescents and adults. Legal blindness is
defined as a visual acuity of 20/200 or less in the better eye with corrective lenses or a peripheral vision
that is restricted to 20 degrees or less (tunnel vision);
however, many individuals labeled legally blind have
some usable vision (10).

Hearing impairment ranges from decreased sensitivity to total deafness. Individuals who are hard of hearing often have some residual hearing that enables
them to understand speech and use the telephone
with the help of a hearing aid (11).

There also are an estimated 40,000 individuals in
the United States with both deafness and blindness,
defined as auditory and visual impairments, the combination of which cause severe communication and
other developmental and educational problems (10).
Women with sensory impairments may have special
communication needs and require the use of assistive
devices when accessing gynecologic health care.

Women with disabilities are more likely to have
lower education levels, to be unemployed, and to
earn less than both men with disabilities and nondisabled women. Although they are just as likely to
have health care coverage, it is more likely to be
publicly funded coverage (Medicare and state
Medicaid programs). Individuals with disabilities
are at great risk of being underinsured. According
to a 2003 survey conducted by the Kaiser Family
Foundation, 73% of nonelderly individuals with disabilities rely on Medicare or Medicaid (12). In that
same survey, 17% reported that they were unable to
find a physician who would accept their health
insurance, 32% reported that they had problems

paying for prescription drugs, and 37% reported that
they postponed or put off care because of cost. One
cross-sectional survey illustrated that only 67% of
women with physical disabilities receive the counseling and routine primary gynecologic care they need
(13).

Both unsupportive environments and negative
stereotypes have been identified as barriers to these
women receiving adequate reproductive health care
services (14). In 1997, 28% of those with severe disabilities lived in poverty (15). Social isolation also is
more prominent because most women with disabilities
are likely to be unmarried and to live alone. Working-
age African-American and Native American women
have the highest incidence of extensive disability,
whereas Asian American women have the lowest incidence (15). Women with disabilities living in rural
areas receive fewer formal or specialized services and
must travel farther to obtain these services (16).

Women With Physical Disabilities

Physical Barriers to Health Care Services

All medical settings need to support the mobility
needs of the patient (5). Physical access barriers range
from doorways too narrow to access by wheelchair to
examination tables and room setups that make transfer from a wheelchair to the table difficult or unsafe.
The ability to obtain accurate weights, critical for pregnant patients, may be prohibited if a scale is not available that can be used by wheelchair users. It may be
impossible to obtain urine specimens if bathrooms are
inaccessible, and mammography may be prohibited if
appropriate equipment is not adaptable for women
with mobility impairments. Title III of the ADA states
that a public accommodation operated by a private
entity, including professional offices of health care
providers, must take steps to ensure that no individual
with a disability is discriminated against on the basis
of her limitation. The ADA requires the reduction of
environmental barriers through both modifications of
physical access and provision of auxiliary aids and
services to individuals with disabilities (5, 17).
Accessible examination tables that raise and lower in
height to accommodate most wheelchair users are one

example of office equipment that is helpful for women with physical disabilities (18). (Several resources are provided in this chapter to help physicians understand their responsibilities under the ADA as well as information on federal tax credits that may be available to offset the additional costs associated with reducing barriers to women with disabilities.)

Tax incentives are available to businesses that incur expenses in removing barriers or increasing accessibility for individuals with disabilities. The "Tax Deduction to Remove Architectural and Transportation Barriers to People with Disabilities and Elderly Individuals" (Title 26, Internal Revenue Code, Section 190) allows a deduction for "qualified architectural and transportation barrier removal expenses not to exceed $15,000 for any taxable year" (19).

Many physical access barriers can be overcome with suggestions from the woman with disabilities herself and the utilization of community resources. If the woman uses a device to assist with mobility or communication or an assistance animal, it can be helpful to discuss with her how best to utilize this assistance during the gynecologic appointment.

Programmatic Access

Many physician offices have tightly scheduled appointments, posing significant challenges for women with disabilities. Women with mobility impairments may rely on wheelchair accessible transportation services, which frequently are unreliable and cumbersome to use. Transportation often poses one of the greatest stressors for women with disabilities and can greatly contribute to difficulty accessing health care services.

Women with disabilities also may need extra time allotted for their appointment. If this is not built into the schedule, it can create significant frustrations for both the provider and patient. When scheduling appointments, asking patients about the need for extra time or services in a nonjudgmental and nonstigmatizing fashion may be one way of accommodating such needs. Creativity and flexibility on the part of each staff member can go a long way in ameliorating these challenges and establishing mutually rewarding and respectful services.

Knowledge Barriers

Knowledge barriers take a variety of forms in the care of women with disabilities. Health care providers may be unfamiliar with the individual's specific disability and its consequences on health, sexual functioning, and reproductive potential. Few health care professionals have received comprehensive information about caring for individuals with disabilities in their medical schools or training programs. This information may be accessible through various means, such as consultation with rehabilitation physicians or other disability providers, further investigation of medical literature, disability organizations, and through discussion with the woman and her family. Many women are well informed about their disabilities and the resources available to them. Issues such as strategies to manage spasticity and contractures during the pelvic examination, potential complications of pregnancy (eg, autonomic dysreflexia in women with spinal cord injuries, bowel impactions, and difficulties identifying labor), and accessing health care services can then be readily addressed.

There has been limited clinical research in the area of health care and women with disabilities. Questions arise about such topics as the risk of using hormone therapy or oral contraceptives in women with mobility impairments who may already have an increased risk of deep vein thrombosis; the best way to approach both primary and secondary osteoporosis in women with disabilities, many of whom will have significant immobility-related osteoporosis; and the risks of pregnancy for women with disabilities and how they may differ by type of disability. Although there are pockets of anecdotal experience and some retrospective studies, much more high quality research, definitive prospective studies, and perhaps pooled databases are needed. In the meantime, addressing health care issues with the best available current information is critical. Using a team approach involving primary care, physiotherapy, nursing, and social service may be helpful.

Attitudinal Barriers

Social psychology research has shown that non-disabled individuals, including health care providers, tend to see the disability as the defining aspect of the individual's life, whereas those who live with disability see it as just one of many variables by which they judge themselves. Consistent with this is the message that women with disabilities want to be viewed as women who have the same issues and concerns as other women; they just also have a disability.

Women with disabilities should be regarded as experts in how their body functions (6). The health care provider needs to be attuned to the woman's concern regarding the side effects of a medication or the alteration of her diet. Many of these women's lives are precisely balanced and slight alterations can have great consequences. Some may rely heavily on the services of attendants, family members, or friends for their basic care needs. Appointments, treatments, and medication administration require consideration of attendant availability.

Misconceptions about sexual interest and activity for women with physical disabilities are commonplace in both the public and health care professionals. In virtually all studies, individuals with physical disabilities report that, in the absence of depression, sexual desire is comparable to nondisabled peers (20, 21). The frequency of sexual activity and behavior as well as sexual satisfaction may be affected by the timing of the onset of the disability. Barriers to social development, decreased opportunity to date, difficulty finding partners, and lack of basic knowledge of sex and sexuality are more likely to be characteristics of adults whose disability began at birth (22). Most problems with sexual activity reported by women with physical disabilities were related to weakness; vaginal dryness; lack of balance; hip or knee pain; spasticity of legs; and reduced, delayed, or absent orgasmic sensation (6). Parents and professionals may attempt to keep girls with physical disabilities isolated because of concerns about sexual victimization and pregnancy. Individuals with acquired disabilities, such as spinal cord injury or complications of stroke, report not only changes in sexual functioning after onset of the disability but also a high degree of unmet needs for counseling and explicit information (for both them and their intimate partners) to adapt to these changes during initial rehabilitation or specialized care. Information about nontraditional and creative approaches to sexual expressions can be very helpful.

Growing research (particularly in the new field of disability studies and in the social sciences) is showing that quality of life is more tightly linked to social supports and degree of community integration than to disability per se (23). Knowledge of important community-based resources, such as Centers for Independent Living (nonresidential centers run by and for individuals with disabilities that provide community resources and training) and peer support services, may help women with disabilities make life-enhancing linkages.

Highlights of Selected Issues

Abuse and Violence

Victimization and abuse by partners are found to be equally prevalent among women with disabilities and women without physical disabilities (62%). However, women with physical disabilities are more at risk for abuse by attendants or health care providers and more likely to experience a longer duration of abuse (24). Many women with physical disabilities rely on a relative, personal attendant, or other type of caregiver for their personal and household needs. This reliance may involve exploitative relationships that often are difficult to uncover. Women who need others for personal assistance may be reluctant to disclose their concerns for fear of retaliation or loss of the essential services performed by the home or personal care provider. Abuse described by women with physical disabilities includes withholding of assistance or assistive devices. This type of abuse is not detected in standard abuse screening measures; however, a four-question abuse assessment tool for those with physical disabilities has been developed (Box 5).

Lack of available alternative resources or accessible shelters as well as fear of losing their children create further obstacles for women with disabilities encountering abuse. This contributes to the longer duration of the abuse. The obstetrician–gynecologist can provide support and information to help the woman with disabilities resolve the abusive situation, as well as provide her with knowledge of the various health consequences of abuse and violence for herself and her children. Given the complexity of the issues often raised, consultation with rehabilitation providers, Centers for Independent Living, and domestic violence programs may best be used to identify local, accessible resources. Some states have mandatory reporting requirements to adult protective services for individuals who are elderly or disabled and are living in an institutional setting. Other states require only that information about community resources be given. Health care providers should be familiar with their state laws, which can be obtained through the state department of social services.

Pregnancy and Parenting

Pregnancy and parenting for women with physical disabilities may have unique medical and social aspects but are rarely precluded by the disability itself. In fact, few physical disabilities directly limit fertility, although

---

Box 5 **Abuse Assessment Screen—Disability**

1. Within the last year, have you been hit, slapped, kicked, pushed, shoved, or otherwise physically hurt by someone?   ❑ YES   ❑ NO

   If YES, who? (circle all that apply)

   Intimate Partner   Care Provider   Health Professional   Family Member

   Other (eg, stranger, clergy)

   Please describe _____

2. Within the last year, has anyone forced you to have sexual activities?   ❑ YES   ❑ NO

   If YES, who? (circle all that apply)

   Intimate Partner   Care Provider   Health Professional   Family Member

   Other (eg, stranger, clergy)

   Please describe _____

3. Within the last year, has anyone prevented you from using a wheelchair, cane, respirator, or other assistive devices?   ❑ YES   ❑ NO

   If YES, who? (circle all that apply)

   Intimate Partner   Care Provider   Health Professional   Family Member

   Other (eg, stranger, clergy)

   Please describe _____

4. Within the last year, has anyone you depend on refused to help you with an important personal need, such as taking your medicine, getting to the bathroom, getting out of bed, bathing, getting dressed, or getting food or drink?   ❑ YES   ❑ NO

   If YES, who? (circle all that apply)

   Intimate Partner   Care Provider   Health Professional   Family Member

   Other (eg, stranger, clergy)

   Please describe _____

McFarlane J, Hughes RB, Nosek MA, Groff JY, Swedlend N, Dolan-Mullen P. Abuse assessment screen-disability (AAS-D): measuring frequency, type, and perpetrator of abuse toward women with physical disabilities. J Womens Health Gend Based Med 2001;10:861–6.

---

certain medications commonly prescribed to women with disabilities may affect ovulation by either altering thyroid function or prolactin levels or by directly suppressing ovulation (21). Health care professionals have the responsibility to provide appropriate reproductive health services to these women or arrange adequate consultation or referral (see "Resources"). Nonbiased preconceptional counseling for couples in which one or both partners has a physical disability may decrease subsequent psychosocial and medical complications of pregnancy.

Some complications are known to occur in pregnant women with specific disabilities. Autonomic hyperreflexia, for example, may occur in pregnant women with spinal cord lesions above T6 as a result of a loss of hypothalamic control over sympathetic spinal reflexes (25). This is in response to pressure in the bladder or rectum caused by distention, manipulation, uterine contractions, infection, decubitus ulcer, or thrombophlebitis. Autonomic hyperreflexia is a medical emergency and is characterized by severe hypertension and bradycardia. During a pelvic examination, ultrasonography, or the course of pregnancy and labor, the obstetrician–gynecologist must be alert for autonomic hyperreflexia and discuss this possibility with the patient. Physical signs include sweating, erection of body hair, nausea, and nasal congestion.

Pregnant women with mobility problems are more susceptible to urinary tract infections, decubitus ulcers, decrease in coordination and balance, and fatigue (26). For more information on the management of pregnancy for women with spinal cord injuries, see "ACOG Resources."

To avoid questions from child protective services staff about the ability of women with disabilities to parent, it is best to handle issues around parenting during the pregnancy. At this time, rehabilitation specialists and community and peer supports can help assess the woman's ability to provide needed infant care and determine any adaptations and equipment necessary to facilitate her independence as a mother (27). The presence of a partner or other individual to assist with particular activities can be discussed before birth to facilitate a safe and successful discharge to home for all concerned (see "Resources" for organizations and publications on parenting).

Cancer Screening

Women with physical disabilities are less likely to have cancer screenings, often because they do not acknowledge their risk of gynecologic cancer (28). It has been reported that women with functional limitations (Box 6) have fewer Pap tests and are somewhat less likely to undergo mammogram screening compared to women without functional limitations (29). As primary health care providers to women, obstetrician–gynecologists should have an awareness of and implement all age-appropriate cancer screening guidelines for their patients, including those with disabilities. Coordination with colleagues may facilitate the conduct of multiple examinations, such as sigmoidoscopy and colposcopy, during the same visit.

Breast Cancer. The three components of adequate breast health screening include breast self-examina-

| Box 6 | Functional Limitations |

A functional limitation is defined as being unable to do any of the following:
- Lift 10 pounds
- Walk up 10 steps without resting
- Walk one quarter of a mile
- Stand for approximately 20 minutes
- Bend down from a standing position
- Reach up over the head or reach out
- Use fingers to grasp or handle something
- Hold a pen or pencil

Use of cervical and breast cancer screening among women with and without functional limitations, United States, 1994–1995. MMWR Morb Mortal Wkly Rep 1998;47:853–6.

tion, clinical examination, and mammography. Barriers to breast self-examination or mammography screening for women with disabilities include: difficulty with hand coordination, inability to reach around the chest, impaired sensation in fingers, and tremors (30, 31). Until recently, many women with disabilities were not trained in breast self-examination. For those women with limited upper body dexterity, modifications to breast self-examination techniques and practice can be used by the woman, her partner, or personal care provider (32) (see Fig. 4 and "Resources").

Mammography remains the best screening procedure for the early detection of breast cancer. Newer types of mammography equipment have been developed to accommodate women with some mobility problems. Resources of this type can be identified within a geographic area at www.bhawd.org. No clinical guidelines have been established for women who are unable to have mammography; however, frequent breast clinical examinations coupled with ultrasonography when indicated have been used. Ultrasonography does not, however, detect microcalcifications often indicative of early malignant breast changes (33).

Cervical Cancer. Women with more severe functional limitations are much less likely to have regular pelvic examinations. The most prevalent cause of not having regular pelvic examinations is difficulty getting on to

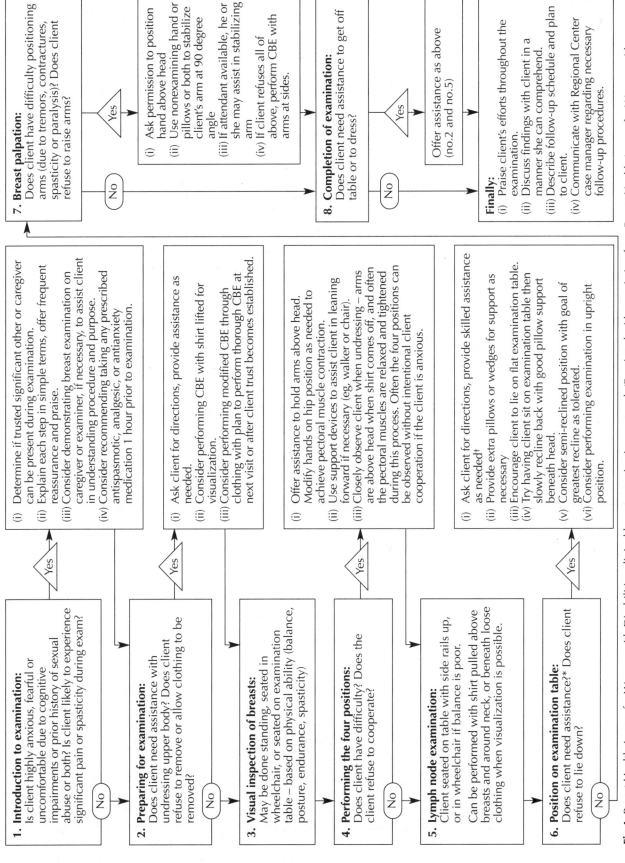

1. Introduction to examination:
Is client highly anxious, fearful or uncomfortable due to cognitive impairments or prior history of sexual abuse or both? Is client likely to experience significant pain or spasticity during exam?

No → / Yes →

(i) Determine if trusted significant other or caregiver can be present during examination.
(ii) Explain each step in simple terms, offer frequent reassurance and praise.
(iii) Consider demonstrating breast examination on caregiver or examiner, if necessary, to assist client in understanding procedure and purpose.
(iv) Consider recommending taking any prescribed antispasmotic, analgesic, or antianxiety medication 1 hour prior to examination.

2. Preparing for examination:
Does client need assistance with undressing upper body? Does client refuse to remove or allow clothing to be removed?

No → / Yes →

(i) Ask client for directions, provide assistance as needed.
(ii) Consider performing CBE with shirt lifted for visualization.
(iii) Consider performing modified CBE through clothing with plan to perform thorough CBE at next visit or after client trust becomes established.

3. Visual inspection of breasts:
May be done standing, seated in wheelchair, or seated on examination table – based on physical ability (balance, posture, endurance, spasticity)

Yes →

(i) Offer assistance to hold arms above head. Modify hands on hip position as needed to achieve pectoral muscle contraction.
(ii) Use support devices to assist client in leaning forward if necessary (eg, walker or chair).
(iii) Closely observe client when undressing – arms are above head when shirt comes off, and often the pectoral muscles are relaxed and tightened during this process. Often the four positions can be observed without intentional client cooperation if the client is anxious.

4. Performing the four positions:
Does client have difficulty? Does the client refuse to cooperate?

No → / Yes →

5. Lymph node examination:
Client seated on table with side rails up, or in wheelchair if balance is poor.
Can be performed with shirt pulled above breasts and around neck, or beneath loose clothing when visualization is possible.

No → / Yes →

(i) Ask client for directions, provide skilled assistance as needed†
(ii) Provide extra pillows or wedges for support as necessary
(iii) Encourage client to lie on flat examination table.
(iv) Try having client sit on examination table then slowly recline back with good pillow support beneath head.
(v) Consider semi-reclined position with goal of greatest recline as tolerated.
(vi) Consider performing examination in upright position.

6. Position on examination table:* Does client need assistance?* Does client refuse to lie down?

No → / Yes →

7. Breast palpation:
Does client have difficulty positioning arms (due to tremors, contractures, spasticity or paralysis)? Does client refuse to raise arms?

No → / Yes →

(i) Ask permission to position hand above head
(ii) Use nonexamining hand or pillows or both to stabilize client's arm at 90 degree angle
(iii) If attendant available, he or she may assist in stabilizing arm
(iv) If client refuses all of above, perform CBE with arms at sides.

8. Completion of examination:
Does client need assistance to get off table or to dress?

No → / Yes →

Offer assistance as above (no.2 and no.5)

Finally:
(i) Praise client's efforts throughout the examination.
(ii) Discuss findings with client in a manner she can comprehend.
(iii) Describe follow-up schedule and plan to client.
(iv) Communicate with Regional Center case manager regarding necessary follow-up procedures.

Fig.4. Breast Health Access for Women with Disabilities clinical breast examination protocol. (Reprinted with permission from Breast Health Access for Women with Disabilities [BHAWD]. A provider's guide to the examination and screening of women with disabilities. Breast Health Access for Women with Disabilities [BHAWD], Alta Bates Summit Medical Center, Rehabilitation Services Department, Berkeley [CA]; 2003.)

*Recommend electrically controlled, high-low exam table with side rails
†Client may prefer to bring own attendant, or clinic provides assistance from trained personnel
Abbreviation: CBE, clinical breast examination

the examination table (28). As mentioned previously, examination tables that lower to facilitate wheelchair transfer have been developed. If these are not yet in place, safe transfer and positioning techniques can be used (see "Resources").

There are important issues to consider when conducting a pelvic examination for women with physical disabilities. The manipulation and positioning in the examination may cause the patient's bowels or bladder to empty, or a full bladder or constipation may trigger spasticity. Therefore, it is important to have the patient empty her bladder and bowels before the examination (6). Mobility limitations of the woman's disability may require alternative positioning for a pelvic examination. Obstetric stirrups have been found to provide the support many women require for optimal positioning during the examination and also to reduce spasms (34) (see "Resources").

Sexually Transmitted Diseases

Women with physical disabilities may have difficulty manipulating barrier methods of contraception, leaving them more vulnerable to contracting STDs, including human immunodeficiency virus (HIV) infection. Therefore, patients who use hormonal contraception or the intrauterine device (IUD) need to be screened for STDs at the same frequency as nondisabled women using these methods (35). Discussion of STD prevention also is beneficial in helping the patient to plan for safe sexual encounters.

Women With Developmental Disabilities

Patients with developmental disabilities may present with a broad range of health concerns, including difficulty maintaining preventive care, poor hygiene, unanticipated pubertal development, the need for family planning and contraception, pregnancy, abnormal uterine bleeding, menopausal issues, and sexual or physical abuse. Some aspects of the provision of comprehensive gynecologic health care, including the performance of a gynecologic examination, cancer screening, sexuality issues, contraception, and screening and treatment for STDs, are unique for women with developmental disabilities. With patience, some modification of the examination, and knowledge of the issues, obstetrician–gynecologists can provide compre-

hensive, individualized reproductive health care and education to this group of women and their caregivers.

Gynecologic Health Care

To determine an appropriate treatment plan for women with developmental disabilities, it is important to consider the following psychosocial factors: whether the individual lives at home or in a domiciliary care setting; whether there is a reliable caregiver present; previous history of sexual abuse; and cognitive factors, including her ability to have consensual intercourse and to relay a personal or family history of gynecologic disease and symptoms.

Routine examinations can be hindered by communication difficulties and potential physical limitations. Adaptations needed may include altering the type of examination, the positioning for the examination, or the frequency or sequence of specific tests. The clinician should allow the patient to become familiar with her and the setting before initiation of the examination. For instance, before having the patient disrobe, the clinician might spend a few moments sitting and conversing with the patient. The clinician may want to talk about a favorite food, pet, or article of clothing. Reminding the woman of this conversation during the examination may help to calm her fears. Gynecologic evaluation is never to be accomplished with physical force or inducement of fear in any patient. Office staff and clinical assistants should be oriented to the special needs of each woman during her visit and examination. If possible, the appointment should be scheduled with extra time allowed and when the attention and support of staff can be optimized.

Consent for Treatment

Before examination, it should be determined who will give consent for the examination and any consequential treatment. It also is important at this time to ascertain if the patient is competent to understand findings and health recommendations or whether this information needs to be transmitted to an identified guardian or caregiver. It often is helpful, with the patient's consent, to have a companion with whom the patient is familiar accompany her to the examination room. Additionally, providers who care for patients with developmental disabilities may find it helpful to provide a short summary of the patient's medical problems for the patient or guardian to keep in their bill-fold along with the name of a contact person and their primary medical provider. This will help emergency room personnel, new providers, or consult physicians when records are not available.

Cancer Screening

Cervical Cancer. Data on Pap tests in women with developmental disabilities are limited. One retrospective review of such patients from a specialty clinic found the incidence of abnormal Pap tests to be 0.3% as compared with 0.6% in the general population. Of note is that only approximately one third of the Pap tests obtained from women with developmental disabilities had an endocervical component, and a Pap test without an endocervical component may be of limited value (36).

For women with developmental disabilities, there are several concerns regarding Pap tests. Often there is inadequate information regarding past medical history, including Pap history, the presence of human papillomavirus (HPV), or sexual risk factors, such as abuse and STDs, leading to a difficulty assessing the risk for cervical cancer and determining an optimal schedule for Pap tests (36). Performing the pelvic examination may be difficult for several reasons, including the inability to communicate with the patient, patient's fear induced by previous encounters with caregivers, accompanying physical disabilities, or the complete inability of the patient to perceive what is taking place. Different examining positions (eg, frog leg) may be helpful (37). In some instances, examination under anesthesia is necessary (see the discussion in section on "Sedation or Anesthesia for Examination.") If the patient with developmental disabilities and her guardian consent to the examination, Pap tests can be done as frequently as she and her physician determine are appropriate and as recommended by ACOG for all women (38).

Some patients come to their gynecologist with a "directive" for a Pap test from a social service agency, community program, or residential institution. There are no laws mandating Pap tests for any group of women. Organizations and institutions will have differing guidelines pertaining to Pap tests. A comprehensive reproductive evaluation often is needed, but it may not need to include a Pap test. If a gynecologist receives such a "mandate," an investigation to identify the source and clarify this request is in order.

Ovarian Cancer. A woman's lifetime incidence of ovarian cancer is 1.72% (39). There are no screening techniques currently available that have proved effective in reducing the disease-specific mortality of ovarian cancer. The use of ultrasound and CA 125 has not been proved effective in population-based screening for ovarian cancer (40), but if the patient has been sedated for a physical examination, transvaginal ultrasonography may be useful.

Sedation or Anesthesia for Examination. The use of sedation to facilitate health care screening has been advocated by some for women whose developmental disabilities otherwise preclude pelvic examination (41). However, this use of sedation has never been evaluated in a systematic fashion. For example, one study revealed that 25% of women with developmental disabilities could not be examined even with sedation (36). Of the patients who were examined with intravenous sedation, the rate of endocervical cells on their Pap tests (30%) was similar to that in women with developmental disabilities examined without sedation. Moreover, there are concerns about the ethics of this approach (42, 43). There is no information on the emotional effects of a pelvic examination in a sedated state. Sedation with oral agents that have a lower risk profile may be considered in patients with a higher level of functioning in consultation with the patient's primary care provider. If sedation is chosen, consent must be obtained from the patient (if legally competent) or the patient's legally designated guardian (44).

Patients whose developmental disabilities prohibit pelvic examination and Pap test without general anesthesia pose an extra challenge to the health care provider. Although the ACOG recommendation for cervical cytology screening is for three normal annual examinations before prolonging the screening interval (38), the risk of general anesthesia 3 years in a row may outweigh the chance of finding a premalignant lesion. This challenge may be compounded by the frequency of incomplete records or unknown Pap history as noted previously. If general anesthesia is to be used, a screening interval of every 3 years can be considered. Several studies that did not specifically include individuals with developmental disabilities have shown the safety of 3-year intervals in women with at least one previous normal Pap test result (45). The sensitivity of screening at extended intervals may be increased by the use of liquid-based cytology.

When planning procedures, providing comprehensive care under a single anesthetic may reduce the risk of repeated general anesthesia. Some hospitals have special clinics for the gynecologic care of women with disabilities and have established programs with other services that may require anesthesia, such as dentistry. When a patient with developmental disabilities is subjected to general anesthesia for gynecologic care, coordination with other providers for health maintenance examinations may be useful. An alternative to anesthesia for a pelvic examination may be pelvic ultrasound imaging at regular intervals, based on age and symptomatology.

Breast Cancer. Breast cancer is the second leading cause of death from cancer among women. One in eight women will develop breast cancer during her lifetime if she lives to age 90 years (39). Nulliparity is one of the associated risk factors for breast cancer. Women with developmental disabilities are living longer than in years past and frequently are nulliparous, thereby increasing their risk for developing breast cancer.

Women with developmental disabilities who live in a supervised setting usually are required to undergo monthly breast examinations by a caregiver as part of their care plan. This, however, may not be done adequately or at all. Although there is some recent discussion about harm versus benefit of the monthly breast self-examination (46), ACOG currently recommends this for women between the ages of 19 and 39 years (47). The provider can discuss and reinforce or teach breast examination techniques to the caregiver and the patient when this is appropriate.

Women with developmental disabilities may face specific problems with screening mammography because the procedure requires cooperation, ability to stand up and move the arms, and the ability to tolerate some discomfort of the breasts. Many women with developmental disabilities cannot comply with one or all of these requirements.

Mammography is the only U.S. Food and Drug Administration-approved examination to help screen for cancer in women who show no signs or symptoms of the disease. Although not appropriate for asymptomatic screening, suspicious areas might be followed up with diagnostic testing requiring minimal discomfort and cooperation, such as ultrasonography.

Sexuality

Sexuality issues facing women with developmental disabilities need to be addressed by parents,

caregivers, and health care professionals. These individuals may be uncomfortable addressing these issues. Consequently, the patients often have limited or no access to appropriate services and counseling. The ability to reproduce usually is not affected by a developmental disability (48). Therefore, reproductive concerns need to be addressed in routine care. Also to be included is an assessment of the patient's risk for abuse and her ability to have a consensual sexual relationship. Parents or caregivers fearful of abuse or pregnancy often request contraception for women with developmental disabilities.

If the parent or guardian is requesting long-term contraception for a woman who is incapable of giving informed consent, the decision to use long-term contraception should be based on a careful assessment. This may involve a multidisciplinary team that includes an advocate appointed for the impaired woman (49). Some states have legislation on issues of consent and permanence concerning contraception for women with developmental disabilities. The clinician can consult the state developmental disabilities council for further information (see "Resources").

Parents and caregivers often are unable to provide clear, easily comprehensible sexuality education to women with developmental disabilities. Physicians can offer guidance to caregivers on various approaches to educating these women about sexual abuse, conception, contraception, and prevention of STDs. Physicians also can educate patients about sexuality issues, using teaching aids and materials that are appropriate to their level of functioning, rather than their biological age (50) (see "Resources").

Contraceptive Issues

It is important to do a thorough assessment and evaluation before initiating any hormonal contraceptive method for a patient with developmental disabilities because patients who begin a hormonal contraceptive method may continue them for many years without reevaluation of the indications and long-term consequences. Such an evaluation also includes a determination of whether the current sexual relationship is consensual. Following this assessment and evaluation, the clinician provides the patient and, when necessary, her caregiver education about method safety; effectiveness; use of the contraceptive; and expected side effects, such as alterations in the menstrual cycle. (See section on "Contraception" for discussion of specific methods of contraception.)

Sterilization

Physicians must adhere to the highest ethical standards when considering sterilization for women with developmental disabilities. Federal, state, and local laws and regulations vary widely on the subject. These laws often protect women in this population but occasionally limit their full reproductive options. The presence of a developmental disability does not, in itself, justify either sterilization or its denial. However, federal funds cannot be used to pay for sterilization in women who have developmental disabilities that preclude their ability to understand the implications of sterilization and give truly informed consent (42). It is incumbent on the physician to determine the capacity of a patient to grant informed consent before any surgical procedure. Physicians need to consider the patient's language and culture, the clarity and degree of bias of the information provided, the setting of counseling, and possible fluctuations in the patient's comprehension because of various stressors or medication. Multiple interviews over a period of time may mitigate these factors, as may enlisting the assistance of special educators, psychologists, attorneys familiar with disability law, or other personnel trained to work with individuals with developmental disabilities. If sterilization is performed, it may be prudent to "hide" the ligation scar in the umbilicus so women with developmental disabilities cannot be identified by potential predators as sterilized women. (See "Resources" for information pertaining to pregnancy and parenting issues for women with developmental disabilities.)

Sexually Transmitted Disease Screening

Limited research has shown that women with developmental disabilities are less aware of the risks that are associated with being sexually active (48). The difficulty in educating women with developmental disabilities, combined with their increased risk for coerced sexual activity and limited capability to use barrier contraception, enhances their risk of contracting STDs. Routine screening for STDs is to be performed. This includes testing for HPV by visual inspection and cervical cytology. In women on whom performing a pelvic examination is difficult, screening for *Neisseria gonorrhoeae* and *Chlamydia trachomatis* can be accomplished by nucleic acid testing of urine, introital swab, or modified sanitary napkin specimens (49, 51, 52).

Sensory Impairments

Communication and mobility are the main issues facing women who have sensory impairments. When possible, these issues should be discussed before the appointment. Teletypewriter devices; professional signers for those whose primary mode of communication is sign language; and materials in large print, on audiotape, or in Braille may all be needed to facilitate communication and foster ongoing health education. (See "Resources" for information on the ADA's legal requirements in this area.)

The gynecologic examination may be traumatic for women with visual impairments if time is not taken to orient her to the surroundings, to allow her to touch an example of the instruments that will be used during the examination, and to give a thorough explanation of what will transpire. If she uses an assistive device, such as a cane, it is important to not move it without her knowledge. Assistance animals should always be allowed to accompany the woman as needed throughout her appointment.

Before the gynecologic examination for the woman with hearing impairments, it may be helpful for the provider to explore how the patient prefers to communicate and her assistance needs. For instance, if a sign language interpreter is used, the patient can determine where that individual will stand. It is helpful to position the drape so it does not interfere with the woman's ability to see the health care provider's face, particularly if she is lip-reading. If appropriate, before the examination the health care provider and woman together should determine how the woman will communicate discomfort or distress. Women with hearing impairments often have difficulty with balance. This is especially important to note when positioning during an examination and in standing after an examination.

Common Issues for Women With Disabilities

Communication Barriers

Good health care is dependent on communication. Language and educational differences between women and their providers are barriers to effective care. Women with disabilities may have additional challenges. Women with brain impairments may have aphasias (impairments in language abilities—including comprehension or expression) or dysarthrias (impairments in speech).

Some individuals with extensive speech impairments may use augmentative communication devices, such as letter boards, eye gaze systems, or computer devices to communicate. Having a communication impairment does not indicate the legal competency of the patient or her ability to participate in her health care decision making. Knowledge of the women's mode of communication and patience in the process is critical to ensure informed health care delivery.

It is important to make every attempt to address and communicate with the woman directly rather than through a family member or personal assistant. For women with cognitive or developmental disabilities, making materials available in pictorial formats or in simple, straightforward language can facilitate communication greatly.

Contraception

There are numerous safe, effective, and easy to use contraceptives available to all women. Female barrier contraceptives, including spermicides and the diaphragm, typically are not recommended for women with mobility and developmental disabilities because of difficult, inconsistent, or improper use. Unless the woman is in a stable, mutually monogamous relationship, the use of condoms for male partners is always recommended to reduce the risk of STDs, regardless of any additional method used by the woman.

Estrogen-Progestin Combined Formulation

Oral Contraceptives. Oral contraceptives commonly are used for birth control as well as for cycle control. The subsequent decrease in menstrual flow, dysmenorrhea, and in the number of bleeding episodes in a year often is beneficial for women with disabilities and may help in the care of patients with heavy menses. Taking the pills regularly may require daily assistance or supervision. Special considerations include cardiac and vascular flow abnormalities (they occur frequently among women with Down syndrome) that may predispose a woman to thromboembolic disease, or the concurrent use of anti-seizure medications that may reduce contraceptive effectiveness.

Nonoral Methods. Safe and effective contraception can now be achieved with a monthly combination estrogen and progestin injection, a transdermal patch, or a vaginal ring. The monthly injection needs to be given every 28 days with a margin of error of 5 days (53). A transdermal patch is changed weekly for 3 weeks, with no patch administered in the fourth week. Menstruation is expected in the fourth week. A new patch is worn the following week (54). A single vaginal ring is worn for 3 weeks and then removed for a week. Menstruation is expected during the week the ring is not worn. A new ring is inserted the following week (55). These methods are very similar to the combined oral contraceptive pill in terms of efficacy and contraindications. They also are likely to provide similar noncontraceptive benefits, such as good cycle control, a decrease in menstrual bleeding, and decrease in dysmenorrhea. A major advantage of these nonoral methods is that they do not require daily administration. There may be, however, the need for assistance or supervision given the periodic removal, reapplication, or insertion of methods; a possibility of inadvertent displacement by the woman; or more health care visits for the injection.

Progestin-Only Formulation

Contraceptive methods using only progestin are safe, effective, and can be used in women who cannot or should not use estrogen because of a high risk of thromobembolic disease. Progestin-only contraceptives can be given as an intramuscular injection, as a pill, as a subdermal implant, or as part of an intrauterine system (56).

Oral administration of this method is likely of limited use for women with developmental disabilities because efficacy is dependent on administration adherence. The pill should be taken at the same time every day (with no pill-free interval). The main side effect of this method is irregular vaginal bleeding, which may be problematic in this population.

Intramuscular Medroxyprogesterone. Medroxyprogesterone is a popular choice for women with disabilities because of its ease of administration, very high efficacy, and relative long duration (3 months). Initial use often results in irregular vaginal bleeding. After prolonged use, complete cessation of menstrual flow is likely. Absence of menstrual flow may be beneficial in patients who have difficulty managing their menses. Caution is advised in the use of medroxyprogesterone for women who are nonweight-bearing or at risk for low bone mineral density because some studies have indicated reduced bone density with prolonged use (56).

Contraceptive Implant. The advantages of contraceptive implants are very high efficacy and long duration of action (up to 5 years). Disadvantages include the need for insertion and removal by a health care professional and a relatively high incidence of unpredictable vaginal bleeding. It is likely that new generations of implants with increased ease of administration and removal will be available soon.

Intrauterine Devices. Research and improvements have made the IUD an attractive contraception choice for many women and may be quite appropriate for women with disabilities. The copper-T380A continues to provide reliable contraception for up to 10 years after insertion. However, it may cause cramping and irregular and sometimes heavy menstrual bleeding, especially in the first months after insertion. These side effects may not be acceptable to women with disabilities or those caring for them. The levonorgestrel intrauterine system is a flexible, plastic, T-shaped device with a reservoir of progesterone and may be left in place for 5 years. An advantage of this system for women with disabilities is that following the first few months after insertion, menstrual bleeding is greatly reduced and some women stop bleeding completely (57). As with all IUDs, it is important to teach the patient or caretaker how to check for placement on a monthly basis. An IUD would not be an appropriate choice for women who may be prone to pulling it out.

Adolescent Women

Adolescents with either physical or developmental disabilities often receive inadequate education or guidance regarding menarche, sexuality, and reproductive care services. Additionally, menarche may pose new behavioral concerns for the caretakers of women with developmental disabilities. The obstetrician–gynecologist may be the first individual to offer information and counseling in this area. With mainstreaming in the public school system, adolescents with disabilities may have little contact with other girls and women with disabilities who can serve as mentors or role models. A positive, respectful experience with an obstetrician–gynecologist in early ado-

lescence can affect the woman's self-esteem and willingness to seek out future reproductive health care services.

Menstrual hygiene may become an important issue for some adolescents with disabilities and those caring for them. To avoid the unpleasant effects and potential danger from prolonged use, tampons usually are not recommended for women who cannot care for their own menstrual hygiene (37). Keeping a menstrual calendar also can be helpful (58).

Perimenopausal Women

Menopausal and postmenopausal women represent an underserved population with regard to general gynecologic and primary care. Women with developmental disabilities or long-term or acquired physical disabilities in this stage of life require care that limits secondary complications and enhances quality of life and social interactions. Detailed analysis of cardiovascular status, a risk profile for osteoporosis, and medication lists are needed for making decisions about prescribing medications. Coordination with other primary care physicians and family members of older women with disabilities is essential to avoid iatrogenic complications, such as those caused by use of multiple medications.

References

1. Disability status of the civilian noninstitutionalized population by sex and selected characteristics for the United States and Puerto Rico: 2000 (PHC–T–32). Washington, DC: U.S. Census Bureau, 2004. Available at: www.census.gov/population/www/cen2000/phc-t32.html. Retrieved September 21, 2004.

2. Nosek MA, Young ME, Rintala DH, Howland CA, Foley C, Bennett JL. Barriers to reproductive health maintenance among women with physical disabilities. J Women's Health 1995;4: 505–18.

3. Fine M, Asch A, editors. Women with disabilities: essays in psychology, culture and politics. Philadelphia (PA): Temple University Press; 1988.

4. Elkins TE, McNeeley SG, Rosen D, Heaton C, Sorg C, DeLancey JO, et al. A clinical observation of a program to accomplish pelvic exams in difficult-to-manage patients with mental retardation. Adolesc Pediat Gynecol 1988;1:195–8.

5. US Department of Justice. A guide to disability rights laws. Washington, DC: USDOJ; 2001

6. Bradshaw KD, Elkins TE, Quint, EH. The patient with physical disabilities: issues in gynecologic care. Raritan (NJ): Ortho–McNeil Pharmaceutical; 1996.

7. LaPlante MP. The demographics of disability. Milbank Q 1991; 69 suppl:55–77.

8. United Cerebral Palsy. UCP: media & public awareness—glossary and definitions. Available at: http://www.ucp.org/ucp_printsub.cfm/53/9/36. Retrieved July 7, 2003.

9. American Association on Mental Retardation. Definition of mental retardation. Washington, DC: AAMR; 2002. Available at: http://www.aamr.org/Policies/faq_mental_retardation.shtml. Retrieved September 21, 2004.

10. North Dakota Deaf Blind service project. Deaf blind services project. Available at: www.state.nd.us/deafblind/. Retrieved July 7, 2003.

11. Ries PW. Prevalence and characteristics of persons with hearing trouble: United States, 1990–91. Vital Health Stat 10 1994;(188): 1–75.

12. The Kaiser Family Foundation. Survey of people with disabilities. The Kaiser Family Foundation, Menlo Park (CA). Publication #6107; 2003.

13. Nosek MA, Howland CA. Breast and cervical cancer screening among women with physical disabilities. Arch Phys Med Rehabil 1997;78:S39–S44.

14. Welner SL. Gynecologic care of the disabled woman. Contemp Ob Gyn 1993;3855–67.

15. McNeil JM. Americans with disabilities: 1997. Current Population Report Series P70–73. Washington, DC: US Dept. of Commerce; 1997.

16. Lishner DM, Richardson M, Levine P, Patrick D. Access to primary health care among persons with disabilities in rural areas: a summary of the literature. J Rural Health 1996;12:45–53.

17. American College of Obstetricians and Gynecologists. Guidelines for women's health care. 2nd ed. Washington, DC: ACOG; 2002: p. 428–32.

18. Mace RL. Removing barriers to health care: a guide for health professionals. Raleigh (NC): North Carolina State University; 1998.

19. Council of Better Business Bureaus' Foundation. Medical offices: access equals opportunity: your guide to the Americans with Disabilities Act. 1992. Publication no. 24–280.

20. Nosek MA, Rintala DH, Young ME, Howland CA, Foley CC, Rossi D, et al. Sexual functioning among women with physical disabilities. Arch Phys Med Rehabil 1996;77:107–15.

21. Sipski ML, Alexander CJ, editors. Impact of disability or chronic illness on sexual function. In: Sexual function in people with disability and chronic illness: a health professional's guide. Gaithersburg (MD): Aspen Publishers; 1997. p. 3–12.

22. Baylor College of Medicine. National study of women with physical disabilities: sexual functioning. Available at: http://www.bcm.tmc.edu/crowd/national_study/sexfunc.htm. Retrieved July 16, 2001.

23. Albrecht GL, Devlieger PJ. The disability paradox: high quality of life against all odds. Soc Sci Med 1999;48:977–88.

24. Young ME, Noesk MA, Howland CA, Chanpong G, Rintala DH. Prevalence of abuse of women with physical disabilities. Arch Phys Med Rehabil 1997;78:S34–8.

25. Pope CS, Markenson GR, Bayer-Zwirello LA, Maissel GS. Pregnancy complicated by chronic spinal cord injury and history of autonomic hyperreflexia. Obstet Gynecol 2001;97:802–3.

26. Villanova University College of Nursing. Disability-related symptoms. Available at: http://www.nursing.villanova.edu/womenwithdisabilities/preg/disability.htm. Retrieved July 16, 2003.

27. Rogers J, Matsumura M. The first step—deciding whether to have a child. In: Mother to be: a guide to pregnancy. Birth for women with disabilities. New York (NY): Demos Publications; 1991. p. 51–91.

28. Welner S. A provider's guide for the care of women with physical disabilities and chronic medical conditions. Chapel Hill (NC): North Carolina Office on Disability and Health; 1999.

29. Use of cervical and breast cancer screening among women with and without functional limitations—United States, 1994–1995. MMWR Morb Mortal Wkly Rep 1998;47:853–6.

30. Breast Health Access for Women with Disabilities. BHAWD highlights of January 1999 conference report. Available at http://www.bhawd.org/sitefiles/Conferen.html. Retrieved July 16, 2003.

31. Thierry JM. Increasing breast and cervical cancer screening among women with disabilities. Womens Health Gend Based Med 2000;9:9–12.

32. Fletcher SW, O'Malley MS, Earp JL, Morgan TM, Lin S, Degnan D. How best to teach women breast self-examination. A randomized controlled trial. Ann Intern Med 1990;112:772–9.

33. Smith RA, Saslow D, Sawyer KA, Burke W, Costanza ME, Evans WP, et al. American Cancer Society guidelines for breast cancer screening: update 2003. CA Cancer J Clin 2003;53:141–69.

34. Ferreyra S, Hughes K. Table manners: a guide to the pelvic examination for disabled women and health care providers. San Francisco (CA): Planned Parenthood Alameda/SanFrancisco; 1991.

35. American College of Obstetricians and Gynecologists. Guidelines for women's health care. 2nd ed. Washington, DC: ACOG; 2002.

36. Quint EH, Elkins TE. Cervical cytology in women with mental retardation. Obstet Gynecol 1997;89:123–6.

37. Bradshaw KD, Elkins TE, Quint EH. The patient with mental retardation: issues in gynecologic care. Raritan (NJ). Ortho-McNeil Pharmaceutical; 1996.

38. Cervical cytology screening. ACOG Practice Bulletin No. 45. American College of Obstetricians and Gynecologists. Obstet Gynecol 2003;102:417–27.

39. Ries LA, Eisner MP, Kosary CL, Hankey BF, Miller BA, Clegg L, et al, editors. SEER cancer statistics review, 1975–2000. Bethesda (MD): National Cancer Institute; 2003. Available at: http://www.seer.cancer.gov/csr/1975-2000. Retrieved July 7, 2003.

40. Screening for ovarian cancer: recommendation statement. U.S. Preventive Services Task Force. Ann Fam Med 2004;2:260–2.

41. Rosen DA, Rosen KR, Elkins TE, Andersen HF, McNeeley SG Jr, Sorg C. Outpatient sedation: an essential addition to gynecologic care for persons with mental retardation. Am J Obstet Gynecol 1991;164:825–8.

42. Brown D, Rosen D, Elkins TE. Sedating women with mental retardation for routine gynecologic examination: an ethical analysis. J Clin Ethics 1992;3:68–75; discussion 76–7.

43. Hoyle D. The autonomy of adult women should be paramount, not the exam. J Clin Ethics 1992;3:76–7.

44. American College of Obstetricians and Gynecologists. Ethics in obstetrics and gynecology. 2nd edition. Washington, DC: ACOG; 2004.

45. Sawaya GF, Kerlikowske K, Lee NC, Gildengorin G, Washington AE. Frequency of cervical smear abnormalities within 3 years of normal cytology. Obstet Gynecol 2000;96:219–23.

46. Baxter N. Canadian Task Force on Preventive Health Care. Preventive health care, 2001 update: should women be routinely taught breast self–examination to screen for breast cancer? CMAJ 2001;164:1837–46.

47. American College of Obstetricians and Gynecologists. Primary and preventive care: periodic assessments. ACOG Committee Opinion 292. Washington, DC: ACOG; 2003.

48. Haefner HK, Elkins TE. Contraceptive management for female adolescents with mental retardation and handicapping disabilities. Curr Opin Obstet Gynecol 1991;3:820–4.

49. American College of Obstetricians and Gynecologists. Health care for adolescents. Washington, DC: ACOG; 2003.

50. Sexuality education of children and adolescents with developmental disabilities. American Academy of Pediatrics. Committee on Children with Disabilities. Pediatrics 1996;97:275–8.

51. Morse SA. New tests for bacterial sexually transmitted diseases. Curr Opin Infect Dis 2001;14:45–51.

52. Alary M, Poulin C, Bouchard C, Fortier M, Murray G, Gingras S, et al. Evaluation of a modified sanitary napkin as a sample self-collection device for the detection of genital chlamydia infection in women. J Clin Microbiol 2001;39:2508–12.

53. Kaunitz AM, Garceau RJ, Cromie MA. Comparative safety, efficacy, and cycle control of Lunelle monthly contraceptive injection (medroxyprogesterone acetate and estradial cypionate injectable suspension) Ortho Novum 7/7/7 oral contraceptive (norethindronelethinyl estradiol triphasic). Lunelle Study Group Contraception 1999;60:179–87.

54. Smallwood GH, Meador ML, Lenihan JP, Shangold GA, Fisher AC, Creasy GW, et al. Efficacy and safety of a transdermal contraceptive system. Obstet Gynecol 2001;98:799–805.

55. Mulders TM, Dieben TO. Use of the novel combined contraceptive vaginal ring NuvaRing for ovulation inhibition. Fertil Steril 2001;75:865–70.

56. American College of Obstetricians and Gynecologists. The use of hormonal contraception in women with coexisting medical conditions. ACOG Practice Bulletin 18. Washington, DC: ACOG; 2000.

57. Andersson K, Odlind V, Rybo G. Levonorgestrel–releasing and copper–releasing (Nova T) IUDs during five years of use: a randomized comparative trial. Contraception 1994;49:56–72.

58. Lunsky Y, Straiko A, Armstrong SC, Havercamp SM, Kluttz-Hile C, Dickens P. Appendix O: sample menstrual calendar. In: Women be healthy: a curriculum for women with mental retardation and other developmental disabilities. Chapel Hill (NC); North Carolina Office on Disability and Health 2002; p. 94.

Resources

ACOG Resources

American College of Obstetricians and Gynecologists. Adolescents' right to refuse long-term contraceptives. In: Health care for adolescents. Washington, DC: ACOG; 2003. p. 63–8.

Obstetric management of spinal cord injuries. ACOG Committee Opinion No. 275. American College of Obstetricians and Gynecologists. Obstet Gynecol 2002;100:625–7.

American College of Obstetricians and Gynecologists. Sterilization of women, including those with mental disabilities. In: Ethics in obstetrics and gynecology. 2nd ed. Washington, DC: ACOG; 2004. p. 56–9.

Other Resources

The resources listed as follows are for information purposes only. Referral to these sources and web sites does not imply the endorsement of ACOG. This list is not meant to be comprehensive. The exclusion of a source or web site does not reflect the quality of that source or web site. Please note that web sites are subject to change without notice.

American Academy of Physical Medicine and Rehabilitation
One IBM Plaza, Suite 2500
Chicago, IL 60611-3604
Tel: (312) 464-9700
E-mail: info@aapmr.org
Web: www.aapmr.org

The American Academy of Physical Medicine and Rehabilitation is a physician member organization focusing on research and advocacy on public policy issues related to disability.

American Foundation for the Blind
11 Penn Plaza, Suite 300
New York, NY 10001
Tel: 800-AFB-LINE (232-5463)
Web: www.afb.org/

The American Foundation for the Blind addresses issues of literacy, independent living, employment, and access through technology for those who are blind or visually impaired.

The Arc of the US
1010 Wayne Avenue, Suite 650
Silver Spring, MD 20910
Tel: (301) 565-5470
Web: www.thearc.org

The Arc is a national organization of and for people with mental retardation and related developmental disabilities and their families. It provides advocacy at the legislative, system, and individual levels and resources for those in need, including those for older women. The Arc is organized by state chapters to supply local information.

Breast Health Access for Women with Disabilities
Alta Bates Summit Medical Center
2001 Dwight Way, 2nd Floor
Berkeley, CA 94704
Tel: (510) 204-4866 (voice); (510) 204-4574 (TDD)
Web: www.bhawd.org

The Breast Health Access for Women with Disabilities web site is designed for women and health professionals. It has pictorial descriptions that can be used for teaching breast self-examination to woman with physical disabilities.

Centers for Independent Living
2323 South Shepherd, Suite 1000
Houston, TX 77019
Tel: (713) 520-0232 (voice); (713) 520-5136 (TTY)
Fax: (713) 520-5785
E-mail: ilru@ilru.org
Web: www.ilru.org

Centers for Independent Living are private, nonprofit corporations in the United States and Canada that provide advocacy, independent living skills training, information, peer counseling and referral to individuals with disabilities.

Center for Research on Women with Disabilities
Department of Physical Medicine and Rehabilitation
Baylor Medical College
3440 Richmond, Suite B
Houston, TX 77064
Tel: (713) 960-0505
E-mail: mnosek@bcm.tmc.edu
Web: www.bcm.tmc.edu/crowd/

The Center for Research on Women with Disabilities at Baylor College of Medicine focuses on issues related to health, aging, civil rights, abuse, and independent living. Researchers develop and evaluate models for interventions to address specific problems affecting women with disabilities. Baylor College also developed Reproductive Health Care for Women with Disabilities, which is a web-based guide designed to inform women with disabilities about reproductive health care. It is available at http://pw2.netcom.com/~jpender1/default_index.html.

Disability Rights Advocates
449 15th Street, Suite 303
Oakland, CA 94612-2821
Tel: (510) 451-8644; (510) 451-8716 (TTY)
Web: www.dralegal.org/

Disabilities Rights Advocates is a nonprofit legal center dedicated to protecting the legal and civil rights of people with disabilities to ensure dignity, equality, and opportunity for all.

Health Promotion for Women with Disabilities Project
Villanova University—College of Nursing
800 Lancaster Avenue
Villanova, PA 19085
Tel: (610) 519-4922
Web: www.nursing.villanova.edu/WomenWithDisabilities

The Health Promotion for Women with Disabilities Project is a comprehensive program that addresses issues shared by women with all types of disabilities throughout the life span. Their web site includes current research, information about women's health issues, resources, and links to related sites.

MammaCare
930 NW 8th Avenue
Gainesville, FL 32601
Tel: 800-MAMCARE (626-2273)
Web: www.mammacare.com

MammaCare offers a system for teaching breast self-examination and has adapted personal learning systems for women with disabilities including women who are blind or deaf.

National Association of Developmental Disabilities Councils
1234 Massachusetts Avenue, NW, Suite 103
Washington, DC 20005
Tel: (202) 347-1234
Web: www.naddc.org/

The National Association of Developmental Disabilities Councils provides support and assistance to member councils to promote a consumer- and family-centered system of services and supports for those with developmental disabilities. There are councils in every state and most territories.

National Institute on Deafness and Other Communication Disorders
National Institutes of Health
31 Center Drive, MSC 2320
Bethesda, MD 20892-2320
Tel: (301) 496-7243; 800-241-1055 (TTY)
Fax: (301) 402-0018
Web: www.nidcd.nih.gov

The National Institute on Deafness and Other Communication Disorders provides health information about human communication and disorders of hearing, balance, smell, taste, voice, speech, and language. Fact sheets, brochures, reports, directories, database searches, and other resources are available for the public and health professionals. Publications are available online and through online ordering.

National Women's Health Information Center
Web: www.4woman.gov/wwd/

The women with disabilities web site of the National Women's Health Information Center provides information, resources, and news for providers, women with disabilities, and families.

North Carolina Office on Disability and Health
Frank Porter Graham Child Development Institute
Campus Box 8185
The University of North Carolina at Chapel Hill
Chapel Hill, NC 27599-8185
Tel: (919) 966-0871
Fax: (919) 966-0862
Web: www.fpg.unc.edu/~ncodh/WomensHealth/

The North Carolina Office on Disability and Health (NCODH) works to promote access to health care by providing training and technical assistance to health care providers and self-care and self-advocacy information to consumers. It developed *Women Be Healthy: A Curriculum for Women with Mental Retardation and Other Developmental Disabilities* in 2002 to enable women with mental retardation and other developmental disabilities to become more active participants in their health care. Its primary emphasis is teaching women about reproductive health and breast/cervical cancer screenings. The facilitators' manual is free to North Carolina residents. Out of state residents may order one free copy, each additional copy may be purchased at $3.00 each. Email: odhpubs@mail.fpg.unc.edu to order a copy. In addition, NCODH and the Center for Universal Design at N.C. State University published *Removing Barriers to Health Care: A Guide for Professionals* in 1998. This book walks the health care provider through the process of making a medical facility physically accessible. It is complete with specific Americans with Disabilities Act requirements, picture illustrations, and some helpful tips on creating accessible environments and services. For more information, contact the Center for Universal Design at (919) 515-3082; Fax (919) 515-3023; http://www.design.ncsu.edu/cud.

Rehabilitation Institute of Chicago
345 East Superior Street, Room 106
Chicago, IL 60611
E-mail: hrcwd@rehabchicago.org
Web: www.ric.org

The Rehabilitation Institute of Chicago publishes the *Resourceful Woman*, which is a free newsletter written by and for women with disabilities. The institute also offers patient care, advocacy, research, and education for health professionals on physical medicine and rehabilitation. The Health Resource Center for Women with Disabilities is part of the Rehabilitation Institute of Chicago. The center created "Learning to Act in Partnership: Women with Disabilities Speak to Health Professionals," which is a 38-minute training video that is designed to give insight into health experiences, needs, and preferences of women with disabilities.

Roeher Institute
Kinsmen Building
York University
4700 Keele Street
Toronto, Ontario M3J 1P3
Canada
Tel: (416) 661-9611
E-mail: info@roeher.ca

The Roeher Institute is a policy-research and development organization dedicated to generating knowledge, information, and skills to secure the inclusion, citizenship, human rights, and equality of people with intellectual and other disabilities. It publishes reports, training materials, awareness tools, and guides in a variety of formats. The institute published *Harm's Way: The Many Faces of Violence and Abuse Against Persons with Disabilities* in 1995. This book examines forms of violence and abuse toward people with disabilities, how people with disabilities define abuse, and factors creating vulnerability. The institute also provides direct responses to requests for references, referrals, research information, public speakers, and technical consulting.

Through the Looking Glass
2198 Sixth Street, Suite 100
Berkeley, CA 94710-2204
Tel: 800-644-2666; 800-804-1616 (TTY)
Web: www.lookingglass.org/

Through the Looking Glass is a center that conducts research, training, and services for families in which a child, parent, or grandparent has a disability or medical issue. Services include adaptive equipment and peer support for parents with disabilities, including parents with developmental disabilities.

U.S. Equal Employment Opportunity Commission
1801 L Street, NW
Washington, DC 20507
Tel: 800-669-3362 (voice) or 800-800-3302 (TDD)—for Americans with Disabilities Act documents; 800-669-4000 (voice) or 800-669-6820 (TDD)—for Americans with Disabilities Act information
Web: www.eeoc.gov

The U.S. Equal Employment Opportunity Commission promotes equal opportunity in employment. Commission employment discrimination, enforcement, and litigation information can be found on its web site.

University of Alabama
Medical Rehabilitation Research and Training Center on Secondary Conditions of Spinal Cord Injury
Department of Physical Medicine and Rehabilitation
1717 6th Avenue South, Room 506
Birmingham, AL 35233-7330
Tel: (205) 934-3283
Web: www.spinalcord.uab.edu

In 1996, the University of Alabama Medical Rehabilitation Research and Training Center on Secondary Conditions of Spinal Cord Injury published a video and study guide that provides CME credit entitled *Reproductive Health for Women with Spinal Cord Injury.*

Waisman Center Cognitive and Developmental Disabilities Resources
Web: www.waisman.wisc.edu/www/mrsites.html

The web site of the Waisman Center provides a list of more than 100 web sites with information for people with developmental disabilities, including job accommodation organizations, specialized health care organizations, and support groups.

Publications
Physician Resources

Council of Better Business Bureau's Foundation
4200 Wilson Boulevard
Arlington, VA 22203
Tel: (703) 247-3656

Medical offices access equals opportunity: your guide to the Americans with Disabilities Act. Publication No. 24-280. 1992. The Council of Better Business Bureau's Foundation published this booklet for physicians with suggestions to comply creatively with requirements of the public accommodations section of the Americans with Disabilities Act for existing businesses.

The patient with mental retardation: issues in gynecologic care and *The patient with physical disabilities: issues in gynecologic care.* Ortho-McNeil Continuing Education Monographs. 1996. These guides contain tips and tools for direct gynecologic care for women with disabilities. They provide pictures of positioning techniques that can be used for women with either physical or developmental disabilities. Videos also are available. The guides and videos are available directly from Ortho-McNeil Pharmaceutical representatives.

Simpson KM. *Table manners and beyond: the gynecological exam for women with developmental disabilities and other functional limitations*. Regional Center of the East Bay and the Women's Health Project of UCP of the Golden Gate. 2001. This is a web-based guide for both patients with developmental, sensory, and physical disabilities and providers. It includes chapters on alternative positioning, transfer techniques, equipment and equipment modifications, the blind and deaf patient, and lists of resources. It is available at http://www.bhawd.org/sitefiles/TblMrs/cover.html. For more information, contact Kathleen Lankasky, klankasky@aol.com, phone (510) 278-0106.

Sipski M, Alexander C. *Sexual function in people with disabilities: a health professional's guide*. Aspen Publications, 1997. This is an indexed manual with an interdisciplinary approach to addressing the medical, social, and psychological aspects of sexual functioning in people with disabilities. It includes chapters on infertility and adolescents. Specific issues for nine common disabilities are addressed.

Stanfield & Co
Box 1983
Santa Monica, CA 90406
Tel: (213) 385-7466

Stanfield & Co published the *GYN exam handbook* and videotapes with a teacher's guide. This resource contains photos, videotapes, and a teacher's guide to educate girls and women with disabilities about breast and pelvic examinations, clinical procedures, and their importance.

Abuse Prevention

Disability, Abuse and Personal Rights Project
PO Box T
Culver City, CA 90230
Tel: (310) 391-2420

The Disability, Abuse and Personal Rights Project published a book entitled *Abuse of children and adults with disabilities* in 1993. This book is a prevention and intervention guidebook for parents and other advocates that addresses vulnerability and identification and reporting of abuse.

Diverse City Press
33 des Floralies
Eastman, Quebec
Canada J0E 1P0
Tel: 877-246-5226

Diverse City Press provides educational materials for people with disabilities and their care providers. A publication pertaining to abuse follows:

Hingsburger D. *Just say know! Understanding and reducing the risk of sexual victimization*. 1995. This book explores the victimization of people with disabilities and discusses ways to reduce the risk of sexual assault.

Employment and Legal Information

Griffin LK. *Informed consent, sexuality, and people with developmental disabilities: strategies for professional decision-making.*

United States Department of Justice. Civil Rights Division. Disability Rights Section. *A guide to disability rights law*. This publication is available at http://www.usdoj.gov/crt/ada/cguide.htm.

U.S. Equal Employment Opportunity Commission and U.S. Department of Justice, Civil Rights Division. *Americans with Disabilities Act: questions and answers*. 1996. This publication is available online at http://www.usdoj.gov/crt/ada/qandaeng.htm. For more information, contact: U.S. Department of Justice, ADA Information Line, 800-514-0301 (voice), 800-514-0383 (TDD).

Sexuality

Bucharme SH, Gill KM. *Sexuality after spinal cord injury*. Brooks Publishing Co. 1997. This guide covers important sexual issues, including anatomy, fertility, sexually transmitted diseases, self-esteem, sexual satisfaction, and parenting. It is available at http://www.brookespublishing.com/.

Hingsburger D. *Fingertips: a guide for teaching about female masturbation*. 2000. A video and workbook developed by Diverse City Press (see contact information under "Abuse Prevenion") aimed at teaching women with developmental disabilities about masturbation.

Gregory MF. *Sexual adjustment: a guide for the spinal cord injured*. Accent Books/Cheever Publishing, 1992. This book is a guide for understanding sexual adjustments written by a rehabilitation counselor married to a man with a spinal cord injury.

Griffin LK. *Informed consent, sexuality, and people with developmental disabilities: strategies for professional decision-making*. ARC Milwaukee, 1996. This book includes examples and discussion of many informed consent scenarios. For information about ordering, contact (414) 774-6255.

Kroll K, Klein EL. *Enabling romance: a guide to love, sex, and relationships for people with disabilities (and the people who care about them)*. No Limits Communications, 2001.

Schwier KM, Hingsburger D. *Sexuality: your sons and daughters with intellectual disabilities guide*. Brook Publishing Co. Inc. 2000. This book offers advice and practical strategies for parents to increase self-esteem and encourage appropriate behavior among children with developmental disabilities. It is available at http://www.brookespublishing.com/.

Parenting Resources

Garee B. *Parenting: tips from parents (who happen to have a disability) on raising children*. Accent Books/Cheever Publishing. 1989. This book contains a collection of articles and information on having and raising children that were written by parents with disabilities.

Rogers J, Matsumura M. *Mother-to-be: a guide to pregnancy and birth for women with disabilities*. Demos Medical Publishing, 1992. This book provides pregnancy and childbirth information for women with disabilities.

Clinics for Women With Disabilities

Disabled Women's Health Center
Spain Rehabilitation Hospital
1717 6th Avenue South
Birmingham, AL 35233
Tel: (205) 934-3330

The Disabled Women's Health Center is located at Spain
Rehabilitation Hospital and offers a clinic specializing in the health
care of women with disabilities.

Rehabilitation Institute of Chicago (see previous listing)

Texas Institute of Rehabilitation and Research
Independent Living Research Unit
5100 Travis Road
Houston, TX 77002-9746
(713) 942-6159
Web: www.tirr.org

The Texas Institute of Rehabilitation and Research offers a continuum
of care for those suffering catastrophic disabling injury or illness.

Primary Care of Lesbians and Bisexual Women in Obstetric and Gynecologic Practice

Key Points

- Practitioners have the responsibility to provide quality care to all women regardless of their sexual orientation.

- Providers of reproductive health care and family planning services should not assume that patients, even if pregnant, are heterosexual.

- Many lesbians are limited in their access to health care due to problems obtaining health insurance, confidentiality concerns, and concerns about disclosure.

- Being a lesbian or a bisexual does not inherently affect an individual's health status. There may be, however, behaviors or risk factors that are more common among lesbian or bisexual women that have health consequences.

- Many physicians incorrectly conclude that lesbian patients do not require a Pap test because they are considered to be in a low-risk category.

- Because most lesbians have been sexually active with men at some point in their lives and because some STDs can be transmitted by exclusive lesbian sexual activity, it is important to consider screening for STDs.

- Adolescents who self-identify as lesbians during high school are at higher risk for suicide, victimization, sexual risk behaviors, and substance use at an earlier age than their peers.

- Sexual orientation should not be a barrier to receiving fertility services to achieve a pregnancy.

- Obstetrician–gynecologists can make their practices more receptive to lesbian and bisexual patients through implementation of a nondiscrimination policy and use with all patients of inclusive language.

Practitioners have the responsibility to provide quality care to all women regardless of their sexual orientation.

In 1999, the Institute of Medicine published its landmark report, *Lesbian Health: Current Assessment and Directions for the Future* (1). The National Institutes of Health and the Centers for Disease Control and Prevention led the effort to support this first-of-a-kind study. The recommendations were broad and overarching. Given the challenge in implementing the recommendations, in March 2000 the National Institutes of Health convened health experts to discuss implementation of these recommendations and examine the research currently available on lesbian and bisexual women. Problems identified in the current research include designing and implementing sound studies because lesbians are a hidden population. There are further challenges in conducting such research, including lack of funding. The experts identified the research gaps and priorities for additional research. The report also recommended that health professional associations and academic institutions disseminate information on lesbian health to health care providers, researchers, and the public (2).

Many peer-reviewed articles on lesbian health support the contention that the lesbian population may have a specific health demographic profile and experience barriers in accessing health care (3). Informing clinicians about the health issues of sexual orientation and homosexuality should enhance health care received by lesbian and bisexual patients. Accurate information about lesbian health concerns is important to obstetricians and gynecologists as women's health care providers, particularly as they care for adolescents and young women who are first discovering and seeking to understand their sexuality—whether homosexual, bisexual, or heterosexual. Practitioners have the responsibility to provide quality care to all women regardless of their sexual orientation. In addition, providers of reproductive health care and family planning services should not assume that patients, even if pregnant, are heterosexual or that adolescent and adult women who say they are bisexual, lesbian, or unsure of their sexual orientation are not in need of routine gynecologic care, including family planning and STD services.

Definition and Prevalence

Sexual orientation can best be thought of as "one component of a person's identity, along with others including culture, ethnicity, gender and personality traits" (4). Although there is no standard definition of a lesbian, those that are used generally include any of three components: 1)attraction, 2) behavior, and 3) identity (1). A lesbian could thus be defined by having same-sex attraction, same-sex sexual behavior, or by claiming for herself a lesbian identity. Sexual orientation falls along a continuum; a woman may not be exclusively heterosexual or homosexual, or she may develop a lesbian orientation over her lifetime (4). A bisexual woman has attraction for or sexual behavior with both sexes, or identifies herself as a bisexual. It is important to note that in 1973 the American Psychiatric Association reclassified homosexuality as sexual orientation/expression, removing from it any connotation of disorder or disease (5, 6). The current opinion of most researchers is that sexual orientation is not a choice (7).

Because of a lack of research and differing definitions, there are no truly accurate prevalence statistics for lesbians or bisexual women in the general U.S. population. Estimates of prevalence in the United States range from 2% to 10% (1). Lesbians are as diverse as the general population of all women and are represented among all subpopulations of women. Therefore, obstetrician–gynecologists will encounter lesbian or bisexual patients, although not all will have disclosed their sexual orientation.

Barriers to Health Care

Lesbians and bisexual women experience many barriers to care. These barriers are discussed as follows.

Confidentiality

Concerns about confidentiality often prevent lesbians and bisexual women from seeking care. This is especially true for the adolescent population.

Insurance

Lesbians are limited in their access to health care insurance for many of the same social and economic reasons as heterosexual women. In addition, lesbians who are unemployed or work in a setting that does not offer health insurance face additional limits in that they are unable to participate in their partners' employment benefits packages (8).

Caregiver Attitudes

Patients may perceive negative attitudes on the part of their caregivers, causing them to hesitate in obtaining routine health maintenance visits. In many surveys about their experience as patients, lesbians reported experiencing ostracism, rough treatment, derogatory comments, or having their life-partners excluded from discussions by their medical practitioners (9, 10). Surveys of physicians (11) and nursing professionals (12) confirm that approximately 30% of caregivers report discomfort when providing care to lesbian patients. They also report that they have received little training about issues of sexual orientation (13, 14).

Concerns About Disclosure

Both patients and health care providers contribute to a healthy physician–patient relationship. Patients have a responsibility to provide accurate information about their lifestyle, health habits, and sexual practices when these factors may affect medical judgment (15). Lesbian and bisexual women often are concerned about disclosing their sexual orientation to health care providers, especially when they have not yet "come out" (16). Positive attitudes of health care providers can increase the likelihood that the patient will disclose information about sexual orientation. If a patient experiences an accepting attitude, she may be more willing to disclose sensitive issues or return for routine care. Suggestions for ways to create a receptive environment for lesbian patients and resources to help accomplish this are included later in this chapter.

Medical Considerations

Being a lesbian or bisexual does not inherently affect an individual's health status. There are no known physiologic differences between lesbians and heterosexual women. For example, there are no differences in serum hormone levels of testosterone, androstenedione, estradiol, and progesterone among lifelong lesbians, lesbians who realized their orientation at a later age, and heterosexual women when measured at the same points in the menstrual cycle (17).

There may, however, be health behaviors or health risk factors that are more common among lesbians or bisexual women that have health consequences. Nulligravidity and low parity are more common in lesbians and bisexual women than among heterosexual women (18, 19). In pooled data from seven national and local studies, only 16% of lesbians ever gave birth to a live child compared with 57% of heterosexual women. Thirty-six percent of lesbians reported ever using oral contraceptives compared with 80% of all women (19). Use of postmenopausal hormones was similar (18). Dysmenorrhea was reported by nearly one half of women in a survey of more than 2,000 lesbians and bisexual women (20). This may be a result of their higher rates of nulligravidity and lower rates of oral contraceptive use. Several studies have reported higher prevalence rates of obesity, tobacco use, and alcohol use. It was reported in the 1994 National Health Interview Survey and the Third National Health and Nutrition Examination Survey (NHANES III) that lesbians and bisexual women eat fewer portions of fruits and vegetables than heterosexual women. However, they were found to have similar exercise patterns and rates of hypertension (18, 19, 21). These combined factors may increase the risk for breast cancer, lung cancer, type 2 diabetes, and cardiovascular disease. In fact, higher rates of heart attack have been reported in the lesbian population (18).

Routine Health Visits

Standard comprehensive gynecologic care is recommended for lesbians and bisexual women, including family planning and STD screening and prevention counseling. The aforementioned risk factors should be considered during provision of this care to determine appropriate medical intervention.

In light of the increased likelihood of risk factors for cardiovascular disease and diabetes, it is particularly important during routine office visits to include counseling for weight control and smoking cessation as needed and to screen for diabetes and lipid status as appropriate for the patient's age and medical history. Risk factors for heart disease also should be considered. Other procedures and treatments that should be considered in this population during a routine health visit are discussed as follows (Box 7).

Vaginitis and Sexually Transmitted Diseases

Although the overall incidence of vaginitis and STDs appear quite low in the lesbian population, all types have been diagnosed and should remain in the differential diagnosis for pelvic pain and vaginal discharge (22). Because most lesbians have been sexually active with men at some point in their lives and because some STDs can be transmitted by exclusive lesbian sexual activity, it is important to consider screening all lesbians and bisexual women for STDs based on the patient's risk factors. They are at risk for STDs based

Box 7   Routine Health Visits

Counseling

- Smoking cessation
- Weight control
- Risk factors for heart disease

Age- or risk-appropriate screening

- Diabetes
- Lipid abnormalities
- Vaginitis and sexually transmitted diseases
- Human immunodeficiency virus and acquired immunodeficiency syndrome

Cancer screening

- Pap tests
- Mammography
- Colon cancer screening

Hormone therapy and osteoporosis evaluation

on the same risk factors as other women, including number of partners and unprotected sex with an infected partner. Exclusive lesbian sexual activity is associated with the lowest rates of all types of vaginitis. Woman-to-woman transmission of hepatitis A and hepatitis B and trichomoniasis has been reported (23). In addition, lesbians have developed yeast, herpes, human papillomavirus (HPV), and gonorrhea, all of which correlate with the extent of their heterosexual activity (20, 24). Lesbians also have developed and may be at higher risk for bacterial vaginosis (25). Skin-to-skin transmission of HPV and herpes can occur with both male-female and same-sex sexual contact.

Human Immunodeficiency Virus and Acquired Immunodeficiency Syndrome

There are reports in the literature of cases of suspected lesbian sexual transmission of the human immunodeficiency virus (HIV) (26, 27). The Institute of Medicine has reviewed the issue and concludes that the risk of transmission of HIV between women is unclear, noting that bisexual women have the highest rates of seropositivity in comparison with both lesbians

and heterosexual women (1). In a convenience sample survey of HIV risk behavior among 1,086 inner-city lesbians and bisexual women, 16% reported sex with a bisexual man, 2.5% injected drugs, 4% had sex with an injection drug-using male, 8% had sex with an injection drug-using female, and 21% engaged in other risky behaviors (28). All patients, regardless of their sexual orientation, should be encouraged to practice safer sex to reduce the risk of transmitting or acquiring HIV. Safer sex practices for lesbians include use of condoms on sex toys, gloves, and dental dams and avoidance of sharing dildos or sex toys. Patients, especially young women, may benefit from anticipatory guidance regarding these safer sex practices given that they may not disclose their sexual orientation or behaviors. In addition, lesbians and bisexual women should be screened for HIV based on the same risk factors as other women (29).

Pap Tests

Routine Pap testing for lesbians and bisexual women is recommended regardless of type of sexual activity (30, 31). The onset and interval for this testing should be based on American College of Obstetricians and Gynecologists (ACOG) recommendations, which state that the first Pap test should take place within 3 years of first vaginal–penile intercourse, but no later than age 21 years; the test should be performed annually until age 30 years. At that time, after three normal tests, testing can occur less frequently. If the patient has had prior dysplasia, it may not be advisable to test less frequently (32). In addition, less frequent testing may not be advisable in the patient who is a current smoker or who has multiple sexual partners (30).

Many physicians incorrectly conclude that lesbian patients do not require a Pap test because they are considered to be in a low-risk category. This is based on the assumption, not always correct, that the patient has not previously had sex with males. In fact, most surveys of lesbians confirm that most lesbians are or have been sexually active with men, especially at younger ages while they were questioning and exploring their orientation (21). In addition, cervical dysplasia has been reported in lesbians who have not had prior intercourse with men, and there is at least one report of HPV transmission by exclusive lesbian sexual contact (30). Lesbians' higher rates of cigarette use (18, 19) also may contribute to an increased risk of cervical dysplasia.

Mammography

The general recommendations for mammography should be followed for all lesbian and bisexual patients (29). At least one study suggests lesbians may get fewer mammograms than the general population (33). Among women participating in the Women's Health Initiative (WHI), lesbians and bisexual women had higher rates of breast cancer than heterosexual women, despite similar mammography screening rates as other study protocol participants (18). The reasons for these findings are unclear but may be related to behavioral risk factors.

Colorectal Cancer Screening

Lesbians in the WHI protocol study were shown to have obtained fecal occult blood tests and to have developed colon cancer at similar rates as heterosexuals and bisexuals (18). In studies of the general population, however, screening may be less frequent. In addition, smoking and drinking alcohol may be linked to a higher risk for colorectal cancer (34, 35). Higher rates of these behaviors among the lesbian population may put them at higher risk for this cancer than the heterosexual population. Lesbians and bisexual women should be screened per ACOG recommendations (29).

Hormone Therapy and Osteoporosis

The ACOG has established general recommendations for hormone therapy and osteoporosis screening. These recommendations should be followed for all lesbian and bisexual patients (36).

Mental Health and Psychosocial Considerations

Clinicians should be alert to the signs and symptoms of depression, substance abuse, and violence in all patients and conduct appropriate screening and intervention (29) (see "Substance Use" and "Intimate Partner Violence and Domestic Violence" chapters).

Depression

The WHI study of women aged 50 to 79 years reports that women who identify as lifetime lesbians, bisexuals, or adult lesbians are more likely to be depressed than heterosexual women (18). When questioned about causes of depressive stress in their lives, most lesbians report stress from isolation and social ascription of inferior status (37, 38) and lack of support from families and friends (39). In some studies, as many as 70–80% of lesbians report that they sought counseling services (40, 41). One half of those who had received counseling had done so for feelings of sadness or depression (40).

Substance Abuse

In stratifying data from the 1996 National Household Survey on Drug Abuse, it was found that lesbians did not differ from heterosexual women in six major psychiatric syndromes, but they were more likely to be classified with alcohol and drug dependency syndromes (42). Although lesbians reported drinking alcohol more frequently during the month than the predominantly heterosexual respondents of the National Household Survey on Drug Abuse, few differences were observed between the two samples for heavy alcohol consumption (43). Compared with all women in the 1994 NHANES III, alcohol use was slightly greater among lesbian women (70% among lesbians compared with 67% among all women) (19).

Violence

In a nationally representative telephone interview sampling of 8,000 United States women by the U.S. Department of Justice in conjunction with the Centers for Disease Control and Prevention, 1% of women reported living with a same-sex intimate partner at least once in their lifetime. Eleven percent of these women reported being raped, physically assaulted, or stalked by a female partner and 30% by a male partner. In comparison, just more than 20% of the women who reported marrying or living only with a male partner reported such violence by the man (44). Just as with heterosexual couples, domestic violence is correlated with abuse of alcohol and drugs (45). Clinicians should be alert to the signs and symptoms of violence in all relationships (see "Intimate Partner Violence and Domestic Violence" chapter). Shelters for victims of abuse should be aware of the need for and be prepared to provide services to lesbian clients.

The Hate Crime Statistics Act requires the federal government to collect data obtained by police agencies about hate crimes based on race and religion but not on sexual orientation. This limits the availability of quality data on this subject. Lesbian and gay youth have been more likely than heterosexual youth to report being threatened, experiencing property damage or physical violence, and missing school because of fear (46). Violence because of their orientation can confer posttraumatic emotional sequelae (47), including depression, diminished self-esteem, and suicidal thoughts (48–50). It also can lead to homelessness. Many of the youth who are homeless left home because of conflicts with parents over their sexual orientation (51). In one study of homeless adolescents in Portland, Oregon, 44.9% of females identified as lesbian or bisexual (52). The distress from violence is compounded by the need for some women to hide their orientation from potential sources of support such as family, friends, and colleagues (53).

The American Psychological Association reviewed the literature regarding sexual abuse of children. It confirmed that neither lesbians nor gay men are more likely to abuse children than are heterosexuals (54, 55).

Lifespan Issues

Adolescence

Children as young as age 10 years can recognize their sexual orientation as attraction to a particular sex (56). By high school, approximately 10% of Minnesota youth responding to a statewide health questionnaire said they were unsure about their orientation, with 4.5% reporting lesbian attraction and 1% having had lesbian behavior (57). Lesbian adolescents must navigate the same developmental tasks as heterosexual peers. This includes accepting their sexual identity and deciding about sexual behaviors (7). They, however, face additional issues, including social stigma, hostility, hatred, and isolation. They may find it difficult to ask for, or they may not find, understanding and acceptance from their parents and family. Youth who self-identify as lesbian or gay during high school are at higher risk for suicide, victimization, sexual risk behaviors, and substance use at an earlier age than their peers (46, 58). Lesbian or bisexual girls also are at heightened risk for tobacco use and eating disorders. This also is true for girls reporting same-sex attractions who indicate that they are primarily attracted to males and do not describe themselves as lesbian or bisexual (59, 60). It is, therefore, important to ask about sexual activity with males or females, attraction to males or females, and self-identification as lesbian or bisexual (see suggested questions later in this chapter).

Counseling may be very helpful for young people who are uncertain about their orientation or have difficulty expressing their sexuality. Lesbian adolescents may benefit from assistance from a counselor or health care provider in exploring issues pertaining to when and to whom they disclose their sexual identity (58). Further, therapy can assist a lesbian adolescent in coping with difficulties faced at home, school, or in the community. However, therapy directed specifically at changing sexual orientation is contraindicated because it can provoke guilt and anxiety while having no demonstrated potential for achieving changes in orientation. So-called reparative therapy and the "transformational ministries" use psychology and religion to shame nonheterosexual children into changing their orientation. These groups use social stigmatization as the primary means to motivate nonheterosexuals to change their sexual orientation. Such therapies have been shown to be ineffective and harmful (61). More constructive therapeutic goals for such youth should be to create and maintain self-confidence and honest relationships with family and friends. Families may experience stress and require information and assistance while supporting a child's questioning of sexual orientation (7). Referral to organizations such as Advocates for Youth; the Gay, Lesbian and Straight Education Network; the Gay-Straight Alliance Network; and Parents, Families & Friends of Lesbians & Gays may be helpful (see "Resources").

Aging Lesbians

Age, poverty, and health issues can render the older lesbian invisible (62). For some aging lesbians, acceptance of the aging process and high levels of life satisfaction are associated with connection to and activity in the lesbian community (62, 63). Currently, many lesbian seniors find they must give up their gay identity as they progress into senior age and enter retirement communities with a generation that is still predominantly homophobic (63).

Family Issues

Lesbian Parenting

Although most lesbians are nulligravid (18, 19), many of these same women have reared nonbiological children who were adopted from their partners' prior marriages to men or were products of their domestic partners' insemination. In a study comparing heterosexual couples with lesbian couples seeking fertility services, there were no observed differences in self-esteem, psychiatric symptomatology, or relationship adjustment, except that lesbians reported greater family cohesion than heterosexuals (64). Lesbian and heterosexual mothers in another study had similar scores on self-reported stress, adjustment, competence, and quality of the relationship with their families (65). Among women seeking fertility services, the clinical pregnancy rates and complications were similar between lesbian and heterosexual women (66).

Lesbians desiring insemination should be advised to use the services of an established sperm bank to reduce transmission of infectious diseases and genetic abnormalities from unscreened sperm sources and to establish custody. It may be valuable to refer them to an attorney who can help them establish parental authority for both the biological mother and the lesbian co-parent.

Sexual orientation should not be a barrier to receiving fertility services to achieve a pregnancy. However, lesbians and other unmarried women are still sometimes refused fertility services (1). In a survey of members of the Society of Assisted Reproduction Technology, it was reported that only 55% of responding members would offer lesbian couples the option to receive donated embryos. This percentage is similar to that for single women (59%) and unmarried heterosexual couples (61%); 100% of responding members would offer married couples the option to receive donated embryos (67). Obstetrician–gynecologists who elect not to provide fertility services to lesbian couples or individuals should refer them for these services.

Lesbians should have equal access to co-parenting and second parent adoption rights. The American Academy of Pediatrics has recently issued a policy statement that supports legislative and legal efforts to provide the possibility of adoption of the child by the second parent or co-parent in same-sex-parent-families (68). The American Medical Association recently voted to support state legislation that allows adoption by same-sex partners (69). A comprehensive review of multiple published studies of children raised in gay and lesbian households concluded that being raised in a household of this type does not influence a child's development of gender identity, sex-role behavior, sexual orientation, self-concept, locus of control, moral judgment, intelligence, or development of peer relationships (54). Lesbians seeking to adopt a child

should be encouraged to confer with an attorney. The laws on adoption vary by state. Some states have codified into law prohibitions against either individual gay or lesbian adoption or second parent adoption. However, in most states, court decisions have set the legal precedent for adoption by gay and lesbian parents (70). New laws legalizing same-sex marriage in certain states also may affect this issue. In this constantly evolving context, lesbian patients would be well-advised to contact an attorney to keep abreast of the latest legal decisions in their states.

Family-of-Choice and Lesbian Family Relationships

The definition of "family" for lesbian couples often involves creation of a network of close and accepting friends as a family-of-choice, especially if their family-of-origin has rejected them (71). More than 60% of lesbians are observed to be in long-term relationships (40). Lesbians who do not hide their homosexuality have better self-esteem (72, 73) and satisfaction with their relationships (74). Relationship instability in lesbian couples can occur because of the same common relational conflicts observed in all couples, but it can be compounded by effects of cultural homophobia: dealing with disdain, issues surrounding disclosure of sexual identity, and maintaining a positive self-concept in a hostile dominant culture (75, 76).

An important consideration for lesbians in committed relationships is whether to obtain powers of attorney for medical decisions for one another or a medical conservatorship or guardianship in case they become incapacitated and are unable to make their own decisions (77). These are available at most hospitals and should be signed well in advance of admission for elective surgeries. Without these arrangements, a lesbian may be unable to make decisions for her incapacitated domestic partner. Some cities and states offer same-sex marriages, civil unions, or domestic partner registration. Some lesbians may object to these contracts and registries as evidence of their second-class citizenship, but they may be the only way to protect their families. These contracts may not be honored in states other than those in which they were written and may be void in the countries in which homosexuality is still illegal. It is important to note that as a result of the U.S. Supreme Court decision in *Lawrence v. Texas* (No. 02-102) on June 26, 2003, all remaining state sodomy laws making homosexuality illegal were struck down (78). Many state sodomy laws had been repealed before this decision.

Changes in the Patient Care Setting

In light of the barriers to health care faced by lesbian and bisexual patients, efforts to ensure that the health care setting is more receptive to and appropriately addresses the needs of this population are warranted, especially given that most, if not all, obstetrician–gynecologists are caring for a number of lesbian and bisexual women already. The sexual orientation of these individuals may or may not have been disclosed. There are numerous ways obstetrician–gynecologists can accomplish this in their practices. Specific suggestions for changes in the office setting include:

1. Inform receptionists and other office staff that lesbian and bisexual patients are welcome in the practice and should be treated with the same respect as other patients.

2. Modify office registration forms and questionnaires that require patients to identify their relational and behavioral statuses to obtain more accurate and useful information. For example:

   - Are you single, married, widowed, divorced, or domestic partner?
   - Are you sexually active with anyone—male, female, both male and female partners, not sexually active?
   - Who are you attracted to—males, females, or both males and females?
   - Do you consider yourself heterosexual, lesbian, bisexual, transsexual, transgender, or asexual?

   The form can state that response to these questions is optional. If the patient does not answer these questions, she can be asked in person. If the patient has concerns about confidentiality, the health care provider can either not write down the answer to the question or code the response.

3. Have a nondiscrimination policy for your office staff posted in the reception area. For example: "This office appreciates the diversity of women and does not discriminate based on race, age, religion, disability, marital status, sexual orientation, or perceived gender."

4. Use inclusive language with all patients and generic terms such as "partner" or "spouse" rather than "boyfriend" for any patient until you know the patient.

5. Providers can be a resource for health information about sexual orientation and gender issues for both patients and their families. Concerned families can be encouraged to obtain counseling or contact Parents, Family, and Friends of Lesbians and Gays (http://www.pflag.org) for information and support. Patients can be provided with patient education materials produced by ACOG on lesbian health (see "Resources") or similar informational brochures that list community resources. These resources can be displayed in the reception area.

References

1. Institute of Medicine (US). Lesbian health: current assessment and directions for the future. Washington, DC: The Institute; 1999.

2. U.S. Department of Health and Human Services. Scientific workshop on lesbian health 2000: steps for implementing the IOM report. Washington, DC: USDHHS; 2004. Available at: http://www.4woman.gov/owh/pub/factsheets/Lesbian.pdf. Retrieved August 9, 2004.

3. O'Hanlan KA. Do we really mean preventive medicine for all? Am J Prev Med 1996;12:411–4.

4. American Psychological Association. Just the facts about sexual orientation and youth: a primer for principals, educators and school personnel. Washington, DC: APA; 2002. Available at: http://www.apa.org/pi/lgbc/publications/justthefacts.html. Retrieved August 10, 2004.

5. American Psychiatric Association. Homosexuality and civil rights. APA position statement. Washington, DC: APA; 1973. Available at: http://www.psych.org/edu/other_res/lib_archives/archives/730010.pdf. Retrieved August 31, 2004.

6. American Psychiatric Association. Diagnostic and statistical manual of mental disorders: DSM–IV–TR. 4th ed., text revision. Washington, DC: APA; 2000.

7. Frankowski BL. Sexual orientation and adolescents. American Academy of Pediatrics Committee on Adolescence. Pediatrics 2004;113:1827–32.

8. O'Hanlan KA. Domestic partnership benefits at medical universities. JAMA 1999;282:1289, 1292.

9. Stevens PE, Hall JM. Stigma, health beliefs and experiences with health care in lesbian women. Image J Nurs Sch 1988;20:69–73.

10. Kass NE, Faden RR, Fox R, Dudley J. Homosexual and bisexual men's perceptions of discrimination in health services. Am J Public Health 1992;82:1277–9.

11. Mathews WC, Booth MW, Turner JD, Kessler L. Physicians' attitudes toward homosexuality—survey of a California County Medical Society. West J Med 1986;144:106–10.

12. Eliason MJ, Raheim S. Experiences and comfort with culturally diverse groups in undergraduate pre-nursing students. J Nurs Educ 2000;39:161–5.

13. Albarran JW, Salmon D. Lesbian, gay and bisexual experiences within critical care nursing, 1988–1998: a survey of the literature. Int J Nurs Stud 2000;37:445–55.

14. Risdon C, Cook D, Willms D. Gay and lesbian physicians in training: a qualitative study. CMAJ 2000;162:331–4.

15. American College of Obstetricians and Gynecologists. Patient testing. In: Ethics in obstetrics and gynecology. 2nd ed. Washington, DC: ACOG; 2004. p. 26–8.

16. Stevens PE, Hall JM. Abusive health care interactions experienced by lesbians: a case of institutional violence in the treatment of women. Response 1990;13(3):23–7.

17. Dancey CP. Sexual orientation in women: an investigation of hormonal and personality variables. Biol Psychol 1990;30:251–64.

18. Valanis BG, Bowen DJ, Bassford T, Whitlock E, Charney P, Carter RA. Sexual orientation and health: comparisons in the women's health initiative sample. Arch Fam Med 2000;9:843–53.

19. Cochran SD, Mays VM, Bowen D, Gage S, Bybee D, Roberts SJ, et al. Cancer–related risk indicators and preventive screening behaviors among lesbians and bisexual women. Am J Public Health 2001;91:591–7.

20. Johnson SR, Smith EM, Guenther SM. Comparison of gynecologic health care problems between lesbians and bisexual women. A survey of 2,345 women. J Reprod Med 1987;32:805–11.

21. O'Hanlan KA. Lesbian health and homophobia: perspectives for the treating obstetrician/gynecologist. Curr Prob Obstet Gynecol Fertil 1995;18:97–133.

22. Patel A, DeLong G, Voigl B, Medina C. Pelvic inflammatory disease in the lesbian population—lesbian health issues: asking the right questions [abstract]. Obstet Gynecol 2000;95:29S–30S.

23. Marrazzo JM. Sexually transmitted infections in women who have sex with women: who cares? Sex Transm Infect 2000;76:330–2.

24. Sherman KJ, Daling JR, Chu J, Weiss NS, Ashley RL, Corey L. Genital warts, other sexually transmitted diseases, and vulvar cancer. Epidemiology 1991;2:257–62.

25. Marrazzo JM, Koutsky LA, Eschenbach DA, Agnew K, Stine K, Hillier SL. Characterization of vaginal flora and bacterial vaginosis in women who have sex with women. J Infect Dis 2002;185:1307–13.

26. Marmor M, Weiss LR, Lyden M, Weiss SH, Saxinger WC, Spira TJ, et al. Possible female-to-female transmission of human immunodeficiency virus [letter]. Ann Intern Med 1986;105:969.

27. Chu SY, Buehler JW, Fleming PL, Berkelman RL. Epidemiology of reported cases of AIDS in lesbians, United States 1980–89. Am J Public Health 1990;80:1380–1.

28. Einhorn L, Polgar M. HIV-risk behavior among lesbians and bisexual women. AIDS Educ Prev 1994;6:514–23.

29. American College of Obstetricians and Gynecologists. Guidelines for women's health care. 2nd ed. Washington, DC: ACOG; 2002.

30. O'Hanlan KA, Crum CP. Human papillomavirus-associated cervical intraepithelial neoplasia following lesbian sex. Obstet Gynecol 1996;88:702–3.

31. Marrazzo JM, Stine K, Koutsky LA. Genital human papillomavirus infection in women who have sex with women: a review. Am J Obstet Gynecol 2000;183:770–4.

32. Cervical cytology screening. ACOG Practice Bulletin No. 45. American College of Obstetricians and Gynecologists. Obstet Gynecol 2003;102:417–27.

33. Koh AS. Use of preventive health behaviors by lesbian, bisexual, and heterosexual women: questionnaire survey. West J Med 2000;172:379–84.

34. Giovannucci E, Stampfer MJ, Colditz GA, Rimm EB, Trichopoulos D, Rosner BA, et al. Folate, methinone, and alcohol intake and risk of colorectal adenoma. J Natl Cancer Inst 1993;85:875–84.

35. U.S. Department of Health and Human Services. The health consequences of smoking: a report of the Surgeon General. Washington, DC: USDHHS; 2004. Available at: http://www.cdc.gov/tobacco/sgr/sgr_2004/chapters.htm. Retrieved August 6, 2004.

36. Osteoporosis. ACOG Practice Bulletin No. 50. American College of Obstetricians and Gynecologists. Obstet Gynecol 2004;103:203–16.

37. Safren SA, Heimberg RG. Depression, hopelessness, suicidality, and related factors in sexual minority and heterosexual adolescents. J Consult Clin Psychol 1999;67:859–66.

38. Savin-Williams RC. Verbal and physical abuse as stressors in the lives of lesbian, gay male, and bisexual youths: associations with school problems, running away, substance abuse, prostitution, and suicide. J Consult Clin Psychol 1994;62:261–9.

39. Oetjen H, Rothblum ED. When lesbians aren't gay: factors affecting depression among lesbians. J Homosex 2000;39:49–73.

40. Bradford J, Ryan C, Rothblum ED. National Lesbian Health Care Survey: implications for mental health care. J Consult Clin Psychol 1994;62:228–42.

41. Welch S, Collings SC, Howden-Chapman P. Lesbians in New Zealand: their mental health and satisfaction with mental health services. Aust N Z J Psychiatry 2000;34:256–63.

42. Cochran SD, Mays VM. Relation between psychiatric syndromes and behaviorally defined sexual orientation in a sample of the US population. Am J Epidemiol 2000;151:516–23.

43. Skinner WF, Otis MD. Drug and alcohol use among lesbian and gay people in a southern U.S. sample: epidemiological, comparative, and methodological findings from the Trilogy Project. J Homosex 1996;30:59–92.

44. Tjaden P, Theonnes N. Prevalence of intimate partner violence among same-sex cohabitants. In: Extent, nature, and consequences of intimate partner violence: findings from the National Violence against Women Survey. Washington, DC: National Institute of Justice; 2000. p. 29–31.

45. Schilit R, Lie GY, Montagne M. Substance use as a correlate of violence in intimate lesbian relationships. J Homosex 1990; 19:51–65.

46. Garofalo R, Wolf RC, Kessel S, Palfrey SJ, DuRant RH. The association between health risk behaviors and sexual orientation among a school-based sample of adolescents. Pediatrics 1998;101:895–902.

47. Herek GM, Gillis JR, Cogan JC. Psychological sequelae of hate-crime victimization among lesbian, gay, and bisexual adults. J Consult Clin Psychol 1999;67:945–51.

48. Waldo CR, Hesson-McInnis MS, D'Augelli AR. Antecedents and consequences of victimization of lesbian, gay, and bisexual young people: a structural model comparing rural university and urban samples. Am J Community Psychol 1998;26:307–34.

49. Garnets LD, D'Augelli AR. Empowering lesbian and gay communities: a call for collaboration with community psychology. Am J Community Psychol 1994;22:447–70.

50. Otis MD, Skinner WF. The prevalence of victimization and its effect on mental well–being among lesbian and gay people. J Homosex 1996;30:93–121.

51. Farrow JA, Deisher RW, Brown R, Kulig JW, Kipke MD. Health and health needs of homeless and runaway youth. A position paper of the Society for Adolescent Medicine. J Adolesc Health 1992;13:717–26.

52. Noell JW, Ochs LM. Relationship of sexual orientation to substance use, suicidal ideation, suicide attempts, and other factors in a population of homeless adolescents. J Adolesc Health 2001;29:31–6.

53. Larson DG, Chastain RL. Self–concealment: conceptualization, measurement, and health implications. J Soc Clin Psychol 1990;9:439–55.

54. American Psychological Association. Lesbian and gay parenting. Washington, DC: APA; 1995. Available at: http://www.apa.org/pi/parent.html. Retrieved August 31, 2004.

55. Jenny C, Roesler TA, Poyer KL. Are children at risk for sexual abuse by homosexuals? Pediatrics 1994;94:41–4.

56. D'Augelli AR, Hershberger SL. Lesbian, gay, and bisexual youth in community settings: personal challenges and mental health problems. Am J Community Psychol 1993;21:421–48.

57. Remafedi G, Resnick M, Blum R, Harris L. Demography of sexual orientation in adolescents. Pediatrics 1992;89:714–21.

58. Lesbian and gay youth: care and counseling. Adolesc Med 1997;8:207–374.

59. Austin SB, Ziyadeh N, Fisher LB, Kahn JA, Colditz GA, Frazier AL. Sexual orientation and tobacco use in a cohort study of US adolescent girls and boys. Arch Pediatr Adolesc Med 2004; 158:317–22.

60. Austin SB, Ziyadeh N, Kahn JA, Camargo CA Jr, Colditz GA, Field AE. Sexual orientation, weight concerns, and eating disordered behaviors in adolescent girls and boys. J Am Acad Child Adolesc Psychiatry 2004;43:1115–23.

61. Davison GC. Constructionism and morality in therapy for homosexuality. In: Gonsiorek JC, Weinrich JD, editors. Homosexuality: research implications for public policy. Newbury Park (CA): Sage; 1991. p. 137–48.

62. Quam JK, Whitford GS. Adaptation and age-related expectations of older gay and lesbian adults. Gerontologist 1992; 32:367–74.

63. Brogan M. The sexual needs of elderly people: addressing the issue. Nurs Stand 1996;10:42–5.

64. Jacob MC, Klock SC, Maier D. Lesbian couples as therapeutic donor insemination recipients: do they differ from other patients? J Psychosom Obstet Gynaecol 1999;20:203–15.

65. McNeill KF, Rienzi BM, Kposowa A. Families and parenting: a comparison of lesbian and heterosexual mothers. Psychol Rep 1998;82:59–62.

66. Ferrara I, Balet R, Grudzinskas JG. Intrauterine donor insemination in single women and lesbian couples: a comparative study of pregnancy rates. Hum Reprod 2000;15:621–5.

67. Kingsberg SA, Applegarth LD, Janata JW. Embryo donation programs and policies in North America: survey results and implications for health and mental health professionals. Fertil Steril 2000;73:215–20.

68. Coparent or second-parent adoption by same-sex parents. Committee on Psychosocial Aspects of Child and Family Health. American Academy of Pediatrics. Pediatrics 2002;109:339–40.

69. American Medical Association. Partner co-adoption. AMA House of Delegates Resolution 204. Chicago (IL): AMA; 2004.

70. Bennett L. The state of the family: laws and legislation affecting gay, lesbian, bisexual and transgender families. Washington, DC: Human Rights Campaign Foundation; 2002.

71. Kurdek LA, Schmitt JP. Perceived emotional support from family and friends in members of homosexual, married, and heterosexual cohabiting couples. J Homosex 1987;14(3–4):57–68.

72. LaSala MC. Lesbians, gay men, and their parents: family therapy for the coming-out crisis. Fam Process 2000;39:67–81.

73. Morrow DF. Coming-out issues for adult lesbians: a group intervention. Soc Work 1996;41:647–56.

74. Berger RM. Passing: impact on the quality of same-sex couple relationships. Soc Work 1990;35:328–32.

75. Ridge SR, Feeney JA. Relationship history and relationship attitudes in gay males and lesbians: attachment style and gender differences. Aust N Z J Psychiatry 1998;32:848–59.

76. Igartua KJ. Therapy with lesbian couples: the issues and the interventions. Can J Psychiatry 1998;43:391–6.

77. Peterkin A, Risdon C. Caring for lesbian and gay people: a clinical guide. Toronto: University of Toronto Press; 2003.

78. Lawrence v. Texas, No. 02–102 (U.S. June 26, 2003). Available at: http://a257.g.akamaitech.net/7/257/2422/26jun20031200/www.supremecourtus.gov/opinions/02pdf/02-102.pdf. Retrieved October 18, 2004.

Resources

ACOG Resources

American College of Obstetricians and Gynecologists. Lesbian health. ACOG Patient Education Pamphlet AP108. Washington, DC: ACOG; 2000.

American College of Obstetricians and Gynecologists. Lesbian teens. ACOG Tool Kit for Teen Care Fact Sheet FS009. Washington, DC: ACOG; 2003.

Other Resources

The resources listed as follows are for information purposes only. Referral to these sources and web sites does not imply the endorsement of ACOG. This list is not meant to be comprehensive. The exclusion of a source or web site does not reflect the quality of that source or web site. Please note that web sites are subject to change without notice.

Advocates for Youth
2000 M Street NW, Suite 750
Washington, DC 20036
Tel: (202) 419-3420
Fax: (202) 419-1448
Web: www.advocatesforyouth.org

Advocates for Youth is dedicated to creating programs and advocating for policies that help young people make informed and responsible decisions about their reproductive and sexual health. Advocates provides information, training, and strategic assistance to youth-serving organizations, policymakers, youth activists, and the media in the United States and the developing world. This organization established YouthResource (http://www.youthresource.com), which is a web site created by and for gay, lesbian, bisexual, transgender, and questioning (GLBTQ) young people 13- to 24-years-old. It takes a holistic approach to sexual health by offering support, community resources, and peer-to-peer education about issues of concern to GLBTQ young people.

American Academy of Pediatrics
141 Northwest Point Boulevard
Elk Grove Village, IL 60007-1098
Tel: (847) 434-4000
Fax: (847) 434-8000
Web: www.aap.org

The American Academy of Pediatrics is an organization of 60,000 pediatricians committed to the attainment of optimal physical, mental, and social health and well-being for all infants, children, adolescents, and young adults. It has developed materials for patients and physicians that pertain to gay and lesbian youth and conducts advocacy efforts for this population as well.

Bisexual Resource Center
PO Box 1026
Boston, MA 02117-1026
Tel: (617) 424-9595
Web: www.biresource.org

The goals of the Bisexual Resource Center, a nonprofit, educational organization, are to conduct research and provide education, a public forum, and a support network on bisexuality.

Children of Lesbians and Gays Everywhere
3543 18th Street, #1
San Francisco, CA 94110
Tel: (415) 861-KIDS (5437)
Fax: (415) 255-8345
Web: www.colage.org

Children of Lesbians and Gays Everywhere is the only national and international organization specifically supporting young people with gay, lesbian, bisexual, and transgender parents.

Gay and Lesbian Medical Association
459 Fulton Street, Suite 107
San Francisco, CA 94102
Tel: (415) 255-4547
Web: www.glma.org

The Gay and Lesbian Medical Association (GLMA) works to maximize the quality of health services for lesbian, gay, bisexual, and transgendered people and to foster a professional climate in which its members can reach their full potential. GLMA's focus is to increase the visibility of the specific health concerns of lesbian, gay, bisexual, and transgendered patients and offer programs and services that the organization is in a unique position to provide, such as continuing medical education, the lesbian health fund, and providers advocacy network.

The Gay & Lesbian National Hotline
PMB #296
2261 Market Street
San Francisco, CA 94114
Tel: 888-THE GLNH (843-4564)
Web: www.glnh.org/home.htm

The Gay & Lesbian National Hotline is a nonprofit, tax-exempt organization dedicated to meeting the needs of the gay, lesbian, bisexual, transgendered, and questioning community by offering free and anonymous information, referrals and peer-counseling. Peer counselors are available Monday-Friday, 4 PM–midnight and Saturday noon–5PM EST.

The Gay, Lesbian and Straight Education Network
121 West 27th Street
Suite 804
New York, NY 10001
Tel: (212) 727-0135
Fax: (212) 727-0254
Web: www.glsen.org

The Gay, Lesbian and Straight Education Network works to ensure safe and effective schools for all students.

Gay-Straight Alliance Network
160 14th Street
San Francisco, CA 94103
Tel: (415) 552-4229
Fax: (415) 552-4729
Web: www.gsanetwork.org

The Gay-Straight Alliance Network is a youth-led organization that connects school-based Gay-Straight Alliances (GSAs) to each other and community resources. Through peer support, leadership development, and training, GSA Network works to support young people in starting, strengthening, and sustaining GSAs and build the capacity of GSAs to create safe environments in schools so that students can support each other and learn about homophobia and other oppressions; educate the school community about homophobia, gender identity, and sexual orientation issues; and fight discrimination, harassment, and violence in schools.

Go Ask Alice!
Web: www.goaskalice.columbia.edu/

Go Ask Alice! is the health question and answer Internet service produced by Alice! Columbia University's Health Education Program—a division of Columbia University Health and Related Services. The mission of Go Ask Alice! is to increase access to, and use of, health information by providing factual, in-depth, straight-forward, and nonjudgmental information to assist readers' decision-making about their physical, sexual, emotional, and spiritual health. "Alice!" answers questions about relationships; sexuality; sexual health; emotional health; fitness; nutrition; alcohol, nicotine and other drugs; and, general health. Questions specific to lesbian women focus on safer sex between women (http://www.goaskalice.columbia.edu/1844.html) and worries about sexuality (http://www.goaskalice.columbia.edu/1722.html).

Human Rights Campaign
Lesbian Health
1640 Rhode Island Avenue NW
Washington, DC 20036-3278
Tel: (202) 628-4160
Fax: (202) 347-5323
Web: www.hrc.org

Founded in 1980, the Human Rights Campaign (HRC) lobbies Congress and works to educate the public on a wide array of topics affecting gay, lesbian, bisexual, and transgendered Americans, including workplace, family, discrimination, and health issues. Their web site includes the latest news affecting this population. The HRC site offers many of the same resources that their staff uses to educate congressional leaders and the public on critical issues. Links are provided to send messages to U.S. senators and representatives on particular issues of concern. Information also is provided on state laws affecting lesbian women.

Kaiser Permanente
National Diversity Department
One Kaiser Plaza, 22 Lakeside
Oakland, CA 94612
Tel: (501) 271-6663

The Kaiser Permanente National Diversity Department developed monographs to provide a comprehensive overview of health care for populations, including those who are lesbian, gay, bisexual, and transgendered. The books contain sections on demographics, health beliefs, risk factors, major diseases, infectious diseases and special areas of clinical focus including obstetrics and gynecology, childhood and adolescent health and mental health. The monographs also contain a list of web-based resources and an extensive bibliography.

LesbianSTD.com
Web: depts.washington.edu/wswstd

This web site features an overview of sexually transmitted diseases (STDs) and their transmission between women; a question and answer forum where readers can get questions answered; an index of previous questions and answers; a listing of lesbian health research studies currently enrolling women; research data from current studies; and a bibliography and links to other relevant sites. The goal of the site is to provide information and resources regarding STDs in women who have sex with women and to further the collective knowledge about lesbian STDs through research.

National Mental Health Association
2001 N Beauregard Street, 12th Floor
Alexandria, VA 22311
Tel: (703) 684-7722; 800-969-NMHA (6642); 800-433-5959 (TTY)
Fax: (703) 684-5968
Web: www.nmha.org

The National Mental Health Association (NMHA) is the country's oldest and largest nonprofit organization addressing all aspects of mental health and mental illness. With more than 340 affiliates nationwide, NMHA works to improve the mental health of all Americans, especially the 54 million individuals with mental disorders, through advocacy, education, research, and service. They have developed numerous resources on lesbian and gay issues.

The Mautner Project
1707 L Street, NW, Suite 230
Washington, DC 20036
Tel: (202) 332-5536
Fax: (202) 332-0662
Web: www.mautnerproject.org

The Mautner Project is a national organization dedicated to lesbians with cancer, their partners, and caregivers. Its mission is to provide the following: direct services to lesbians with cancer, their partners and caregivers; education and information to the lesbian community about cancer; education to the health care community about the special concerns of lesbians with cancer and their families; and advocacy on lesbian health issues in national and local arenas. Resources for providers include: "Tools For Caring About Lesbian Health" training package, which includes an 18-minute video, discussion guide, and an Optimal Care Kit (provides English and Spanish breast and cervical cancer brochures, shower card, sample nondiscrimination statement, suggestions for inclusive intake forms, checklist for optimal care, and an expanded lesbian health bibliography). Their "Removing the Barriers" CD-ROM contains a newly updated trainer guide, participant handbook, and Power-Point slides.

MEDLINEPlus Gay/Lesbian Health
Web: www.nlm.nih.gov/medlineplus/gayandlesbianhealth.html

The National Library of Medicine's MEDLINEPlus information pages are designed to direct users to a variety of resources to help them research their health questions. Access to MEDLINE, organizations, statistics, and full text materials is provided in an integrated environment. The Gay/Lesbian Health page provides information specifically on these topics.

National Gay and Lesbian Task Force
1325 Massachusetts Avenue, NW
Suite 600
Washington, DC 20005
Tel: (202) 393-5177
Fax: (202) 393-2241
Web: www.thetaskforce.org/

The National Gay and Lesbian Task Force Foundation was the first national lesbian, gay, bisexual and transgender (LGBT) civil rights and advocacy organization. It trains state and local activists and leaders and organizes broad-based campaigns to defeat anti-LGBT referenda and advance pro-LGBT legislation. They provide research and policy analysis on issues pertaining to LGBT individuals.

The National Latina/o Lesbian, Gay Bisexual & Transgender Organization
1420 K Street, NW Suite 400
Washington, DC 20005
Tel: 888-633-8320
Fax: (202) 408-8478
Web: www.llego.org/

The National Latina/o Lesbian, Gay Bisexual & Transgender Organization works to accomplish the following: 1) to form a national organization to address issues of concern to lesbian, gay, bisexual, and transgendered Latinas/os at the local, state, regional, national and international levels; 2) to create a forum of awareness, under-standing, and recognition of lesbian, gay, bisexual, and transgendered Latina/o identities, legal rights, relationships, and roles; 3) to formu-late and sustain a national health agenda that includes the impact of HIV/AIDS, breast cancer, and other health-related issues in Latino/a communities; 4) to develop a supportive network that will facilitate the sharing of information and resources; and 5) to educate and sensi-tize Latina/o and non-Latina/o communities by actively working against sexism, racism, homophobia, and discrimination.

The National Women's Health Information Center
8550 Arlington Boulevard, Suite 300
Fairfax, VA 22031
Tel: 800-994-WOMAN (800-994-9662); 888-220-5446 (TTY)
Web: www.4woman.gov

The National Women's Health Information Center is the federal gateway to women's health information. It compiles selected infor-mation on lesbian health through the Lesbian Health page.

Parents, Family, and Friends of Lesbians and Gays
1726 M Street, NW
Suite 400
Washington, DC 20036
Tel: (202) 467-8180
Fax: (202) 467-8194
Web: www.pflag.org

Parents, Families & Friends of Lesbians & Gays is a national nonprof-it organization with more than 80,000 members and supporters and more than 460 affiliates in the United States. It promotes the health and well-being of gay, lesbian, bisexual, and transgendered persons, and their families and friends through: support, to cope with an adverse society; education, to enlighten an ill-informed public; and advocacy, to end discrimination and to secure equal civil rights.

Sexuality Information and Education Council of the United States
130 West 42nd Street, Suite 350
New York, NY 10036-7802
Tel: (212) 819-9770
Fax: (212) 819-9776
Web: www.siecus.org

The Sexuality Information and Education Council of the United States develops, collects, and disseminates sexuality information, promotes comprehensive education about sexuality, and advocates for the right of individuals to make responsible sexual choices. Of particular relevance to lesbian health is its fact sheet entitled, *Lesbian, Gay, Bisexual and Transgender Youth Issues*, which can be obtained at http://www.siecus.org/pubs/fact/fact0013.html, and their annotated bibliography, *Lesbian, Gay, Bisexual, and Transgender Sexuality and Related Issues*, which can be obtained at http://www.siecus.org/pubs/biblio/bibs0005.html.

Society for Adolescent Medicine
1916 Copper Oaks Circle
Blue Springs, MO 64015
Tel: (816) 224-8010
Web: www.adolescenthealth.org

The Society for Adolescent Medicine, established in 1968, is a multi-disciplinary organization committed to improving the physical and psychosocial health and well being of all adolescents. One of the society's goals is to promote the availability of special training to adolescent health for all appropriate professionals. The society has a Special Interest Group on Lesbian, Gay, Bisexual and Transgender Adolescent Health. This group has created a speakers bureau listing to be disseminated to professional groups that sponsor local, region-al, or national conferences and training seminars. This list contains adolescent health specialists with expertise in health care of lesbian, gay, bisexual, and transgendered adolescents.

Health Care for Transgendered Individuals

Key Points

- Transgendered individuals have a strong desire to be the opposite gender and have significant discomfort with their assigned gender role. They strongly believe that they were born into a body with the wrong physical gender. This is not an issue of choice for them.

- Health care providers and researchers should treat transgendered individuals with respect and dignity. Health care providers who are morally opposed to providing care to this population should refer them elsewhere for care.

- Some transgendered individuals are involved in high-risk sexual behaviors and activities as a means of providing income, placing them at risk for human immuno-deficiency virus (HIV) and acquire immunodeficiency syndrome (AIDS).

- Hormonal therapy to maintain acquired gender characteristics can place transgendered individuals at risk for health problems, including cancer and heart and liver disease.

- Nondiscriminatory attitudes and communication styles should be developed in policies and practices for providing health care to all who seek services.

- Office and support staff should develop and maintain sensitive attitudes and practices for all patients, their families, and significant others, including transgendered individuals.

- Providers and researchers need to have appropriate sensitivity to barriers to health care faced by transgendered individuals.

- Providers and researchers need to be aware of specific health care needs for transgendered individuals.

- Maintaining confidentiality and obtaining informed consent are critical when treating transgendered patients. Transgendered individuals often cite the potential for breaches in privacy and confidentiality as a barrier to care. Privacy and confidentiality issues must be considered carefully in the context of referrals.

Transgender is an umbrella term to describe the full range of individuals who have a strong belief, often from childhood onwards, that they were born into a body with the wrong physical gender . . .

Transgender is an umbrella term to describe the full range of individuals who have a strong belief, often from childhood onwards, that they were born into a body with the wrong physical gender and incorporate one or more aspects, traits, social roles, or characteristics of the other gender (1). Transgenderism includes transsexuals (individuals who have had sex-reassignment surgery on their breasts ["top surgery"] and their genitals ["bottom surgery"]), androgynes (those with an androgynous presentation and whose behavior combines both genders or is gender-neutral), intersexuals (those who are born with sex chromosomes, external genitalia, or an internal reproductive system that is not considered standard for either male or female), and cross-dressers (clinically known as transvestism) (1). Cross-dressing by either gender is a fetish for using the clothing of the opposite sex for purposes of emotional satisfaction or erotic arousal, usually by men for women's clothing. Generally speaking, it is important to differentiate drag queens and kings (those who cross-dress only for entertainment purposes, for sex-industry purposes, to challenge social stereotypes, or for personal satisfaction) from transvestites because there is rarely an erotic component for drag queens and kings (2). Each of these populations have a unique set of needs and priorities.

Transgendered individuals can live full- or part-time as members of the opposite gender. Regardless, all transgendered individuals should be consistently referred to by the pronouns of their self-identified gender.

Prevalence rates of transgendered populations are not clearly established. Approximately 1 in 30,000 males and 1 in 100,000 females seek reassignment surgery worldwide (3). Other data suggest that there are 25,000 transsexuals in the United States, with 60,000 candidates for surgery and long waiting lists for those who provide this surgery (4). Thus, transgendered individuals constitute a small but substantial population.

The obstetrician–gynecologist may be called on to provide care for females who desire sex-reassignment surgery, called female-to-male transsexuals, or for women who have had their surgery as previously phenotypic men, called male-to-female transsexuals. The specific needs of each are different (2). Obstetrician–gynecologists can expect to be called on to perform annual examinations or to address specific gynecologic problems or concerns (Box 8). Obstetrician–gynecolo-

---

Box 8   General Gynecologic Care Considerations

- Provide routine health maintenance and preventive care as with all patients

- Address specific health needs related to long-term use of hormone therapy and other medications

- Screen and provide care for health issues related to lifestyle, emotional, and socioeconomic factors

- Ensure privacy and confidentiality of medical records and information when transferring records and making referrals

- Provide necessary and appropriate information on patients' rights and possible associated consequences

---

gists will need to determine if their professional liability insurance covers the examination of male organs. This, along with the physician's knowledge of male anatomy, can be helpful in determining the need for referral. It is important to note that in many states, transsexuals can obtain a new or amended birth certificate that indicates their new sexual identity following sex-reassignment surgery (5). This legal status may be a determining factor of professional liability coverage.

Health care providers can help to improve the health status of transgendered individuals by learning to adequately assess and treat this population; address their special clinical needs (eg, sexually transmitted diseases [STDs]); provide specific preventive services (eg, preventive cancer surveillance); offer psychologic assessments and support; maintain confidentiality; and acknowledge concerns about potential conflicts affecting durable power of attorney (in terms of "families of choice" versus "families of origin"). Physical and emotional issues of this lifestyle and the effects of aging, as in all other individuals, affect the health status of this population and can be addressed by health care providers. Health care providers who are morally opposed to providing care to this population should refer them elsewhere for care.

Care of transgendered individuals often requires special considerations that can best be addressed by physicians with expertise and experience in this area. This chapter will primarily focus on one part of this population—transsexuals. Sources for additional information pertaining to transsexuals as well as to other individuals in the transgendered community can be found in the "Resources" section at the end of this chapter.

Gender Identity and Gender Identity Disorder

Gender identity, sexual orientation, and sexual identity are distinct issues. They are all fundamental to self-identification and social status, with strong cultural, biologic, and psychologic components. Gender identity is a perception of oneself as either male or female. Sexual orientation is an erotic attraction to men, women, or both (2). Lesbian, gay, and bisexual applies to sexual identity in terms of sexual behavior, affection, attraction, and self-identity as lesbian, gay, or bisexual (4). Transgender applies to gender identity.

Transgenderism involves both a strong desire to be the opposite gender and significant discomfort with one's assigned gender or gender (social) role (3). Although the developmental etiology is largely unknown, one theory of gender identity development suggests that various sex hormones affect the developing fetal brain (6). Studies of the multiple sexual-dimorphic nuclei in the brain suggest that transsexuals possess the neuroanatomy appropriate to their self-perceived gender, but not their phenotypic gender (6).

Under the definition of the *Diagnostic and Statistical Manual of Mental Disorders*, 4th edition, transgenderism is not in itself a mental disorder. Severe distress or functional impairment due specifically to a preoccupation with gender identity must be present for a diagnosis of gender identity disorder in any of its several forms (children, adolescent, adults; not otherwise specified; transvestic fetishism). This preoccupation will severely interfere with and impair daily functioning. Genital mutilation and autocastration in presurgical males and breast mutilation in presurgical females rarely have been reported (3). Distress or impairment based on social prejudices (see following discussions) does not fulfill the diagnostic criteria.

The transgender community is a specific population with distinct as well as shared concerns and issues with the lesbian, gay, and bisexual communities. Transgendered individuals manifest a full range of sex-ual presentations and orientations. Both male-to-female and female-to-male transpersons can be attracted to women, men, both, or neither. Often transgendered individuals are or have identified as lesbian, gay, or bisexual but remain uncertain as to their sexual role. This may be caused in part by an individual's confusion between gender and sexual identity when expressing sexuality. Although gender identity issues often are seen as pathologic, some advocates suggest that it may be gender nonconformity rather than pathology (2). The confusion may also be a function of societal ignorance, with transgendered individuals incorrectly being identified categorically as lesbian or gay. Thus, until recently, information about transgendered individuals came from the combined lesbian, gay, bisexual, and transgender literature. Approx-imately 50 years of advocacy and grassroots movements have led to an improved understanding of health issues and concerns in the lesbian, gay, and bisexual communities. Many of these apply to and are shared with the transgender community (7).

Health Issues and Concerns in the Transgender Community

Barriers to Health Care

The social marginalization of transgendered individuals, including extreme harassment, discrimination, and rejection, increases the likelihood that the individual will be of a low socioeconomic status. The condition may be more severe when the transgendered individual is young; of color; or trades sex for drugs, services, and survival with an associated risk of HIV seropositivity.

Awareness that many believe this lifestyle to be pathologic is fundamental to understanding the problems transgendered populations face accessing health care. This belief can lead to discrimination, bias, and stereotyping. Lack of knowledge and sensitivity in the general and health care communities, coupled with lack of awareness and understanding for general and specific health needs on the part of the individual, eventually leads to inadequate access to, underutilization of, and disparities within the health care system for these populations (Table 5). Underutilization also may be caused by feelings of shame, low self-esteem, isolation, anxiety, and depression in certain individuals. There are inade-

Table 5. Social and Behavioral Factors and Health Concerns Relevant to Transgendered Populations

Sexual Behavior	Cultural Factors	Disclosure of Sexual Orientation, Gender Identity	Prejudice and Discrimination	Concealed Sexual Identity
■ Human immunodeficieny virus and acquired immunodeficiency syndrome ■ Hepatitis A and hepatitis B ■ Enteritis ■ Human papillomavirus and other sexually transmitted diseases ■ Bacterial vaginosis ■ Anal cancer	■ Body culture: eating disorders ■ Socialization: drugs, alcohol ■ Parenting: insemination, cryopreservation, mental health concerns ■ Gender polarity in dominant culture	■ Psychologic adjustment, depression, anxiety, suicide ■ Conflicts with family, lack of social support ■ Physical/economic dislocation	■ Provider bias, lack of sensitivity ■ Harassment and discrimination in medical encounters, employment, housing, and child custody ■ Limited access to care or insurance coverage ■ Pathologizing of gender-variant behavior ■ Violence against transsexual and transgendered populations	■ Reluctance to seek preventive care ■ Delayed medical treatment ■ Incomplete medical history; concealed risks, related complications, social factors

Modified from Kluwer Academic Publishers, Journal of the Gay and Lesbian Medical Association, 4 (3):102–51, 2000. Lesbian, gay, bisexual, and transgender health: findings and concerns. Dean L, Meyer IH, Robinson K, Sell RL, Sember R, Silenzio V, et al; table 1. Reprinted with kind permission of Springer Science and Business Media.

quate resources for care of the transgendered community, and there is no public health infrastructure for them. These issues result in poor health status and an underserved population. Studies indicate that most transsexuals and transgendered individuals primarily use the medical system specifically to obtain hormones and injection apparatus (8, 9).

Societal issues that affect health status reflect lower socioeconomic conditions through discrimination in housing, employment, and employment-related benefits; discrimination in nursing homes, senior citizen centers, and domestic violence shelters; interference with basic civil rights (eg, hate crimes and other violence); and stress related to discrimination in the workplace. Such events are underreported because of a lack of social, legal, and judicial support.

Health insurance usually fails to provide coverage to committed partners and often offers no coverage for special procedures (fertility services), medications (contraceptive pills for noncontraceptive use), and psychologic support services in general or for transgendered individuals. Sex-reassignment surgery often

is considered cosmetic or experimental and, therefore, not covered by insurance.

Mental Health Needs

Transgendered individuals typically isolate themselves, with an increased risk for depression, low self-esteem, substance abuse, suicidal ideation, and suicidal acts (3, 10, 11). Eating disorders also may be a problem in this population (4). These self-destructive behaviors are especially high in transgendered adolescents and presurgical transgendered patients, especially males who wish to be females (3, 11). Long-term victimization resulting from physical and sexual assaults, harassment, and discrimination may lead to posttraumatic stress disorder. Unexplained somatic symptoms may be manifestations of this disorder and suggest screening for this syndrome. When initially learning about their partner's transgenderism, the effect on significant others reportedly includes concerns over their own sexual identity and psychologic reactions to the disclosure that resemble posttraumatic stress disorder (12).

Human Immunodeficiency Virus, Acquired Immunodeficiency Syndrome, and Other Sexually Transmitted Diseases

The risk and prevalence of STDs is not known in the transgendered community, but it is reportedly higher for transgendered sex workers (prostitutes), especially male-to-female transsexuals, when compared with female sex workers. A recent analysis of several studies on HIV prevalence reveals that prevalence varies between 11% and 68% in studies on male-to-female sex workers (8). It also is reported that there is an increased risk of HIV for male-to-female transsexuals because this population may resort to prostitution as a primary source of income because of the high cost of sex-reassignment surgery, unemployment, and lack of insurance coverage (8, 13). Transgendered sex workers are more likely to engage in anal receptive intercourse as a means to earn money. Some are prone to engage in unprotected intercourse because of client request and lack of awareness of safe sex practices or because it may make them feel more feminine to be submissive and responsive (14). Additionally, many men will pay considerably more to engage in unprotected sex. Therefore, screening for human papillomavirus-related cancers and HIV, hepatitis B, and other STDs should be offered routinely for transgendered patients.

Risks for HIV are exacerbated with associated drug abuse, especially crack cocaine. Needle sharing for drugs, including blackmarket hormone injections, is common. Many transgendered individuals incorrectly believe that blackmarket hormone injections are more effective than pills, some cannot afford the pills, and others do not have health insurance to cover the therapy (15). Concern has been raised about complications from simultaneous administration of anti-HIV drugs and hormone injections (12). This has not been confirmed by research.

Sex Reassignment

Once a commitment has been made to change gender, the transition period lasts approximately 2 years. The process is very complex and involves significant psychologic and clinical support (see discussion under "Clinical Aspects of Transsexualism"). Follow-up studies indicate significant patient satisfaction with surgical outcomes and improved psychologic and clinical functioning (11, 16, 17). There are a relatively small percentage of individuals, however, who are dissatisfied with their surgery. Characteristics that may be predictive of postsurgical dissatisfaction include the following factors: alcoholism, drug addiction, heterosexual experience, married, older age, lack of family and social support, and psychologic instability (16).

Research

There are few exclusive studies on transgendered individuals, and those that exist are small, not randomized, and subject to bias. Generally, medical research does not identify sexual preference or gender identity, and those that do infrequently stratify for transgendered individuals. There has been inadequate or even denied funding for research in transgendered communities. However, in the past few years, cooperative efforts have emerged among various research and policy-forming agencies. These include the Department of Health and Human Services along with the Gay and Lesbian Medical Association/Lesbian Health Fund and the National Institute of Mental Health working with the American Psychological Association. The Department of Health and Human Services includes sexual orientation in its Healthy People 2010 directives on public health infrastructure and access to care, community education, programs, immunizations, infectious diseases (including HIV and other STDs), mental health, cancer, nutrition, substance and tobacco abuse, family planning, and injury and violence prevention (4). Research is needed to help health care clinicians to provide appropriate care for transgendered individuals. Standards of care have been developed by the Harry Benjamin International Gender Dysphoria Association (HBIGDA) (18), but others in the field of transgender health do not agree with these standards, which do not provide guidance for clinicians managing the care of transgendered individuals who choose not to undergo surgery. In addition, many patients are unwilling to conform to the HBIGDA requirements needed to start the treatments that prepare them for surgery (19).

Clinical Aspects of Transsexualism

Female-to-Male Transsexualism

Many women who transition to men see themselves as the opposite sex as early as childhood. On request by these young women or their parents, clinicians should refer them to a clinic with knowledge and expertise on transsexualism (see "Resources"). The clinical aspects of female-to-male transsexualism are shown in Box 9.

Before female-to-male sex-reassignment surgery, it is recommended that the candidate live ostensibly as a male for at least 1 year. In addition, a total of at least 3 months of counseling often is recommended before initiation of hormone therapy (18). Counseling during hormone therapy also may be helpful. Specific consent forms should be used for each stage of the transition. There are absolute and relative contraindications to hormone therapy (Box 10). When present, caution should be used if the patient is to be treated with this therapy. If the patient has a substance abuse problem, treatment to address that problem should be encour-

aged. The patient should not, however, be asked to choose between substance abuse treatment and hormone therapy (20). Substance abuse is only a contraindication for hormone therapy if there is resultant hepatic dysfunction. Because it may cause masculinization of a female fetus, patients should be advised that testosterone is contraindicated during pregnancy and encouraged to use barrier methods of contraception before surgery if at risk for pregnancy.

Methyl-testosterone injections every 2 weeks, or other androgen therapies, usually are sufficient to suppress menses and induce masculine secondary sex characteristics. The patient may request injection supplies (needles, syringes) if they are to self-administer the testosterone. Self-administration is not recommended for the first 3 months because careful moni-

---

Box 9   Clinical Aspects of Female-to-Male Transsexualism

Common medications taken:
- Methyltestosterone (or other androgen therapies)

Sex-reassignment surgery:
- Hysterectomy
- Vaginectomy
- Mastectomy
- Construction of phallus/scrotum. (May also include salpingo-oophorectomy, metoidioplasty, and urethroplasty.)

Clinical concerns (general):
- Low high-density lipoprotein cholesterol level
- High low-density lipoprotein cholesterol level
- Heart disease
- Liver disease
- Hepatic tumors

Organ specific examination and clinical concerns:
- Breast: Risk of breast cancer may be similar to that of biologic women if mastectomy has not been performed. Consider mammography as per current guidelines for biologic women (if mastectomy has not been performed).
- Vagina: visual inspection needed if present
- Cervix: Pap test is needed if cervix is present

- Uterus: endometrial hyperplasia/cancer has been reported
- Ovaries: bimanual examination of ovaries is needed if present. If a vaginectomy has been performed, a rectal examination to assess the ovaries can be conducted.
- Male genitalia: examination for scarring, urethral stricture
- Prostate: not applicable

Side effects of androgen therapy in female-to-male transsexuals:
- Fluid and sodium retention
- Increased erythropoiesis
- Decreased carbohydrate tolerance
- Decreased serum high-density lipoprotein cholesterol
- Liver abnormalities
- Obesity
- Emotional or psychiatric problems
- Sleep apnea

General recommendations:
- Yearly general physical examination
- Yearly examination of residual female organs
- Lipid level evaluation

| Box 10 | **Absolute and Relative Contraindications to Androgen Therapy and Estrogen Therapy in Transexual Patients** |

- Severe diastolic hypertension
- Ischemic cardiac episodes or electrocardiographic or ultrasound examination evidence of significant cardiac dysfunction. A variety of cardiac diseases, such as rheumatic heart disease, valvular defects, conduction disturbances, cardiomyopathies, or recent myocarditis, should be included in this category
- Thrombophlebitis or thromboembolic disease
- Cerebrovascular disease
- Hepatic dysfunction as evidenced by liver function abnormalities, history of chronic hepatitis, drug abuse, or heavy alcohol intake
- Impairment of renal function
- Refractory migraine headaches, seizures, or retinal lesions

- Brittle or poorly controlled diabetes mellitus
- Hyperprolactinemia
- Family history of breast cancer in one or more first-degree relatives
- Current or past history of heavy cigarette consumption (greater than 20 cigarettes per day)
- Marked obesity, particularly with a waist-to-hip ratio > 0.85 and > 0.9 in genetic females and males, respectively. This together with the presence of noninsulin-dependent diabetes mellitus puts the patient at risk with hormone therapy.
- Hypertriglyceridemia or hypercholesterolemia in genetic females, whereas estrogens may benefit the genetic males with hypercholesterolemia.

Modified with permission from Futterweit W. Endocrine therapy of transsexualism and potential complications of long-term treatment. Arch Sex Behav 1998;27:209–26, Kluwer Academic/Plenum Publishers.

toring of effects by a physician is needed (2). Use of needles also may be a relapse trigger for the patient in early recovery from substance abuse (20). Consultation with a mental health provider may, therefore, be warranted. Serum cholesterol and lipid levels should be monitored because testosterone can decrease high-density lipoprotein cholesterol levels. Additional complications of testosterone therapy for female-to-male transsexuals are high lipid levels, heart disease, liver disease and hepatic tumors, male pattern baldness, fluid and sodium retention, increased erythropoiesis, decreased carbohydrate tolerance, obesity, emotional or psychiatric problems, sleep apnea, and acne (21). Endometrial hyperplasia and carcinoma also have been reported (21, 22). Smoking increases the risk of coronary artery disease in individuals using testosterone (2).

Some patients may request mastectomies, which can be performed with circum-areolar incisions with excellent cosmesis. Hysterectomy and vaginectomy are part of the surgical process. Surgery is available to make functional phalluses (with both sexual and urinary function) and anatomic testicles. Salpingo-oophorectomy, metoidioplasty, and urethroplasty also may be done. Hot flashes may ensue after oophorecto-my despite the testosterone dose. Very low doses of estrogen can be considered, but this treatment has not been evaluated in studies.

In addition to a yearly general physical examination, gynecologic evaluation is recommended if total hysterectomy, vaginectomy, or oophorectomy have not been performed. Age-appropriate screening and evaluation for breast and cervical cancers is appropriate in all female-to-male patients with these organs. Visual inspection of the vagina and bimanual examination of the ovaries is needed in this population if these organs are still present. If a vaginectomy has been performed, a rectal examination to assess the ovaries can be conducted. Ultrasound examination may be useful if this examination is not adequate. Examination of the male genitalia for scarring and urethral stricture also is needed.

Some presurgical patients are so focused on their surgery and the transition period that they are unaware of or do not foresee a time in their lives when raising a child might be desirable. During the counseling process, patients should be counseled about reproductive options. Biologic females do not have a readily available option for gamete preservation other than cryopreservation of fertilized embryos in the event that they may want to choose biologic parenting later. Cryopreservation of oocytes is experimental, and patients should be counseled that this is not routinely available, is costly, is not covered by insurance, and has not been successful to date. As other options become available, they should be presented to the individual. Counseling also can include the psychologic aspects of potential progeny (23).

Male-to-Female Transsexualism

The first step for males who wish to change sex to females is to initiate estrogen therapy. The clinical aspects of male-to-female transsexualism are shown in Box 11. Counseling beginning 3 months before initiation of estrogen therapy is recommended (18). Counseling during hormone therapy also may be useful. Cryopreservation of banked sperm can be offered before initiating therapy. High-dose estrogen therapy will suppress gonadotropins and result in cessation of spermatogenesis. Complications of estrogen therapy in male-to-female transsexuals are those typically reported with high dose estrogen therapy, primarily venous thromboembolism (24). Smoking increases this risk (2). Other reported complications are liver dysfunction, weight gain, emotional lability, hypertension, and heart disease (19). Benign pituitary tumors (prolactinoma) have been reported, but the relationship between estrogen excess and these tumors is unclear (25). Breast cancer also has been reported (26). There are absolute and relative contraindications to this therapy (see Box 10). When present, caution should be used if the patient is to be treated with estrogen therapy.

It is recommended that sex-reassignment surgery not be performed until after the candidate has been living as an overt female taking hormones for at least 1 year (18). Surgery usually involves penile and testicular excision and remodeling the skin of the penile shaft into a neovagina, preserving portions of the glans penis as a clitoris or neocervix, and fashioning an opening for the urethra beneath the clitoris. Other techniques include use of bowel segments, peritoneum, or colon segments. Sometimes a neovagina is extended by adding a split thickness skin graft from the anterior or posterior thigh, the buttocks, or the lower abdomen between the umbilicus and the pubic hair. The final result usually includes a neovagina that has a functional orgasmic sexual response and the appearance of female external genital structures (2).

Box 11   Clinical Aspects of Male-to-Female Transsexualism

Common medications taken:
- Estrogen (often high dose) therapy
- Spironolactone

Sex-reassignment surgery:
- Penile and testicular excision
- Construction of vagina
- Breast implants

Clinical concerns (general):
- Fistula formation
- Thromboembolic disease

Organ specific:
- Breast: mammography should be conducted for male-to-female individuals according to age-specific guidelines of a biologic female
- Vagina: examine for stricture or stenosis and cancer screening.* Annual pelvic examination needed.
- Cervix: in patients who have a neocervix created from the glans penis, routine cytological examination of the neocervix may be indicated
- Uterus: not applicable
- Ovaries: not applicable
- Male genitalia: may have problems with residual erectile tissue
- Prostate: same risk of prostate cancer as biologic males as prostate is not removed in most surgeries

General recommendations:
- Yearly general physical examination
- Prostate and prostate specific antigen examinations as per clinical judgment

*Squamous cell cancer of neovagina has been reported.

However, the neovagina must be dilated postoperatively to prevent contracture. Breast implants also may be desired.

Reported complications of surgery include vaginal and urethral stenosis, fistula formation, problems with remnants of erectile tissue, and pain. Because spirono-lactone has been shown to reduce beard hair (27), some recommend its use as an adjuvant to the estrogen therapy to reduce unwanted hair growth in the vagina when a skin graft is used to extend a neovagina.

Examination of a male-to-female transsexual requires attention to both the newly created female anatomy and the residual male anatomy. Age-appropriate screening for breast and prostatic cancer is appropriate for male-to-female patients. Biologic males undergoing estrogen treatment should be monitored for breast cancer and encouraged to engage in routine self-examination. Mammography should be conducted for male-to-female individuals according to age-specific guidelines for a biologic female (18). The yearly examination also should include an assessment of the prostate, when age-appropriate because this is not removed in most surgeries. A serum prostate specific antigen assay can be offered. Often the prostate is too small to identify, but if any nodularity is identified, biopsy should be considered. There are no cases reported of postoperative prostatic carcinoma in male-to-female transsexuals.

Opinion varies regarding the need for Pap testing in this population. The Standards of Care for Gender Identity Disorders developed by HBIGDA recommend regular medical screening according to established guidelines for the patient's age (18). Routine vaginal cytologic screening in biologic women who have had a hysterectomy with removal of the cervix for benign conditions is not recommended (28). These recommendations also apply to male-to-female trans-sexuals. In patients who have a neocervix created from the glans penis, routine cytologic examination of the neocervix may be indicated. The glans are more prone to cancerous changes than the skin of the penile shaft, and intraepithelial neoplasia of the glans is more likely to progress to invasive carcinoma than is intraepithelial neoplasia of other penile skin (29).

Annual pelvic examinations are done to reinforce that the individual is female, to examine for stricture or stenosis, and to confirm the surgery was successful. If necessary, cancer screening can be done in male-to-female transsexuals who have undergone vaginoplasty (29). It should be noted that squamous cell carcinomas have been documented in neovaginas, usually occurring 10 or more years after vaginoplasty. They occurred regardless of vaginoplasty technique (skin grafts, bowel segments, peritoneum, or colon segments) (29).

The obstetrician–gynecologist may be consulted for stenosis of the vaginal graft and may need to surgically revise a contracted introitus to accommodate sexual activity. Revision also will require vaginal dilation because estrogen cream alone will not prevent or treat a graft from contracture. Use of estrogen to change the graft into estrogenized tissue has not been studied but probably occurs. It is important to note that estrogen does not work on keratinized tissue, but skin grafts are not keratinized. The obstetrician–gynecologist also may be asked to instruct in dilation of the neovagina (30).

Recommendations

The American Public Health Association has recommended guidelines for clinical practice and research (1). These include:

- Providers and researchers need to be aware of specific health care needs of transgendered individuals and have appropriate sensitivity to barriers to access to care.
- Unless their sexual orientation includes this in their preferred gender role, male-to-female and female-to-male transsexuals are not to be equated with homosexuals.
- Transgendered individuals should not be expected or forced to conform to narrow, socially defined gender roles.

Providers must always maintain awareness of the needs of transgendered individuals in terms of genetic factors related to their phenotypic gender, lifestyle, aging, and environmental factors, as well as their current gender. The long-term use of hormonal medications may increase the risk for certain cancers, while the genotype of the transgendered individual will still affect the risk of gender-specific cancers. As such, all routine health maintenance and preventive care should be provided as indicated. Additional research is needed to clarify this care.

With respect to lowered socioeconomic status, poor access to care, stigmatization, prejudice, and exposure to unsafe sexual practices, physicians are urged to be aware of and screen the transgendered population for violence; tobacco and substance abuse; alcoholism; and infectious diseases, such as tuberculosis for which individuals in lower socioeconomic populations are at risk (31).

Privacy and confidentiality issues must be carefully considered in the context of referrals. The physician who refers the patient should have an informed consent process, as should the consultant physician. Transgendered individuals often cite the potential for breaches in privacy and confidentiality as a barrier to care. Confidentiality is critical for physicians to maintain the trust of the patient when referring the patient to a physician who has expertise in transgender issues. A thorough informed consent is key. Maintaining confidentiality and obtaining informed consent also are critical when treating transgendered patients. It is important to inform patients about data collection that includes references to sexual orientation or gender identity, including how and when such information might be disclosed. Lastly, transgendered minors should be informed of their legal rights to care without parental consent and of the possibility and possible consequences of any mandatory reporting (32). For instance, the physician should explain that if the patient discloses any risk of bodily harm to herself or others, confidentiality will be breached. Furthermore, state laws may mandate the reporting of physical or sexual abuse of minors.

Obstetrician–gynecologists should be prepared to assist or refer individuals who wish to change their gender identity. As with other clinical and psychosocial issues not frequently recognized or seen, establishing referral patterns and resources is suggested, especially for mental health issues. Resources for patients can include access to Internet sites that will in turn provide information on advocacy and other support services in the local community (see "Resources").

Physicians are urged to eliminate barriers to access to care through their own individual efforts. To allow for appropriate sensitivity to needs, physicians are urged to identify the sexual orientation and gender identity status of all their patients as a routine (universal) part of their clinical encounters and should recognize that transgendered individuals may not identify themselves. There are nonjudgmental methods for inquiring about sexual orientation and gender identity status. Questions should be framed in ways that do not make assumptions and use language that is inclusive, allowing the patient to decide when and what to disclose.

Physicians are asked to treat transgendered individuals with dignity and respect and to help overcome ignorance and fear about this population in the health care community. Other recommendations include (33):

- Develop nondiscriminatory attitudes and communication styles in policies and practices for providing health care to all who seek services.

- Ensure that office and support staff develop and maintain similar sensitivity, attitudes, and practices for all patients, their families, and significant others, including transgendered individuals.

- Provide safe and confidential treatment.

- Ensure confidentiality of all records, especially identification of sexual orientation and gender identity.

- Provide necessary and appropriate information on patients' rights to confidential care.

References

1. The need for acknowledging transgendered individuals within research and clinical practice. APHA Policy Statement No. 9933. American Public Health Association. Am J Public Health 2000;90:482–4.

2. Israel GE, Tarver DE 2nd. Transgender care: recommended guidelines, practical information and personal accounts. Philadelphia (PA): Temple University Press; 1997.

3. American Psychiatric Association. Diagnostic and statistical manual of mental disorders. 4th ed, text rev. Washington, DC: APA; 2000.

4. Gay and Lesbian Medical Association. Healthy people 2010 companion document for lesbian, gay, bisexual, and transgender (LGBT) health. San Francisco (CA): GLMA; 2001.

5. Minter S. Representing transsexual clients: selected legal issues. San Francisco (CA): National Center for Lesbian Rights; 2003. Available at: www.nclrights.org/publications.pubs/tgclients.pdf. Retrieved October 29, 2003.

6. Zhou JN, Hoffman MA, Gooren LJ, Swaab DF. A sex difference in the human brain and its relation to transsexuality. Nature 1995;378 (6552):68–70.

7. Lee R. Health care problems of lesbian, gay, bisexual and transgender patients. West J Med 2000;172:403–8.

8. Clements-Nolle K, Marx R, Guzman R, Katz M. HIV prevalence, risk behaviors, health care use, and mental health status of transgender persons: implications for public health intervention. Am J Public Health 2001;91:915–21.

9. Moriarty HJ, Thiagalingam A, Hill PD. Audit of service to a minority client group: male to female transsexuals. Int J STD AIDS 1998;9:238–40.

10. Dixen JM, Maddever H, Van Maasden J, Edwards PW. Psychosocial characteristics of applicants evaluated for surgical gender reassignment. Arch Sex Behav 1984;13:269–76.

11. Fleming M, Cohen D, Salt P, Jones D, Jenkins S. A study of pre- and postsurgical transsexuals: MMPI characteristics. Arch Sex Behav 1981;10:161–70.

12. Dean L, Meyer IH, Robinson K, Sell RL, Sember R, Silenzio V, et al. Lesbian, gay, bisexual, and transgender health: findings and concerns. J Gay Lesbian Med Assoc 2000;4:101–51.

13. Pang H, Pugh K, Catalan J. Gender identity disorder and HIV disease. Int J STD AIDS 1994;5:130–2.

14. Boles J, Elifson KW. The social organization of transvestite prostitution and AIDS. Soc Sci Med 1994;39:85–93.

15. Nemoto T, Luke D, Mamo L, Ching A, Patria J. HIV risk behaviours among male-to-female transgenders in comparison with homosexual or bisexual males and heterosexual females. AIDS Care 1999;11:297–312.

16. Seil D. Transsexuals: the boundaries of sexual identity and gender. In: Cabaj RP, Stein TS, editors. Textbook of homosexuality and mental health. Washington, DC: American Psychiatric Press; 1996. p. 743–62.

17. Mate-Kole C, Freschi M, Robin A. A controlled study of psychological and social change after surgical gender reassignment in selected male transsexuals. Br J Psychiatry 1990; 157:261–4.

18. Harry Benjamin International Gender Dysphoria Association. The standards of care for gender identity disorders. Dusseldorf: Symposion; 2001.

19. White JC, Townsend MH. Transgender medicine: issues and definitions [editorial]. J Gay Lesbian Med Assoc 1998;2:1–3.

20. Substance Abuse and Mental Health Services Administration, Center for Substance Abuse Treatment. A provider's introduction to substance abuse treatment for lesbian, gay, bisexual, and transgender individuals. Rockville (MD): SAMSHA; 2001.

21. Futterweit W. Endocrine therapy of transsexualism and potential complications of long-term treatment. Arch Sex Behav 1998;27:209–26.

22. Futterweit W, Deligdisch L. Histopathological effects of exogenously administered testosterone in 19 female to male transsexuals. J Clin Endocrinol Metab 1986;62;16–21.

23. Green R. Transsexuals' children. Int J of Transgenderism (online journal) 1998;2(4). Available at: http://www.symposion.com/ijt/ijtc0601.htm. Retrieved October 29, 2003.

24. van Kesteren PJ, Asscheman H, Megens JA, Gooren LJ. Mortality and morbidity in transsexual subjects treated with cross-sex hormones. Clin Endocrinol (oxf) 1997;47:337–42.

25. Kovacs K, Stefaneanu L, Ezzat S, Smyth HS. Prolactin-producing pituitary adenoma in a male-to-female transsexual patient with protracted estrogen administration: a morphologic study. Arch Pathol Lab Med 1994;118:562–5.

26. Ganley I, Taylor EW. Breast cancer in a trans-sexual man receiving hormone replacement therapy. Br J Surg 1995;82:341.

27. Prior JC, Vigna YM, Watson D. Spironolactone with physiological female steroids for presurgical therapy of male-to-female transsexualism. Arch Sex Behav 1989;18:49–57.

28. Cervical cytology screening. ACOG Practice Bulletin No. 45. American College of Obstetricians and Gynecologists. Obstet Gynecol 2003;102:417–27.

29. Lawrence AA. Vaginal neoplasia in a male-to-female transsexual: case report, review of the literature, and recommendations for cytological screening. Int J Transgenderism (online Journal) 2001;5(1). Available at: http://www.symposion.com/ijt/ijtvo05no01.htm. Retrieved October 29, 2003.

30. Nonsurgical diagnosis and management of vaginal agenesis. ACOG Committee Opinion No. 274. American College of Obstetricians and Gynecologists. Obstet Gynecol 2002; 100:213–6.

31. Centers for Disease Control and Prevention. HIV-related tuberculosis in a transgender network—Baltimore, Maryland and New York City area, 1998–2000. MMWR Morb Mortal Wkly Rep 2000;49:317–20.

32. The Gay, Lesbian, Bisexual and Transgender Health Access Project. Boston (MA): GLBTHAP; 2001. Available at: http://www.Glbthealth.org. Retrieved November 24, 2003.

33. Clark ME, Landers S, Linde R, Sperber J. GLBT Health Access Project: a state-funded effort to improve access to care. Am J Public Health 2001;91:895–6.

Resources

The resources listed as follows are for information purposes only. Referral to these sources and web sites does not imply the endorsement of ACOG. This list is not meant to be comprehensive. The exclusion of a source or web site does not reflect the quality of that source or web site. Please note that web sites are subject to change without notice.

Advocates for Youth
2000 M Street NW, Suite 750
Washington, DC 20036
Tel: (202) 419-3420
Fax: (202) 419-1448
www.advocatesforyouth.org.

Advocates for Youth is dedicated to creating programs and advocating for policies that help young people make informed and responsible decisions about their reproductive and sexual health. Advocates provides information, training, and strategic assistance to youth-serving organizations, policymakers, youth activists, and the media in the United States and the developing world. This organization established YouthResource (http://www.youthresource.com), which is a web site created by and for gay, lesbian, bisexual, transgender, and questioning (GLBTQ) young people 13- to 24-years-old. It takes a holistic approach to sexual health by offering support, community resources, and peer-to-peer education about issues of concern to GLBTQ young people.

Children of Lesbian and Gays Everywhere
3543 18th Street, #1
San Francisco, CA 94110
Tel: (415) 861-KIDS (5437)
Fax: (415) 255-8345
Web: www.colage.org

Children of Lesbian and Gays Everywhere is the only national and international organization specifically supporting young people with gay, lesbian, bisexual, and transgender parents.

The Gay, Lesbian, Bisexual and Transgender Health Access Project
100 Boylston Street, Suite #815
Boston, MA 02116
Tel: (617) 988-2605
Fax: (617) 988-8708
Web: www.glbthealth.org

The goal of the Gay, Lesbian, Bisexual and Transgender (GLBT) Health Access Project is to strengthen the Massachusetts Department of Public Health's ability to foster the development of comprehensive, culturally appropriate health promotion policies and health care services for GLBT people through a variety of venues including community awareness, policy development, advocacy, direct service, and prevention strategies. GLBT published *Community Standards of Practice for Provision of Quality Health Care Services for Gay, Lesbian, Bisexual and Transgendered Clients*, which can be accessed through their web site.

Gay and Lesbian Medical Association
459 Fulton Street, Suite 107
San Francisco, CA 94102
Tel: (415) 255-4547
Fax: (415) 255-4784
Web: www.glma.org

The Gay and Lesbian Medical Association (GLMA) works to maximize the quality of health services for lesbian, gay, bisexual, and transgendered people (LGBT). Efforts include policy advocacy efforts, especially those dedicated to expand LGBT access to high-quality health care. It holds a number of conferences and seminars designed for LGBT physicians and medical students as well as for a growing number of researchers, policy makers, and other health care professionals. These conferences provide continuing medical education credit to physicians and to other health care professionals on subjects that include HIV/AIDS, lesbian health, mental health, primary care, and many other LGBT health-related topics. It organizes and mobilizes members of the LGBT medical community through GLMA*PAN*, which is an alert system used to encourage physicians and other health care providers to advocate for administrative and legislative changes to promote LGBT health and civil rights. The GLMA online health care referrals program allows web site visitors to search an on-line database to locate a health care provider near their home or work. Everyone listed in the referral program is a member of GLMA who has indicated that he or she is a licensed health care professional who is willing to be listed for referral purposes. It also publishes the *Journal of the Gay and Lesbian Medical Association*, which is a multidisciplinary, peer-reviewed journal devoted to the study of the health of LGBT populations.

Gender Education and Advocacy
PO Box 33724
Decatur, GA 30033-0724
Tel: (770) 939-0244
E-mail: aegis@gender.org
Web: www.gender.org

Gender Education and Advocacy is a national organization focused on the needs, issues and concerns of gender variant people in society. It seeks to educate and advocate for all human beings who suffer from gender-based oppression in its many forms. Gender Education & Advocacy provides a list of surgeons known to conduct sexual reassignment surgery at www.gender.org/resources/srs.html.

Gender Public Advocacy Coalition
1743 Connecticut Avenue, Fourth Floor
Washington, DC 20009-1108
Tel: (202) 462-6610
Fax: (202) 462-6744
E-mail: gpac@gpac.org
Web: www.gpac.org

The Gender Public Advocacy Coalition works to end discrimination and violence caused by gender stereotypes by changing public attitudes, educating elected officials, and expanding legal rights.

Harry Benjamin International Gender Dysphoria Association, Inc.
1300 South Second Street, Suite 180
Minneapolis, MN 55454
Tel: (612) 625-1500
Fax: (612) 626-8311
Web: www.hbigda.org

The Harry Benjamin International Gender Dysphoria Association is a professional organization devoted to the understanding and treatment of gender identity disorders. They have approximately 350 members from around the world in fields such as psychiatry, endocrinology, surgery, psychology, sexology, counseling, sociology, and law. It provides opportunities for scientific interchange among professionals through its biennial conferences and publications. It develops and publishes standards of care for the treatment of gender identity disorders, which are designed to promote the health and welfare of persons with gender identity disorders.

Human Rights Campaign
1640 Rhode Island Avenue, NW
Washington, DC 20036-3278
Tel: (202) 628-4160; (202) 216-1572 (TTY)
Fax: (202) 347-5323
Web: hrc.org

The Human Rights Campaign (HRC) works to mobilize grassroots action in diverse communities and increase public understanding through education and communication strategies. It is a bipartisan organization that works to advance equality based on sexual orientation and gender expression and identity, to ensure that gay, lesbian, bisexual, and transgendered Americans can be open, honest and safe at home, at work, and in the community. It works to educate the public on a wide array of topics affecting gay, lesbian, bisexual, and transgendered Americans, including workplace, family, and discrimination issues. The Human Rights Campaign Foundation, an affiliated organization of HRC, engages in extensive research and provides public education and programming.

International Foundation for Gender Education
PO Box 540229
Waltham, MA 02454-0229
Tel: (781) 899-2212
Fax: (781) 899-5703
E-mail: info@ifge.org
Web: www.ifge.org

The International Foundation for Gender Education (IFGE), founded in 1987, is an advocacy and educational organization that promotes the self-definition and free expression of individual gender identity. However, IFGE is not a support group. It is an information provider and clearinghouse for referrals about all things that are transgressive of established social gender norms.

Intersex Society of North America
4500 9th Avenuw NE, Suite 300
Seattle, WA 98105
Tel: (206) 633-6077
Fax: (206) 633-6049
E-mail: info@isna.org
Web: www.isna.org

The Intersex Society of North America is devoted to systemic change to end shame, secrecy, and unwanted genital surgeries for people born with an anatomy that is often considered atypical by the general public.

Kaiser Permanente
National Diversity Department
One Kaiser Plaza, 22 Lakeside
Oakland, CA 94612
Tel: (501) 271-6663

The Kaiser Permanente National Diversity Department developed monographs to provide a comprehensive overview of health care for populations, including those who are lesbian, gay, bisexual, and transgendered. The books contain sections on demographics, health beliefs, risk factors, major diseases, infectious diseases, and special areas of clinical focus including obstetrics and gynecology, childhood and adolescent health, and mental health. The monographs also contain a list of web-based resources and an extensive bibliography.

The Lesbian, Gay, Bisexual and Transgender Community Center
208 West 13th Street
New York, NY 10011
Tel: (212) 620-7310; 800-662-1220 (TDD/TTY)
Web: www.gaycenter.org

The Lesbian, Gay, Bisexual and Transgender Community Center facilitates many health-related, civic, and cultural programs. In addition, one of the center's prime functions is to provide affordable meeting space for gay and lesbian organizations. The center publishes the *National Directory of Lesbian, Gay, Bisexual and Transgender Community Centers*. This resource is available on the center's web site.

National Coalition for LGBT Health
1407 S Street, NW
Washington, DC 20009
Tel: (202) 797-3516
Fax: (202) 797-4430
E-mail: coalition@lgbthealth.net
Web: www.lgbthealth.net

The National Coalition for LGBT Health is committed to improving the health and well-being of lesbian, gay, bisexual, and transgendered individuals through federal advocacy that is focused on research, policy, education, and training. It has workgroups focusing on the areas of data collection, policy, cultural competency and education, access, and health disparities.

National Gay and Lesbian Task Force
1325 Massachusetts Avenue, NW
Suite 600
Washington, DC 20005
Tel: (202) 393-5177
Fax: (202) 393-2241
Web: www.thetaskforce.org/

The National Gay and Lesbian Task Force was the first national lesbian, gay, bisexual and transgender (LGBT) civil rights and advocacy organization. It trains state and local activists and leaders and organizes broad-based campaigns to defeat anti-LGBT referenda and advance pro-LGBT legislation. It provides research and policy analysis on issues pertaining to LGBT individuals.

The National Latina/o Lesbian, Gay Bisexual & Transgender Organization
1420 K Street, NW Suite 400
Washington, DC 20005
Tel: 888-633-8320
Fax: (202) 408-8478
Web: www.llego.org/

The National Latina/o Lesbian, Gay Bisexual & Transgender Organization works to accomplish the following: 1) to form a national organization to address issues of concern to lesbian, gay, bisexual, and transgendered Latinas/os at local, state, regional, national, and international levels; 2) to create a forum of awareness, understanding, and recognition of lesbian, gay, bisexual, and transgender Latina/o identities, legal rights, relationships, and roles; 3) to formulate and sustain a national health agenda that includes the impact of HIV/AIDS, breast cancer, and other health-related issues in Latino/a communities; 4) to develop a supportive network that will facilitate the sharing of information and resources; and 5) to educate and sensitize Latina/o and non-Latina/o communities by actively working against sexism, racism, homophobia, and discrimination.

OutProud
369 Third Street, Suite B-362
San Rafael, CA 94901-3581
E-mail: info@outproud.org
Web: www.outproud.org

OutProud is the web site of the National Coalition for Gay, Lesbian, Bisexual & Transgender Youth. It serves the needs of these young men and women by providing advocacy, information, resources, and support. It provides outreach and support to gay, lesbian, bisexual, and transgendered teens who are coming to terms with their sexual orientation and to those contemplating coming out. In addition, the coalition works to effect change at a grassroots level by catalyzing and fostering the development of a new generation of youth activists.

Renaissance Transgender Association
987 Old Eagle School Road, Suite 719
Wayne, PA 19087
Tel: (610) 975-9119
E-mail: info@ren.org
Web: www.ren.org

The mission of the Renaissance Transgender Association is to provide comprehensive education and caring support to transgendered individuals and those close to them. This is accomplished by offering a variety of carefully selected programs and resources focused on the factors affecting their lives.

Sexuality Information and Education Council of the United States
130 West 42nd Street, Suite 350
New York, NY 10036-7802
Tel: (212) 819-9770
Fax: (212) 819-9776
Web: www.siecus.org

The Sexuality Information and Education Council of the United States develops, collects, and disseminates sexuality information, promotes comprehensive education about sexuality, and advocates for the right of individuals to make responsible sexual choices. Of particular relevance to transgender health is their fact sheet entitled, *Lesbian, Gay, Bisexual and Transgender Youth Issues*, which can be obtained at http://www.siecus.org/pubs/fact/fact0013.html, and their annotated bibliography, *Lesbian, Gay, Bisexual, and Transgender Sexuality and Related Issues*, which can be obtained at http://www.siecus.org/pubs/biblio/bibs0005.html.

Society for Adolescent Medicine
1916 Copper Oaks Circle
Blue Springs, MO 64015
Tel: (816) 224-8010
Web: www.adolescenthealth.org

The Society for Adolescent Medicine, established in 1968, is a multidisciplinary organization committed to improving the physical and psychosocial health and well being of all adolescents. One of the society's goals is to promote the availability of special training in adolescent health for all appropriate professionals. The society has a Special Interest Group on Lesbian, Gay, Bisexual and Transgender Adolescent Health. This group has created a speakers bureau listing to be disseminated to professional groups that sponsor local, regional, or national conferences and training seminars. This list contains adolescent health specialists with expertise in health care of lesbian, gay, bisexual, and transgendered adolescents.

Transgender Law and Policy Institute
Tel: (917) 686-7663
E-mail: info@transgenderlaw.org
Web: www.transgenderlaw.org

The Transgender Law and Policy Institute (TLPI) is a nonprofit organization dedicated to engaging in advocacy for transgendered people. The TLPI brings experts and advocates together to work on law and policy initiatives designed to advance transgender equality. The TLPI tracks current developments in legal and public policy issues affecting transgendered people and their families and writes summaries of these trends for activists, policymakers, and the media. The TLPI provides legal, medical, and social science resources to attorneys and others advocating on behalf of transgendered individuals. The TLPI makes freely available litigation, legislative, and education advocacy materials for use by other advocates for transgendered people.

Clinics With Expertise in Treating Transgendered Individuals

Fenway Community Health
7 Haviland Street
Boston, MA 02115
Tel: (617) 267-0900; 888-242-0900; (617) 859-1256 (TTY)
Web: www.fenwayhealth.org

Fenway Community Health provides medical and mental health care to Boston's gay, lesbian, bisexual, and transgendered community, and to those who live and work in the neighborhood. They are a nationally recognized leader in HIV care and research.

University of Minnesota
Center for Sexual Health
Tel: (612) 625-1500
Web: www.med.umn.edu/fp/phs/tgs.htm

The Center for Sexual Health serves the special health needs of the transgender community. Clinical services provided include psychological, physical, and psychiatric evaluations; individual, group, couple, and family psychotherapy; evaluation and treatment of children and adolescents; physical health care, including prescriptions of appropriate medications and hormones; recommendations for sex reassignment surgery; ongoing support for transgendered individuals; counseling for intersexuality; and sex therapy.

Tom Waddell Health Center
50 Lech Walesa (Ivy) Street
San Francisco, CA 94102
Tel: (415) 554-2727
Web: www.dph.sf.ca.us/chn/HlthCtrs/transgender.htm

The Transgender Clinic of Tom Waddell Health Center has been in operation since November of 1993 and is committed to providing quality, integrated health care in an atmosphere of trust and respect. The center is a multidisciplinary primary care clinic focusing primarily on the needs of underserved populations of inner-city San Francisco. They offer nutritional, mental health, and social services and work closely with community organizations.

Health and Health Care of Incarcerated Adult and Adolescent Females

Key Points

- Most incarcerated women are of reproductive age, making reproductive health care a priority area for this population.

- Generally, pregnant inmates, because of their disadvantaged backgrounds, are at higher risk for poor pregnancy outcomes than the general population. Many facilities do not offer adequate prenatal care or routine abortion services.

- Behavioral profiles and anecdotal evidence suggest that inmates are disproportionately affected by sexually transmitted diseases (STDs).

- Many incarcerated women have substance abuse problems, histories of sexual abuse, and histories of domestic violence. Rates of anxiety and depression also are particularly high in this population.

- Adolescent female offenders have many of the same health problems as adult women, including high-risk pregnancies, substance abuse, poor mental health, STDs, human immunodeficiency virus (HIV) and acquired immunodeficiency syndrome (AIDS), and physical or sexual abuse histories.

- Incarcerated females of all ages should receive reproductive health care, including adequate prenatal care or abortion services, as per American College of Obstetricians and Gynecologists (ACOG) guidelines.

- The type of care that can be provided will depend on the length of incarceration. The period of incarceration, however long or short, provides a window of opportunity for improving the health status of this population.

- Health professionals and institutions should consider ways to become further involved with correctional health care to ensure adequate provision of health care services to incarcerated adult and adolescent females.

. . . it is likely that as a result of their disadvantaged backgrounds, a disproportionate number of incarcerated women have acute and chronic illnesses and undetected health problems.

Between 1990 and 1998, the number of women in jail and prison increased 60% and 88%, respectively (1). Where female offenders are housed depends on the nature of their offense, the length of their sentence, whether they would be a risk to others or themselves, and their age. Adult women can be housed in federal prisons, state prisons, and local jails. Federal prisons hold individuals who have been convicted of or are awaiting trial for violating a federal law. Those who have been convicted of violating a state law are sentenced to time either in a state prison or a local jail. Prisons typically hold inmates with sentences of 1 year or more. Jails are operated locally and incarcerate unsentenced individuals and individuals serving sentences of 1 year or fewer (2). Female juvenile offenders (younger than 18 years) can be housed in juvenile detention homes, usually operated locally, or in residential correctional facilities (learning/training schools or ranches), usually under the state department of juvenile corrections. These offenders include alleged or adjudicated juveniles or status offenders (those who committed an act that would not be considered an offense if done by an adult, such as curfew violation). Most states allow certain categories of offenders younger than 18 years to be incarcerated in adult prisons and jails where they may be segregated from or housed with older inmates (3).

Overcrowding has resulted in both adult and adolescent female offenders frequently being sent to inappropriate and often dangerous settings. Of the 103 federal institutions, only 12 operate facilities that house women alone (4). Of the more than 1,400 state prisons, only 92 house women alone (5). Most facilities, therefore, are not well-equipped to address the unique needs of adult or adolescent females. Increased attention to the needs of incarcerated females is warranted to ensure appropriate medical care.

Characteristics of Incarcerated Females

Adult Women

At mid-year 2003, 100,102 women (6.9% of all prison inmates) were incarcerated in federal or state prisons (6). There also were 81,650 women in local jails. The median age of women offenders in state prison was 33 years; it was lower in local jails (31 years) and slightly higher (36 years) in federal prisons. Nearly

one quarter of female federal prison inmates are at least 45 years old. Although women of racial and ethnic minority groups represent 26% of the United States female population, they account for 64%, 67%, and 71% of women in jails, state prisons, and federal prisons, respectively. Many of these women are from economically, educationally, socially, and emotionally disadvantaged environments. Only 40% of women in state prison were employed full-time before their arrests. Nearly 30% of female inmates reported receiving welfare assistance before the arrest that brought them to prison (1).

Most women in correctional facilities are incarcerated for nonviolent crimes. Drug offenses are the most common felonies committed by women in both the federal (72%) and state (34%) prison systems, and are the second most common offense committed by women in local jails (30%). Property offenses (when property is unlawfully damaged or taken through means such as shoplifting, burglary, or vandalism) are the most common offense of women in local jails (34%) (Table 6). Nearly one in three women in state prison claims to have committed her offense to finance drug purchases (1). An increase in violent offenders accounted for 49% of the growth in the female population in state prisons between 1995 and 2001 (7). An estimated 28% of violent female offenders are juveniles (1).

Adolescents

In 2002, 29% of juveniles arrested were female. Law enforcement agencies made 654,000 arrests of women younger than 18 years that year. Between 1993 and 2002, arrests of juveniles generally increased more for females than for males in several categories, including simple assault, drug abuse violations, liquor law viola-

Table 6. Offenses of Women in Prison or Jail, 1998

Most Serious Offense	Percentage of Women Offenders		
	State Prison	Federal Prison	Local Jails
Violent offenses	28	7	12
Property offenses	27	12	34
Drug offenses	34	72	30
Public-order offenses	11	8	24

Greenfeld, LA, Snell TL. Women offenders. Bureau of Justice Statistics Special Report. Washington, DC: U.S. Department of Justice; 1999. NCJ 175688. Available at http://www.ojp.usdoj.gov/bjs/pub/pdf/wo.pdf. Retrieved September 3, 2004.

tions, driving under the influence, and curfew and loitering. In the case of aggravated assault, the rate for males decreased whereas the rates for females increased. There were decreases in arrests for both male and female juveniles for larceny-theft, motor vehicle theft, vandalism, weapons, and runaways, but the decreases were less for females than males (8). During the 1990–1999 period, there was a surge in the number of female delinquency cases entering detention (a 50% increase compared with 4% for males). The large increase was tied to the growth in the number of delinquency cases involving females charged with person offenses (assault, robbery, rape, and homicide) (a 102% increase compared with a 20% increase for males (9). Still, most (87%) young offenders in residential placement are male (10).

A substantial number of individuals younger than 18 years (6,900) are held in adult jails. Most of these youth were held as adults (6). The number of offenders younger than 18 years admitted to state prison more than doubled from 3,400 in 1985 to 7,400 in 1997. Most of these individuals are males, but 8% of those younger than 18 years held in state prison are female (3). Adult settings are not prepared to address adolescent girls' needs. Often, rather than protecting the adolescent, many adult settings neglect adolescents' needs and may further victimize them because this environment increases their vulnerability to suicide and sexual assault (11).

Pregnant and Parenting Incarcerated Females

In 1997, 6% of the women who entered local jails and 5% who entered state prison were pregnant (1). It is likely that these percentages underestimate the pregnant population because many facilities do not routinely screen for pregnancy (12). In 1998, more than 1,400 women gave birth to an infant in prison (13). Data on adolescent pregnancy in juvenile detention centers are sparse. A national survey of juvenile facilities found that roughly two thirds of 261 correctional facilities housed between one and five pregnant adolescents on any given day. Moreover, 60% of the facilities that reported housing pregnant youths reported having had one or more obstetric complications (14). In a study of girls in the California juvenile justice system, 29% of the girls interviewed had been pregnant one or more times, and 16% had been pregnant while in custody. Of those girls who had been

pregnant in custody, 23% had miscarried and 29% had been placed in physical restraints at some point, usually during transport (15).

Most adult women under correctional sanction have minor children. In 1998, an estimated 70% of women in local jails, 65% of women in state prisons, and 59% of women in federal prisons had minor children (1). The total number of children with incarcerated mothers in state prison increased from more than 56,000 in 1991 to more than 117,000 in 1998. When including children with mothers in jail or federal prison, the number increases to more than 230,000 (1, 16). The number of incarcerated female minors who are parents is unknown. Researchers estimate that in 1 year there could be between 500 and 1,000 adolescent mothers who are incarcerated (14). One study has indicated that 83% of incarcerated adolescent women who were mothers reported that they had been separated from their infants within the first 3 months of their children's lives. In addition, 54% of adolescents who were mothers had not had a single visit with their children while in detention or placement (15). With mothers often being the primary caregivers, the imprisonment can affect markedly the structure and stability of the children's care. According to the Department of Justice, most children whose mothers are in prison live with grandparents or relatives other than their fathers. Ten percent of children with mothers in state prison are in the care of a foster home, institution, or agency (17).

Health Services for Incarcerated Women

Once an individual enters a correctional facility, her health needs become the responsibility of the institution. Generally speaking, correctional health care is delivered in one of three ways:

1. In-house services managed by the warden or, less often, services by health personnel who are not directly supervised by the warden
2. Arrangements with local hospitals and clinics for on-site or transported examinations and procedures
3. Contracting with a firm or agency that provides and manages services on-site

Historically, correctional health care was delivered via sick call, meaning an inmate must notify a guard or other designated authority of her need for medical attention. Adequate sick call requires a professional evaluation by trained personnel (18). Many facilities are now recognizing that provision of primary care and health education also are needed. However, this recognition often does not result in the provision of comprehensive care, and some facilities still have only a sick call system for health care.

The considerable increase in inmate populations is adding to the existing strain on an already limited and stressed correctional health care delivery system. Because women are a minority in most facilities, health services tailored to their needs frequently are severely limited. One of the objectives of the Federal Bureau of Prisons for fiscal year 2003 was to ensure all of its facilities housing female offenders offer programs that effectively meet the physical, social, educational, and psychologic needs of this population (4).

Improvements in bringing quality health care to correctional facilities that have taken place are diluted by the problem of overcrowding and the limited resources to provide such services. Twenty-three states report operating their prisons at 100% or more of their highest capacity, and the federal system in 2003 was estimated to be operating at 39% over capacity (19). Overcrowding also is a problem in juvenile custody facilities (20). There continue to be medical personnel staffing shortages nationally. This is compounded by the difficulties in appealing to and retaining medical staff to work in correctional facilities (21).

Health Service Standards

There are no federal or state mandates requiring correctional health facilities to obtain any type of accreditation. There are organizations that assess the quality of correctional health care and set infrastructural standards. The Joint Commission on Accreditation of Health Care Organizations routinely surveys and accredits facilities within the federal prison system. In addition to the Joint Commission on Accreditation of Health Care Organizations, the National Commission on Correctional Health Care, and the American Correctional Association accredit correctional facilities. However, national uniform standards are not applied to all state and local correctional facilities and incarceration programs, and there is no one organization or agency to which all facilities are accountable.

The National Commission on Correctional Health Care develops health care standards for jails, prisons, and juvenile facilities. These standards provide recom-

mendations about inmate care and treatment, health promotion and disease prevention, health records, medical–legal issues, special inmate needs and services, personnel and training, and health care services support (22–24).

The American Correctional Association also develops health care standards for correctional facilities, addressing services, programs, and operations necessary for the proper management of correctional facilities. Issues covered include administrative and financial management, staff training and development, sanitation, food service, rules, and discipline. The standards reflect policies and procedures that protect the health and safety of both staff and offenders.

The American Public Health Association is another source of standards for health services in correctional institutions. Its standards define the scope of services that are necessary to provide adequate health care to incarcerated populations. They are based on principles of public health and constitutional standards developed through litigation (25).

Health of Incarcerated Adult and Adolescent Females and Related Care

Although few studies have been done, it is likely that as a result of their disadvantaged backgrounds, a disproportionate number of incarcerated women have acute and chronic illnesses and undetected health problems. Outlined in Table 7 are recommendations for care of incarcerated adult and adolescent females. Areas of specific need are addressed as follows.

Reproductive Health

Most incarcerated women are of reproductive age, making reproductive health care a priority area. In 1997, 90% of women in state prisons received a gynecologic examination at the time of their admission. In local jails, only 22% received this care (1). The latter data may be secondary to the length of incarceration or less developed or available health care services in local jails.

Pregnancy

Generally, pregnant inmates, because of their disadvantaged backgrounds, are at higher risk for poor preg-

Table 7. Recommended Care for Incarcerated Adult and Adolescent Females

Care	Prison*	Jail*	Juvenile Facilities
Intake	History—question about current medical problems, immunization status, sexual activity, menstrual cycle; number of pregnancies and outcomes; history of medical problems, chronic illness, hospitalizations, breast disease and gynecologic problems; domestic violence, sexual and physical abuse; care and safety of minor children at home	Same as in prison	Same as in prison, but also screen for eating disorders
	Mental health assessment	Same as in prison	Same as in prison bearing in mind that adolescents in correctional facilities are at higher risk for suicide than those in general population
	Examination[†]—pelvic and breast, Pap test, baseline mammography based on ACOG guidelines	Same as in prison, except Pap test and mammography should only be done if incarceration will be long enough for information to be useful	Same as in jail except mammography is unlikely to be needed. Pap test should be performed on high-risk adolescents
	Laboratory work—STD tests, HIV test, pregnancy tests, tuberculin skin test based on ACOG guidelines	Same as in prison, except tuberculin skin test should only be done if incarceration will be long enough for information to be useful	Same as in jail
Pregnancy care	Pregnancy counseling and abortion services	Same as in prison	Same as in prison
	HIV tests and treatment to prevent perinatal HIV transmission for HIV positive pregnant women	Same as in prison	Same as in prison
	Assessment for substance abuse and initiation of treatment; prompt initiation of methadone treatment for women addicted to heroin is critical	Same as in prison	Same as in prison
	Perinatal care per ACOG guidelines	Same as in prison	Same as in prison
	Provision of dietary supplements	Same as in prison	Same as in prison
	Delivery services in a licensed hospital that has facilities for high-risk pregnancies	Same as in prison	Same as in prison
Preventive care	Additional tests, examinations, and care based on ACOG guidelines	Same as in prison	Same as in prison
	Health education on contraception; pregnancy; tobacco, alcohol, and substance abuse cessation; and parenting	Same as in prison	Same as in prison
	Comprehensive HIV and STD testing, treatment, and prevention programs	Same as in prison	Same as in prison bearing in mind that adolescents, especially those in correctional facilities, are at higher risk for STDs than the adult population

(continued)

Table 7. Recommended Care for Incarcerated Adult and Adolescent Females *(continued)*

Care	Prison*	Jail*	Juvenile Facilities
Preventive care	Contraceptive services, including emergency contraception, based on medical need or potential risk for pregnancy	Same as in prison, noting that contraceptive services are very important with short-term incarceration	Same as in jail
	Provide immunizations as necessary per ACOG guidelines	Same as in prison	Same as in prison
Care for older women	Hormone therapy, if indicated	Same as in prison	Not applicable
	Screening, treatment, and prevention programs for osteoporosis	Same as in prison	Osteoporosis prevention programs may be useful
Mental health	Medication management, suicide prevention, crisis intervention, substance abuse programs, linkage to social services and community substance abuse programs upon release	Same as in prison	Same as in prison, noting that incarceration is a risk factor for suicide among adolescents

Abbreviations: ACOG, The American College of Obstetricians and Gynecologists; HIV, human immunodeficiency virus; STDs, sexually transmitted diseases.

*If a juvenile is housed in an adult prison or jail, the recommendations under the juvenile facilities column should be followed

†The request by either a patient or a physician to have a chaperone present during a physical examination should be accommodated regardless of the physician's sex.

Data from American College of Obstetricians and Gynecologists. Health care for adolescents. Washington, DC: ACOG; 2003; American Academy of Pediatrics, American College of Obstetricians and Gynecologists. Guidelines for perinatal care. 5th ed. Elk Grove Village (IL): AAP; Washington, DC: ACOG; 2002; Primary and preventive care: periodic assessments. ACOG Committee Opinion No. 292. American College of Obstetricians and Gynecologists. Obstet Gynecol 2003;102:1117–24; Cervical cancer screening in the adolescent female. ACOG Committee Opinion No. 300. American College of Obstetricians and Gynecologists. Obstet Gynecol 2004;104:885-9; Sexually transmitted diseases in adolescents. ACOG Committee Opinion No. 301. American College of Obstetricians and Gynecologists. Obstet Gynecol 2004;104:891-8; American Public Health Association. Standards for health services in correctional institutions. 3rd ed. Washington, DC: APHA; 2003; Anno B. Correctional health care: guidelines for the management of an adequate delivery system. Washington, DC: National Institute of Corrections; 2001; National Commission on Correctional Health Care. Standards for health services in jails. Chicago (IL): NCCHC; 2003; National Commission on Correctional Health Care. Standards for health services in prison. Chicago (IL): NCCHC; 2003; National Commission on Correctional Health Care. Standards for health services in juvenile detention and confinement facilities. Chicago (IL): NCCHC; 2004; and Health care for children and adolescents in the juvenile correctional care system. American Academy of Pediatrics. Committee on Adolescence. Pediatrics 2001;107:799–803; American College of Obstetricians and Gynecologists. Ethics in obstetrics and gynecology. 2nd ed. Washington, DC: ACOG; 2004.

nancy outcomes than the general population. Many facilities do not offer adequate prenatal care or routine abortion services (26). Eighty percent of incarcerated pregnant women received some prenatal care during their admission into state prisons; only 50% received such care in local jails (1). Only approximately two thirds of juvenile facilities provide prenatal services and only 30% provide parenting classes (14). Studies indicate that birth outcomes can be improved by providing adequate prenatal care to incarcerated women (27, 28).

Sexually Transmitted Diseases

Behavioral profiles and anecdotal evidence suggest that inmates are disproportionately affected by STDs (12). A total of 3–28% have syphilis, 4–6% have chlamydia cervicitis, and 0.7–7.4% are infected with gonorrhea (13). Data, however, are incomplete. In 1997, a study revealed that routine or mandatory syphilis screening policies were in place in 88% of state and federal prison systems, but only 28% and 20%, respectively, have policies for gonorrhea and chlamydia testing (12). In local jails, only 42% have routine or mandatory screening policies for syphilis

and only 27% and 4%, respectively, have testing policies for gonorrhea and chlamydia. Given the high prevalence of STDs among incarcerated females, they may be at higher risk for cervical cancer, but this risk has not been adequately evaluated.

Human Immunodeficiency Virus

In 2002, 3% of all female inmates in state prisons were HIV-positive (29). Routine screenings are not performed in all correctional facilities; therefore, data on prevalence rates of HIV and AIDS are incomplete. Each state, the District of Columbia, and the federal Bureau of Prisons test inmates for HIV based on certain criteria. Specifically, most jurisdictions (51 out of 52) test inmates if they have HIV-related symptoms or if the inmate requests a test. Fifteen jurisdictions test high-risk groups. Only 20 jurisdictions test all incoming inmates (30). High-risk behaviors for HIV transmission, including sex, drug use, sharing of injection materials, and tattooing, occur in correctional facilities, and HIV transmission among correctional inmates has been shown to occur (12).

Mental Health

Often the behaviors that are related to being arrested (eg, drug use) are symptoms associated with previous psychological trauma and trauma-related disorders (31). Many incarcerated women have substance abuse problems, histories of sexual abuse, and histories of domestic violence. Rates of anxiety and depression also are particularly high in this population. Anxiety remains high throughout incarceration for women with young children, whereas it dissipates for women without children (32). Nearly one fourth of female state prison and local jail inmates were identified as mentally ill. More than 30% of mentally ill females in state prison, just under 25% of mentally ill females in federal prison, and nearly 50% of those in local jails did not receive mental health services while incarcerated (33).

Physical and Sexual Abuse

Nearly 60% of incarcerated women in state prisons and nearly 50% in local jails had been physically or sexually abused at some time during their lives (1). The prison environment may foster sexual aggression among inmates and sexual exploitation by staff. Rates of sexual abuse vary by institution. In one facility, 27% of incarcerated women reported sexual coercion; in another facility, 8% of incarcerated women reported sexual coercion (33). The serious physical and psychologic harm caused by sexual abuse is well-known (see the "Sexual Assault" chapter.) These consequences may be more severe when resulting from prison sexual abuse given, for example, the high rates of STDs and HIV and AIDS in this population.

Substance Abuse

Incarcerated women are more likely than their male counterparts to be drug users (1). Approximately six in 10 women in state prison indicated they were using drugs in the month before their offense, and five in 10 described themselves as daily users of drugs. Just more than one half of women confined in state prisons reported drinking alcohol in the year before the current offense. Daily drinkers accounted for approximately 25% of female inmates. Slightly more than 55% of female substance abusers in state prisons had ever been in substance abuse treatment; 20% of women had received such treatment since prison admission (1). Prompt identification of pregnant women who are addicted to heroin is important so that methadone can be started and maintained throughout the pregnancy. Substance abuse can continue during incarceration despite efforts to prevent drugs from entering correctional facilities. Effective treatment programs, therefore, are essential.

Tuberculosis

In recent years, the incidence of tuberculosis has decreased both in the overall U.S. population and among correctional facility inmates. It still remains higher, though, among inmates. Overcrowding can exacerbate the problem. Most prison systems appear to follow the guidelines of the Centers for Disease Control and Prevention regarding screening for tuberculosis, isolation and treatment, and preventive therapy. Adherence to these guidelines is lower, however, among city and county jail systems (12).

Special Concerns With Adolescents

Little research has been done on adolescent offenders' health concerns, and what has been reported usually covers both males and females. However, it is clear that adolescent female offenders have many of the same health problems as adult women, including high-risk pregnancies, substance abuse, poor mental health, STDs, HIV and AIDS, and physical or sexual abuse histories (35). A study of adolescent females entering various juvenile facilities indicate that between 16% and 27% had chlamydia and between 6% and 17% had gonorrhea (36). The overall positivity for both chlamydial and gonococcal infections was higher at the juvenile facility than at the adult facility in the same city. Nearly 70% of girls in the juvenile justice system have histories of physical abuse, compared with approximately 20% of adolescent females in the general population. More than 70% of girls in the juvenile justice system and in shelters report sexual abuse and assault (37). Another study indicated that 92% of juvenile female offenders had experienced some form of emotional, physical, or sexual abuse (15). It also is important to note that incarceration is a risk factor for adolescent suicide (38). A recent survey of juvenile detention facilities indicates that two thirds of these facilities hold youth who are waiting for community mental health treatment. Some of these youth have no criminal charges pending against them. In other cases, these youth have been charged with crimes but are unable to be released and must stay incarcerated for extended periods because of lack of available treatment facilities (39).

Financing Correctional Health Care Services

Legislative appropriations determine most of the funds that are allocated to operate correctional facilities, including those that cover the cost of health care. The increasing costs of health care make it difficult for correctional facilities to improve health care for incarcerated women. The average annual expense per inmate for health care in prison increased from $901 in 1982 to $2,640 in 1998 (18). It is difficult to determine how much of this increase was caused by expansion in staffing, services, and other health care programs versus increasing health care costs in general.

Restrictions on Medicaid financing apply to adults and most adolescents in secure confinement, such as juvenile detention centers. Those in other settings, such as group homes or residential treatment facilities, may be eligible for Medicaid and the benefits of the Early and Periodic Screening, Diagnosis, and

Treatment program (40). This service is Medicaid's comprehensive and preventive child health program for individuals younger than 21 years. It includes periodic screening, vision, dental, and hearing services.

Recommendations

Given the growing population of incarcerated adult and adolescent females, increased attention to the needs of this population is warranted to ensure receipt of appropriate medical care during incarceration. Global efforts are needed to increase funding for the provision of health care services to incarcerated women, research pertaining to the health needs of this population, and efforts to more appropriately serve this population. In addition, local and individual efforts by health care professionals and correctional health care facilities and staff can be undertaken to improve the health and care of incarcerated adults and adolescent females. Specific recommendations are shown in Box 12.

Box 12   Recommendations to Improve the Health and Care of Incarcerated Adult and Adolescent Females

Global

- Data are needed on the health needs of incarcerated women and adolescents, the services they receive, the qualifications of the provider, the location of the service, and the outcome of these services.

- Future health care reform legislation at the state and federal level should include funding to increase access to necessary health care and availability of qualified providers for incarcerated females.

- Adolescents should be detained or incarcerated only in facilities with developmentally appropriate programs and staff trained to deal with their unique needs. If they must be housed in adult correctional facilities, they should be separated from the adult population by sight and sound and provided with a developmentally appropriate environment (1).

- Adolescents with serious mental disorders should not be placed in detention when they do not have any criminal charges pending

against them. The placement of adolescents who have serious mental disorders who have been charged with crimes and are able to be released from incarceration into a community mental health facility should be completed in a timely fashion.

Health care professionals and correctional health care facilities and staff

- Correctional facilities should move away from the reactive sick call method of service delivery and develop a continuum of care providing appropriate initial screenings for physical and mental health problems, in-house services or referrals to medical experts in the community for follow-up on identified problems, and health education and other efforts aimed at disease prevention and health promotion. Adequate prerelease planning to link individuals with the resources they will need once no longer incarcerated is essential. Policymakers must allocate more funds for these purposes and medical and public health professionals can assist in these reforms.

(continued)

Box 12   Recommendations to Improve the Health and Care of Incarcerated Adult and Adolescent Females *(continued)*

—Incarcerated females of all ages should receive reproductive health care, including adequate prenatal care or abortion services, per American College of Obstetricians and Gynecologists guidelines (2–4). The type of care that can be provided will depend on the length of incarceration. The period of incarceration, however long or short, provides a window of opportunity for improving the health status of this population.

—Applying physical restraints to pregnant women should be needed only very rarely, in extreme situations, for short periods. If restraint is needed after the first trimester, it should be performed with the individual on her side, not flat on her back or stomach. If she needs to be restrained for more than several minutes, she should be allowed to lie on her side, preferably on her left side. Pressure should not be applied either directly or indirectly to the abdomen while restraining the patient.

—As the population of incarcerated women ages and the number of incarcerated women increases, attention will need to be directed to older women's health issues. One of the most common issues will be menopause and morbidities associated with it and appropriate screening for organ system disease.

—Increased attention is needed to address incarcerated women's mental health needs (5). This includes efforts to eradicate sexual abuse in correctional facilities.

—If hospitalization or other off-site health care is needed, efforts should be undertaken to ensure that receipt of treatment prescribed, such as medications, is received once the patient returns to the correctional care facility.

■ Funding should be readily available to increase the training and skills of health care providers and other staff in correctional facilities. Training should cover proper management of the pregnant woman to ensure that an appropriate schedule of prenatal care is provided.

■ Health professionals should consider ways to become further involved with correctional health care, such as gaining representation on the boards of correctional health organizations, working in correctional facilities to provide services to incarcerated women and adolescents, or undertaking efforts to ensure that the medical needs of these individuals are being addressed appropriately.

■ Medical schools, nursing schools, and schools of public health should consider working collaboratively with correctional facilities on efforts to improve direct care to inmates. One way to accomplish this is for educational institutions to expand the population of women deemed eligible for services that are provided as part of the training of medical residents and other students to include incarcerated females. They can then contract with correctional health facilities for provision of these services.

■ Health care providers can facilitate the provision of care to incarcerated females in private practice settings through activities such as allowing incarcerated women to enter the practice through an alternate entrance or offering care off-hours or times designated for this population.

1. Health care for children and adolescents in the juvenile correctional care system. American Academy of Pediatrics. Committee on Adolescence. Pediatrics 2001;107:799–803.
2. American College of Obstetricians and Gynecologists. Health care for adolescents. Washington, DC: ACOG; 2003.
3. American College of Obstetricians and Gynecologists. Guidelines for women's health care. 2nd ed. Washington, DC: ACOG; 2002.
4. Primary and preventive care: periodic assessments. ACOG Committee Opinion No. 292. American College of Obstetricians and Gynecologists. Obstet Gynecol 2003;102:1117–24.
5. Hardyman PL, Van Voorhis P. Developing gender–specific classification systems for women offenders. Washington, DC: U.S. Department of Justice; 2004. Available at: http://www.nicic.org/Downloads/PDF/2004/018931.pdf. Retrieved October 29, 2004.

References

1. Greenfeld LA, Snell TL. Women offenders. Bureau of Justice Statistics Special Report. Washington, DC: U.S. Department of Justice; 1999. NCJ 175688. Available at http://www.ojp.usdoj.gov/bjs/pub/pdf/wo.pdf. Retrieved September 3, 2004.

2. Baldwin KM, Jones J. Health issues specific to incarcerated women: information for state maternal and child health programs. Baltimore (MD): Women's and Children's Health Policy Center, Johns Hopkins University, School of Public Health. Available at: http://www.med.jhu.edu/wchpc_/Publications/prison.pdf. Retrieved September 13, 2004.

3. Strom KJ. Profile of state prisoners under age 18, 1985–97. Bureau of Justice Statistics Special Report. U.S. Department of Justice. Office of Justice Programs. USDOJ: Washington, DC; 2000.

4. Bureau of Prisons. State of the Bureau 2003: accomplishments and goals. Washington, DC: U.S. Department of Justice; 2003. Available at: http://www.bop.gov/ipapg/ipasob2003.pdf. Retrieved October 29, 2004.

5. National Institutes of Corrections Information Center. Current issues in the operation of women's prisons. Longmont (CO): NICIC; 1998. Available at: http://www.nicic.org/pubs/1998/014784.pdf. Retrieved September 3, 2004.

6. Harrison PM, Karberg JC. Prison and jail inmates at midyear 2003. Bureau of Justice Statistics Bulletin. Washington, DC: U.S. Department of Justice; 2004. Available at: http://www.ojp.usdoj.gov/bjs/pub/pdf/pjim03.pdf. Retrieved October 29, 2004.

7. Harrison PM, Beck AJ. Prisoners in 2002. Bureau of Justice Statistics Bulletin. Washington, DC: U.S. Department of Justice; 2003. NCJ 200248. Available at: http://www.ojp.usdoj.gov/bjs/pub/pdf/p02.pdf. Retrieved September 3, 2004.

8. Snyder HN. Juvenile arrests 2002. Office of Juvenile Justice and Delinquency Prevention. Juvenile Justice Bulletin. Washington, DC: U.S. Department of Justice; 2004. NCJ 204608. Available at: http://www.ncjrs.org/pdffiles1/ojjdp/204608.pdf. Retrieved February 16, 2005.

9. Harms P. Detention in delinquency cases, 1990–1999. OJJDP fact sheet. Washington, DC: U.S. Department of Justice; 2003. Available at: http://www.ncjrs.org/pdffiles1/ojjdp/fs200307.pdf. Retrieved September 3, 2004.

10. Sickmund M. Juvenile offenders in residential placement: 1997–1999 juvenile offenders and victims national report series. Washington, DC: U.S. Department of Justice; 2002. Available at: http://www.ncjrs.org/pdffiles1/ojjdp/fs200207.pdf. Retrieved September 3, 2004.

11. Soler M. Health issues for adolescents in the justice system. J Adolesc Health 2002;31(suppl):321–33.

12. Hammett TM, Maruschak LM. 1996–1997 update: HIV/AIDS, STDs, and TB in correctional facilities. Washington, DC: U.S. Department of Justice; 1999. NCJ 176344. Available at: http://ncjrs.org/pdffiles1/176344.pdf. Retrieved September 3, 2004.

13. Women, injection drug use, and the criminal justice system. Atlanta (GA): Centers for Disease Control and Prevention; 2001. Available at: http://www.cdc.gov/idu/facts/cj-women.pdf. Retrieved September 3, 2004.

14. Breuner CC, Farrow JA. Pregnant teens in prison. Prevalence, management, and consequences. West J Med 1995;162:328–30.

15. Acoca L, Dedel K. No place to hide: understanding and meeting the needs of girls in the California juvenile justice system. Oakland (CA): National Council on Crime and Delinquency; 1998.

16. Snell TL, Morton DC. Women in prison: survey of state prison inmates, 1991. Bureau of Justice Statistics Special Report. Washington, DC: U.S. Department of Justice; 1994. NCJ-145321. Available at: http://www.ojp.usdoj.gov/bjs/pub/pdf/wopris.pdf. Retrieved September 3, 2004.

17. Mumola CJ. Incarcerated parents and their children. Bureau of Justice Statistics Special Report. Washington, DC: U.S. Department of Justice; 2000. NCJ 182335. Available at: http://www.ojp.usdoj.gov/bjs/pub/pdf/iptc.pdf. Retrieved September 3, 2004.

18. Anno BJ. Correctional health care: guidelines for the management of an adequate delivery system. Washington, DC: National Institute of Corrections; 2001.

19. Harrison PM, Beck AJ. Prisoners in 2003. Bureau of Justice Statistics Bulletin. Washington, DC: U.S. Department of Justice; 2004. NCJ 205335. Available at: http://www.ojp.usdoj.gov/bjs/pub/pdf/p03.pdf. Retrieved February 16, 2005.

20. Snyder HN, Sickmund M. Juvenile offenders and victims: 1999 national report. Washington, DC: Office of Juvenile Justice and Delinquency Prevention; 1999. Available at: http://www.ncjrs.org/html/ojjdp/nationalreport99/toc.html. Retrieved September 3, 2004.

21. Acoca L. Defusing the time bomb: understanding and meeting the growing health care needs of incarcerated women in America. Crime Delinq 1998;44:49–69.

22. National Commission on Correctional Health Care. Standards for health services in jails. Chicago (IL): NCCHC; 2003.

23. National Commission on Correctional Health Care. Standards for health services in juvenile detention and confinement facilities. Chicago (IL): NCCHC; 2004.

24. National Commission on Correctional Health Care. Standards for health services in prisons. Chicago (IL): NCCHC; 2003.

25. American Public Health Association. Standards for health services in correctional institutions. 3rd ed. Washington, DC: APHA; 2003.

26. Smith BV, Dailard C. Incarceration. In: Allen KM, Phillips JM, editors. Women's health across the lifespan: a comprehensive perspective. Philadelphia (PA): Lippincott-Raven; 1997. p. 464–78.

27. Martin SL, Kim H, Kupper LL, Meyer RE, Hays M. Is incarceration during pregnancy associated with infant birthweight? Am J Public Health 1997;87:1526–31.

28. Kyei-Aboagye K, Vragovic O, Chong D. Birth outcome in incarcerated, high-risk pregnant women. J Reprod Med 2000;45:190–4.

29. Maruschak LM. HIV in prisons and jails, 2002. Bureau of Justice Statistics Bulletin. Washington, DC: U.S. Department of Justice; 2004. NCJ 205333. Available at: http://www.ojp.usdoj.gov/ bjs/pub/pdf/hivpj02.pdf. Retrieved February 16, 2005.

30. Maruschak LM. HIV in prisons, 2000. Bureau of Justice Statistics Bulletin. Washington, DC: U.S. Department of Justice; 2002. NCJ 196023. Available at: http://www.ojp.usdoj.gov/ bjs/pub/pdf/hivp00.pdf. Retrieved October 29, 2004.

31. Jordan BK, Schlenger WE, Fairbank JA, Caddell JM. Prevalence of psychiatric disorders among incarcerated women: II. Convicted felons entering prison. Arch Gen Psychiatry 1996;53: 513–9.

32. Fogel CI, Martin SL. The mental health of incarcerated women. West J Nurs Res 1992;14:30–40; discussion 41–7.

33. Ditton PM. Mental health and treatment of inmates and probationers. Bureau of Justice Statistics Special Report. Washington, DC: U.S. Department of Justice, Office of Justice Programs; 1999. NCJ 174463. Available at: http://www.ojp.usdoj.gov/ bjs/pub/pdf/mhtip.pdf. Retrieved September 3, 2004.

34. Struckman-Johnson C, Struckman-Johnson D. Sexual coercion reported by women in three midwestern prisons. J Sex Res 2002;39:217–27.

35. Health care for children and adolescents in the juvenile correctional care system. American Academy of Pediatrics. Committee on Adolescence. Pediatrics 2001;107:799–803.

36. High prevalence of chlamydial and gonoccocal infection in women entering jails and juvenile detention centers—Chicago, Birmingham, and San Francisco, 1998. MMWR Morb Mortal Wkly Rep 1999;48:793–6.

37. Lederman CS, Brown EN. Entangled in the shadows: girls in the juvenile justice system. Buffalo Law Rev 2000;48:909–25.

38. American College of Obstetricians and Gynecologists. Health care for adolescents. Washington, DC: ACOG; 2003.

39. Incarceration of youth who are waiting for community mental health services in the United States. Washington, DC: United States House of Representatives; 2004. Available at: http://www.house.gov/reform/min/pdfs_108_2/pdfs_inves/pdf _health_mental_health_youth_incarceration_july_2004_rep.pdf. Retrieved September 3, 2004.

40. National Commission on Correctional Health Care. Health care funding for incarcerated youths. NCCHC Position Statement. Chicago (IL): NCCHC; 1993. Available at: http://www.ncchc.org/resources/statements/funding.html. Retrieved September 3, 2004.

Resources

The resources listed as follows are for information purposes only. Referral to these sources and web sites does not imply the endorsement of ACOG. This list is not meant to be comprehensive. The exclusion of a source or web site does not reflect the quality of that source or web site. Please note that web sites are subject to change without notice.

American Correctional Association

4380 Forbes Boulevard
Lanham, MD 20706-4322
Tel: 800-ACA-JOIN
Web: www.aca.org

The American Correctional Association (ACA) is a professional organization for all individuals and groups, both public and private, which share a common goal of improving the justice system. This organization offers professional development and educational opportunities and has developed standards for correctional facilities. These standards are the basis for ACA accreditation of correctional facilities. The ACA works to build relationships with the educational community and influence their research agendas. The association works with correctional agencies to implement valid research findings. The ACA also promotes continuing education and the expansion of degree programs relevant to corrections.

American Correctional Health Services Association

250 Gatsby Place
Alpharetta, GA 30022-6161
Tel: 877-918-1842
Fax: (770) 650-5789
Web: www.corrections.com/achsa/

The mission of the American Correctional Health Services Association (ACHSA) is to be the voice of the correctional health care profession and serve as an effective forum for communication addressing current issues and needs confronting correctional health care. The ACHSA provides support, skill development, and education programs for health care personnel, organizations, and decision-makers involved in correctional health care. The association holds annual multidisciplinary training conferences designed to provide education on the latest developments in correctional health care. In addition, ACHSA has state and regional chapters that conduct local training conferences.

American Jail Association

1135 Professional Court
Hagerstown, MD 21740-5853
Tel: (301) 790-3930
Web: www.corrections.com/aja/

The American Jail Association (AJA) is a national, nonprofit organization that exists to support those who work in and operate the nation's jails. Through its publications, technical assistance, Certified Jail Manager program, on-site and regional training seminars, and the annual training conference and jail expo, AJA disseminates information to jail personnel, the criminal justice community, and the population of all communities that operate jails.

American Public Health Association

800 I Street, NW
Washington, DC 20001-3710
Tel: (202) 777-APHA (2742)
Fax: (202) 777-2532
Web: www.apha.org

The American Public Health Association (APHA) is an association of individuals and organizations working to improve the public's health and to achieve equity in health status for all. The APHA works to promote the scientific and professional foundation of public health practice and policy, advocate the conditions for a healthy global society, emphasize prevention, and enhance the ability of members to promote and protect environmental and community health. It has a Task Force on Correctional Health Care Standards that developed the third edition of "Standards for Health Services in Correctional Institutions" in early 2003.

Bureau of Justice Statistics, Sourcebook of Criminal Justice Statistics
Web: www.albany.edu/sourcebook

The *Sourcebook of Criminal Justice Statistics* brings together data from more than 100 sources about all aspects of criminal justice in the United States. These data are displayed in more than 600 tables. This sourcebook is available online and is updated periodically. The sourcebook is supported by the U.S. Department of Justice, Bureau of Justice Statistics.

The Corrections Connection
159 Burgin Parkway
Quincy, MA 02169
Web: www.corrections.com

The Corrections Connection is a news source working to improve the lives of corrections professionals and their families. They provide an open forum where practitioners exchange ideas, resources, case studies, and new technologies. Links to numerous corrections-related web sites are provided through their web site, including links to state correctional departments.

Council of Juvenile Correctional Administrators
170 Forbes Road, Suite 106
Braintree, MA 02184
Tel: (781) 843-2663
Fax: (781) 843-1688
Web: www.cjca.net/sitecode/cjca_home.html

The Council of Juvenile Correctional Administrators (CJCA) is a national nonprofit organization dedicated to the improvement of youth correctional services and practices. The CJCA initiates and facilitates the exchange of ideas and philosophies among administrators from all jurisdictions at three annual meetings as well as through regular communications, including a quarterly newsletter and web site. The CJCA serves as a clearinghouse for members seeking referrals for practices and services and the public. It also contributes to research on juvenile corrections practices and the causes of crime and delinquency and to the development and application of youth correction standards and accreditation.

Federal Bureau of Prisons
320 First Street, NW
Washington, DC 20534
Tel: (202) 307-3198
Web: www.bop.gov

The Federal Bureau of Prisons was established to provide administrative oversight and support to the federal prison system. The bureau works to protect public safety by ensuring that federal offenders serve their sentences of imprisonment in institutions that are safe, humane, cost-efficient, and appropriately secure. The bureau undertakes efforts to reduce future criminal activity by encouraging inmates to participate in a range of programs that have been proven to help them adopt a crime-free lifestyle upon their return to the community.

National Commission on Correctional Health Care
1145 W Diversey Parkway
Chicago, IL 60614
Tel: (773) 880-1460
Fax: (773) 880-2424
Web: www.ncchc.org

The mission of the National Commission on Correctional Health Care (NCCHC) is to improve the quality of health care in jails, prisons, and juvenile confinement facilities. The NCCHC is a not-for-profit organization that offers resources to help correctional health care systems provide efficient, high quality care. The NCCHC's *Standards for Health Services* provide guidelines for managing the delivery of medical and mental health care within correctional systems. They are written in separate volumes for prisons, jails, and juvenile confinement facilities and cover the general areas of care and treatment, health records, administration, personnel, and medical–legal issues. In addition to the standards, NCCHC publishes position statements and clinical guidelines to assist correctional health care practitioners in the many medical, ethical, administrative, and legal aspects of their work. In support of its mission, NCCHC also offers numerous other programs, services and resources, such as facility accreditation, technical assistance, quality reviews, research studies, and educational programs and conferences.

National Juvenile Detention Association
Eastern Kentucky University
EKU-301 Perkins Building
521 Lancaster Avenue
Richmond, KY 40475-3102
Tel: (859) 622-6259
Fax: (859) 622-23333
Web: www.njda.com

The National Juvenile Detention Association (NJDA) works to advance the science, processes, and art of juvenile detention services through the overall improvement of the juvenile justice profession. Although NJDA is primarily focused on juvenile detention issues, the association is committed to improving all facets of juvenile justice.

Office of Juvenile Justice and Delinquency Prevention
810 Seventh Street, NW
Washington, DC 20531
Tel: (202) 307-5911
Web: ojjdp.ncjrs.org

The mission of the Office of Juvenile Justice and Delinquency Prevention (OJJDP) is to provide national leadership, coordination, and resources to prevent and respond to juvenile delinquency and victimization. The OJJDP works to accomplish this by supporting states and local communities in their efforts to develop and implement effective and coordinated prevention and intervention programs and improve the juvenile justice system so that it protects the public safety, holds offenders accountable, and provides treatment and rehabilitative services tailored to the needs of families and each individual juvenile. *Juvenile Female Offenders: A Status of the States* is a recent publication of OJJDP that describes state programs for at-risk girls and juvenile female offenders. It is available online at http://www.ojjdp.ncjrs.org/pubs/gender.

Society of Correctional Physicians
1300 West Belmont Avenue
Chicago, IL 60657-3200
Tel: 800-229-7380
Fax: (773) 880-2424
Web: www.corrdocs.org

The Society of Correctional Physicians was formed in 1993 to provide a forum for the support, education, and professional development of physicians delivering health care in correctional settings. It aims to promote, improve, and, if necessary, defend the standards of care extended by its members. The society advocates for correctional health care issues, including research efforts and outcomes within served populations, examination of treatment issues specific to the incarcerated, and the effective delivery of high quality health care to inmate–patients.

Stop Prison Rape
3325 Wilshire Boulevard, Suite 340
Los Angeles, CA 90010
Tel: (213) 384-1400
Fax: (213) 384-1411
E-mail: info@spr.org
Web: www.spr.org

Stop Prisoner Rape seeks to end sexual violence against men, women, and youth in all forms of detention. It has three goals for its work: to push for policies that ensure institutional accountability, to change society's attitudes toward prisoner rape, and to promote access to resources for survivors of sexual assault behind bars.

U.S. Department of Justice
950 Pennsylvania Avenue, NW
Washington, DC 20530-0001
Tel: (202) 353-1555
Web: www.usdoj.gov

The mission of the U.S. Department of Justice is to enforce the law and defend the interests of the United States according to the law; to ensure public safety against threats foreign and domestic; to provide federal leadership in preventing and controlling crime; to seek just punishment for those guilty of unlawful behavior; to administer and enforce the nation's immigration laws fairly and effectively; and to ensure fair and impartial administration of justice for all Americans. The Federal Bureau of Prisons is housed in the U.S. Department of Justice as is the National Institute of Corrections.

U.S. Department of Justice, National Institute of Corrections
320 First Street, NW
Washington, DC 20534
Tel: 800-995-6423; (202) 307-3106
Fax: (202) 307-3361
Web: www.nicic.org

The National Institute of Corrections (NIC) is an agency within the U.S. Department of Justice, Federal Bureau of Prisons. The institute provides training, technical assistance, information services, and policy/program development assistance to federal, state, and local corrections agencies. Through cooperative agreements, NIC awards funds to support its program initiatives. The institute also works to influence correctional policies, practices, and operations nationwide in areas of emerging interest and concern to correctional executives and practitioners as well as public policymakers.

Special Issues

Substance Use: Obstetric and Gynecologic Implications

Key Points

- Substance use, abuse, and dependence affect women and men differently and can have serious implications for women's health. Among them are adverse effects on reproductive function and pregnancy.

- Key areas in which obstetrician–gynecologists can have an effect are prevention, screening, testing, brief intervention, and referral.

- Obstetrician–gynecologists are responsible for prescribing appropriately, encouraging healthy behaviors by providing appropriate information and education, and identifying and referring patients already abusing drugs.

- Asking questions of all patients about their history and levels of use of alcohol and other drugs helps to indicate when further investigation is needed.

- Substance abuse and dependence occur across the lifespan and without regard to ethnic background, socioeconomic status, or sexual orientation.

- Women who abuse substances rarely abuse a single substance. Those who abuse illicit substances frequently also abuse tobacco or alcohol or both. The potential effect of multiple substance abuse must be taken into account when attempting to evaluate the effects of individual substances on the fetus or on pregnancy outcome.

- Fetal alcohol syndrome (FAS) is the most common preventable cause of mental retardation; FAS and other alcohol-related defects and disorders are 100% preventable if a woman does not drink during pregnancy.

- Education and brief intervention preformed by the obstetrician–gynecologist can be very effective in reducing alcohol-exposed pregnancies.

- Comprehensive prenatal care has been shown to ameliorate many of the maternal and neonatal complications associated with substance abuse.

Because substance abuse and dependence are medical conditions, health care providers have a key role to play in prevention and treatment.

The Disease of Addiction

Addiction is a chronic, relapsing behavioral disorder affecting the functioning of the brain and other major organs. It is not a moral problem, an indication of bad character, a sign of weakness, or a failure of the will. Addiction hijacks the brain's reward system, the mesolimbic dopaminergic pathway extending from the ventral tegmentum to the nucleus accumbens. All addictive drugs act on this system; the resulting pleasurable effects reinforce the drug-taking behavior. Despite popular misconception, the issue of whether or not a drug can produce physical dependence has little bearing on whether or not its use can lead to addiction. If a substance can produce compulsive drug-seeking and use in spite of adverse consequences, then it has addictive potential (1). Table 8 lists the *Diagnostic and Statistical Manual of Mental Disorders*, 4th edition (DSM-IV) criteria for substance abuse and dependence. The use of these terms in this book refers to DSM-IV definitions.

Until recently, most research into drug abuse focused on male subjects, yet women and men often demonstrate different biologic responses to drugs, different patterns of use, different reasons for using, and different responses to treatment. Conclusions derived from research conducted primarily in men are not necessarily generalizable to women; therefore, current trends emphasize the importance of investigating how drugs of abuse specifically affect women, and how the course of the disease of addiction may vary between the sexes.

Because substance abuse and dependence are medical conditions, health care providers have a key role to play in prevention and treatment. This role may include screening patients by use of questionnaires; providing education, treatment, and referral; guiding and referring high-risk patients; advising patients about social and support groups; practicing safe prescription writing; and addressing the needs of adolescents. Obstetrician–gynecologists are central figures in women's health care and, thus, need to be knowledgeable about substance abuse and dependence both in general and in areas of specific concern to women.

Substance use, abuse, and dependence affect not only the individual, but also families, communities,

Table 8. Diagnostic and Statistical Manual of Mental Disorders Criteria for Substance Abuse and Dependence

Substance Abuse	Substance Dependence

Substance abuse, which is a separate diagnosis from substance dependence, is defined as a maladaptive pattern of substance use with one or more of the following criteria over a 1-year period:
 	
1. Repeated substance use that results in an inability to fulfill obligations at home, school, or work.
 	
2. Repeated substance use when it could be physically dangerous (such as driving a car).
 	
3. Repeated substance-related legal problems, such as arrests.
 	
4. Continued substance use despite interpersonal or social problems that are caused or made worse by use.
	Substance dependence is a maladaptive pattern of substance use, leading to clinically significant impairment or distress, as manifested by three (or more) of the following, occurring at any time in the same 12-month period:
	
	1. Tolerance, as defined by either of the following:
	  a) A need for markedly increased amounts of the substance to achieve intoxication or desired effect
	  b) Markedly diminished effect with continued use of the same amount of the substance
	
	2. Withdrawal, as manifested by either of the following:
	  a) The characteristic withdrawal syndrome for the substance
	  b) The same (or a closely related) substance is taken to relieve or avoid withdrawal symptoms
	
	3. The substance is often taken in larger amounts or over a longer period than was intended.
	
	4. There is a persistent desire or unsuccessful efforts to cut down or control substance use.
	
	5. A great deal of time is spent in activities necessary to obtain the substance, use the substance, or recover from its effects.
	
	6. Important social, occupational, or recreational activities are given up or reduced because of substance use.
	
	7. The substance use is continued despite knowledge of having a persistent or recurrent physical or psychological problem that is likely to have been caused or exacerbated by the substance.

workplaces, and society in general. Complications related to illegal and prescribed or controlled drugs, alcohol, and tobacco constitute a significant national health problem and a large economic detriment. The subject of women and tobacco dependence is discussed in another chapter in this book. The National Institute on Drug Abuse and the National Institute on Alcohol Abuse and Alcoholism estimated that the economic cost of alcohol and drug abuse is in the hundreds of billions of dollars. In 1998, the estimated cost of alcohol abuse alone was $184.6 billion (2). It is important to note that most individuals who abuse substances use more than one substance (ie, are polysubstance abusers) making it difficult to determine the effect of one particular drug. Information on specific drugs of abuse is given later in this chapter.

In addition to the harmful effects associated with specific drugs, substance abuse also poses more general risks associated with unhealthy life styles, such as malnutrition. Some individuals may trade sex for drugs, exposing themselves to sexually transmitted diseases. Individuals who share needles while using drugs risk contracting blood-borne infections, such as human immunodeficieny virus (HIV) or the hepatitis B and hepatitis C viruses. Drug abuse is more than twice as likely to be associated with HIV and acquired immunodeficiency syndrome (AIDS) in women than in men (3). Drug use leads to a number of adverse social consequences, such as poor judgment and impaired decision making; increased unprotected sex; and increased arguments, fights, domestic violence, and child abuse. The neurobehavioral effects of alcohol and drug use have been cited as the precipitating factor in injuries and deaths of the substance user and others. The 1996 National Household Survey on Drug and Alcohol Abuse (NHSDA) indicated that 14% of women respondents reported driving within 2 hours of alcohol use during the past year (4). In the same survey, 4% of women reported driving within 2 hours of drug use. Of the 15,000 motor vehicle crashes during the year 2002 involving a female driver in which a fatality occurred, 15% of the drivers had a blood alcohol concentration of more than 0.01 g/dL (5).

The true prevalence of substance abuse by pregnant women is difficult, if not impossible, to establish. In urban populations receiving care at large medical centers, routine urine testing at the time of labor has demonstrated rates of illicit substance abuse of 20% or higher (6). Because of the high-risk populations surveyed, however, many feel that these studies overestimate the magnitude of the problem in the general population.

Although there are some women who seem to be at high risk for substance abuse, physicians should not be biased about who might be using drugs. In a cross-sectional study of substance abuse by pregnant women in Pinellas County, Florida, all patients who presented for prenatal care from a public- or private-sector health care provider had urine samples analyzed for evidence of recent alcohol or illicit substance abuse (7). There was no difference in the prevalence of recent substance abuse when those with private insurance were compared with medically indigent patients.

Epidemiology

Gender

The 2003 NHSDA completed by the Substance Abuse and Mental Health Services Administration (SAMHSA) found significant gender-related differences in the use and abuse of alcohol (8).

- Females aged 12 years or older were less likely than males in that age group to report past month alcohol use, 43.2% versus 57.3%.

- Male adolescents had higher rates of binge use and heavy drinking than females, but females and males aged 12–17 years had almost equal rates of past month alcohol use (18.3% and 17.1% respectively).

- Male college students aged 18–22 years are more likely to report current, heavy, and binge alcohol use than females; however, a significant number of females in college report current use (59.2%), heavy alcohol use (11.7%), and binge drinking (33.5%).

Some studies have reported that women who are white, unmarried, younger, and working full time outside the home are more likely than other women to drink alcohol (8).

The 2003 NHSDA also reported on gender differences for illicit drug use. Illicit drugs include marijuana, hashish, cocaine (including crack), heroin, hallucinogens, inhalants, or any prescription-type psychotherapeutic drugs used nonmedically. Women were less likely than men to report current illicit drug use (6.5% versus 10%) but had approximately the same rates of the nonmedical use of psychotherapeutics (approximately 2.7%) (8).

- Among adolescents, boys had slightly higher rates than girls of any drug use and of marijuana use in 2003, but girls were more likely than boys to use psychotherapeutic drugs for nonmedical purposes (3.8% vs 2.7%) (Fig. 5) (8).

- Overall, only one half as many females as males meet the criteria for dependence on or abuse of illicit drugs or alcohol; however, females and males aged 12–17 years show almost equal rates of abuse or dependence. (10).

Pregnancy

The use of alcohol in the past month by age and pregnancy status is presented in Table 9. Those in the youngest group of pregnant females were more likely to report binge and heavy alcohol use than older pregnant women (11). Based on data collected in 2000 and 2001 by the NHSDA and other broad-based data collection projects:

- Patterns of drinking before pregnancy often predict use patterns during pregnancy (12). Among nonpregnant women aged 15–44 years, 49.8% used alcohol, and 20.5% were binge drinkers (11).

- A total of 12.9% of pregnant women used alcohol, and 4.6% reported binge drinking (11). The Centers for Disease Control and Prevention (CDC) reported similar rates of use, with 12.8% of pregnant women reporting alcohol use and 3.3% reporting binge drinking in a 1999 survey (13).

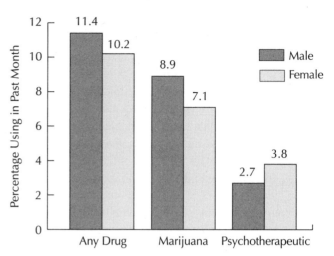

Fig. 5. Past month illicit drug use among youths aged 12–17 years by gender: 2003. (Substance Abuse and Mental Health Services Administration. Results from the 2003 National Household Survey on Drug Abuse: Volume I. Summary of national findings. Rockville [MD]: SAMHSA; 2004. Available at: http://oas.samhsa.gov/nhsda/2k3nsduh/2k3ResultsW.pdf. Retrieved October 21, 2004.)

- The CDC also reported that pregnant women who had any alcohol use were more likely than other pregnant women to be older than 30 years, unmarried, and employed (13).

- Unlike women younger than 30 years, women older than 30 years are less likely to reduce alcohol use when they learn they are pregnant. This effect may be caused by greater alcohol dependency (10, 14).

Table 9. Percentages of Females Aged 15–44 Years Reporting Past Month Use of Alcohol, by Pregnancy Status and Age: 1999 and 2000

	Pregnancy Status and Age (y)					
	15–17		**18–25**		**26–44**	
Past Month Use	Pregnant	Nonpregnant	Pregnant	Nonpregnant	Pregnant	Nonpregnant
Alcohol	8.6	26.1	10.1	53.6	14	50.2
Binge alcohol use*	7	16.4	4.8	29.6	3.1	17.1
Heavy alcohol use†	2	3.3	0.9	7.6	0.5	3

*Five or more drinks on the same occasion at least once in the 30 days before the survey (includes heavy use)
†Five or more drinks on the same occasion on at least 5 different days in the past 30 days
Substance Abuse and Mental Health Services Administration. Substance use among pregnant women during 1999 and 2000. NHSDA Report. Rockville (MD): SAMHSA; 2002. Available at: http://www.oas.samhsa.gov/2k2/preg/preg.pdf. Retrieved August 11, 2004.

The 2000 and 2001 NHSDA surveys and other current data-gathering initiatives reported on pregnant women's use of illicit drugs:

- A total of 3.3% of pregnant women aged 15–44 years were reported to have used an illicit drug in the past month. This rate was significantly lower than the rate reported for women in the same age group who were not pregnant (10.3%) (11).

- Among young pregnant women aged 15–17 years, the rate of illicit drug use was almost the same as that for nonpregnant women, 12.9% and 13.5%, respectively (11).

- Pregnant adolescents are more likely to use illicit drugs than older pregnant women (Fig. 6) (11).

- Among pregnant women aged 15–44 years, current use of illicit drugs does not vary by race or Hispanic origin (8).

- In 1999, the primary substances of abuse among nonpregnant females aged 15–44 years admitted for treatment included alcohol (38%), cocaine (20%), and opiates (19%) (11). For pregnant women entering treatment, the primary substances of abuse were cocaine (27%), followed by alcohol (24%) and opiates (19%) (Fig. 7) (11).

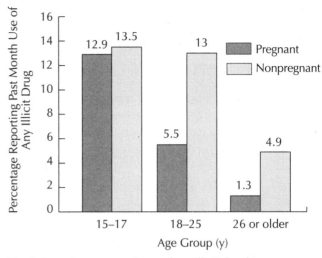

Fig. 6. Reporting past month use of any illicit drug by pregnancy status and age: 1999 and 2000. (Substance Abuse and Mental Health Services Administration. Substance use among pregnant women during 1999 and 2000. NHSDA Report. Rockville [MD]: SAMHSA; 2002. Available at: http://www.oas.samhsa.gov/2k2/preg/preg.pdf. Retrieved August 11, 2004.)

- In 1999, approximately 28% of pregnant women admitted to treatment were referred through the criminal justice system, and 28% were self-referrals. Between 1995 and 1999, the percent of pregnant women referred to treatment by a health professional decreased from 14% to 11% (15).

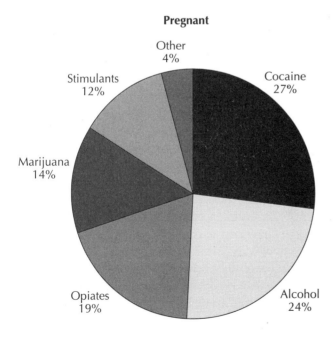

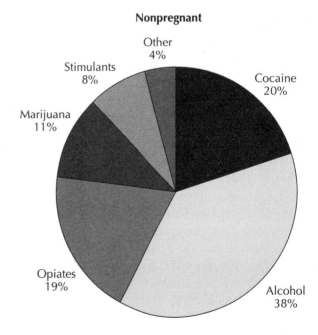

Fig. 7. Primary substance of abuse among women aged 15–44 years admitted to treatment by pregnancy status: 1999. (Substance Abuse and Mental Health Services Administration. Pregnant women in substance abuse treatment. The DASIS Report. Rockville [MD]: SAMHSA; 2002. Available at: http://www.oas.samhsa.gov/2k2/pregTX/pregTX.pdf. Retrieved August 12, 2004.)

Substance Abuse in Women and the Role of the Obstetrician–Gynecologist

Obstetrician–gynecologists have important opportunities for substance abuse intervention. Three of the key areas in which they can have an effect are 1) prescribing appropriately, 2) encouraging healthy behaviors through providing appropriate information and education, and 3) identifying and referring patients already abusing drugs. The woman's health care clinician is in a position to warn her about the adverse effects of tobacco, excessive alcohol, and drug use. Routine screening and intervention for all patients for substance abuse can improve women's present and future health and might help to avert or decrease prenatal substance exposure.

Occasions for substance abuse screening and prevention exist in daily practice. Two examples are pregnancy and visits for medical problems that may be exacerbated by substance abuse. Awareness of populations that may be at higher risk for substance abuse can aid clinicians in targeting their prevention efforts. At-risk populations may include biologic daughters of alcoholic or drug-abusing parents, spouses and partners of an alcoholic or drug abusing individual, women who have experienced a traumatic life event (divorce or separation, death of spouse or significant other, job loss, retirement, rape or sexual abuse, or witness a traumatic event), women with a chronic disabling or painful condition, health care professionals, women who have a psychiatric disorder (eg, depression, psychosis, anxiety, hyperactivity, posttraumatic stress disorder), and women who are victims of current or past intimate partner violence.

Clinicians should recognize presenting symptoms that might be associated with substance use problems. Frequently, psychologic problems associated with substance abuse or dependence are brought to the attention of the clinician by a relative. Vague physical symptoms, such as fatigue, insomnia, headaches, sexual problems, and loss of appetite, prompt early suspicion of substance use; however, definitive psychologic and physical evidence of substance abuse usually does not become apparent until late in the disease process. Importantly, most users of illicit drugs have no signs on physical examination (16). A careful history by a trusted clinician remains the most sensitive means of detecting drug use and abuse (16).

Discovery of substances taken by a patient may be prohibited because she may have consumed an adulterated substance (the composition of the substance taken is unknown to the patient), the patient may fear action by child welfare agencies, or the phenomenon of patient denial. In these circumstances, the clinician can use any local knowledge of what drugs are "on the street," combined with information from emergency departments, observation of the patient's behavioral status (eg, hallucinations, agitation, drowsiness), physical examination (eg, alcoholic fetor, white powder in nares), and, with her permission, perform tests for specific drugs to inform the clinician in counseling her.

Higher rates of eating disorders, panic disorders, posttraumatic stress disorder, and depression are found among women with alcohol use disorders (17). Women who develop alcohol dependence often are more likely than men to deny that they have a problem and to minimize the problems associated with their drinking (18). However, when they do seek help for problem drinking, it often is from their primary care providers (17). Therefore, it is essential that women be screened and diagnosed so they can receive appropriate intervention, referral, and treatment.

Misuse of Prescription and Over-the-Counter Drugs

The nonmedical use of prescription drugs, defined as taking a prescription drug that was "not prescribed for the user, or that the user took only for the experience of feeling it caused," is increasing (8). Seven percent of the U.S. population reports using prescription sedatives for nonmedical reasons at least once (19). Thus, it is important for clinicians to remain alert for signs of drug-seeking behavior. Patients may complain of losing prescriptions or medications and repeatedly report running out of medications before the time that would be expected if medications were taken as prescribed. They often seek narcotic or tranquilizer prescriptions from multiple physicians or claim that another physician, who is now unavailable, prescribed a certain narcotic that now needs to be refilled. They may insist on a particular drug by brand name and claim that nothing else works or demand an immediate prescription of a strong narcotic for chronic illness (20). Adolescents and young adults may be frequent abusers of over-the-counter drugs, particularly cold, allergy, and antinausea medications, taking large doses, multiple drugs or recompounding or refining packaged medications. Health care providers should be alert to symptoms of overdose of these common drugs.

When prescribing potentially addictive substances, it is important for the clinician to assess carefully the risks posed by that treatment and consider nonpharmacologic treatments or nonaddicting medications whenever possible. Potentially addictive drugs should be prescribed initially at a dose adequate to relieve symptoms and then be reduced gradually to the smallest effective dose. However, it is important to not undertreat pain out of fear of causing addiction. In some cases, drug-seeking behavior by patients with undertreated pain may be mistaken for addiction; this is referred to as pseudo-addiction (21). Opioid drugs have legitimate use in the management of both cancer pain and chronic nonmalignant pain if warranted by the clinical picture. However, the opioids best at alleviating pain also have the most abuse liability (see the "Opioids" section later in chapter) (22).

It is advisable that the physician take a thorough history of alcohol use and prescription, over-the-counter, and illicit drug use before prescribing drugs with a dependence liability. A history of drug abuse or dependence is not an absolute contraindication; many patients with such histories can benefit from opioid pain relief (23). Appropriate measures to reduce drug misuse in all patients include medication contracts, discussion of reasonable goals, prescribing suitable amounts of pain medication, writing out numbers to prevent alteration of dose or quantity, monitoring with drug screens and pill counts, and careful documentation of the rationale of the prescription (24).

At times, the physician may encounter a patient who obtains prescriptions for medications that can be resold for profit. This "entrepreneur" often refuses diagnostic testing, intramuscular injections, or medications for immediate consumption. She encourages providers to prescribe a maximum amount of pills or asks for a number that is easily converted to a greater one (for example, 10 can become 40 or 100 with a stroke of a pen) (25). This patient knows exactly what she wants and will adamantly refuse an alternative. Patient-generated pressure to prescribe in the face of the physician's feeling of hesitancy is a classic indicator of a drug-seeking behavior. An initial refusal to prescribe by the physician that eventually changes to a willingness to prescribe in the face of patient pressure is considered by some experts to be pathognomomonic of prescription

drug abuse (20). An effective response by the physician is to stick to the principle of requiring a formal physician–patient relationship before prescribing medication. Components of this relationship can include a complete history, obtaining confirmatory medical records from other practitioners and hospitals, a thorough physical examination, and the obtaining of indicated diagnostic tests (16). The physician may shift the focus of the encounter to the patient while still refusing to prescribe by making statements such as, "I'm feeling pushed by you to write a prescription today that is not medically indicated. I'm concerned about you, and we need to talk about your use of these substances." The physician's fear of confrontation and time constraints play into the hands of chemically dependent patients, who have a stronger relationship with the prescription than they do with the physician (20).

It is important for clinicians to educate patients about the effects of drugs prescribed to them, including activities to be avoided while taking the medication and potential interactions with other medications and substances they are known to be using. The potential for a drug to produce dependence needs to be clearly stated as well as the effect of the medication when mixed with other substances. The clinician should warn about the dangers of misuse of a drug and assess the patient's understanding (see Box 13 for substance abuse prevention prescribing pointers).

Because some substances, such as ephedra, have been marketed in the past as a "natural" supplement, many patients are not aware of the health risks associated with their use. Additionally, many patients do not inform their physicians about their use of "alternative medicine" (26) and do not think of herbal remedies as drugs. It is, therefore, important to specifically ask about the use of vitamins, supplements, and traditional medicines. It is important for health care providers to educate patients about the risks of these supplements, explaining that the herbal supplements are not regulated by the U.S. Food and Drug Administration (FDA) or any other agency and that "natural" does not necessarily mean safe, as many natural products can be just as potent and risky as pharmaceuticals.

Brief Intervention and Motivational Interviewing

Brief interventions and motivational interviewing as part of primary health care can help reduce the risk of developing substance dependence. There are several motivational models for behavioral change. The Stages Model of the Process of Change is useful in determining where a patient is in the process of change (27). The stages of change include precontemplation, contemplation, action, maintenance, and relapse (Table 10). Research has shown that the best strategy for helping patients is to try to move them to the next step in the change process (28). For those women who may be stuck in the precontemplation and contemplation stages, a group meeting with medical providers, family, close friends, and co-workers at which, in the framework of care and concern, each group member states the effects of the patient's substance use and the consequences of not accepting treatment. This intervention can markedly support the patient's desire for treatment (16).

In a brief intervention, the clinician follows five steps (known as the 5A's) within a 3–10 minute conversation. These steps are: *Ask* (screening for use, amount, frequency), *Assess* (determining how problematic the behavior is for the patient or others), *Advise* (making a clear statement that the behavior is detrimental to the patient's health or the health of her fetus), *Assist* (suggesting how the patient can receive help, referring for treatment, supplying further information on the behavior, setting goals), and *Arrange* follow-up (making a follow-up appointment for the provider to reassess). Women who use alcohol, narcotics or cocaine heavily require intervention directly followed by referral for treatment to a professional trained in addiction medicine.

Motivational interviewing involves a directive, client-centered counseling style for eliciting behavior change by helping patients to explore and resolve ambivalence. Compared with nondirective counseling, it is more focused and goal-directed (29). Although the technique requires some training, brief encounters using motivational interviewing techniques can be accomplished in the primary care setting.

A recent study confirmed that brief intervention and motivational interviewing are effective techniques in reducing harmful drinking patterns among women of childbearing age (30). In another study, conducted by the CDC, women who received motivational interviewing were able to reduce the risk for alcohol-exposure during pregnancy by decreasing their alcohol consumption risk, increasing contraception use, or both (31) (Fig. 8). In fact, among high-risk women overall, 69% of high-risk women were able to reduce

Table 10. Stages of Change

Stage	Mechanism	Patient Needs
Precontemplation	Patient does not believe a problem exists	Evidence of problem and its consequences
Contemplation	Patient recognizes a problem exists and is considering treatment	Support and encouragement to initiate treatment Information on treatment options Referral to a specific treatment program
Action	Patient begins treatment	Ongoing support Follow-up to support success
Maintenance	Patient incorporates drug-free living into daily life	Initiate steps to break cycle of addiction: weekly contact, peer support groups, family or group therapy.
Relapse	Patient returns to regular drug use. This is an expected part of the recovery process.	Institute prevention strategies: ■ Alter lifestyle to reduce outside influence ■ Develop drug-free socialization ■ Identify social pressures that influence use and rehearse avoidance strategies ■ Learn ways to cope with negative feelings

American College of Obstetricians and Gynecologists. Illicit drug abuse and dependence in women: a slide lecture presentation. Washington, DC: ACOG; 2002.

<table>
<tr><td></td></tr>
</table>

Box 13 | Substance Abuse Prevention Prescribing Pointers

When considering prescribing potentially addictive drugs:

- Assess option of alternative treatments
  —Nonpharmacologic treatments
  —Nonaddicting medications

- Determine risk of developing abuse or dependence

- Order an initial dose sufficient to provide analgesia, then taper to smallest effective dose

Prescribing suggestions for potentially addictive drugs

- Write for the shortest period of time for treatment

- Avoid more than one refill

- Avoid telephone refills

- Reassess at frequent intervals

- Prescribe to be taken on a fixed schedule rather than as needed

- Taper, rather than discontinue if used long term

- On the prescription write the amount to be dispensed numerically and by word to minimize ability for alteration

American College of Obstetrics and Gynecologists. Illicit drug abuse and dependence in women: a slide lecture presentation. Washington, DC: ACOG; 2002.

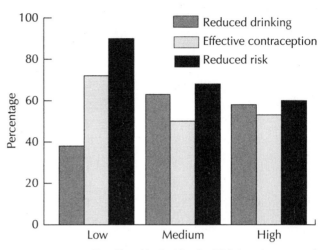

Fig. 8. Baseline alcohol intake among women and choices for reducing risk of an alcohol exposed pregnancy. (Motivational intervention to reduce alcohol-exposed pregnancies—Florida, Texas, and Virginia, 1997–2001. MMWR Morb Mortal Wkly Rep 2003;52:441–4.)

ful effects of excessive drinking, such as increased breast cancer risk, show up above a certain threshold of alcohol consumption. Intervenous drug users who cannot or will not enter treatment should be encouraged to take advantage of needle-exchange programs, if available in the local community, because they may reduce the risk of HIV infection for some users (33). To reduce the risk of pregnancy and, thus, reduce future exposure to a fetus, it is important to encourage women who abuse substances to use effective contraception. For those adolescents and women who are using alcohol, it is key to reinforce the message of refraining from driving or other situations requiring full attention.

Screening Questionnaires

The use of alcohol and other drugs should be determined when taking a medical history. Direct questioning of patients about their substance use is preferable to a vague inquiry (34). Many of the studies that validated the use of screening questionnaires originally did not include women. However, several screening questionnaires have recently been validated for use with women. These screening tools, known by their acronyms, are the TWEAK, AUDIT, T-ACE, and 5 P's (Box 14). Some studies have suggested that the TWEAK questionnaire was the optimal screening tool for women with heavy drinking or alcohol abuse and

their risk for an alcohol-exposed pregnancy. Given this capacity for dramatic improvement, physicians have an obligation to be therapeutic—in this case to learn the techniques of screening and brief intervention—and to inform themselves as they would if a new test or therapy were developed for any other recognized disease entity (32).

Risk Reduction

Women who are unable or unwilling to stop using substances should be advised to at least cut down on their substance use because negative outcomes may have a dose-dependent effect. For example, some of the harm-

Box 14 Substance Abuse Questionnaires

AUDIT Questionnaire

1. How often do you have a drink containing alcohol?
   (0) Never
   (1) Monthly or less
   (2) 2–4 times per month
   (3) 2 to 3 times per week
   (4) 4 or more times per week

2. How many drinks containing alcohol do you have on a typical day when you are drinking?
   (0) 1 or 2
   (1) 3 or 4
   (2) 5 or 6
   (3) 7 to 9
   (4) 10 or more

3. How often do you have six or more drinks on one occasion?
   (0) Never
   (1) Less than monthly
   (2) Monthly
   (3) Weekly
   (4) Daily or almost daily

4. How often during the last year have you found that you were not able to stop drinking once you started?
   (0) Never
   (1) Less than monthly
   (2) Monthly
   (3) Weekly
   (4) Daily or almost daily

5. How often during the last year have you failed to do what was normally expected from you because of drinking?
   (0) Never
   (1) Less than monthly
   (2) Monthly
   (3) Weekly
   (4) Daily or almost daily

6. How often during the last year have you needed a first drink in the morning to get yourself going after a heavy drinking session?
   (0) Never
   (1) Less than monthly
   (2) Monthly
   (3) Weekly
   (4) Daily or almost daily

7. How often during the last year have you had a feeling of guilt or remorse after drinking?
   (0) Never
   (1) Less than monthly
   (2) Monthly
   (3) Weekly
   (4) Daily or almost daily

8. How often during the last year have you been unable to remember what happened the night before because you had been drinking?
   (0) Never
   (1) Less than monthly
   (2) Monthly
   (3) Weekly
   (4) Daily or almost daily

9. Have you or someone else been injured as a result of your drinking?
   (0) No
   (2) Yes, but not in the last year
   (4) Yes, during the last year

10. Has a relative or friend, or a doctor or other health care worker been concerned about your drinking or suggested you cut down?
   (0) No
   (2) Yes, but not in the last year
   (4) Yes, during the last year

The minimum score (for nondrinkers) on the AUDIT is 0 and the maximum possible score is 40. A score of 8 or more indicates a strong likelihood of hazardous or harmful alcohol consumption. (Available online at http://www.niaaa.nih.gov/publications/insaudit.htm.)

Reprinted with permission from World Health Organization. AUDIT, the Alcohol Use Disorders Identification Test: guidelines for use in primary health care. 2nd ed. Geneva: WHO; 2000.

(continued)

Box 14 **Substance Abuse Questionnaires** *(continued)*

5 P's Screening Questions

Did any of your **PARENTS** have a problem with using alcohol or drugs?	Yes*	No	No answer	
Do any of your friends (**PEERS**) have a problem with drug or alcohol use?	Yes*	No	No answer	
Does your **PARTNER** have a problem with drug or alcohol use?	Yes*	No	No answer	
Before you knew you were pregnant (**PAST**), how often did you drink beer, wine, wine coolers, or liquor?	Not at all	Rarely*	Sometimes*	Frequently*
In the past month (**PRESENT**), how often did you drink beer, wine, wine coolers, or liquor?	Not at all	Rarely*	Sometimes*	Frequently*

*Considered positive responses

Kluwer Academic Publishers, Maternal and Child Health Journal, 8 (3):137–47, 2004. Improving screening for alcohol use during pregnancy: the Massachusetts ASAP program. Kennedy C, Finkelstein N, Hutchins E, Mahoney J; table 1. Reprinted with kind permission of Springer Science and Business Media.

TWEAK

T   **T**OLERANCE: How many drinks can you hold? If five or more drinks—score 2 points

W   Have close friends or relatives **W**ORRIED or complained about your drinking in the past year?—If "Yes" 2 points

E   **E**YE OPENER: Do you sometimes take a drink in the morning when you get up?—If "Yes" 1 point

A   **A**MNESIA: Has a friend or family member every told you about things you said or did while you were drinking that you could not remember?—If "Yes" 1 point

K (C)   Do you sometimes feel the need to **C**UT DOWN on your drinking? If "Yes" score 1 point.

The TWEAK is used to screen for pregnant at-risk drinking defined here as the consumption of 1 ounce or more of alcohol per day while pregnant. A total score of 2 or more points indicates a positive screen for pregnancy risk drinking.

Reprinted with permission from Chan AW, Pristach EA, Welte JW, Russell M. Use of the TWEAK test in screening for alcoholism/heavy drinking in three populations. Alcohol Clin Exp Res 1993;17:1188–92.

T-ACE

T   **T**OLERANCE: How many drinks does it take to make you feel high? More than two drinks is a positive response—score 2 points

A   Have people **A**NNOYED you by criticizing your drinking? If "Yes"—score 1 point.

C   Have you ever felt you ought to **C**UT DOWN on your drinking? If "Yes"—score 1 point.

E   **E**YE OPENER: Have you ever had a drink first thing in the morning to steady your nerves or get rid of a hangover? If "Yes"—score 1 point.

A total score of 2 or more points indicates a positive screen for pregnancy risk drinking.

Reprinted from Am J Obstet Gynecol, Vol 160, Sokol RJ, Martier SS, Ager JW. The T-ACE questions: practical prenatal detection of risk drinking. p. 863-8; discussion 868–70, 1989, with permission from Elsevier.

(continued)

Box 14   **Substance Abuse Questionnaires** *(continued)*

CRAFFT Substance Abuse Screen for Adolescents

C   Have you ever ridden in a **C**AR driven by someone (including yourself) who was high or had been using alcohol or drugs?

R   Do you ever use alcohol or drugs to **R**ELAX, feel better about yourself or fit in?

A   Do you ever use alcohol or drugs while you are by yourself **A**LONE?

F   Do you ever **F**ORGET things you did while using alcohol or drugs?

F   Do your **F**AMILY or friends ever tell you that you should cut down on your drinking or drug use?

T   Have you ever gotten in **T**ROUBLE while you were using alcohol or drugs?

Scoring: Two or more positive items indicate the need for further assessment.

Reprinted with permission from: Knight JR, Sheritt L, Shrier LA, Harris SK, Chang G. Validity of the CRAFFT substance abuse screening test among adolescent clinic patients. Arch Pediatr Adolesc Med 2002;156:607–13. Copyright © 2002, American Medical Association. All rights reserved.

Note: A standard drink is defined as a shot of liquor, a glass of wine, or a can of beer (12 oz of beer, 5 oz of table wine, and 1.5 oz of 80-proof distilled spirits). Source: United States Department of Agriculture, United States Department of Health and Human Services. Dietary guidelines for Americans 2005. 6th ed. Washington, DC: USDA; USHHS; 2005.

dependence (35). In another recent study, the standard AUDIT and modified AUDIT-C questionnaires were both sensitive (0.81 and 0.84, respectively) and specific (0.86 and 0.85, respectively) for the diagnosis of at-risk drinking in female Veterans Affairs patients. Although all of these screening questionnaires were developed for use in detecting alcohol use, it is possible to use them for detecting other drug use by adding the term drugs or a specific list of drugs of concern to the screening instrument (34).

During pregnancy, any amount of alcohol or substance use is considered to be "at-risk" use. Screening questionnaires designed specifically for office detection of risk drinking among pregnant women include the T-ACE and 5 P's. The T-ACE is a four-question screen that is considered to have excellent utility in sidestepping the denial syndrome. The T-ACE had demonstrated a sensitivity of 69% and specificity of 96% (36). The 5 P's was designed as a broad catch substance abuse screening tool for pregnant women in need of education, as well as intervention and treatment. This tool has been modified in recent years to include a question on peer alcohol use and to use multiple-choice answers for some questions (37).

The CRAFFT test is used to identify substance abuse in adolescents. This test has proved to be a valid means of screening adolescents for substance-related problems and disorders that may be common in some general clinic populations (38).

To improve disclosure rates for substance abuse, a system of regular screening should be instituted within an office setting. The tools mentioned previously can be self-administered questionnaires; however, care must be taken to ensure privacy during completion and secure and confidential handling of the completed form. As the clinician or staff member reviews the completed form with the woman, additional information can be obtained to further assess problem substance use.

Laboratory Testing

Laboratory drug tests can help identify or confirm a substance abuse problem overlooked by other detection methods when used appropriately and with prior and current informed consent. Although drug testing can be done on blood, hair, sweat, saliva, and nails, urine testing generally is the most practical option for the clinician's office. Urine testing is easy and inexpensive and provides a reasonable testing window for commonly used drugs (a few days in most cases). Mass-produced test kits generate immediate results that can be discussed with the patient. These kits test for the most common drugs of abuse or their metabolites (nicotine, alcohol, codeine-morphine, amphetamine-methamphetamine, phencyclidine "PCP," marijuana, cocaine); however, they do not detect lysergic acid diethylamide "LSD," 3,4-methylenedioxy-methamphetamine "MDMA" (also known as ecstasy), and synthetic opiates or stimulants. If necessary, a urine sample can be retested. Accepted standards for testing exist, including quantitative results (39). Urine samples can be vulnerable to dilution, substitution, and adulteration. Urine testing kits offer less reliability than off-site gas chromatography or mass spectrometry testing. These more expensive measures can be used as a backup, if necessary. Drug testing laboratories must be certified by the U.S. Department of Health and Human Services (39).

All tests can have false-positive and false-negative results, which is why a physician or other qualified individual should interpret all tests. False-positive test results for opiates caused by poppy-seed consumption can be avoided by setting the threshold for a positive test at a sufficiently high level and by testing for presence of a metabolite specific to heroin. In the absence of other clinical evidence of heroin use, opiate test results should be considered negative (39). A test is not in itself a diagnosis. Testing alone cannot confirm intoxication, abuse, or dependence. However, when combined with a thorough history and physical examination and appropriate screening questionnaires, drug testing can help the obstetrician–gynecologist provide better care, including appropriate interventions, to the patient (39).

From an ethical perspective, the most important principles involve a trusting patient–physician relationship, a focus on the benefits the patient may derive from testing, and an appreciation that patients make choices about their medical care. It is incumbent on the the medical provider, as part of the procedure in obtaining consent for testing, to provide information about the nature and purpose of the test to the patient and how the results will guide management (40). As with other confidential medical information, the results of such tests should under no circumstances be made available to police or government agencies unless specifically required by law. Seeking obstetric–gynecologic care should not expose a woman to criminal or civil penalties or the loss of custody of her children. Because of the possible implications of a positive drug screen, the rights of patients to autonomy and privacy are to be respected (16).

Confidentiality is as essential to the physician–patient relationship with adolescents as it is with adults (32). Many state laws protect the confidentiality of minors with regard to substance abuse detection and treatment (41). The American Academy of Pediatrics recommends that parental permission is not sufficient for involuntary drug testing of the adolescent with decisional capacity and that testing be conducted noncovertly, confidentially, and with informed consent in the same context as for other medical conditions (32, 42).

Treatment and the Obstetrician–Gynecologist

The role of the obstetrician–gynecologist includes referral with consultation and pretreatment for substance abuse. Pretreatment is the major contribution of the obstetrician–gynecologist or primary health care provider. It can be defined as providing immediate intervention that goes beyond screening to help the patient to come to terms with her substance abuse problem, even during the precontemplation phase when she may not be ready to accept treatment. The obstetrician–gynecologist can maintain the patient in the health care system, provide counseling on the risks and dangers of substance abuse, and treat the patient respectfully even when she continues to decline specific drug rehabilitation. Approximately 50% of patients who refused drug treatment eventually accepted it after a latent period during which they often tried their own solutions (43).

Physicians may be unaware of options and community resources available for substance abuse intervention and treatment. It is important for the clinician to identify an individual to whom patients can be referred for further assessment. Hospital social workers may be of help in obtaining this information. There are several important roles the obstetrician–gynecologist fills in the diagnosis and treatment of substance abuse that benefits these patients. Often, encouragement and support provided by the physician may lead the patient to reduce or eliminate substance use. This aids in preventing medical and psychosocial complications of substance use. Patient education, early diagnosis, and referral for treatment are key parts of total patient care for women with substance abuse issues. As the most significant health care practitioner for many women, the obstetrician–gynecologist may be influential in a patient's decision to accept treatment or referral.

The obstetrician–gynecologist may wish to offer treatment for low-level substance abuse. This may consist of follow-up office visits to monitor substance use, substance abuse, or treatment compliance.

Providing additional information through directed readings and educational materials about substance abuse is beneficial. The description and availability of local residential and outpatient services for addiction detoxification and treatment can be located through the SAMHSA web site (see "Resources"). Self-help and other treatment programs like Narcotics Anonymous, Alcoholics Anonymous, and Al Anon are important resources. Family members may be involved to help address different aspects of the substance abuse problem. In larger metropolitan areas, support groups specifically for women have been established (44).

The obstetrician–gynecologist can be effective in encouraging a patient's participation in the engagement and maintenance of her treatment and in planning for relapse prevention. For these patients, prescribing potentially addictive medications should be avoided. Treatment or referral for medical or psychiatric complications and co-morbidities can be managed in accordance with the physician's expertise in this field and the patient's wishes.

The role of the obstetrician does not end following referral of a pregnant woman to a drug or alcohol rehabilitation program. By design, these programs are highly regimented. Special consideration for women who are pregnant may require professional advocacy. For instance, many drug rehabilitation programs do not allow medications that have not been approved by the program's governing authority. The obstetrician may need to provide information on medications prescribed and ensure that the patient is receiving them. It also is important for the rehabilitation program to notify the clinician of medications prescribed by the program for the pregnant patient. Prenatal care appointments may coincide with mandatory program activities. The obstetrician's communication with the rehabilitation program staff will help to ensure comprehensive, coordinated care for the patient.

Pharmacologic Agents Used in Treatment

Patients in treatment programs for drugs may be taking supplemental pharmacologic agents. The three most commonly used agents are disulfiram, methadone, and naltrexone. Disulfiram is used to ensure abstinence from alcohol in conjunction with supportive therapy. When treating pregnant women, it is important to note that disulfiram has been associated with increased fetal risk of limb abnormality (45). Ingestion of alcohol while tak-

ing this medication results in profuse vomiting, hyperventilation, throbbing headache, and profuse sweating. Liver functions should be monitored every 6 months in these patients. Disulfiram should never be administered to a patient who is intoxicated or without her full knowledge. A new pharmaceutical, naltrexone injection, has been marketed to reduce heavy drinking; however, studies to date have demonstrated this treatment is only effective for men (46).

Methadone is used to treat narcotic withdrawal. This long-acting narcotic is used in maintenance treatment of narcotic addiction. Levomethadyl acetate, a methadone derivative, has been developed for thrice-weekly use. Buprenorphine, approved by the FDA in 2002, has been suggested as a promising alternative for maintenance therapy of opiate-dependent subjects because it produces limited withdrawal symptoms, results in reduced heroin self-administration, and has a longer duration of action. It is administered sublingually and may be combined with naloxone to decrease the potential for abuse by injection. Limited use of this agent in pregnancy has been reported in Europe with apparent less severe neonatal abstinence syndrome observed compared to neonates born of methadone-maintained women (47). A physician holding a current Drug Enforcement Administration waiver may prescribe these agents. Clonidine has been useful in reducing symptoms during opioid detoxification, particularly during pregnancy (48).

Naltrexone is used to block the "high" associated with opioid drug use. It is used in detoxified, formerly opioid-dependent patients to help prevent relapse. Patients with intact families and jobs benefit most from this treatment. Naltrexone implants have been used successfully to manage pregnant, heroin-dependent patients (49). Several studies have demonstrated promise in treating both cocaine and heroin addiction with auricular acupuncture in combination with counseling or pharmacologic measures (50).

Pregnancy and Substance Use

Substance use by pregnant women continues to be one of the leading causes of complications in modern obstetrics. The frequency of abuse of more than one substance, especially with alcohol and tobacco, makes interpretation of the literature difficult; however, there is little doubt that substance abuse is associated with an increased risk of poor pregnancy outcomes. Furthermore, prenatal care utilization and abstinence from substance use are associated with improved perinatal outcomes. Despite the positive impact of perinatal care, however, continued abuse of substances during pregnancy can result in infant impairment.

Most drugs of abuse alter the blood flow to the uteroplacental site and, therefore, affect the pregnancy outcome. Although substance use in pregnancy is a major public health problem, it often takes decades to identify its effects in humans. Alcohol consumption has been reported for most of human history, yet even FAS was not discovered until recently. For some harmful effects on the fetus, animal studies provide the only available information and suggest that drugs of abuse are dangerous to the fetus as well as the pregnant woman.

The effect to the fetus of maternal drug use has multiple determinants, including time of insult, diet and other host factors, the number of different drugs taken, the route or method of use, and the duration of use. Because engagement in high-risk activities during drug seeking and using periods is common, it is important to offer repeat HIV and sexually transmitted disease testing for pregnant women who use alcohol and other drugs and encourage condom use.

A recent survey of obstetrician–gynecologists found that 87% reported they ask their pregnant patients about drug use. Among women reporting drug use, 97% of clinicians discussed adverse effects and 95% advised abstinence. Forty-five percent reported that they referred patients for treatment, and one third reported performing periodic drug screens (51). In another survey, only 20% of obstetrician–gynecologists reported that abstinence from alcohol use was the safest way to avoid all four of the adverse pregnancy outcomes cited (spontaneous abortion, birth defects, FAS, and central nervous system impairment). Sixty-three percent of providers from this second study stated that they needed referral resources for patients with alcohol problems (52).

Caution should be used when looking at prevalence data in regards to substance abuse during pregnancy. There may be a tendency for women to underreport use (53). When asked retrospectively, women may report higher levels of alcohol use during pregnancy. Antenatal self-reported alcohol use has been found to be predictive of adverse outcomes (54).

Drug Testing in Pregnancy

Drug testing can help to save the lives and improve outcomes for women and their neonates. Misrepresentation and denial are part of the disease of addiction, with the result that patients may give inaccurate or misleading histories in which they minimize their use and the fetus's exposure. In one recent study, 11% of the women self-reported illicit substance use, but 43% of the 3,000 infants tested positive for illicit substances (55). However, false-negative and false-positive drug test results exist as a result of the woman's diet, other substances used, method, and carefulness of collection and elapsed time. Typical detection times for various substances are reported in Table 11. Confirmation of testing is always possible using gas chromatograph or mass spectrometry; however, such testing is expensive. Random testing, commonly used in addiction treatment programs, is not appropriate for use in a general obstetric–gynecologic practice. If the physician feels the need for continuous monitoring and random testing, a substance abuse specialist or team should monitor the patient.

Both meconium and neonatal hair samples have been used to document substance abuse by pregnant women. Although this approach has its limitations, these samples may help identify neonates who may be at risk for developing long-term sequelae as a result of in utero exposure and who may benefit from early identification and intervention. State law governs the practice of testing for prenatal drug exposure in neonates. Information on this testing can be obtained by contacting the state's child welfare agency.

Some states have mandatory reporting laws if a woman has a positive test result for illegal drugs during pregnancy. All health care providers should famil-

Table 11. Typical Urine Drug and Drug Metabolite Detection Times

Drug	Detection Time*
Marijuana (THC), acute use	3 days
Marijuana (THC), chronic use	30 days
Cocaine	1–3 days
Heroin	1 day
Methadone	3 days

*The amount of time that a drug or drug metabolite remains detectable in urine can very depending on the amount and frequency of use, metabolic rate, body mass, age, overall health, drug tolerance, and urine pH. Detection times for hair follicle, blood and saliva tests are much higher.

American College of Obstetricians and Gynecologists. Illicit drug abuse and dependence in women: a slide lecture presentation. Washington, DC: ACOG; 2002.

iarize themselves with state laws governing testing and reporting. There may be instances when mandated reporting measures endanger the relationship of trust between the physician and patient, placing the obstetrician in an adversarial relationship with the patient, and possibly creating conflict with the therapeutic obligation. If pregnant women become reluctant to seek medical care because they fear being reported for alcohol or illegal drug use, these strategies will actually increase the risks to the woman and the fetus rather than reduce the consequences of substance abuse (32). Substance abuse does not by itself guarantee child neglect or prove inadequate parenting capacity (57).

The issue of reporting substance abuse; special issues for girls and adolescent women; and the ethical rationale for universal screening questions, brief intervention, and referral to treatment may be found in American College of Obstetricians and Gynecologists (ACOG) Committee Opinion number 294 "At-Risk Drinking and Illicit Drug Use: Ethical Issues in Obstetric and Gynecologic Practice" (see "ACOG Resources").

Improving Outcomes in Pregnancy

On diagnosis of a substance abuse problem, it is important for the pregnant woman to have a thorough assessment and intervention by an American Society of Addiction Medicine-certified physician or other physician qualified in addiction medicine or a substance abuse-pregnancy counselor (see "Resources"). If these individuals are not available, the obstetrician–gynecologist needs to identify an individual to whom patients can be referred for further assessment. Drug and alcohol use exposes the woman and fetus to numerous untested, complex compounds that interfere with judgment and make numerous other high-risk behaviors more likely. Residential treatment and group, community outpatient, and faith-based programs have been very effective at reducing the consequences of substance use during pregnancy.

Additionally, "drug" use during pregnancy is a misnomer, because polysubstance abuse is almost always involved. Thus, even if the effects of individual drugs were known completely, outcome measures studying multiple drugs and the effect of their interactions would be so complex as to approach impossibility. Early identification and intervention are essential if prevention fails.

Prenatal and Early Postpartum Care

Comprehensive prenatal care has been shown to ameliorate the maternal and neonatal complications associated with substance abuse. For example, among pregnant women who use cocaine, multidisciplinary prenatal care may improve obstetric outcomes compared with users who receive little or no prenatal care (58). The favorable pregnancy outcomes seen in opiate addicts enrolled in methadone maintenance programs throughout pregnancy attest to the beneficial effects of these programs in concert with prenatal care (59).

The pregnant woman who abuses substances often has a multitude of nonmedical problems. Some of these women are unemployed, are undereducated, live in substandard housing, have psychiatric disorders and other co-morbidities, are victims of partner violence, or are homeless. Because of the close association of substance abuse and partner violence, especially during pregnancy, the discovery of one problem should signal a search for others (see the "Intimate Partner Violence and Domestic Violence" chapter). Even when the pregnant woman who abuses substances remains in her abusive relationship, incorporating a strong social support system can improve the chance of a drug-free delivery. Therefore, where possible, it is helpful to have a multidisciplinary team of health care and social service providers to address the multiple problems of pregnant women who abuse substances. At each prenatal encounter, substance abuse treatment should be offered to those who have not quit.

A substance abuse history should be taken from all patients as part of the medical and obstetric history. Those with significant alcohol use need to be counseled regarding the risk and effects of FAS. It also is important to counsel pregnant women who abuse substances about the potential risks of preterm delivery, fetal growth restriction, fetal death, and possible long-term neurobehavioral effects of continued substance abuse. A self-administered questionnaire embedded with a relational and "broad-catch" screening tool (such as the 5 P's) offers the prenatal provider a platform to educate pregnant women on substance use and, when appropriate, provide brief intervention counseling (37). Following screening, all pregnant women, regardless of substance use history, should be educated as to the harmful effects of substance use and the necessity to refrain from use.

Because growth restriction is a relatively frequent finding among fetuses of women who abuse substances, accurate assessment of gestational age is essential for optimal management. Early ultrasound examination confirmation of gestational age may obviate the need for more intensive testing or intervention later in pregnancy. Furthermore, because of the possibility of structural anomalies of the fetuses of women who abuse alcohol, a fetal anatomic survey may be indicated.

Drug abuse also may be associated with serious complications during labor and obstetric anesthesia administration. Complications may result from intoxication and include increased risk of aspiration, respiratory depression, lack of the ability to cooperate or to control musculature, and altered responses to pain. Labor, particularly prolonged labor, may precipitate drug withdrawal, producing a wide range of autonomic reactions. In addition, many drugs produce specific neurologic, cardiovascular, or hematologic dysfunctions that affect the choice of and response to obstetric anesthesia (60). These are included in the discussion of substances of abuse as follows. It is critical that health care providers delivering anesthesia and caring for the newborn be informed of the woman's substance abuse. Fetal well-being needs to be documented throughout labor. The infant may need prolonged observation for signs of withdrawal and for potential future developmental abnormalities.

It is important to encourage women who abuse substances to receive treatment throughout the postpartum period. This includes counseling the breastfeeding woman that the infant may be exposed through her milk to the substances she is using. Women whose infants are at risk for neurobehavioral disabilities need to be informed of the importance of early and frequent developmental examinations. A number of states mandate the reporting and monitoring of these women and their exposed infants. Specific information on state-level requirements can be accessed through a state's child protection department.

Substances of Abuse

The specific effects of commonly abused substances are outlined in Table 12 at the end of this chapter.

Tobacco use is addressed in the "Smoking and Women's Health" chapter.

Alcohol

Alcohol-related mortality (heart disease, cirrhosis, accidents, overdose) represents a leading cause of preventable death. Chronic alcohol abuse results in multiple adverse health effects, raising the risk of many types of cancer, and increasing the incidence of malnutrition, including deficiencies in thiamine, riboflavin, pyridoxine, niacin, and vitamin C. In 2002, 17,419 individuals were killed and 258,000 were injured in alcohol-related motor vehicle crashes (5).

Men and women differ in their metabolism of alcohol. Women achieve higher blood alcohol levels than men after consuming the same amount of alcohol, even after adjusting for body weight. This effect may be caused in part by the lower percentage of body water in women (61). Lower levels of gastric alcohol dehydrogenase in women, leading to reduced first-pass metabolism, also may play a role (62). Women eliminate alcohol at a faster rate than men, which results in increased exposure to acetaldehyde and may contribute to an increased risk of liver disease (62). The menstrual cycle does not appear to affect alcohol metabolism, subjective response, or degree of impairment (63).

More than one half of all women in the United States consume alcohol (64). It is important to remember that light to moderate drinking can have beneficial cardiovascular effects for both men and women; however, the benefit of alcohol consumption for women has much stricter amount limits than for men. (65). One recent study found that women who consume light to moderate amounts of alcohol may have a lower risk of type 2 diabetes mellitus (66).

Women are more vulnerable than men to the toxic effects of alcohol. At all levels of alcohol consumption, women have a higher risk of alcohol-induced liver disease and cirrhosis than do men who drink comparable amounts (67). Women's risk of developing liver disease increases significantly when 7–13 drinks per week are consumed; men have to drink twice as much to face the same risk (67). Estrogen appears to increase the liver's sensitivity to the toxic effects of ethanol; metabolic differences between men and women also may play a role in increasing vulnerability to liver disease among female drinkers (68).

Alcohol consumption is linked to an increased risk of breast cancer. Recent data indicate that women who drink between two and five drinks per day have up to a 41% increased incidence of breast cancer, and risk increases linearly with consumption throughout this range (69, 70). Higher levels of alcohol consumption were not associated with additional risk (70). The relationship between lower levels of alcohol consumption and breast cancer is less clear. Even one drink per day may be associated with a 10% increase in risk (71), although not all studies have demonstrated this (72).

Women are more vulnerable than men to alcoholic cardiomyopathy, developing this condition at lower levels of lifetime alcohol consumption, shorter durations of alcoholism, and lower daily doses of alcohol than alcoholic men (73). Women who die from alcohol-related causes lose more potential years of life than their male counterparts (74).

Alcohol is the most common teratogen to which a fetus is exposed, and alcohol consumption during pregnancy is a leading preventable cause of mental retardation, developmental delay, and birth defects in the fetus. This is not surprising given the high prevalence of alcohol use among women of childbearing age (49.8%) and the high rate of unintended pregnancy in the United States (49%) (8, 75). Birth defects associated with prenatal alcohol exposure can occur in the first 3–8 weeks of pregnancy, before a woman even realizes she is pregnant (76).

Ethanol freely crosses the placenta and the fetal blood–brain barrier. The deleterious effects of ethanol are presumed to be mediated by direct toxicity as well as through toxic metabolites, such as acetaldehyde. In addition, the poor nutritional status of women who use alcohol heavily may play a role in the teratogenic effect. There is substantial evidence that fetal toxicity is dose-related and that the exposure time of greatest risk is the first trimester (77). The most severe effects are on the fetal brain; however, this organ continues to develop throughout gestation. Although a clear threshold could not be defined, Ernhart and colleagues found a trend of increased abnormalities with increasing exposure (77). Anatomic abnormalities in the child were clearly defined among children whose mothers drank more than six drinks per day. Most of the effects of maternal alcohol use on the fetus are not immediately apparent.

There is no established safe level of alcohol use during pregnancy. Women who are pregnant or at risk for pregnancy should not drink alcohol. Although consumption of small amounts of alcohol early in pregnancy is unlikely to cause serious fetal problems, patients are best advised to refrain from alcohol entirely. Because brain growth continues throughout pregnancy, even women who drank heavily in early pregnancy can reduce the risk of further harm to the fetus by cessation of alcohol use.

During labor, acute alcohol intoxication poses a significant risk of pulmonary aspiration. Symptoms of acute alcohol withdrawal can occur 6–48 hours after consumption, producing severe physical symptoms, including vomiting, tachycardia, hypertension, delirium, seizures, and cardiac failure. The sequelae of chronic alcohol use, such as malnutrition, neuropathy, and coagulopathy, are to be considered when making a determination on appropriate anesthesia for labor and delivery (60).

Heavy use of alcohol may lead to a neonatal abstinence syndrome characterized by jitteriness, irritability, and poor feeding. These effects may occur within the first 12 hours of life. This syndrome is less common and less severe than that seen following opiate withdrawal. Short-term treatment with barbiturates is sometimes necessary to ameliorate the symptoms.

Fetal alcohol syndrome was first described in 1973; however, the deleterious effect of alcohol has been suspected for centuries. A congenital syndrome, FAS is characterized by alcohol use during pregnancy and three findings: 1) growth restriction (which may occur in the prenatal period, the postnatal period, or both), 2) facial abnormalities, and 3) central nervous system dysfunction (78). In addition to a history of maternal alcohol use during pregnancy, at least one finding from each of these three categories must be present to make the diagnosis of FAS (78). The facial abnormalities include shortened palpebral fissures, low-set ears, midfacial hypoplasia, a smooth philtrum, and a thin upper lip. Central nervous system abnormalities that are considered part of FAS include microcephaly; mental retardation; and behavioral disorders, such as attention deficit disorder.

Performance deficits in children with FAS are striking. Intelligence is profoundly affected in some; the average intelligence quotient of children with FAS is in the borderline range of functioning (ie, in the low 70s), although they can range from intellectually deficient (intelligence quotient scores less than 70) to average (intelligence quotient scores between 90 and 109) (79). Affected children may display fine motor dysfunction. Irritability is common in infancy, and hyperactivity is a common finding in later childhood.

Skeletal abnormalities and structural cardiac defects are seen with increased frequency in the children of women who use alcohol during pregnancy but are not required for the diagnosis of FAS. These skeletal anomalies include abnormalities of position or function or both and, occasionally, abnormal palmar crease patterns. The most common cardiac structural anomalies are ventricular septal defects, but other cardiac anomalies also may occur.

Some children who are adversely affected by maternal alcohol use do not meet all the criteria for the diagnosis of FAS. These children may have an isolated physical abnormality and be classified as having an alcohol-related birth defect (ARBD). Cranio-facial birth defects occur mainly during embryogenesis. However, neurodevelopmental abnormalities, such as problems with cognitive development (intelligence, communication skills, memory, and learning ability), visual or spatial skills, and motor development occur beyond 8 weeks of gestation. This is called alcohol-related neurodevelopmental disorder (ARND) (formerly fetal alcohol effects) (80).

The exact risk incurred by maternal alcohol use is difficult to establish because the complex pattern of symptoms associated with FAS can make diagnosis difficult. Recent data indicate that the prevalence of FAS in the United States ranges from 0.3 to 1.5 cases per 1,000 live births, with a higher prevalence among Native American and African-American populations (13). Among women who already have a child with FAS, the risk of having another child with FAS in the absence of intervention is 75% for each pregnancy (81). Moreover, even low levels of alcohol consumption (two or fewer drinks per week) have been associated with increased aggressive behavior in children (82).

Many cases of FAS or ARND go undiagnosed until several years after the birth because symptoms often are not immediately apparent. Long-term effects of ARBD and ARND include failure to thrive, dental malalignment and malocclusion, as well as eustachian tube dysfunction from midfacial hypoplasia. Recurrent otitis media is a frequent complication. Ocular development may be impaired, resulting in severe degrees of myopia. Prenatal alcohol exposure has been linked to increased rates of problem drinking in young adulthood (83).

Marijuana

Marijuana is derived from the plant *Cannabis sativa*. Other forms of cannabis, which vary in potency, include sinsemilla, hashish, and hash oil. Its principal psychoactive ingredient is 1,9-tetrahydrocannabinol, which is present in large quantities in each marijuana cigarette. This lipophilic substance accumulates in fatty tissues for days before being metabolized by the liver and eliminated in the feces.

Marijuana usually is smoked as a cigarette (called a joint) or in a pipe or bong. Marijuana also has appeared in blunts, which are cigars that have been emptied of tobacco and refilled with marijuana, sometimes in combination with another drug, such as cocaine. Marijuana also can be mixed into foods or used to brew a tea. Compared with smoking tobacco, smoking cannabis involves inhaling more smoke for a longer period, resulting in a fivefold increase in concentrations of carboxyhemoglobin. Thus, marijuana smokers retain the products of combustion longer than the average cigarette smoker does (84).

Marijuana affects different organs systems of the body, including the pulmonary, cardiovascular, gonadal, immune, and nervous systems. Effects may vary with duration of use. The symptoms associated with the chronic use of marijuana are similar to those of tobacco use, such as daily cough and phlegm production, more frequent acute chest illnesses, a heightened risk of lung infections, and a greater tendency toward obstructed airways. Cancer of the respiratory tract and lungs can result from both tobacco and marijuana use; marijuana smoke contains 50–70% more carcinogenic hydrocarbons than does tobacco smoke (84). Marijuana smokers have more alterations in bronchial mucosa than nonsmokers, and several studies have suggested an association between marijuana smoking and head and neck cancers, but future long-term studies are needed (85). There is an association with marijuana use and respiratory cancer (86).

Marijuana also can have significant cardiovascular effects. Acutely, marijuana increases blood pressure levels and the heart rate (87). Marijuana causes increased cardiac output and decreased exercise performance and peripheral vascular resistance, which is not problematic in most healthy young women who use the drug but is very risky for those with cardiovascular disease (87).

Those who have taken high doses of marijuana may experience acute psychosis, which includes hallucinations, delusions, and depersonalization. Although the etiology of these symptoms remains unknown, they appear to occur more frequently when a high dose of cannabis is consumed in food or drink rather than smoked.

Whereas findings in humans have been inconsistent, animal studies have shown that cannabinoids can alter several hormonal systems. Hormonal systems that are acutely altered in animals include activation of the hypothalamic–pituitary–adrenal axis and suppression of gonadal steroids, thyroid hormone, growth hormone, and prolactin (88).

Because of high lipid solubility and large molecular weight, cannabinoid metabolites can be detected in the urine of those who use the drug for days to weeks—much longer than for alcohol and most other illicit substances. Given that marijuana is a common component in polysubstance abuse, the presence of cannabinoid metabolites in the urine may identify patients who are at high risk for being current users of tobacco or other substances as well.

There is no evidence that marijuana is safe for the childbearing woman, but it does not appear to be a significant teratogen in humans. Marijuana may be detected in maternal amniotic fluid. Heavy cannabis use may increase the risk of low birth weight (89). Prenatal marijuana exposure may be linked to impairment in executive functioning (90) and other circumscribed deficits in cognitive functioning in the child (91). One long-term study of adolescents who were exposed to marijuana prenatally found that marijuana had different long-term effects than those exposed to cigarettes. Whereas tobacco affected functioning, marijuana appeared to have an impact on the application of skills, such as sustained attention, analytical skills, and problems of visual integration (90). Initial reports suggested an increased frequency of meconium-stained amniotic fluid and precipitous labor in those who heavily use marijuana, but these results have not been reproduced (92).

Cocaine

Cocaine is a lipophilic alkaloid extracted from the leaves of *Erythroxylon coca*. Highly addictive, it generally is consumed by snorting, "freebasing" (inhaling cocaine vapors combined with an organic solvent), smoking the alkaloid itself as "crack," and less commonly by injection. Cocaine's major site of action is at

the nerve terminal, where it inhibits dopamine, norepinephrine, and serotonin uptake. This results in intense vasoconstriction, arrhythmia, and a concomitant increase in blood pressure levels (93). Associated adverse consequences are seizures, cerebrovascular accidents, psychosis, nasal septal perforation, malnutrition, and hyperthermia.

Cocaine appears to be metabolized through a number of different pathways in humans. Plasma and liver esterases act on cocaine to form ecgonine methyl ester, a water-soluble compound that accounts for 30–50% of the cocaine metabolites found in urine. In addition, there appears to be spontaneous nonenzymatic hydrolysis of cocaine to benzoyl ecgonine, which also is excreted primarily in the urine. This compound also accounts for 30–50% of the cocaine metabolites found in urine and is the compound that most commercially available enzyme assays are designed to detect in urine tested for evidence of recent cocaine use (94). Meconium analysis has been reported to have a high sensitivity in detecting prenatal exposure to cocaine, especially when coupled with maternal interview (55, 95).

Crack is a crystalline purified compound that is extracted from the powered form of cocaine by a solvent and crystallized with an inorganic base. Crack is water-soluble and heat labile, whereas cocaine is not. It can, therefore, be vaporized by heat and then inhaled or dissolved in water and injected intravenously, thus reaching peak serum concentration more rapidly than inhaled cocaine. Crack also is cheaper than cocaine. The cost of cocaine powder limits the number of doses an addict takes, while crack can be repeated far more often; another dose often is used to relieve the "let-down" after the first dose.

Cocaine use during pregnancy is linked with placental abruption, preterm birth, and low birth weight. This may be a primary effect of vasoconstriction and an increase in uterine contractions or may be associated with concomitant maternal cigarette smoking (96, 97). The initial reports of myriad pregnancy complications caused by cocaine and crack use have not been validated (96); however, cocaine use during pregnancy has been linked to microcephaly in the infant as well as subtle cognitive and motor development abnormalities in the child (97).

It is difficult to separate the role played by cocaine in adverse pregnancy outcomes from other factors associated with cocaine use, such as smoking, malnutrition, lack of prenatal care, older maternal age, and presence of infectious disease in the woman (96). Cocaine does cross the placenta (96) and also passes into breast milk, but the effects on breastfeeding require further study (96, 98). Recent and well-controlled data suggest that prenatal cocaine exposure does not lead to either acute neonatal toxicity or a withdrawal syndrome (99).

During labor and delivery, it is important to consider the following for a woman who uses cocaine: cocaine-induced thrombocytopenia, ephedrine-resistant hypotension and hypertension, arrhythmias, and myocardial ischemia. The patient may have altered pain perception, experiencing pain despite adequate anesthesia levels (60).

Opioids

Opioids are a class of drugs derived from opium and synthetic compounds with similar actions. The prototypical opioid is morphine. Heroin (diacetylmorphine) is more potent on a gram-for-gram basis but is believed to exert its effects chiefly by being metabolized to morphine. Codeine is methylated morphine and also is metabolized to the parent compound. Other opioids, such as meperidine, methadone, and oxycodone, are structurally dissimilar to morphine but share its pharmacologic properties, probably because they all stimulate mu-opioid receptors. These agents produce euphoria, somnolence, and decreased sensitivity to pain. Adverse effects of opioid use include constipation, nephrotic syndrome, and overdose. Opioid use can lead to tolerance, in which an increased dose is needed to have the same effect.

Heroin

Heroin is the most widely abused opioid drug and can be injected, smoked, or snorted. Heroin often is sold combined ("cut") with other white powdery substances, some of which may be toxic. Additionally, this adulteration makes it difficult for users to accurately calculate how much of the active drug they are taking, thus running the risk of unintentional overdose.

Acutely, heroin use produces drowsiness, dry mouth, constipation, skin flushing, and respiratory depression. Chronic use can lead to liver disease and respiratory complications such as pneumonia; in addition, if the drug is injected, it can lead to increased risk of HIV, hepatitis infection, endocarditis, and abscesses.

The chief risk in heroin overdose is respiratory depression, which can be fatal; however, the effects of overdose can be rapidly reversed. Most heroin overdoses involve the concomitant use of heroin and other drugs, in particular alcohol and benzodiazepines (100).

Discontinuation of heroin use can lead to withdrawal, with symptoms including restlessness, muscle aches, nausea, vomiting, and craving for the drug. Withdrawal symptoms peak 2–3 days after cessation of use and markedly diminish after 1 week. Contrary to popular belief and numerous portrayals in television and film, heroin withdrawal is less severe than that associated with many other drugs and is almost never fatal.

Heroin use poses a significant dependence liability. However, it is certainly possible to terminate use, especially with access to proper treatment. Many heroin users "mature out" and spontaneously stop using it in their 30s and 40s. Young heroin users face greater obstacles to entering detoxification and rehabilitation programs because they often lack access to health care and a supportive social structure (101). Heroin users can be treated with maintenance doses of methadone, another opioid that does not produce the intense high of heroin.

Buprenorphine, a nonopioid, has recently been approved for the treatment of heroin dependence within an outpatient setting. Several thousand qualified U.S. physicians are currently dispensing buprenorphine and buprenorphine with nalorxone. (see "Resources" for online directory access). These medications, administered by the sublingual route, have been identified as a safe treatment to reduce the use of and craving for opiates (102); however, reimbursement for this treatment by Medicaid or Medicare currently is not available.

The use, misuse, and diversion of methadone and other opioid medications are increasing (22). According to recent Florida autopsy data, prescription drugs (particularly methadone and oxycodone) are more likely to be found in lethal levels than illegal drugs, 60% versus 40%, respectively (103).

Oxycodone

Oxycodone (oxycontin) is a synthetic opioid legitimately used to treat chronic pain. It has become popular as a recreational drug, particularly in rural areas. Oxycodone for nonmedical purposes is obtained from diversion from legitimate sources. Oxycodone use can produce dependence, and as with other opioids, overdose can be fatal.

Fentanyl

Fentanyl, a synthetic opioid, is medically used in anesthesia and for treating pain but also is occasionally abused. Transdermal fentanyl patches, used to treat pain, are sometimes diverted for illicit use. Some medical personnel with access to anesthetic drugs have developed dependence on fentanyl, which they generally administer intravenously. Fentanyl users run a high risk of fatal overdose because the drug is 50–100 times more potent than morphine (96). Synthetic opioids are not detected on standard urine drug screens.

Opioid addiction during pregnancy poses serious health threats to both the woman and the fetus. Studies analyzing the pregnancy outcomes of heroin addicts have demonstrated rates of stillbirth, fetal growth restriction, preterm birth, and neonatal mortality three to seven times higher than those of the general population (104). Whether these problems are a direct effect of the narcotics and intermittent withdrawal or a result of the myriad health and social problems typical of narcotic addicts is difficult to establish. A recent study has begun to delineate environmental versus potential toxicological effects in children exposed prenatally to heroin. Children born to heroin-dependent women who were adopted soon after birth and raised in a positive environment had normal intellectual function, unlike those who remained with biological parents, but higher rates of inattention, behavioral problems, and attention deficit/hyperactivity disorder (ADHD) persisted (104).

Abrupt withdrawal from opiates during pregnancy is not recommended because maternal withdrawal symptoms threaten the fetus, and abrupt withdrawal may precipitate use of other street drugs, with even more problematic effect (105). For pregnant opioid-dependent women, addiction medicine specialists usually advocate methadone maintenance therapy at a dose that will prevent craving and eliminate withdrawal symptoms, generally 50–150 mg per day (36). Studies have indicated that neonatal withdrawal among infants of women who were on low-dose methadone while pregnant is similar to those of women who were on high-dose methadone (59). Methadone withdrawal during pregnancy is not recommended because of the increased risk of spontaneous

abortion and premature labor (36). Buprenorphine appears to be safe and effective during pregnancy (pregnancy category C) according to a recent review (106).

Discussion of a labor and delivery plan with the opioid user may decrease intrapartum complications. Women with an opioid addiction, fearing withdrawal during labor, may overdose before hospital admission. To prevent acute opioid withdrawal syndrome, opioid replacement therapy should be continued throughout labor. Thrombosed peripheral veins may require the use of a central venous access (60).

The newborn infant of a narcotic addict is at risk for neonatal abstinence syndrome, a severe, potentially fatal, narcotic withdrawal syndrome. As many as two thirds of infants born to heroin addicts will develop signs and symptoms of neonatal abstinence syndrome. Approximately 60% of infants born to women on methadone maintenance exhibit neonatal abstinence syndrome; however, withdrawal symptoms for these infants are less severe than for infants of women who use street heroin (105). Narcotic abstinence syndrome is characterized by a high-pitched cry, poor feeding, hypertonicity, tremors, irritability, sneezing, sweating, vomiting, diarrhea, and, occasionally, seizures. In cases of maternal heroin use, the signs of neonatal abstinence syndrome usually appear 24–72 hours after birth. Signs of neonatal abstinence syndrome occur 1–2 days later in infants born to women taking methadone because it has a longer half-life. Occasionally, neonatal abstinence syndrome symptoms do not appear until 10 days of life—after the infant has been discharged.

Inhalants

Use of inhalants ("glue sniffing," solvent abuse) tends to be found primarily among adolescents. These substances are lipophilic and readily pass through the respiratory tract. Acutely, inhalant use may be accompanied by arrhythmias leading to sudden death; suffocation also poses a serious risk of fatality. Chronic use may cause bone marrow toxicity, liver damage, renal failure, peripheral neuropathy, atrophy, parethesias, cerebellar signs, and organic brain syndrome.

The possibility exists for adverse effects of inhalant use in pregnancy. Data from occupational exposure to some of the abused solvents have suggested an increased risk of spontaneous abortion and fetal malformations. There are no well-controlled studies in this area. Published case reports suggest an association with fetal growth restriction and craniofacial and neurobehavioral abnormalities (107). Among children exposed to inhalants prenatally, there also is some evidence of cognitive, speech, and motor deficits (107). When maternal inhalant use is suspected, it may be beneficial for the clinician to perform a neurologic examination before intrapartum anesthesia administration to detect any sensory or motor deficits (60).

Stimulants

Stimulant drugs include methamphetamine, methylphenidate, ephedra, and khat. Stimulants are sympathomimetics that act on the noradrenergic and dopaminergic neurons of the central and peripheral nervous system, increasing neurotransmitter release and blocking reuptake. They produce feelings of euphoria and energy that users experience as pleasurable.

The central nervous system effects of stimulants may have significant implications regarding the choice of anesthesia for labor and delivery. Fetal distress, placental abruption, and other obstetric emergencies secondary to stimulant abuse may necessitate an emergency cesarean delivery. Physiologic interactions should be considered on a case-by-case basis (60).

Methamphetamine

Methamphetamine (also known as meth, ice, and crystal meth) use is most prevalent in the western United States, Midwest, and rural areas, and is increasing elsewhere. Methamphetamine is inexpensive and readily available because clandestine laboratories can be set up almost anywhere. Methamphetamine can be smoked, sniffed, administered orally, or injected; preference varies by region. Many methamphetamine users alternate between brief, intense periods of frequent drug administration, a "binge," and abstinence at other times. During periods of repeated use, tolerance to the drug develops, enabling users to administer amounts that would be fatal under other circumstances.

Acutely, methamphetamine use can result in blood pressure changes, tachycardia, arrhythmias, insomnia, irritability, nausea, vomiting, anorexia (93), and, rarely, stroke (108). Methamphetamine may exacerbate tics, such as those associated with Tourette's syndrome (93). Chronic use can be detected by hair analysis (109). Ephedrine and certain monoamine oxidase inhibitors

can result in false-positive findings for methamphetamine on drug screens (96).

Methamphetamine can produce psychiatric symptoms, such as psychosis, hallucinations, anxiety, panic, depression, self-mutilation (110), and skin picking (111). There have been occasional reports of recurrences of methamphetamine-induced psychosis or flashbacks, even after discontinuation of the drug (112). Methamphetamine use may be linked to abnormal brain chemistry, neuronal damage, and psychotic symptoms that persist even after periods of abstinence (113).

Discontinuation of methamphetamine use can produce withdrawal, with symptoms such as depression anxiety, fatigue, paranoia, and aggression (111). In treatment, relapse of former users is common, given the dysphoria and craving they experience, and the widespread availability of the drug (114). Studies on d-amphetamine indicate that women experience more subjective stimulation from the drug during the follicular phase of the menstrual cycle; thus, women who are trying to discontinue use may be more successful if they stop during the luteal phase, when the drug effects are less potent (115).

Methamphetamine use in pregnancy is associated with an increase in growth restriction; this effect may be dose-related and is exacerbated if the woman also smokes cigarettes (116). There are occasional reports of withdrawal symptoms in the neonate (116). Methamphetamine crosses into breast milk, but the effects of this on the infant require further study (96, 98).

Amphetamines

Amphetamines may appeal to women for a variety of reasons. Unlike most other drugs, many women report that the use of amphetamines increases their enjoyment of sex and their likelihood of having sex. Some women may be more likely to have unsafe sex while under the influence of this drug (117). Amphetamines may be medically used to suppress appetite; some women may view the weight loss resulting from illicit use as desirable. D-amphetamine improves concentration and performance on repetitive tasks (96); this effect, combined with the decreased need for sleep produced by the drug, has been posited as a reason why the drug may be seen by some women as a way to help cope with a busy and stressful life.

Methylphenidate

Methylphenidate is a phenylethylamine structurally and pharmacologically similar to amphetamines. It is the most commonly used drug in the treatment of ADHD. Methylphenidate is classified as a Schedule II drug, indicating a high potential for abuse. Methylphenidate is used recreationally to produce an amphetaminelike high; it can be taken orally, snorted, or dissolved and injected (96). Illicitly available methylphenidate has been diverted from legitimate supplies, such as in the case of children selling their medication to their classmates. The nonmedical use of methylphenidate is most prevalent among young individuals. The acute effects of methylphenidate include tachycardia, agitation, irritability, and hypertension (118). At least one case of death linked to overdose from nasal administration has been reported (119). Concerta, the extended-release form of methylphenidate, may have less abuse potential (120).

Ephedra

Ephedra, also sold under the names ma huang and herbal ecstasy, is a naturally occurring stimulant used as a dietary supplement, weight loss aid, a substitute for illegal stimulants, and in traditional Chinese medicine. The active components of ephedra are ephedrine and related alkaloids (96). Commercial preparations often combine ephedra with other substances, such as caffeine, which increase its stimulant effects. In December 2003, the FDA issued a consumer alert on the safety of dietary supplements containing ephedra that calls for consumers to immediately stop buying and using ephedra products. The FDA also has banned the sale of dietary supplements containing ephedrine alkaloids because they present an "unreasonable risk of illness or injury" (121).

The health risks of ephedra include cardiovascular complications, stroke, myocardial infarction, and sudden death (122). These risks are not limited to individuals with a history of cardiovascular problems or to those who have taken large doses of ephedra-containing products (122). Combined ephedra-caffeine preparations have cardiovascular effects similar to synthetic amphetamines; these effects can be seen after a single dose (123). It is important to note that a reputable laboratory produced the preparation used in the cited trial specifically for this purpose and the concentration of active ingredients was known and standardized. This had not been the case in commercially available ephedra products, where the amount of ephedrine varied greatly from brand to brand and even from lot to lot, which increased the likelihood of accidental overdose and concomitant adverse effects (124). There currently are no available data on the use of ephedra during pregnancy.

Khat

Khat (also spelled "qat") is a natural stimulant related to ephedrine and amphetamine. Khat is widely used in East Africa and on the Arabian peninsula, where khat leaves are chewed over a period of several hours to slowly release the drug cathionine (96). Because of its anorexic effects, Muslims may use khat during Ramadan fasting to ward off hunger. Currently, there are little data on the safety of khat use in humans, although anecdotal evidence suggests an association with increased susceptibility to myocardial infarction (125). Khat is illegal and not commonly used in the United States, but knowledge of this drug may be useful for health care providers who work with immigrant populations native to regions where khat use is popular. Khat chewing during pregnancy may be linked to low-birth-weight neonates (126).

Hallucinogens

Lysergic Acid Diethylamide

Lysergic acid diethylamide (also known as acid and LSD) induces perceptual changes by binding to 5-hydroxytryptamine receptors (96). Lysergic acid diethylamide is produced in underground laboratories and generally sold soaked on squares of blotter paper and taken orally (96). Risk factors for LSD use in sexually active young women include white ethnicity, being younger than 18 years, a history of physical abuse, and severe symptoms of depression (127). It is estimated that approximately one half of all young women who report trying lysergic acid diethylamide do not continue using it (127).

Lysergic acid diethylamide is not associated with the development of dependence, perhaps because frequent LSD administration markedly decreases the drug's effects. The available evidence does not suggest that LSD use results in long-term neurotoxicity, but more study is needed to definitively answer this question (128). Lysergic acid diethylamide overdose is unlikely (96). Hallucinogen-induced persistent perceptual disorder, popularly known as "flashbacks," has been reported as a consequence of LSD use; however, neither the etiology of this phenomenon nor the percentage of affected users is currently known (129). There is no evidence that LSD or other hallucinogens cause chromosomal damage, as was once reported (130).

Lysergic acid diethylamide is not detected on standard drug screens (96). Additionally, other substances, such as fentanyl and mucolytics, may result in false-positive results on urine screens for LSD (131).

Although there are no known deleterious effects of this group of drugs on human pregnancy, there have been few controlled studies, and the drug should be considered dangerous until proved otherwise. There have been no studies on the potential long-term effects on neurodevelopment in the neonate. The psychotomimetic effects of LSD are produced at extremely low concentrations. It is believed that LSD passes into breast milk; therefore, LSD is contraindicated during lactation (132).

Phencyclidine

Phencyclidine (PCP), often classified as a hallucinogen, is in fact a dissociative anesthetic that acts as an N-methyl-D-aspartate antagonist at low doses and an indirect agonist at sigma receptors at high does. Synthesized illicitly, PCP is most often smoked but also can be snorted, injected, or swallowed. Occasionally, leaves soaked in PCP are sold as marijuana. Acutely, PCP causes hallucinations and methamphetaminelike effects (96). Phencyclidine intoxication is associated with violent acts, but this effect is more common in individuals who have a history of violent behavior (133). Other side effects may include paranoia, delusions, and suicidal thoughts. Most PCP-related deaths also involve accidents or trauma; there are few overdose fatalities caused by PCP alone (96).

Phencyclidine use during pregnancy has been associated with irritability, jitteriness, hypertonicity, poor feeding, and abnormal neurobehavior in the offspring resolving by age 2 years (132). Women consuming PCP should not breastfeed because the drug is passed into the breast milk (132).

Sedatives and Hypnotics

Most sedative and hypnotic drugs of abuse, such as benzodiazepines and barbiturates, are legal prescription drugs that may be misused for their psychoactive effects. Benzodiazepines are gamma-aminobutyrate-agonists widely used as anxiolytics, sedatives or hypnotics, muscle relaxants, and anticonvulsants. They also are used in alcohol detoxification. Commonly prescribed benzodiazepines include alprazolam, diazepam, lorazepam, clonazepam, and chlordiazepoxide.

Although benzodiazepines have a legitimate role in medical treatment, they also have considerable dependence liability. Benzodiazepines should not be used as a long-term treatment, especially when other less addictive drugs are available. For example, selective serotonin reuptake inhibitors also are effective against anxiety, without the risk of abuse and dependence. The attitude of the physician, as perceived by the patient, influences the frequency and duration of use of benzodiazepines (134); thus, good communication about the proper use of these drugs is essential. There is considerable use of benzodiazepines by individuals for whom the drug was not prescribed; in these cases, benzodiazepines are obtained by diversion from medical use.

Benzodiazepines are prescribed more often to women than to men; unlike most other drugs, benzodiazepine dependence is more common in women than men (135). Benzodiazepine dependence is more likely to develop when the drugs are used for long periods or at high doses (135), an important consideration to keep in mind when prescribing. There is an increased risk of dependence in individuals who abuse alcohol and other drugs or who also take antidepressants (135). The role of benzodiazepine half-life in the dependence liability of a particular drug is a subject of debate (135). Patients who use benzodiazepines daily or almost daily, such as patients with chronic illnesses, have higher rates of prolonged use (136).

Benzodiazepines produce subjective effects similar to those of alcohol and cause dose-dependent performance impairment (137). When used alone, benzodiazepines are relatively safe against overdose but can be fatal when combined with alcohol (138).

The abrupt cessation of benzodiazepine use can result in potentially fatal withdrawal symptoms, in particular seizures. Benzodiazepine doses should be tapered off gradually to avoid these complications. Side effects seen during even tapered withdrawal may include insomnia, anxiety, headache, and agitation, but it is unclear whether these are caused by the withdrawal itself or the underlying condition for which the drug was used (24, 135). Although older women do not fit the stereotype of a population likely to abuse drugs, they are at risk for prescription drug abuse, in particular benzodiazepines.

Benzodiazepines often are prescribed inappropriately to older patients, who are at risk for prolonged use of the drug (136). Older individuals who use benzodiazepines show an increased risk of functional decline, but this may be caused by the underlying condition for which the benzodiazepine was prescribed, and not to the drug itself (139). Increased rates of urinary incontinence are associated with benzodiazepine use in the elderly (140).

In pregnancy, as at other times, benzodiazepines should be used at the lowest dose necessary and for the shortest amount of time possible. Prescribing a smaller dose to be taken two or three times per day, rather than one larger dose once per day, may reduce the incidence of problems relating to high peak concentrations of benzodiazepine. It is preferable to use drugs with known histories and safety records (141).

Most of the data on benzodiazepines in pregnancy come from studies of diazepam (pregnancy category D). The available data indicate that diazepam probably is not teratogenic. Some older studies suggested that diazepam might increase the risk of cleft lip or palate and inguinal hernia, but this has not been confirmed (132). Diazepam should be avoided or tapered in the weeks before delivery to minimize the risk of withdrawal or floppy infant syndrome. Diazepam is not recommended during breastfeeding because it is passed into breast milk and may cause lethargy in the infant (141).

Club Drugs

There are numerous club drugs, including MDMA (ecstasy), flunitrazepam (Rohypnol), gamma-hydroxybutyrate (GHB), and ketamine. In addition to the recreational use associated with dance parties and raves (underground dance and drug events), many club drugs reportedly have been used to facilitate acquaintance rape (see "Sexual Assault" chapter). However, whereas media attention focuses heavily on "date rape drugs" such as GHB, flunitrazepam, and ketamine, clinicians need to be aware—and educate their patients—that the number one date rape drug by far is alcohol (142).

Ecstasy

Ecstasy, also known as X or E, is perhaps the best-known club drug and often is used at raves, either alone or in combination with other drugs. It is taken orally in pill form (96). It is important to note that although ecstasy is supposed to consist of MDMA only, products sold as ecstasy often contain a variety of other substances instead of or in addition to MDMA. Commonly substituted compounds include 3,4-methylenedioxyamphetamine, 3,4-methylene-dioxyethamphetamine (known as Eve), and para-methoxyamphetamine. Some of these alternate drugs, especially paramethoxyamphetamine, are significantly more toxic than MDMA, and their use has resulted in fatalities (143). Even with the use of testing kits, it is difficult for consumers to know if the ecstasy they ingest is in fact MDMA (144), which itself has an undeserved reputation of safety among users. Although most ecstasy users use multiple substances at the same time, there have been MDMA-related deaths in which MDMA is the only drug detected.

Subjective effects often reported by MDMA users include feelings of stimulation, hallucinations, a sense of well-being, feelings of empathy and closeness to others (145), as well as the stimulatory properties common to amphetamines. Because of this pattern of subjective experience, MDMA and similar drugs often are classified as enactogens. There are isolated reports of MDMA dependence; however, many individuals who start using MDMA as adolescents or young adults spontaneously stop in their 20s (146).

Use of MDMA can lead to lethally high body temperatures, especially when taken during strenuous physical activity like dancing or in a warm environment, such as a crowded nightclub (147). The risks of MDMA-associated hyperthermia are widely known among consumers of this drug and drinking large doses of water often is suggested as a remedy. However, when combined with excessive fluid consumption, MDMA use can bring about life-threatening hyponatremia, possibly by causing inappropriate secretion of antidiuretic hormone (148). Use of MDMA also produces acute cardiovascular and hormonal effects, increasing blood pressure level; heart rate; and levels of prolactin, cortisol, and dehydro-epiandrosterone (145). Other side effects of MDMA include bruxism, anorexia, and ataxia (143). It has been suggested that MDMA may suppress the immune system (149). Rarely, liver damage has been reported, although the role of MDMA itself, as opposed to contaminants or other co-administered drugs, is unclear (96).

The most worrisome side effect of MDMA is its potential for neurotoxicity. It appears to cause persistent impairment of the brain's serotonergic system (150). It is possible, but not certain, that the brain may recover eventually from these changes if MDMA use is discontinued (150). Users of MDMA perform more poorly on tests of cognitive function than do users of other drugs (151). Users of MDMA also have higher rates of anxiety disorders, eating disorders, and major depression than the general population, but it is not known whether the increased incidence of these disorders is causally associated with their drug use (152).

Because MDMA, like other club drugs, is used recreationally by young individuals, it is ingested by many women of childbearing age. A prospective follow-up of 136 infants exposed to MDMA in utero suggests it increases the risk of congenital abnormalities, particularly cardiovascular and musculoskeletal (153). However, women who use MDMA during pregnancy seem to have higher rates of other risk factors for complications, such as smoking, heavy drinking, and exposure to other drugs, making determination of the causal role of MDMA difficult (154).

Flunitrazepam

Flunitrazepam, a benzodiazepine, is used recreationally to produce pleasurable subjective effects similar to those of alcohol (155). Sometimes referred to by the street names "roofies" or "rophies," this drug is taken orally in pill form or dissolved into a drink. Flunitrazepam is not legally available in the United States; its use appears more prevalent in regions near the Mexican border or in areas with high rates of travel to Mexico or other countries where the drug is sold legally (156). Flunitrazepam is widely available in Europe, Mexico, and Columbia for the treatment of severe sleep disorders.

Flunitrazepam acts rapidly and produces visual and gastrointestinal disturbances, urinary retention, disinhibition, relaxation of voluntary muscles, hypotension, and psychomotor impairment, the actual degree of which often is underestimated by users (157). Flunitrazepam generally is taken with alcohol or other drugs (155), a finding of concern given that benzodiazepines potentiate the effects of alcohol, and, thus,

increases the risk of overdose. Like other benzodiazepines, flunitrazepam can cause dependence (158) and produce withdrawal symptoms when discontinued (159). Many recreational flunitrazepam users are unaware of the health risks associated with this drug (155). The effects of flunitrazepam in pregnancy are unknown and the drug clearly is passed into breast milk (93).

Gamma-hydroxybutyrate

Gamma-hydroxybutyrate (GHB) occurs naturally within the body as a by-product of gama-aminobutyric acid (GABA) metabolism. Exogenous GHB, classified as a dissociative anesthetic (96), was recently approved by the FDA as a treatment for narcolepsy (160). The nonmedical use of GHB originally became popular among bodybuilders because of its strength-enhancing properties, and then crossed over to the dance club and rave scene when its intoxicating effects became known (96).

Gamma-hydroxybutyrate produces effects similar to those of alcohol (161); users report feelings of euphoria (162). Exogenous GABA binds to GHB and GABA receptors and may act by increasing the GABA pool in the central nervous system (163). Although many individuals use GHB only occasionally (162), some users report taking the drug every few hours around the clock because of its short half-life (161).

Most GHB intended for recreational purposes is synthesized in clandestine laboratories; it often is sold under the names "liquid ecstasy," "grievous bodily harm," and "Georgia home boy." Gamma-hydroxybutyrate is taken orally (96), most commonly in liquid form; some users report a salty or soapy taste (96). Because of its illicit manufacture, the actual concentration of the drug can vary widely (162).

Many case reports indicate that GHB use can lead to dependence on the drug (164). Acute GHB intoxication can produce vomiting, bradycardia, and respiratory depression. Gamma-hydroxybutyrate acts synergistically with alcohol and other central nervous system depressants, thus increasing the risk of respiratory depression (163), a serious concern given that GHB often is used in combination with other drugs (162). Many users report experiencing an overdose on at least one occasion (162). The main risk in overdose is respiratory depression, sometimes to the point of coma (163). Most users who come to medical attention recover without lasting ill effects.

Table 12. Effects of Commonly Abused Substances

Depressants

	Nervous System	Cardiovascular System	Gastrointestinal/ Renal System	Musculoskeletal System	Behavior
Alcohol	Impaired psychologic and cognitive functioning (1)	Women achieve higher blood alcohol concentration levels more quickly when consuming the same amount as men (2).	Women have more periods of alcohol hepatitis leading to cirrhosis or cancer, and are at greater risk of liver disease by drinking less and over a shorter time (3).	Decreases bone formation ***Moderate*** Increases parathyroid hormone, calcitonin, and estrogen (4) Decreases bone loss in post-menopausal women (5) ***Chronic*** Decreases vitamin D formation (4)	Psychologic and social effects are more severe for women. Increased psychosexual dysfunction, anxiety, low self-esteem and bulimia, suicidal ideation, and self-harm (6)
Barbiturates	***Short-term*** Central nervous system depression, death, shock syndrome, apnea ***Chronic*** Insomnia, weight loss, and seizures	***Short-term*** Tachycardia, hypotension, circulatory collapse, vasodilator ***Chronic*** Postural hypotension ***Delivery*** Postpartum hemorrhage	***Short-term*** Anuria ***Chronic*** Nausea and vomiting	***Short-term*** Areflexia ***Withdrawal*** Weakness ***Chronic*** Muscle twitches	***Short-term*** Paradoxical excitement, euphoria in those with severe pain, excitement or hyperactivity in children ***Chronic*** Anxiety, severe hallucinations, and delirium
Benzodiazepines	Psychosis, delirium, depersonalization ***Short-term*** Slurred speech, confusion, coma, seizures (1) ***Withdrawal*** Dysphoria, anorexia, insomnia, blurred vision, memory and concentration impairment, paresthesia, hallucinations (1)	***Short-term*** Hypotension (1)	***Withdrawal*** Vomiting, diarrhea, and abdominal cramps	***Short-term*** Impaired coordination, diminished reflexes (1) ***Dependence*** Ataxia ***Withdrawal*** Tremors, muscle cramps (1)	Anxiety, agitation, irritability, confusion, abnormal behavior, hyperexcitability, excessive extroversion, and worsening depression or suicidal ideation (1)
Flunitrazepam	***Short-term*** Visual disturbances and anterograde amnesia	Hypotension	***Short-term*** Gastrointestinal disturbances and urinary retention	***Short-term*** Disinhibition and relaxation of voluntary muscles	—

Stimulants

	Nervous System	Cardiovascular System	Gastrointestinal/ Renal System	Musculoskeletal System	Behavior
Cocaine	***Short-term*** Unconsciousness, convulsions, and death	***Short-term*** Increased heart rate	***Short-term*** Nausea and vomiting	***Short-term*** Tremors and increased reflexes	***Short-term*** Nervousness, restlessness, excitement, euphoria, dysphoria, hallucinations, and anxiousness

Reproductive System	Skin	Respiratory System	Passed Into Breast Milk?	Interactions/Immune Response	Effects on Pregnancy and Neonate
Short-term Impairs libido and sexual gratification (7) Unintended pregnancy (8) **Chronic** Inadequate functioning of ovaries, hormonal deficiencies, sexual dysfunction, and infertility (9, 10, 11) Increased risk of breast cancer.	Acceleration of the aging process (12)	Strongly increases the risk of cancers of the oral cavity, pharynx, and larynx (13)	Yes	Depresses immune response (14)	Smaller weight, height, head circumference, palpebral fissure width (15) Increased risk for attention deficit hyperactivity disorder (16) Decreased learning and memory skills (15) Risk of stillbirth and infant mortality (17)
Impairs libido and sexual gratification (18)	**Short-term** Cold, clammy, bulbous, cutaneous lesions, sweat gland necrosis	**Short-term** Respiratory depression, respiratory arrest, central hypoventilation, laryngospasm, bronchospasm, and coughing	Yes	Decreased effectiveness of oral contraceptives Interacts with other central nervous system depressants, corticosteroids, tricyclic antidepressants, disulfiram, oral anticoagulants, and codeine (18) Contraindicated with griseofulvin and doxycycline (18)	Increased fetal abnormalities, hemorrhagic disease of the newborn, withdrawal symptoms, and respiratory distress (19)
Changes in libido, menstrual irregularities, failure to ovulate, gynecomastia, and galactorrhea (1)	**Withdrawal** Sweating	**Short-term** Respiratory depression, apnea	Yes	Interactions with alcohol, disulfiram, azole antifungal, macrolide antibiotics, human immunodeficiency virus protease inhibitors, calcium channel blocking agents, fluvoxamine, nefazodone, and sympathomimetic drugs (1) **Chlordiazepoxide** May cause a false-positive result in the Granindex pregnancy test (19)	**Chronic use** Increased risk of congenital malformations, withdrawal symptoms in the newborn (19) **Use before delivery** Increased fetal heart rate, hypoactivity, hypotonicity, hypothermia, apnea, feeding problems, and hyperbilirubinemia (19)
—	—	—	Yes	Side effects increased with alcohol	—
Data not adequate to prove reproductive damage in humans	**Chronic** Ischemic mucosal damage and perforation of septum	**Short-term** Irregular Cheyne-Stokes respiration	Yes	Contraindicated with epinephrine or vasopressors	Placental abruption, maternal death (20) Subtle cognitive and motor changes (21)

(continued)

Table 12. Effects of Commonly Abused Substances *(continued)*

Stimulants *(continued)*

	Nervous System	Cardiovascular System	Gastrointestinal/ Renal System	Musculoskeletal System	Behavior
Methamphetamine	*Short-term* Insomnia, dizziness, headache, blurred vision, and anorexia (1) *Long-term* Neurotoxic symptoms similar to Parkinson's (22) Dependence and addiction, psychosis (23, 24)	*Short-term* Hypertension, hypotension, tachycardia, palpitations, arrhythmia, and stroke (21) *Injection users* Pericarditis (23)	*Short-term* Nausea, vomiting, abdominal cramps, diarrhea, constipation, dry mouth, and unpleasant taste (1)	*Short-term* Tremor, exacerbation of motor tics, vocal tics, and Tourette's disorder	*Short-term* Nervousness, irritability, talkativeness, hyperexcitability May have violent behavior and paranoia (23)
Methylphenidate	*Short-term* Headache, seizures, and coma (1) *Long-term* Insomnia	*Short-term* Angina, tachycardia, cardiac arrhythmia, and palpitation (1) *Long-term* Anemia	*Short-term* Vomiting and nausea (1) *Long-term* Hepatic coma and abnormal liver function	*Short-term* Hyperreflexia and twitching (1) *Long-term* Tics in children with attention deficit hyper-activity disorder (1)	*Short-term* Confusion, delirium, euphoria, hallucinations, toxic psychosis, and agitation (1) *Long-term* Nervousness, jitteriness, and social withdrawal (1)
Nicotine	*Toxicity* Dizziness (1) *Withdrawal* Difficulty concentrating, depression, headache, drowsiness, and electroencephalo-gram changes (1)	Increased cardiovascular disease (1) *Withdrawal* Bradycardia, hypotension	*Toxicity* Abdominal pain (1) *Withdrawal* Gastrointestinal disturbances (1)	*Toxicity* Tremor and weakness (18)	*Toxicity* Insomnia (1) *Withdrawal* Irritability, anxiety, restlessness, impatience, hostility, and frustration (1)
Amphetamine	*Acute* Psychosis, disorientation, delusions, and hallucinations (1) *Chronic* Dependence, can look like schizophrenia (1)	*Acute* Palpitations, tachypnea, hypertension or hypotension, heart block, extra systoles, and chest pain (1)	*Acute* Nausea, vomiting, diarrhea, and abdominal cramps (1)	Tremor, exacerbation of motor and phonic tics of Tourette's disorder	*Acute* Confusion, delirium, belligerence, restlessness, panic, suicidal or homicidal tendencies *Chronic* Continuous chewing or teeth grinding movements (1)
MDMA	Confusion, insomnia, drug craving, and blurred vision (25) *Long-term* Brain cell damage and paranoia	Tachycardia, hypertension, and heart failure (25)	Hepatic failure, nausea and vomiting, electrolyte disturbances, and kidney failure (26)	Muscle tension and involuntary teeth clenching (25)	Confusion, amnesia, impaired cognition, impulsiveness, aggression, depression, and anxiety

Reproductive System	Skin	Respiratory System	Passed Into Breast Milk?	Interactions	Effects on Pregnancy and Neonate
Changes in libido	*Injection users* Skin abscesses (23)	Rapid respiration (22)	Yes (18)	Contraindicated with monoamine oxidase inhibitors and history of drug abuse (18)	Teratogenic and embryocidal in animals. Preterm delivery, low birth weight, agitation with neonatal withdrawal (10) Neurotoxic response in male offspring (23)
Adequate data not available to prove in humans	*Street use* Superficial abscesses (1) **Long-term** Rash, exfoliate dermatitis, and easy bruising (1)	*Street use* Pulmonary talc granulomata (1) *Long-term* Upper respiratory tract infection (1)	Most likely yes	Contraindicated with monoamine oxidase inhibitors (1) Inhibits metabolism of tricyclic antidepressants, selective serotonin reuptake inhibitors, coumarin, anti-coagulants, anti-convulsants *Other interactions* Pressor agents	Adequate studies not available to prove teratogenic in humans (18).
Earlier menopause Decreases fertility in women and men	*Toxicity* Rash and sweating (1)	Chronic obstructive pulmonary disease and lung cancer (1)	Yes	Amitriptyline, desipramine, aminophylline, clomipramine, doxepin, amoxapine, dyphylline, theophylline, riluzole, oxtriphylline, and imipramine Contraindicated with oral contraceptives in female smokers older than 35 years	Increased risk for stillbirth, low birth weight neonates, fetal growth restriction, spontaneous abortion, and perinatal mortality (1)
Adequate data not available to prove in humans	*Chronic* Ulcers of lip and tongue (1)	Pulmonary hypertension, respiratory failure (1)	Yes	Contraindicated with monoamine oxidase inhibitors, general anesthesia (1), tricyclic antidepressants, and antihypertensives (18)	Intrauterine growth restriction, premature delivery, increased maternal and neonatal morbidity
Increased libido and decreased sexual performance	Hyper-thermia, sweating, and chills (25)	Tachypnea	Yes	Alcohol, cocaine, phencyclidine, and lysergic acid diethylamide	Possible increased risk of cardiovascular and musculoskeletal defects (27) Possible impaired memory and cognition (28)

(continued)

Table 12. Effects of Commonly Abused Substances *(continued)*

Stimulants *(continued)*

	Nervous System	Cardiovascular System	Gastrointestinal/ Renal System	Musculoskeletal System	Behavior
Khat	Hyperactivity, psychosis, and mydriasis (29)	Risk of myocardial infarction, tachycardia, and hypertension (29, 30)	Anorexia and constipation (29)	Hyperactivity (29)	Loquacity, emotional instability, manic behavior (29)

Opiate Agonists

	Nervous System	Cardiovascular System	Gastrointestinal/ Renal System	Musculoskeletal System	Behavior
Methadone	***Short-term*** Miosis ***Long-term*** Severe psychologic or physical dependence	Red eyes caused by vasodilatation Females have serum concentrations 25% higher than men	Decreased gastric motility, constipation, reduction in gastric, biliary, and pancreatic secretions	Twitching (18)	Nervousness and confusion (18)

Opiods

	Nervous System	Cardiovascular System	Gastrointestinal/ Renal System	Musculoskeletal System	Behavior
Codeine, fentanyl, morphine, and oxycodone	Euphoria, sedation, and dysphoria (18)	Bradycardia and orthostatic hypotension (18)	Vomiting, nausea, constipation, abdominal pain, diarrhea, and difficulty urinating (18)	Smooth muscle hypotonicity; skeletal and thoracic muscle rigidity	Confusion, anxiety, and depression (18)
Heroin	Euphoria, drowsiness, and coma; highly addictive	Hypotension, bradycardia, venous sclerosis, and septicemia	Constipation and stomach cramps	Muscle cramps	Disorientation, delirium, and reduced anxiety ***Withdrawal*** Anxiety and irritability

Hallucinogens

	Nervous System	Cardiovascular System	Gastrointestinal/ Renal System	Musculoskeletal System	Behavior
Lysergic acid diethylamide (LSD)	Heightened sensorium, synesthesia, hallucinations, sleeplessness, and dilated pupils (34)	Tachycardia and hypertension	Anorexia and dry mouth (34)	Tremors (34)	Paranoia, unpredictable, changing emotions, long lasting psychoses (34)
Phencyclidine (PCP)	***Short-term*** Delusions, suicidal thoughts, and hallucinations ***High dosage*** Seizures and coma	***Moderate dosage*** Hypertension and tachycardia ***High dosage*** Hypotension and bradycardia	Nausea and vomiting ***High dosages*** Acute renal failure	Muscle rigidity and loss of coordination (35) ***Adolescents*** Interference with growth and developmental hormones (35)	***Short-term*** Paranoia, violence, agitation, irritability, and feeling invulnerable Addictive craving and compulsion (35)

Reproductive System	Skin	Respiratory System	Passed Into Breast Milk?	Interactions	Effects on Pregnancy and Neonate
Adequate data not available to prove in humans.	Adequate data not available to prove in humans	Adequate data not available to prove in humans	Adequate data not available to prove in humans	Ampicillin, Amoxycillin (31)	Decreased maternal weight gain and risk of low birth weight (32)
Adequate data not available to prove in humans (18)	Puritis, flushing, and sweating (18)	Cough suppression, depressed respiration	Yes	Antianxiolytics, antipsychotics, barbiturates, monoamine oxidase inhibitors, central nervous system depressants, protease inhibitors, alcohol	Respiratory depression (18) Effective prenatal maintenance treatment decreases newborn complications (33)
Possible impaired fertility and reduced sex drive (18)	Uticaria (1)	Respiratory depression and hypoventilation (18)	Yes, may cause drowsiness and respiratory depression in infant (18).	Potentiate central nervous system depressants, phenothiazines, tricyclic antidepressants, monoamine oxidase inhibitors, and alcohol (18) *Fentanyl* Macrolide antibiotics, certain azole derivatives, antinfective agents, most human immunodeficiency virus protease inhibitors (18)	Respiratory depression, withdrawal, irritability, excessive crying, tremors, hyperreflexia, fever, vomiting, and diarrhea (18) Morphine shown to be teratogenic in rodents (19)
Adequate data not available to prove in humans	Cyanosis of nails and lips, flushing of skin, severe itching, and boils	Slow, shallow, labored breathing	Yes	Immune reactions with the substances added to heroin may contribute to arthritis	*Withdrawal* Intrauterine death from meconium aspiration, low birth weight, increased perinatal mortality Impaired behavioral, perceptual, and organizational abilities
None documented	Hyper-thermia and sweating (34)	Hyperventlation is common	Yes	—	—
Enhances sexual pleasure	Flushing and profuse sweating (35)	Rapid, shallow respirations (35)	Yes	Alcohol, crack cocaine, heroin, and MDMA	Irritability, jitteriness, hypertonicity, and poor feeding

(continued)

Table 12. Effects of Commonly Abused Substances *(continued)*

Hallucinogens *(continued)*

	Nervous System	Cardiovascular System	Gastrointestinal/ Renal System	Musculoskeletal System	Behavior
Marijuana	Impaired memory and learning, tolerance Impaired balance, posture, psychosis, toxic psychosis (36)	Dilated blood vessels in eyes, hypertension, tachycardia, and increased risk of myocardial infarction (36)	Higher THC serum levels and increased central nervous system effects when digested	Impaired coordination (36)	Depression, anxiety, personality disturbances, and memory loss Long-term use can lead to addiction (36).

Dissociative Anesthetics

	Nervous System	Cardiovascular System	Gastrointestinal/ Renal System	Musculoskeletal System	Behavior
Ketamine	Distorted perceptions of sight and sound, hallucinations, flashbacks, amnesia Cerebral anoxia with large doses (37, 38)	Hypertension and heart rate abnormalities (38)	*Large doses* Vomiting (38)	Impaired coordination and muscle rigidity (38)	Impaired perception and paranoid ideation (37) Dependence and tolerance with frequent use (37, 38)

Inhalant

	Nervous System	Cardiovascular System	Gastrointestinal/ Renal System	Musculoskeletal System	Behavior
Various substances	Damage to nerve sheath (toluene), cognition, vision, and hearing Dementia Lack of oxygen to brain (nitrous oxide) Glassy, glazed, or watery eyes and loss of appetite	Irregular and rapid heart rhythms, cardiac failure, Sudden Sniffing, Death (butane, propane, aerosols), red blood cell damage (amyl nitrite, butyl nitrate, benzene), increased risk of leukemia (benzene), reduced oxygen carrying capacity of blood (methylene chloride), blackouts, depression of heart muscle function (nitrous oxide, hexane)	Liver damage (freon, toluene), cirrhosis of the liver (trichloroethylene), and kidney damage (toluene)	Alterations in motor coordination and limb spasms (nitrous oxide, hexane)	Behavioral changes, slurred speech, problems in school, excitability, and irritability

Steroids

	Nervous System	Cardiovascular System	Gastrointestinal/ Renal System	Musculoskeletal System	Behavior
Testosterone	Psychotic manifestations, affective disorders (1)	Cardiovascular disease (1)	Hepatotoxicity and fluid retention (1)	Tears of muscles and tendons Inhibition of bone growth in adolescents	Increased aggression and antisocial behavior (1)

Reproductive System	Skin	Respiratory System	Passed Into Breast Milk?	Interactions	Effects on Pregnancy and Neonate
Potentially affects reproductive hormones in females (36)	Associated with burning and stinging of the mouth and throat (36)	Increased respiratory infections, cough with phlegm production, chronic obstructive-pulmonary disease, and increased risk of head and neck cancers (36)	Yes	Immune system impairment (36)	Altered response to visual stimuli and increased tremulousness\n\nChildren have more behavioral problems (36)
Enhancement of sexual and sensory experience (37)	Increased salivary secretions	Respiratory depression (38) and increased bronchial secretions	Most likely yes	Fentanyl (39)	Depression of the newborn if used at the time of delivery (19)
Reproductive system damage (benzene, trichloroethylene), associated with unsafe sex, increased risk of HIV, AIDS, and hepatitis	Paint or other products on face, spots or sores around nose or mouth	Asphyxiation, suffocation, choking and respiratory obstruction (freon)	Yes	Suppressed immunologic function (amyl nitrite, butyl nitrate, benzene)	—
Clitoral enlargement, menstrual irregularities, androgenic alopecia, deepened voice, breast atrophy, and inhibition of gonadotropin secretion (1)	Acne	Insufficient data	Not known (1)	Increases oral anticoagulant action\n\nInterferes with total serum thyroxine measurement (1)	Clitoral hypertrophy, abnormal vaginal development, and persistent urogenital sinus (1)

(continued)

Table 12. Effects of Commonly Abused Substances *(continued)*

1. American Society of Health-System Pharmacists. AHFS drug information: 2004. Bethesda (MD): ASHSP; 2004.
2. Frezza M, di Padova C, Pozzato G, Terpin M, Baraona E, Lieber CS. High blood alcohol levels in women. The role of decreased gastric alcohol dehydrogenase activity and first-pass metabolism [published errata appear in N Engl J Med 1990;323:553; N Engl J Med 1990;322:1540]. N Engl J Med 1990;322:95–9.
3. Maher JJ. Exploring alcohol's effects on liver function. Alcohol Health Res World 1997;21:5–12.
4. Sampson HW. Alcohol's harmful effects on bone. Alcohol Health Res World 1998;22:190–4.
5. Turner R, Sibonga JD. Effects of alcohol use and estrogen on bone. Alcohol Res Health 2001;25:276–81.
6. Petrakis IL, Gonzalez G, Rosenheck R, Krystal JH. Comorbidity of alcoholism and psychiatric disorders: an overview. Alcohol Res Health 2002;26:81–9.
7. Emanuele MA, Wezeman F, Emanuele NV. Alcohol's effects on female reproductive function. Alcohol Res Health 2002:26:274–81.
8. Naimi TS, Lipscomb LE, Brewer RD, Gilbert BC. Binge drinking in the preconception period and the risk of unintended pregnancy: implications for women and their children. Pediatrics 2003;111:1136–41.
9. Gabriel K, Hofmann C, Glavas M, Weinberg J. The hormonal effects of alcohol use on the mother and fetus. Alcohol Health and Research World 1998;22:170–7.
10. Alcohol and Hormones. Alcohol Alert. NIAAA 1994 No. 26 PH 352. Bethesda (MD): National Institute on Alcohol Abuse and Alcoholism;1994. Available at: http://www.niaaa.nih.gov/publications/aa26.htm. Retrieved July 26, 2004.
11. Tolstrup JS, Kjaer SK, Holst C, Sharif H, Munk C, Osler M, et al. Alcohol use as predictor for infertility in a representative population of Danish women. Acta Obstet Gynecol Scand 2003;82:744-9
12. Spencer RL, Hutchinson KE. Alcohol, aging, and the stress response. Alcohol Res Health 1999;23:272–83.
13. Bernard V, Blangiardo M, Carlo La Vecchia C, Corrao G. Alcohol consumption and the risk of cancer: a meta-analysis. Alcohol Res Health 2001;25:263–70.
14. Kovacs EJ, Messingham KA. Influence of alcohol and gender on immune response. Alcohol Res Health 2002;26:257–63.
15. Prenatal exposure to alcohol. In: 10th special report to the US Congress on Alcohol and Health: highlights from current research. Bethesda (MD): National Institutes of Health; 2000. NIH Publication No. 00-1583. p. 283–322.
16. Richardson GA, Ryan C, Willford J, Day NL, Goldschmidt L. Prenatal alcohol and marijuana exposure effects on neuropsychological outcomes at 10 years. Neurotoxicol and Teratol 2002;24:309–20.
17. Kesmodel U, Wisborg K, Olsen SF, Henriksen TB, Secher NJ. Moderate alcohol intake during pregnancy and the risk of stillbirth and death in the first year of life. Am J of Epidemiol 2002;155:305–12.
18. PDR: physicians' desk reference; 2004. 5th ed. Montvale (NJ): Thompson PDR; 2004.
19. Briggs GG, Freeman RK, Yaffe SJ. Drugs in pregnancy and lactation. 6th edition. Philadelphia (PA): Lippincott Williams and Wilkins; 2002.
20. Martin K. New animal model simulates human exposure, confirms harm from prenatal cocaine. NIDA Notes 2003;18(1):5, 14.
21. Singer LT, Salrator A, Arendt R, Minnes S, Farkas K, Kliegman R. Effects of cocaine/polydrug exposure and maternal psychological distress on infant birth outcomes. Neurotoxicol Teratol 2002;24:127–35.
22. Methamphetamine. NIDA Info Facts. Bethesda (MD): National Institutes of Health; 2003. Available at: http://www.drugabuse.gov/infofax/methamphetamine.html. Retrieved July 26, 2004.
23. Methamphetamine: abuse and addiction. National Institute on Drug Abuse Research Report Series. Bethesda (MD): National Institutes of Health; 2002. Available at: http://www.nida.nih.gov/PDF/RRMetham.pdf. Retrieved July 26, 2004.
24. Heller A, Babula N, Lew R, Heller B, Won L. Gender-dependent enhanced adult neurotoxic response to methamphetamine following fetal exposure to the drug. J Pharmacol Exp Ther 2001;298:769–79.
25. MDMA (Ecstasy). NIDA Info Facts. National Institutes of Health; Bethesda (MD):2004. Available at: http://www.drugabuse.gov/PDF/infofacts/MDMA04.pdf. Retrieved July 26, 2004.
26. Doyon S. The many faces of ecstasy. Curr Opin Pediatr 2001;13:170–6.
27. McElhatton PR, Bateman DN, Evans C, Pughe KR, Thomas SH. Congenital anomalies after prenatal ecstasy exposure. Lancet 1999;354:1441–2.
28. Broening HW, Morford LL, Inman-Wood SL, Fukumura M, Vorhees CV. 3,4-methylene-dioxymethamphetamine (ecstasy)-induced learning and memory impairments depend on the age of exposure during early development. J Neurosci 2001;21:3228–35.
29. Drugs and chemicals of concern: khat, quat, tschat, miraa (cathinone, cathine). Washington, DC: US Dept. of Justice, Drug Enforcement Administration; 2001. Available at: http://www.deadiversion.usdoj.gov/drugs_concern/khat/summary.htm. Retrieved July 26, 2004.
30. Alkadi HO, Noman MA, Al-Thobhani AK, Al-Mekhlafi FS, Raja'a YA. Clinical and experimental evaluation of the effect of khat-induced myocardial infarction. Saudi Med J 2002;23:1195–8.
31. Attef OA, Ali AA, Ali HM. Effect of khat chewing on the bioavailability of ampicillin and amoxycillin. J Antimicrob Chemother 1997;39:523–5.
32. Abdul Ghani N, Eriksson M, Kristiansson B, Qirbi A. The influence of khat-chewing on birth-weight in full-term infants. Soc Sci Med 1987;24:625–7.
33. Berghella V, Lim PJ, Hill MK, Cherpes J, Chennat J, Kaltenbach K. Maternal methadone dose and neonatal withdrawal. Am J Obstet Gynecol 2003;189:312–7.
34. LSD. NIDA Info Facts. Bethesda (MD): National Institutes of Health; 1999. Available at:http://www.drugabuse.gov/Infofax/lsd.html. Retrieved July 26, 2004.
35. PCP (Phencyclidine). NIDA Info Facts. Bethesda (MD): National Institutes of Health; 2003. Available at: http://www.drugabuse.gov/PDF/infofacts/PCP04.pdf. Retrieved July 26, 2004.
36. Marijuana. NIDA Info Facts. Bethesda (MD): National Institutes of Health; 2004. Available at: http://www.drugabuse.gov/Infofax/marijuana.html. Retrieved July 26, 2004.

Table 12. Effects of Commonly Abused Substances *(continued)*

37. Lim DK. Ketamine associated psychedelic effects and dependence. Singapore Med J 2003;44:31–4.

38. National Clearinghouse for Drug and Alcohol Information. Ketamine: a fact sheet. Rockville (MD): NCADI, 2004. Available at: http://www.health.org/nongovpubs/ketamine/. Retrieved July 26, 2004.

39. Nadeson R, Tucker A, Bajunaki E, Goodchild CS. Potentiation by ketamine of fentanyl antinociception. I. An experimental study in rats showing that ketamine administered by non-spinal routes targets spinal cord antinociceptive systems. Br J Anaesth 2002;88:685–91.

Gamma-hydroxybutyrate withdrawal syndrome is similar to that seen in withdrawal from alcohol and benzodiazepines (161, 163). Symptoms include agitation, psychosis, tachycardia, hallucinations, hypertension, and insomnia (163, 164). Withdrawal appears to occur more commonly in individuals who use GHB regularly, taking it around the clock, rather than those who binge occasionally (163).

The legal, readily available, industrial solvents gamma-butyrolactone and 1,4-butanediol are sometimes substituted for GHB because they are rapidly converted to GHB when ingested and produce similar effects (96, 163). Both substances are associated with withdrawal syndrome similar to that of GHB (165). Gamma-butyrolactone is sometimes referred to as "Blue Nitro." There are no data on the safety of GHB in pregnancy.

Ketamine

Ketamine is a dissociative anesthetic used legally in veterinary and human medicine, where it is classified as a Schedule III drug. An N-methyl-D-aspartate-receptor antagonist, ketamine produces changes in perception, hallucinations, depersonalization, and derealization (166). The nonmedical use of ketamine often is associated with dance parties and raves, where it frequently is used in combination with other drugs (167). Individuals who partake of the drug in such venues often refer to it by the names "Special K," "Vitamin K," and "Cat Valium." Ketamine is administered mainly by snorting and less frequently by injection and orally (167). Illicitly used ketamine is obtained by diversion from legal sources (96).

At high doses, ketamine can produce tachycardia, rhabdomyolysis (168), vomiting, amnesia, delirium, and agitation (167); however, the use of ketamine poses few overdose risks, except possibly aspiration from vomiting in unconscious users (96). The case literature contains reports of ketamine dependence (169), and regular, chronic use of ketamine may be linked to memory impairment (170).

There are no data on the safety of ketamine use during pregnancy. However, animal studies suggest that N-methyl-D-aspartate-blocking drugs damage the developing fetal brain in rats (171).

Sexual Assault

Considerable media attention has focused on the use of flunitrazepam, GHB, and ketamine as "date rape drugs" because of their ability to produce amnesia, weakness, and loss of consciousness (157, 172). These drugs can be introduced into a victim's drink without her knowledge because they lack odor and strong taste, and in the case of GHB and ketamine, color. To reduce the likelihood of criminal misuse of flunitrazepam, the manufacturer now adds a dye to the odorless and tasteless drug so that it will turn blue when slipped into a drink. The obstetrician–gynecologist should counsel adolescents and women who date that they should never drink anything that is blue, leave a drink unattended, or accept a drink directly from a stranger. Despite their notoriety, only a small minority of acquaintance rape cases (less than 5%) involves the use of these drugs (142, 173) (see "Sexual Assault" chapter).

Standard urine drug screens do not detect flunitrazepam, GHB, or ketamine. When it is necessary to confirm the presence of these drugs, as for forensic reasons, special urine tests are available (174, 175). However, even specialized testing can produce misleading results. Flunitrazepam may be mistaken for other benzodiazepines, and testing is unreliable below a certain threshold (176). The presence of ketamine may result in a false positive test result for PCP. Hair analysis may be useful in sexual assault cases because it can detect a single exposure to a drug (177, 178).

References

1. Leshner AI. Addiction is a brain disease, and it matters. Science 1997;278:45–7.

2. National Institute on Alcohol Abuse and Alcoholism. Updating estimates of the economic costs of alcohol abuse in the United States: estimates, update methods and data. Rockville (MD): NIAAA; 2000.

3. Leshner AI. Meeting the challenge of reducing health disparities. NIDA Notes 2001;16(1). Available at: http://www.drugabuse.gov/NIDA_Notes/NNVol16N1/DirRepVol16N1.html. Retrieved August 11, 2004.

4. Substance Abuse and Mental Health Administration. Driving after drug or alcohol use report. Rockville (MD): SAMHSA; 2003. Available at: http://oas.samhsa.gov/driverrprt/fnldrf14.html. Retrieved August 13, 2004.

5. National Highway Traffic Safety Administration (NHTSA). Traffic safety facts 2002: a compilation of motor vehicle crash data from the Fatality Analysis Reporting System and the General Estimates System. Washington, DC: US Department of Transportation; 2004.

6. Gillogley KM, Evans AT, Hansen RL, Samuels SH, Batra KK. The perinatal impact of cocaine, amphetamine, and opiate use detected by universal intrapartum screening. Am J Obstet Gynecol 1990;163:1535-42.

7. Chasnoff IJ, Landress HJ, Barrett ME. The prevalence of illicit-drug or alcohol use during pregnancy and discrepancies in mandatory reporting in Pinellas County, Florida. N Engl J Med 1990;322:1202-6.

8. Substance Abuse and Mental Health Services Administration. Results from the 2003 National Household Survey on Drug Abuse: Volume I. Summary of national findings. Rockville (MD): SAMHSA; 2004. Available at: http://oas.samhsa.gov/nhsda/2k3nsduh/2k3ResultsW.pdf. Retrieved October 21, 2004.

9. Day NL, Cottreau CM, Richardson GA. The epidemiology of alcohol, marijuana, and cocaine use among women of childbearing age and pregnant women. Clin Obstet Gynecol 1993;36:232-45.

10. Grant BF, Dawson DA. Age of onset of drug use and its association with DSM-IV drug abuse and dependence: results from the National Longitudinal Alcohol Epidemiologic Survey. J Subst Abuse 1998;10:163-73.

11. Substance Abuse and Mental Health Services Administration. Substance use among pregnant women during 1999 and 2000. NHSDA Report. Rockville (MD): SAMHSA; 2002. Available at: http://www.oas.samhsa.gov/2k2/preg/preg/pdf. Retrieved August 11, 2004.

12. Substance Abuse and Mental Health Services Administration. Summary of findings from the 1999 National Household Survey on Drug Abuse. Rockville (MD): SAMHSA; 2000.

13. Alcohol use among women of childbearing age—United States, 1991-1999 (published erratum appears in MMWR Morb Mortal Wkly Rep 2002;51:308]. MMWR Morb Mortal Wkly Rep 2002;51:273-6.

14. Ebrahim SH, Diekman ST, DeCoufle P, Tully M, Floyd RL. Pregnancy-related alcohol use among women in the United States—1988-95. Prenat Neonatal Med 1999;4:39-46.

15. Substance Abuse and Mental Health Services Administration. Pregnant women in substance abuse treatment. The DASIS Report. Rockville (MD): SAMHSA; 2002. Available at: http://www.oas.samhsa.gov/2k2/pregTX/pregTX.pdf. Retrieved August 12, 2004.

16. American College of Obstetricians and Gynecologists. Illicit drug abuse and dependence in women: a slide lecture presentation. Washington, DC: ACOG; 2002.

17. Becker KL, Walton-Moss B. Detecting and addressing alcohol abuse in women. Nurse Pract 2001;26(10):13-6, 19-23; quiz 24-5.

18. Gold MS, Aronson MD. Screening and diagnosis of patients with alcohol problems. In: UpToDate. Available at: http://www.uptodate.com/physicians/fp_toclst.asp. Retrieved February 18, 2005.

19. Goodwin RD, Hasin DS. Sedative use and misuse in the United States. Addiction 2002;97:555-62.

20. Longo LP, Parran T Jr, Johnson B, Kinsey W. Addiction: part II. Identification and management of the drug-seeking patient. Am Fam Physician 2000;61:2401-8.

21. Weissman DE, Haddox JD, Opioid pseudoaddiction—an iatrogenic syndrome. Pain 1989;36:363-6.

22. Zacny J, Bigelow G, Compton P, Foley K, Iguchi M, Sannerud C. College on Problems of Drug Dependence taskforce on prescription opioid non-medical use and abuse: position statement. Drug Alcohol Depend 2003;69:215-32.

23. Weaver M, Schnoll S. Abuse liability in opioid therapy for pain treatment in patients with an addiction history. Clin J Pain 2002;18(suppl):S61-9.

24. Zitman FG, Couvee JE. Chronic benzodiazepine use in general practice patients with depression: an evaluation of controlled treatment and taper-off: report on behalf of the Dutch Chronic Benzodiazepine Working Group. Br J Psychiatry 2001;178:317-24.

25. Midwest Medical Insurance Company Risk Management Committee. Drug seeking patients: avoid getting caught in their trap. RMS Bulletin 1997;91(3). Available at: http://www.ramseymed.org/bulletin/91-3/16.htm. Retrieved August 11, 2004.

26. Eisenberg DM, Davis RB, Ettner SL, Appel S, Wilkey S, Van Rompay M, et al. Trends in alternative medicine use in the United States, 1990-1997: results of a follow-up national survey. JAMA 1998;280:1569-75.

27. Prochaska JO, Norcross JC, DiClemente CC. Changing for good: the revolutionary program that explains the six stages of change and teaches you how to free yourself from bad habits. New York (NY): W. Morrow; 1994.

28. Nikita MB, Levin FR. Drug abuse. In: Rakel RE, Bope ET, editors. Conn's current therapy. 2004 ed. Philadelphia (PA): Saunders; 2004. p. 1145-50.

29. Rollnick S, Miller WR. What is motivational interviewing? Behav Cogn Psychother 1995;23:325-34.

30. Babor TF, Steinberg K, Anton R, Del Boca F. Talk is cheap: measuring drinking outcomes in clinical trials. J Stud Alcohol 2000;61:55-63.

31. Motivational intervention to reduce alcohol-exposed pregnancies—Florida, Texas, and Virginia, 1997-2001. MMWR Morb Mortal Wkly Rep 2003;52:441-4.

32. At-risk drinking and illicit drug use: ethical issues in obstetric and gynecologic practice. ACOG Committee Opinion No. 294. American College of Obstetricians and Gynecologists. Obstet Gynecol 2004;103:1021–31.

33. Monterroso ER, Hamburger ME, Vlahor D, DesJarlais DC, Ouellet LJ, Altice FL, et al. Prevention of HIV infection in street-recruited injection drug users. The Collaborative Injection Drug User Study (CIDUS). J Acquir Immune Defic Syndr 2000;25:63–70.

34. American College of Obstetricians and Gynecology. Guidelines for Women's Health Care, 2nd ed. Washington, DC: ACOG; 2002.

35. Bradley KA, Boyd-Wickizer J, Powell SH, Burman ML. Alcohol screening questionnaires in women: a critical review. JAMA 1998;280:166–71.

36. Substance Abuse and Mental Health Services Administration. Pregnant, substance-using women: Treatment Improvement Protocol (TIP). Series 2. Rockville (MD): SAMHSA; 1995.

37. Kennedy C, Finkelstein N, Hutchins E, Mahoney J. Improving screening for alcohol use during pregnancy: the Massachusetts ASAP program. Matern Child Health J 2004;8:137–47.

38. Knight JR, Sherritt L, Shrier LA, Harris SK, Chang G. Validity of the CRAFFT substance abuse screening test among adolescent clinic patients. Arch Pediatr Adolesc Med 2002;156:607–13.

39. Jacobs WS, DuPont R, Gold MS. Drug testing and the DSM-IV. Psychiatric Ann 2000;30:583–8.

40. American College of Obstetricians and Gynecology. Patient testing. In: Ethics in obstetrics and gynecology. 2nd ed. Washington, DC: ACOG; 2004. p. 26–8.

41. Adger H, Macdonald DI, Wenger S. Core competencies for involvement of health care providers in the care of children and adolescents in families affected by substance abuse. Pediatrics 1999;103:1083–4.

42. Testing for drugs of abuse in children and adolescents. American Academy of Pediatrics Committee on Substance Abuse. Pediatrics 1996;98:305–7.

43. Burkett G, Gomez-Marin O, Yasin SY, Martinez M. Prenatal care in cocaine-exposed pregnancies. Obstet Gynecol 1998;92:193–200.

44. Washburn AM, Fullilove RE, Fullilove MT, Keenan PA, McGee B, Morris KA, et al. Acupuncture heroin detoxification: a single-blind clinical trial. J Subst Abuse Treat 1993;10:345–51.

45. Reitnauer PJ, Callanan NP, Farber RA, Aylsworth S. Prenatal exposure to disulfiram implicated in the cause of malformations in discordant monozygotic twins. Teratology 1997;56:358–62.

46. Alkermes announces statistically significant reduction in heavy drinking in alcohol dependent patients in Phase III clinical trial of Vivitrex. 2003 Press Release. Cambridge (MA): Alkermes, Inc.; 2003. Available at: http://www.alkermes.com/news/index.asp?id=252. Retrieved August 5, 2004.

47. Schindler SD, Eder H, Ortner R, Rohrmeister K, Lauger M, Fischer G. Neonatal outcome following buprenorphine maintenance during conception and throughout pregnancy. Addiction 2003;98:103–10.

48. Dashe JS, Jackson GL, Olscher DA, Zane EH, Wendel GD Jr. Opioid detoxification in pregnancy. Obstet Gynecol 1998;92:854–8.

49. Hulse G, O'Neil G. Using naltrexone implants in the management of the pregnant heroin user. Aust N Z J Obstet Gynaecol 2002;42:569–73.

50. Avants SK, Margolin A, Holford TR, Kosten TR. A randomized controlled trial of auricular acupuncture for cocaine dependence. Arch Intern Med 2000;160:2305–12.

51. Floyd RL, Belodoff B, Sidhu J, Schulkin J, Ebrahim SH, Sokol RJ. A survey of obstetrician–gynecologists on their patients' use of tobacco and other drugs during pregnancy. Prenat Neonatal Med 2001;6:201–7.

52. Diekman ST, Floyd RL, DeCoufle P, Schulkin J, Ebrahim SH, Sokol RJ. A survey of obstetrician–gynecologists on their patients' alcohol use during pregnancy. Obstet Gynecol 2000;95:756–63.

53. Kaskutas LA. Understanding drinking during pregnancy among urban American Indians and African Americans: health messages, risk beliefs, and how we measure consumption. Alcohol Clin Exp Res 2000;24:1241–50.

54. Jacobson SW, Chiodo LM, Sokol RJ, Jacobson JL. Validity of maternal report of prenatal alcohol, cocaine, and smoking in relation to neurobehavioral outcome. Pediatrics 2002;109:815–25.

55. Lester BM, Elsohly M, Wright LL, Smerigglio VL, Verter J, Bauer CR, et al. The Maternal Lifestyle Study: drug use by meconium toxicology and maternal self-report. Pediatrics 2001;107:309–17.

56. Davis SK. Comprehensive interventions for affecting the parenting effectiveness of chemically dependent women. J Obstet Gynecol Neonatal Nurs 1997;26:604–10.

57. Smith BD, Test MF. The risk of subsequent maltreatment allegations in families with substance-exposed infants. Child Abuse Negl 2002;26:97–114.

58. MacGregor SN, Keith LG, Bachicha JA, Chasnoff IJ. Cocaine abuse during pregnancy: correlation between prenatal care and perinatal outcome. Obstet Gynecol 1989;74:882–5.

59. Brown HL, Britton KA, Mahaffey D, Brizendine E, Hiett AK, Turnquest MA. Methadone maintenance in pregnancy: a reappraisal. Am J Obstet Gynecol 1998;179:459–63.

60. Kuczkowski KM. Labor analgesia for the drug abusing parturient: is there cause for concern? Obstet Gynecol Surv 2003;58:599–608.

61. Mumenthaler MS, Taylor JL, O'Hara R, Yesavage JA. Gender differences in moderate drinking effects. Alcohol Res Health 1999;23:55–64.

62. Baraona E, Abittan CS, Dohmen K, Moretti M, Pozzato G, Chayes ZW, et al. Gender differences in pharmacokinetics of alcohol. Alcohol Clin Exp Res 2001;25:502–7.

63. Holdstock L, de Wit H. Effects of ethanol at four phases of the menstrual cycle. Psychopharmacology (Berl) 2000;150:374–82.

64. Schoenborn CA, Adams PF. Alcohol use among adults: United States, 1997–98. Advance data from vital and health statistics; no. 324. Hyattsville (MD): National Center for Health Statistics; 2001.

65. Rimm E. Alcohol and cardiovascular disease. Curr Atheroscler Rep 2000;2:529–35.

66. Wannamethee SG, Comargo CA Jr, Manson JE, Willett WC, Rimm EB, et al. Alcohol drinking patterns and risk of type 2 diabetes mellitus among younger women. Arch Intern Med 2003;163:1329–36.

67. Becker U, Deis A, Sorensen TR, Gronbaek M, Borch-Johnsen K, Muller CF, et al. Prediction of risk of liver disease by alcohol intake, sex, and age: a prospective population study. Hepatology 1996;23:1025–9.

68. Sato N, Lindros KO, Baraona E, Ikejima K, Mezey E, Jarvelainen HA, et al. Sex difference in alcohol-related organ injury. Alcohol Clin Exp Res 2001;25(suppl ISBRA):40S–45S.

69. Hamajima N, Hirose K, Tajima K, Rohan T, Calle EE, Heath CW Jr, et al. Alcohol, tobacco and breast cancer—collaborative reanalysis of individual data from 53 epidemiological studies, including 58,515 women with breast cancer and 95,067 women without the disease. Collaborative Group on Hormonal Factors in Breast Cancer. Br J Cancer 2002;87:1234–45.

70. Smith-Warner SA, Speigelman D, Yaun SS, van den Brandt PA, Folsom AR, Goldbohm RA, et al. Alcohol and breast cancer in women: a pooled analysis of cohort studies. JAMA 1998;279 (7):535–40.

71. Ellison RC, Zhang Y, McLennan CE, Rothman KJ. Exploring the relation of alcohol consumption to risk of breast cancer. Am J Epidemiol 2001;154:740–7.

72. Zhang Y, Kreger BE, Dorgan JF, Splansky GL, Cupples LA, Ellison RC. Alcohol consumption and risk of breast cancer: the Framingham Study revisited. Am J Epidemiol 1999;149:93–101.

73. Fernandez-Sola J, Nicolas-Arfelis JM. Gender differences in alcoholic cardiomyopathy. J Gend Specif Med 2002;5(1):41–7.

74. John U, Hanke M. Alcohol-attributable mortality in a high per capita consumption country—Germany. Alcohol Alcohol 2002;37:581–5.

75. Henshaw SK. Unintended pregnancy in the United States. Fam Plann Perspect 1998;30:24–9, 46.

76. United States Department of Health and Human Services. Healthy people 2010. Understanding and Improving Health and Objectives for Improving Health. Washington, DC: USDHHS; 2000.

77. Ernhart CB, Sokol RJ, Martier S, Moron P, Nadler D, Ager JW, et al. Alcohol teratogenicity in the human: a detailed assessment of specificity, critical period, and threshold. Am J Obstet Gynecol 1987;156:33–9.

78. Rosett HL. A clinical perspective of the Fetal Alcohol Syndrome. Alcohol Clin Exp Res 1980;4:119–22.

79. Mattson SN, Schoenfeld AM, Riley EP. Teratogenic effects of alcohol on brain and behavior. Alcohol Res Health 2001;25:185–91.

80. Mitchell KT. Fetal alcohol syndrome and other alcohol related birth defects: identification and implications. NADD Bulletin 2001;4:11–14.

81. Burd L, Cox C, Fjelstad K, McCulloch. Screening for Fetal Alcohol Syndrome: Is it feasible and necessary? Addict Biol 2000;5:127–39.

82. Sood B, Delaney-Black V, Covington C, Nordstrom-Klee B, Ager J, Templin T, et al. Prenatal alcohol exposure and childhood behavior at 6 to 7 years: I. Dose-response effect. Pediatrics 2001;108:E34.

83. Baer JS, Sampson PD, Barr HM, Connor PD, Streissguth AP. A 21-year longitudinal analysis of the effects of prenatal alcohol exposure on young adult drinking. Arch Gen Psychiatry 2003;60:377–85.

84. Henry JA, Oldfield WL, Kon OM. Comparing cannabis with tobacco. BMJ 2003;326:942–3.

85. Hashibe M, Ford DE, Zhang ZF. Marijuana smoking and head and neck cancer. J Clin Pharmacol 2002;42 (suppl):103S–107S.

86. Tashkin DP, Baldwin GC, Sarafian T, Dubinett S, Roth MD. Respiratory and immunologic consequences of marijuana smoking. J Clin Pharmacol 2002;42(suppl):71S–81S.

87. Jones RT. Cardiovascular system effects of marijuana. J Clin Pharmacol 2002;42(suppl):58S–63S.

88. Brown TT, Dobs AS. Endocrine effects of marijuana. J Clin Pharmacol 2002;42(suppl):90S–96S.

89. Fergusson DM, Horwood LJ, Northstone K. Maternal use of cannabis and pregnancy outcome. ALSPAC Study Team. Avon Longitudinal Study of Pregnancy and Childhood. BJOG 2002;109:21–7.

90. Fried PA. Adolescents prenatally exposed to marijuana: examination of facets of complex behaviors and comparisons with the influence of in utero cigarettes. J Clin Pharmacol 2002; 42(suppl):97S–102S.

91. Richardson GA, Ryan C, Willford J, Day NL, Goldschmidt L. Prenatal alcohol and marijuana exposure: effects on neuropsychological outcomes at 10 years. Neurotoxicol Teratol 2002;24:309–20.

92. Fried PA, Buckingham M, Von Kulmiz P. Marijuana use during pregnancy and perinatal risk factors. Am J Obstet Gynecol 1983;146:992–4.

93. American Society of Health—System Pharmacists. AHFS drug information: 2004. Bethesda (MD): ASHSP; 2004.

94. Stewart DJ, Inaba T, Lucassen M, Kalow W. Cocaine metabolism: cocaine and norcocaine hydrolysis by liver and serum esterases. Clin Pharmacol Ther 1979;25:464–8.

95. Ostrea EM Jr, Knapp DK, Tannenbaum L, Ostrea AR, Romero A, Salari V, et al. Estimates of illicit drug use during pregnancy by maternal interview, hair analysis, and meconium analysis. J Pediatr 2001;138:344–8.

96. Karch SB. Karch's pathology of drug abuse. 3rd ed. Boca Raton (FL): CRC Press; 2002.

97. Singer LT, Salrator A, Arendt R, Minnes S, Farkas K, Kliegman R. Effects of cocaine/polydrug exposure and maternal psychological distress on infant birth outcomes. Neurotoxicol Teratol 2002;24:127–35.

98. The transfer of drugs and other chemicals into human milk. American Academy of Pediatrics Committee on Drugs. Pediatrics 2001;108:776–89

99. Eyler FD, Behnke M, Garvan CW, Woods NS, Wobie K, Conlon M. Newborn evaluations of toxicity and withdrawal related to prenatal cocaine exposure. Neurotoxicol Teratol 2001;23: 399–411.

100. Gossop M, Stewart D, Treacy S, Marsden J. A prospective study of mortality among drug misusers during a 4-year period after seeking treatment. Addiction 2002;97;39–47.

101. Tarabar AF, Nelson LS. The resurgence and abuse of heroin by children in the United States. Curr Opin Pediatr 2003;15:210–5.

102. Fudala PJ, Bridge TP, Herbert S, Williford WO, Chiang CN, Jones K, et al. Office-based treatment of opiate addiction with a sublingual-tablet formulation of buprenorphine and naloxone. Buprenorphine/Naloxone Collaborative Study Group. N Engl J Med 2003;349:949–58.

103. Florida Department of Law Enforcement. 2003 report of drugs identified in deceased persons by Florida Medical Examiners. Tallahassee (FL): FDLE; 2004. Available at: http://www.fdle.state.fl.us/publications/examiner_drug_report_2003.pdf. Retrieved August 11, 2004.

104. Dashe JS, Sheffield JS, Olscher DA, Todd SJ, Jackson GL, Wendel GD. Relationship between maternal methadone dosage and neonatal withdrawal. Obstet Gynecol 2002;100:1244–9.

105. Greene CM, Goodman MH. Neonatal abstinence syndrome: strategies for care of the drug-exposed infant. Neonatal Netw 2003;22(4):15–25.

106. Johnson RE, Jones HE, Fischer G. Use of buprenorphine in pregnancy: patient management and effects on the neonate. Drug Alcohol Depend 2003;70(suppl):S87–S101.

107. Jones HE, Balster RL. Inhalant abuse in pregnancy. Obstet Gynecol Clin North Am 1998;25:153–67.

108. Petitti DB, Sidney S, Quesenberry C, Bernstein A. Stroke and cocaine or amphetamine use. Epidemiology 1998;9:596–600.

109. Saito T, Yamamoto I, Kusakabe T, Huang X, Yukawa N, Takeichi S. Determination of chronic methamphetamine abuse by hair analysis. Forensic Sci Int 2000;112:65–71.

110. Kratofil PH, Baberg HT, Dimsdale JE. Self-mutilation and severe self-injurious behavior associated with amphetamine psychosis. Gen Hosp Psychiatry 1996;18:117–20.

111. Hall W, Hando J, Darke S, Ross J. Psychological morbidity and route of administration among amphetamine users in Sydney, Australia. Addiction 1996;91:81–7.

112. Yui K, Goto K, Ikemoto S, Ishiguro T, Kamada Y. Increased sensitivity to stress and episode recurrence in spontaneous recurrence of methamphetamine psychosis. Psychopharmacology (Berl) 1999;145:267–72.

113. Ernst T, Chang L, Leonido-Yee M, Speck O. Evidence for long-term neurotoxicity associated with methamphetamine abuse: A 1H MRS study. Neurology 2000;54:1344–49.

114. Rawson RA, Gonzales R, Brethen P. Treatment of methamphetamine use disorders: an update. J Subst Abuse Treat 2002;23:145–50.

115. White TL, Justice AJ, de Wit H. Differential subjective effects of D-amphetamine by gender, hormone levels and menstrual cycle phase. Pharmacol Biochem Behav 2002;73:729–41.

116. Smith L, Yonekura ML, Wallace T, Berman N, Kuo J, Berkowitz C. Effects of prenatal methamphetamine exposure on fetal growth and drug withdrawal symptoms in infants born at term. J Dev Behav Pediatr 2003;24:17–23.

117. Rawson RA, Washton A, Domier CP, Reiber C. Drugs and sexual effects: role of drug type and gender. J Subst Abuse Treat 2002;22:103–8.

118. Klein-Schwartz W, McGrath J. Poison centers' experience with methylphenidate abuse in pre-teens and adolescents. J Am Acad Child Adolesc Psychiatry 2003;42:288–94.

119. Massello W 3rd, Carpenter DA. A fatality due to the intranasal abuse of methylphenidate (Ritalin). J Forensic Sci 1999;44:220–1.

120. Ciccone PE. Attempted abuse of concerta [letter]. J Am Acad Child Adolesc Psychiatry 2002;41:756.

121. U.S. Food and Drug Administration. FDA announces plans to prohibit sales of dietary supplements containing ephedra. Rockville (MD): FDA; 2003. Available at: http://www.fda.gov/oc/initiatives/ephedra/december2003. Retrieved August 12, 2004.

122. Samenuk D, Link MS, Homoud MK, Contreras R, Theoharides TC, Wang PJ, et al. Adverse cardiovascular events temporally associated with ma huang, an herbal source of ephedrine [published erratum appears in Mayo Clin Proc 2003;78:1055]. Mayo Clin Proc 2002;77:12–6.

123. Haller CA, Jacob P 3rd, Benowitz NL. Pharmacology of ephedra alkaloids and caffeine after single-dose dietary supplement use. Clin Pharmacol Ther 2002;71:421–32.

124. Gurley BJ, Gardner SF, Hubbard MA. Content versus label claims in ephedra-containing dietary supplements. Am J Health Syst Pharm 2000;57:963–9.

125. Alkadi HO, Noman MA, Al-Thobhani AK, Al-Mekhlafi FS, Raja'a YA. Clinical and experimental evaluation of the effect of Khat-induced myocardial infarction. Saudi Med J 2002;23:1195–8.

126. Eriksson M, Ghani NA, Kristiansson B. Khat-chewing during pregnancy effect upon the off–spring and some characteristics of the chewers. East Afr Med J 1991;68:106–11.

127. Rickert VI, Siqueira LM, Dale T, Wiemann CM. Prevalence and risk factors for LSD use among young women. J Pediatr Adolesc Gynecol 2003;16:67–75.

128. Halpern JH, Pope HG Jr. Do hallucinogens cause residual neuropsychological toxicity? Drug Alcohol Depend 1999;53:247–56.

129. Aldurra G, Crayton JW. Improvement of hallucinogen persisting perception disorder by treatment with a combination of fluoxe-

tine and olanzapine: case report. J Clin Psychopharmacol 2001;21:343–4.

130. Long SY. Does LSD induce chromosomal damage and malformations? A review of the literature. Teratology 1972;6:75–90.

131. Rohrich J, Zorntlein S, Lot Z, Becker J, Kern T, Rittner C. False-positive LSD testing in urine samples from intensive care patients. J Anal Toxicol 1998;22:393–5.

132. Briggs GG, Freeman RK, Yaffe SJ. Drugs in pregnancy and lactation: a reference guide to fetal and neonatal risk. 6th ed. Baltimore (MD): Williams & Wilkins; 2002.

133. Fishbein DH. Female PCP-using jail detainees: proneness to violence and gender differences. Addict Behav 1996;21:155–72.

134. van Hulten R, Bakker AB, Lodder AC, Teeuw KB, Bakker A, Luefkens HG. The impact of attitudes and beliefs on length of benzodiazepine use: a study among inexperienced and experienced benzodiazepine users. Soc Sci Med 2003;56:1345–54.

135. de las Cuevas C, Sanz E, de la Fuente J. Benzodiazepines: more "behavioural" addiction than dependence. Psychopharmacology (Berl) 2003;167:297–303.

136. Isacson D. Long-term benzodiazepine use: factors of importance and the development of individual use patterns over time—a 13-year follow-up in a Swedish community. Soc Sci Med 1997;44:1871–80.

137. Bramness JG, Skurtveit S, Morland J. Clinical impairment of benzodiazepines—relation between benzodiazepine concentrations and impairment in apprehended drivers. Drug Alcohol Depend 2002;68:131–41.

138. Baca-Garcia E, Diaz-Sastre C, Saiz-Ruiz J, deLeon J. How safe are psychiatric medications after a voluntary overdose? Eur Psychiatry 2002;17:466–70.

139. Gray SL, LaCroix AZ, Blough D, Wagner EH, Koepsell TD, Buchner D. Is the use of benzodiazepines associated with incident disability? J Am Geriatr Soc 2002;50:1012–18.

140. Landi F, Cesari M, Russo A, Onder G, Sgadari A, Bernabei R. Benzodiazepines and the risk of urinary incontinence in frail older persons living in the community. Silvernet–HC Study Group. Clin Pharmacol Ther 2002;72:729–34.

141. Iqbal MM, Sobhan T, Ryals T. Effects of commonly used benzodiazepines on the fetus, the neonate, and the nursing infant. Psychiatr Serv 2002;53:39–49.

142. Slaughter L. Involvement of drugs in sexual assault. J Reprod Med 2000;45:425–30.

143. Ling LH, Marchant C, Buckley NA, Prior M, Irving RJ. Poisoning with the recreational drug paramethoxyamphetamine ("death"). Med J Aust 2001;174:453–5.

144. Winstock AR, Wolff K, Ramsey J. Ecstasy pill testing: harm minimization gone too far? Addiction 2001;96:1139–48.

145. Harris DS, Baggott M, Mendelson JH, Mendelson JE, Jones RT. Subjective and hormonal effects of 3,4-methylenedioxy-methamphetamine (MDMA) in humans. Psychopharmacology (Berl) 2002;162:396–405.

146. von Sydow K, Lieb R, Pfister H, Hofler M, Wittchen HU. Use, abuse and dependence of ecstasy and related drugs in adolescents and young adults–a transient phenomenon? Results from a longitudinal community study. Drug Alcohol Depend 2002; 66:147–59.

147. Teter CJ, Guthrie SK. A comprehensive review of MDMA and GHB: two common club drugs. Pharmacotherapy 2001;21: 1486–513.

148. Hartung TK, Schofield E, Short AI, Parr MJ, Henry JA. Hyponatraemic states following 3,4-methylenedioxymethamphetamine (MDMA, 'ecstasy') ingestion. QJM 2002;95:431–7.

149. Pacifici R, Zuccaro P, Farre M, Pichini S, DiCarlo S, Roset PN, et al. Cell-mediated immune response in MDMA users after repeated dose administration: studies in controlled versus non-controlled settings. Ann N Y Acad Sci 2002;965:421–33.

150. Buchert R, Thomasius R, Nebeling B, Petersen K, Obrocki J, Jenicke L, et al. Long-term effects of "ecstasy" use on serotonin transporters of the brain investigated by PET. J Nucl Med 2003;44:375–84.

151. Fox HC, McLean A, Turner JJ, Parrott AC, Rogers R, Sahakian BL. Neuropsychological evidence of a relatively selective profile of temporal dysfunction in drug-free MDMA ("ecstasy") poly-drug users. Psychopharmacology (Berl) 2002;162:203–14.

152. Lieb R, Schuetz CG, Pfister H, von Sydow K, Wittchen H. Mental disorders in ecstasy users: a prospective-longitudinal investigation. Drug Alcohol Depend 2002;68:195–207.

153. McElhatton PR, Bateman DN, Evans C, Pughe KR, Thomas SH. Congenital anomalies after prenatal ecstasy exposure. Lancet 1999;354:1441–2.

154. Ho E, Karimi–Tabesh L, Koren G, Characteristics of pregnant women who use ecstasy (3, 4-methylenedioxymethamphetamine). Neurotoxicol Teratol 2001;23:561–7.

155. Rickert VI, Wiemann CM, Berenson AB. Prevalence, patterns, and correlates of voluntary flunitrazepam use. Pediatrics 1999;103:E6.

156. Calhoun SR, Wesson DR, Galloway GP, Smith DE. Abuse of flunitrazepam (Rohypnol) and other benzodiazepines in Austin and South Texas. J Psychoactive Drugs 1996;28:183–9.

157. Mintzer MZ, Griffiths RR. Flunitrazepam and triazolam: a comparison of behavioral effects and abuse liability. Drug Alcohol Depend 1998;53:49–66.

158. Simmons MM, Cupp MJ. Use and abuse of flunitrazepam. Ann Pharmacother 1998;32:117–9.

159. Martinez-Cano H, Vela-Bueno A, de Iceta M, Pomalima R, Martinez-Gras I. Benzodiazepine withdrawal syndrome seizures. Pharmacopsychiatry 1995;28:257–62.

160. Center for Drug Evaluation Research (CDER). Xyrem (Sodium Oxybate) questions and answers. Rockville (MD): U.S. Food and Drug Administration; 2002. Available at: http://www.fda.gov/cder/drug/infopage/xyrem/xyrem_qa.htm. Retrieved August 11, 2004.

161. Freese TE, Miotto K, Reback CJ, The effects and consequences of selected club drugs. J Subst Abuse Treat 2002;23:151–6.

162. Degenhardt L, Darke S, Dillon P. GHB use among Australians: characteristics, use patterns and associated harm. Drug Alcohol Depend 2002;67:89–94.

163. Mason PE, Kerns WP 2nd. Gamma hydroxybutyric acid (GHB) intoxication. Acad Emerg Med 2002;9:730–9.

164. Galloway GP, Frederick SL, Staggers FE Jr, Gonzales M, Stalcup SA, Smith DE. Gamma-hydroxybutyrate: an emerging drug of abuse that causes physical dependence. Addiction 1997;92:89–96.

165. Sivilotti ML, Burns MJ, Aaron CK, Greenberg MJ. Pentobarbital for severe gamma-butyrolactone withdrawal. Ann Emerg Med 2001;38:660–5.

166. Klafta JM, Zacny JP, Young CJ. Neurological and psychiatric adverse effects of anaesthetics: epidemiology and treatment. Drug Saf 1995;13:281–95.

167. Dillon P, Copeland J, Jansen K. Patterns of use and harms associated with non-medical ketamine use. Drug Alcohol Depend 2003;69:23–8.

168. Weiner AL, Vieira L, McKay CA, Bayer MJ. Ketamine abusers presenting to the emergency department: a case series. J Emerg Med 2000;18:447–51.

169. Jansen KL, Darracot-Cankovic R. The nonmedical use of ketamine, part two: a review of problem use and dependence. J Psychoactive Drugs 2001;33:151–8.

170. Curran HV, Monaghan L. In and out of the K-hole: a comparison of the acute and residual effects of ketamine in frequent and infrequent ketamine users. Addiction 2001;96:749–60.

171. Ikonomidou C, Bosch F, Miksa M, Bittgau P, Vockler J, Dikranian K, et al. Blockade of NMDA receptors and apoptotic neurodegeneration in the developing brain. Science 1999;283:70–4.

172. Marc B, Baudry F, Vaquero P, Zerrouki L, Hassnaoui S, Douceron H. Sexual assault under benzodiazepine submission in a Paris suburb. Arch Gynecol Obstet 2000;263:193–7.

173. Miotto K, Darakjian J, Basch J, Murray S, Zogg J, Rawson R. Gamma-hydroxybutyric acid: patterns of use, effects and withdrawal. Am J Addict 2001;10:232–41.

174. Walshe K, Barrett Am, Karanagh PV, McNamara SM, Moran C, Shattock AG. A sensitive immunoassay for flunitrazepam and metabolites. J Anal Toxicol 2000;24(4):296–99.

175. Elian AA. A novel method for GHB detection in urine and its application in drug-facilitated sexual assaults. Forensic Sci Int 2000;109:183–7.

176. Wang PH, Liu C, Tsay WI, Li JH, Liu RH, Wu TG, et al. Improved screen and confirmation test of 7–aminoflunitrazepam in urine specimens for monitoring flunitrazepam (Rohypnol) exposure. J Anal Toxicol 2002;26:411–8.

177. Negrusz A, Moore C, Deitermann D, Lewis D, Kaleciak K, Kronstrand R, et al. Highly sensitive micro-plate enzyme immunoassay screening and NCI-GC-MS confirmation of flunitrazepam and its major metabolite 7-aminoflunitrazepam in hair. J Anal Toxicol 1999;23:429–35.

178. Kintz P, Cirimele V, Jamey C, Ludes B. Testing for GHB in hair by GC/MS/MS after a single exposure. Application to document sexual assault. J Forensic Sci 2003;48:195–200.

Resources

ACOG Resources

American College of Obstetricians and Gynecologists. Illegal drugs and pregnancy. ACOG Patient Education Pamphlet AP104. Washington, DC: ACOG; 2002.

American College of Obstetricians and Gynecologists. Having a baby. ACOG Patient Education Pamphlet AP103. Washington, DC: ACOG; 2001.

American College of Obstetricians and Gynecologists. Alcohol and pregnancy. ACOG Patient Education Pamphlet AP132. Washington, DC: ACOG; 2000.

American College of Obstetricians and Gynecologists. Good health before pregnancy: preconceptional care. ACOG Patient Education Pamphlet AP056. Washington, DC: ACOG; 1999.

American College of Obstetricians and Gynecologists. Staying healthy. ACOG Patient Education Pamphlet AP141. Washington, DC: ACOG; 2004.

American College of Obstetricians and Gynecologists. Alcohol and women. ACOG Patient Education Pamphlet AP068. Washington, DC: ACOG; 2000.

American College of Obstetricians and Gynecologists. Illicit drug abuse and dependence in women, a slide lecture presentation. Washington, DC: ACOG; 2002.

At-risk drinking and illicit drug use: ethical issues in obstetric and gynecologic practice. ACOG Committee Opinion No. 294. American College of Obstetricians and Gynecologists. Obstet Gynecol 2004;103:1021–31.

Other Resources

The resources listed as follows are for information purposes only. Referral to these sources and web sites does not imply the endorsement of ACOG. This list is not meant to be comprehensive. The exclusion of a source or web site does not reflect the quality of that source or web site. Please note that web sites are subject to change without notice.

Alcoholics Anonymous World Service, Inc.
PO Box 459, Grand Central Station
New York, NY 10163
Tel: (212) 870 3400
Web: www.alcoholics-anomymous.org

Alcoholics Anonymous (AA) is a fellowship of individuals who share with each other that they may solve their common problem and help others to recover from alcoholism. For professionals working with people who have special needs, AA material and literature are available in Braille, videos in American Sign Language, easy-to-read pamphlets, and most languages. The AA number can be found in any local telephone directory and the local office can supply meeting information and directions.

American Council for Drug Education
164 West 74th Street
New York, NY 10023
Tel: 800-488-DRUG
Web: www.acde.org/

The American Council for Drug Education's prevention and education efforts seek to diminish substance abuse and its impact by translating the most current scientific research into fact-based programs and materials available to all those seeking information on drugs.

American Society of Addiction Medicine
4601 North Park Avenue, Upper Arcade Suite 101
Chevy Chase, MD 20815
Tel: (301) 656-3920
Fax: (301) 656-3815
Web: www.asam.org/

The American Society of Addiction Medicine (ASAM) is an association of physicians dedicated to improving the treatment of alcoholism and other addictions, educating physicians and medical students, promoting research and prevention, and enlightening the medical community and public about these issues. The ASAM recently published the third edition of its textbook, *Principles of Addiction Medicine*, providing an overview of the diagnosis and treatment of addictive disorders, as well as the management of co-occurring medical and psychiatric conditions.

Diversion Control Program
Drug Enforcement Administration
U.S. Department of Justice
Web: www.deadiversion.usdoj.gov

The Diversion Control Program offers a current list and facts about drugs and chemicals of concern.

Hazelden Foundation
CO3, PO Box 11
Center City, MN 55012-0011
Web: www.hazelden.org

The Hazelden Foundation is a nonprofit organization providing high quality, affordable rehabilitation, education, prevention, and professional services and publications in chemical dependency and related disorders. Hazelden is an international provider of treatment, recovery, research and training, offering programs, services, and publications for individuals, families, and communities affected by chemical dependency.

Join Together
One Appleton Street, 4th floor
Boston, MA 02116-5223
Tel: (617) 437-1500
Web: www.jointogether.org

Join Together supports community-based efforts to reduce, prevent, and treat substance abuse nationally and offers up-to-date information on substance abuse news, research and policy to the professional. More recently, Join Together is focusing on strengthening community capacity to expand high-quality drug and alcohol treatment.

Latino Council on Alcohol and Tobacco Prevention
1616 P Street, NW
Washington, DC 20036
Tel: (202) 265-8054
Fax: (202) 265-8056
Web: www.nlcatp.org

The Latino Council on Alcohol and Tobacco Prevention is dedicated to preventing or eliminating tobacco use and reducing alcohol abuse in the Latino community through community education, technical assistance, policy analysis, and advocacy. The Council has an extensive clearinghouse of documents and videos related to alcohol and tobacco issues available at free or low cost.

Monitoring the Future
Web: www.monitoringthefuture.org/

Monitoring the Future, begun in 1975, is a long-term study of American adolescents, college students, and adults through age 40. It is conducted by the University of Michigan's Institute for Social Research and is supported under a series of investigator-initiated, competing research grants from the National Institute on Drug Abuse.

Narcotics Anonymous World Service, Inc.
PO Box 9999
Van Nuys, CA 91409
Tel: (818) 773-9999
Web: www.na.org

A sister organization to Alcoholics Anonymous, Narcotics Anonymous World Service utilizes the same meeting structure and format offering mutual support to combat addiction.

National Association for Children of Alcoholics
11426 Rockville Pike, Suite 100
Rockville, MD 20852
Tel: 888-55-4COAS; (301) 468-0985
E-mail: nacoa@nacoa.org
Web: www.nacoa.org

The National Association for Children of Alcoholics is the national nonprofit membership organization working on behalf of children of alcohol and drug dependent parents. Its mission is to advocate for all children and families affected by alcoholism and other drug dependencies.

The National Center on Addiction and Substance Abuse
Columbia University
633 Third Avenue, 19th floor
New York, NY 10017-6706
Tel: (212) 841-5200
Web: www.casacolumbia.org

The National Center on Addiction and Substance Abuse at Columbia University encourages and disseminates research on the societal and individual costs of substance abuse, and develops and distributes messages and tools to educate the public and assist treatment professionals.

National Council on Alcoholism and Drug Dependence, Inc.
20 Exchange Place, Suite 2902
New York, NY 10005
Tel: (212) 269-7797; 24 Hour Hotline 800-622-2255
Fax: (212) 269-7510
Web: www.ncadd.org

The National Council on Alcoholism and Drug Dependence provides education, information, and assistance to the public. It
advocates prevention, intervention, and treatment through offices
in New York City and Washington, DC, and a nationwide network
of affiliates. It also staffs a 24-hour information hotline that will
refer the caller to a local affiliate office. Callers can also leave
their name and address to receive written information about alcohol and other drug abuse.

National Institute on Alcohol Abuse and Alcoholism
5635 Fishers Ln, MSC 9304
Bethesda, MD 20892-9304
Web: www.niaaa.nih.gov/

The National Institute on Alcohol Abuse and Alcoholism provides
leadership in the national effort to reduce alcohol-related problems by conducting research, coordinating research activities,
translating and disseminating research findings, and collaborating
with other entities involved in alcohol-related work. Publications
of note include:

Women and Alcohol: An Update, which is available at
http://www.niaaa.nih.gov/publicatons/arh26-4/toc26-4.htm. It
features research about sex differences and genetic risk, minority populations, elderly women, osteoporosis risk factors, prenatal alcohol exposure, and other issues.

Alcohol: A Women's Health Issue, which is available at http://
www.niaaa.nih.gov/publications/brochurewomen/women.htm.
This is a 20-page illustrated public education brochure.

Drinking and Your Pregnancy, which is available at
http://www.niaaa.nih.gov/publications/brochure.htm.
This is a 2–page public education facts sheet in a question and
answer format.

NIAAA has an alcohol policy information system, which is available at: http://www.alcoholpolicy.niaaa.nih.gov. This tool provides information on U.S. state and federal laws and regulations
related to alcohol. It also has an underage drinking research initiative (http://www.niaaa.nih.gov/about/underage.htm). This web
site includes statistics, publications, other resources, and links.

National Institute on Drug Abuse
National Institutes of Health
6001 Executive Boulevard, Room 5213
Bethesda, MD 20892-9561
Tel: (301) 443-1124
Web: www.drugabuse.gov

The National Institute on Drug Abuse supports and conducts
research across a broad range of disciplines and ensures the rapid
and effective dissemination and use of the results of that research
to significantly improve drug abuse and addiction prevention,
treatment, and policy. The institute publishes a monthly review of
scientific substance abuse research papers.

Office of National Drug Control Policy
Web: www.whitehousedrugpolicy.gov/

The Office of National Drug Control Policy provides information
on specific drugs, including data, health effects, and monitoring
activity.

Physician Leadership On National Drug Policy
Center for Alcohol and Addiction Studies
Brown University, Box G-BH
Providence, RI 02912
Tel: (401) 444-1817
E-mail: plndp@brown.edu
Web: www.plndp.org

The Physician Leadership On National Drug Policy is a national
organization of physician leaders involved with health care policy. It
has undertaken research reports and has educational materials available for clinicians. Among other resources, the web site contains an
online, downloadable curriculum on substance abuse and women.

Soberrecovery.com—Recovery Resources On-Line
Web: www.soberrecovery.com

Soberrecovery is a web site offering a directory of resources on treatment programs and recovery options for the addicted person, their
family, professional care providers, and the community. It includes a
section for adolescent treatment and programs. The site has a chat
room and direct links to treatment facilities and recovery programs
and lists of AA/NA and other support meetings.

Substance Abuse and Mental Health Services Administration
5600 Fishers Lane
Rockville, MD 20857
Tel: (301) 443-0365
Web: www.samhsa.gov

The Substance Abuse and Mental Health Services Administration
(SAMHSA) is the federal agency charged with improving the quality
and availability of prevention, treatment, and rehabilitative services
to reduce illness, death, disability, and cost to society resulting from
substance abuse and mental illnesses. SAMHSA has a substance
abuse facility locator through which a telephone service links the
caller to a variety of hotlines (Hotline: 1-800-662-HELP; 1-800-662-
9832 [Español]; 1-800-228-0427 [TDD]) that provide treatment
referrals. It is available 24 hours a day. The on-line resource
(http://findtreatment.samhsa.gov) for locating drug and alcohol
abuse treatment programs lists private and public facilities that are
licensed, certified, or otherwise approved for inclusion by their state
substance abuse agency and treatment facilities administered by the
Department of Veterans Affairs, the Indian Health Service, and the
Department of Defense. This site also identifies and links user to
physicians within a state or geographic area licensed to dispense
buprenorphine. A listing of buprenorphine dispensing physicians
can be found at http://buprenorphine.samhsa.gov/bwns_locator/.
These resource links are updated frequently.

SAMHSA Fetal Alcohol Spectrum Disorders Center for Excellence
1700 Research Boulevard, Suite 400
Rockville, MD 20850
Tel: (866) 786-7327
Web: www.fascenter.samhsa.gov

The SAMHSA Fetal Alcohol Spectrum Disorders Center for Excellence provides resources and information on fetal alcohol syndrome to expand the knowledge base and promote best practices. It also supports individuals, families, and communities affected by fetal alcohol syndrome in an effort to improve quality of life.

U.S. Food and Drug Administration
Department of Health and Human Services
Web: www.fda.gov/cder/

The U.S. Food and Drug Administration offers detailed information for providers and consumers on drugs, including over-the-counter drugs.

Treatment and Research Facilities

Division of Addiction Medicine at the University of Florida
University of Florida
PO Box 100183
Gainesville, FL 32610-0183
Tel: (352) 392-6681
Fax: (352) 392-8217
Web: www.psychiatry.ufl.edu/addiction/site/index.htm

The goal of the Division of Addiction Medicine at the University of Florida is to develop a new awareness in the medical community of the significance of the role of prevention and intervention in nicotine, alcohol, and other drug use and is accomplished by enhancing understanding and competency in addiction medicine and drug prevention education of medical students, medical residents, primary care practitioners, and psychiatric specialists.

Fetal Alcohol and Drug Unit
Department of Psychiatry and Behavioral Medicine
University of Washington, School of Medicine
180 Nickerson Street, Suite 309
Seattle, WA 98109
Tel: (206) 543-7155
Fax: (206) 685-2903
Web: depts.washington.edu/fadu/

The Fetal Alcohol and Drug Unit at the University of Washington is dedicated to the prevention, intervention, and treatment of fetal alcohol syndrome (FAS) and alcohol-related neurodevelopmental disorder (ARND). It works to research fetal alcohol and drug effects across the life span, to disseminate information on fetal alcohol and drug effects, to provide consultation for persons of any age thought to be affected by prenatal exposure to alcohol, and to provide training in human behavioral teratology. The unit also provides staffing and curricula for workshops, invited lectures and conferences on FAS/ARND prevention, and intervention at the regional, national, and international level.

Smoking and Women's Health

Key Points

- Cigarette smoking is the largest single risk factor for premature death and avoidable illness in developed countries.

- Smoking in U.S. women has attributed to a 600% increase in the rate of lung cancer deaths; smoking in U.S. women also increases the risk of myocardial infarction to twice that of men.

- Screening for tobacco use can be done efficiently as a vital sign at every clinical visit.

- A brief smoking cessation intervention known as the 5A's is recommended for screening and treating tobacco dependence. Follow-up can then be done at every clinical encounter.

- Smoking cessation interventions delivered by health care providers (eg, physicians, dentists, nurses, psychologists, social workers) markedly increase cessation rates compared with interventions with no health care provider involvement.

Smoking cessation interventions delivered by health care providers markedly increase cessation rates.

- Pharmacologic treatment for smoking cessation (including nicotine replacement therapy and bupropion sustained release) should be offered to all women attempting smoking cessation unless it is contraindicated. These products increase quit rates 1.5- to 2-fold regardless of the treatment setting. They may be used in combination for those experiencing difficulty quitting.

- Comprehensive, individualized smoking cessation programs coupled with the use of nicotine replacement therapy when indicated and proper follow-up care can help women to stop smoking and avoid relapse.

- The clinician may find it helpful to address depression and fear of weight gain in the smoking patient. These are common deterrents to smoking cessation for women.

- Clinicians should routinely assess and intervene with adolescents on tobacco initiation and use, including offering multiple strategies for cessation.

Cigarette smoking is the largest single risk factor for premature death and avoidable illness in developed countries (1). Approximately one fifth of the deaths in the United States are attributable to smoking (2), amounting to more than 440,000 deaths per year (3). The major smoking-attributable deaths involve lung cancer, other respiratory conditions, and cardiovascular disease (1). Multiple studies demonstrate, however, that tobacco use renders deleterious effects on most human organ systems, not only the heart and lung.

Causes of persistent cigarette smoking are multifactorial: pharmacologic, behavioral, genetic, and psychologic. Of all of these factors, nicotine dependence is the most significant reason that smokers sustain tobacco use (4). Despite the overwhelming medical evidence about the harmful effects of smoking, an estimated 22% of women continue to smoke (4). Nicotine addiction often begins early in life, with more than 2,000 additional children and adolescents becoming regular users of tobacco products each day (5). This is especially important because those who start smoking earlier in life are more likely to smoke heavily and become dependent on nicotine than those who begin later in life (6). Approximately 28% of high-school girls in 2001 reported current cigarette smoking (7). Among daily smokers, 81% began smoking at age 18 years or younger, with some studies reporting the average age of initiation of smoking in women to be age 12 or 13 years (6).

Tobacco use results in substantial medical care costs. The Centers for Disease Control and Prevention estimates the annual U.S. costs attributable to smoking to be greater than $50 billion, and the cost of lost productivity and earnings to be at least another $47 billion per year (8). The tobacco industry has been successfully marketing to women since the late 1920s, portraying cigarette smoking to be glamorous, adventurous, slimming, and a symbol of freedom and emancipation. The smoking initiation rate for adolescent girls has corresponded to the yearly increase of this targeted marketing to women (4). In 2004, the American College of Obstetricians and Gynecologists' (ACOG's) Executive Board reaffirmed the 1990 policy stating that it "opposes the unconscionable targeting of women of all ages by the tobacco industry" (see Appendix B).

Women who stop smoking achieve a significant reduction in the risk of disease and premature death (4). Studies show that nearly 75% of women smokers desire to quit, yet only one half of smokers have received advice from their health care providers about smoking cessation (9). Obstetrician–gynecologists can play a key role in promoting smoking prevention and cessation. As primary health care providers for women, obstetrician–gynecologists can be effective in educating women on the health consequences of tobacco use, advising smokers to quit, and assisting patients with smoking cessation counseling and pharmacotherapy.

Effects of Smoking on Women

Smoking is one of the most studied of human behaviors. Thousands of studies have documented its health consequences, yet most have not reported results by sex (4). Nicotine activates the brain's mesolimbic dopaminergic reward system (10) and produces dependence, resulting in withdrawal symptoms with abrupt cessation. Nicotine has been implicated in the development of various diseases through its effects on the microvasculature and on the function of platelets, fibroblasts, red blood cells, and other blood components. In addition, cigarette smoke contains carbon monoxide and at least 60 other toxic substances that exert harmful effects in many human tissues through direct and indirect mechanisms (11). Seven of these compounds are known human carcinogens (12).

Cancer

Cigarette smoking is a major cause of cancer. In most cases, the relative risk for development of cancer increases with dose of tobacco exposure (13). Smoking is responsible for approximately 90% of all lung cancer deaths in U.S. women. In the past 50 years, lung cancer deaths have increased 600% in women and represent the leading cause of cancer mortality for U.S. women (4). The association between lung cancer and tobacco use is dose-dependent; lung cancer risk increases with quantity and duration of lifetime smoking. A higher relative risk also exists with deeper inhalation of smoke and use of nonfiltered cigarettes (14). Adenocarcinoma has become the most common type of lung cancer in smokers (15).

The 2004 Surgeon General's report, *The Health Consequences of Smoking*, states a causal relationship with smoking for cancer of the bladder, cervix, esophagus, renal cell, renal pelvis, larynx, lung, pancreas, and stomach. There is a causal relationship between smoking and acute myeloid leukemia (15). Evidence is suggestive but not sufficient to infer a causal relationship between smoking and colorectal and liver cancers (15). It is yet unclear how and if smoking contributes to a greater risk for some breast cancers.

Smoking predisposes women to the development of a wide range of cervical abnormalities. Tobacco-specific carcinogenic nitrosamine 4-(methylnitrosamino)-1-(3-pyridyl)-1-butanone has been identified in the cervical mucus of women who smoke cigarettes (11). After adjusting for the presence of human papillomavirus (HPV), recent studies report a significant increase in cervical cancer risk in smokers (16). Women who smoke and are infected with oncogenic HPV have a 3.3 relative risk (light smokers 95% confidence interval [CI], 1.6–6.7) to 4.3 relative risk (heavy smokers 95% CI, 2–9.3) of developing invasive cervical cancer (17). Current smoking is a possible co-factor for the development of a significant cervical intraepithelial neoplasia lesion following infection with HPV (4, 18).

Smoking also appears to be a risk factor for mucinous epithelial ovarian cancer, with a 1.9 relative risk (95% CI, 1.3–2.9) (19). Endometrial cancer occurs less frequently in cigarette smokers. The negative association is thought to be caused by the antiestrogenic effect of tobacco use (20).

Other Lung Disease

Cigarette smoking is a primary cause of chronic obstructive pulmonary disease among women, and the risk increases with the amount and duration of smoking. Close to 90% of mortality from chronic obstructive pulmonary disease in the United States can be attributed to smoking, and this rate has been increasing among women in the past 20–30 years. Adolescent girls who smoke have reduced rates of lung growth, and adult women who smoke experience a premature reduction in lung function (15).

Cardiovascular Disease and Stroke

Cigarette smoking is a significant, independent risk factor for cardiovascular disease. The risk increases with the number of cigarettes smoked daily, the total number of years smoking, the degree of inhalation, and early age at initiation of smoking (4). Tobacco use predisposes women to coronary heart disease (CHD), cerebrovascular disease, myocardial infarction, peripheral vascular disease, carotid atherosclerosis, abdominal aortic

aneurysm, stroke, and hypertension. The relative risk for CHD mortality varies by age, sex, and race, ranging from 1.2 to 3 for different demographic groups compared with respective groups that have never smoked (21). In the U.S. Nurses' Health Study, even women who smoked as few as one to four cigarettes per day had twice the risk for CHD as women who had never smoked (22). In women younger than 50 years, the smoking-attributable risk of MI was found to be as high as six times that of nonsmokers. The presence of diabetes increases the relative risk for developing CHD to 7.67 for a woman who smokes 15 or more cigarettes per day as compared with those who never smoked (23). Several recent studies have demonstrated that women smokers are affected more adversely than men, with an increased relative risk of MI twice that of their male counterparts (24–26).

The relative risk of all types of stroke among smokers is approximately 2.5 compared with nonsmokers. The risk of stroke caused by subarachnoid hemorrhage in smokers may be as high as five times that of individuals who do not smoke (27). The evidence is sufficient to infer a causal relationship between smoking and abdominal aortic aneurysm (15).

Overall, women who used oral contraceptives (OCs) were reported to have approximately two times the risk of MI of nonusers. Smokers who used OCs had a risk for MI between 10 and 14 times that of women who neither used OCs nor smoked (28). Because women older than 35 years are already at higher risk of MI and cerebrovascular accidents, OCs are not recommended for smokers older than 35 years (29).

Smoking cessation reduces the risk of cardiovascular disease and stroke, with a substantial decrease in risk noted within 2 years after smoking cessation (30). This beneficial risk reduction applies no matter what age women stop smoking.

Menopause

Women who smoke undergo natural menopause on average 1.5–2 years earlier than nonsmokers (31). Cigarette smoking appears to exert a significant antiestrogenic effect, possibly because of increased 2-hydroxylation of estradiol resulting from the induction of cytochrome P450 (32).

Osteoporosis

Tobacco use also presents a risk factor for low bone mineral density leading to osteoporotic fracture in postmenopausal women. Rates for bone loss are 1.5–2 times greater in current female smokers. Of all hip fractures, one in eight is attributable to cigarette smoking. In current smokers, the risk of hip fracture is estimated to be 17% greater than nonsmokers at age 60 years, increasing to 71% greater at age 80 years (33). Studies suggest that lower bone density in smokers is a partial result of decreased calcium absorption; smokers do not absorb dietary or supplemental calcium as efficiently as nonsmokers (34).

Reproductive Health

Cigarette smoking is a causal factor for decreased fertility in women (15). In a recent analysis of 12 studies, women cigarette smokers were observed to have a 60% increase in the risk of infertility (35). The effect of smoking on fertilization and pregnancy rates has varied widely in studies, but some studies suggest that smoking may be detrimental to those trying to conceive (4). These effects may be related to reported findings of lower peak serum estradiol levels during ovarian stimulation or reduced motility and ciliary function of the epithelium lining of the fallopian tube (36). The compounds found in tobacco smoke affect oocyte and sperm production, tubal motility, embryo cleavage, blastocyst formation, and implantation (37). For women attempting in vitro fertilization, studies have shown smokers to be approximately one half as successful as nonsmokers, and diminished ovarian reserve has been suggested as a key mechanism (37). After conception, women who smoke experience higher rates of spontaneous abortion and ectopic pregnancy than nonsmokers (37, 38).

Menstrual irregularity, secondary amenorrhea, and dysmenorrhea occur more frequently in smokers than in nonsmokers. There is limited or inconsistent evidence to suggest that smoking decreases the risk for endometriosis and uterine fibroids. A protective effect is plausible because of its systemic antiestrogenic effect, but this mechanism has not been examined extensively (4).

Effects on Pregnancy

Maternal smoking during pregnancy is the most important modifiable risk for adverse fetal health. As a result, ACOG recommends that substance use, including tobacco use, be included in counseling during a women's reproductive years, particularly as part of preconceptional care (39). The perinatal complications associated with maternal tobacco use include preterm delivery, prema-

ture rupture of membranes, spontaneous abortion, ectopic pregnancy, low birth weight, intrauterine growth restriction, placental abruption, placenta previa, stillbirth, and sudden infant death syndrome (SIDS) (15). A causal relationship is suggested between maternal smoking and oral clefts (15).

An estimated 12% of U.S. women smoke during pregnancy, with rates as high as 19% for adolescents and 28% for those with 9–11 years of education (5). The continued use of tobacco products during pregnancy accounts for 15% of all preterm births, 20–30% of all low-birth-weight infants, and a 150% overall increase in perinatal mortality (38). Carbon monoxide and nicotine are thought to be the main ingredients in cigarettes responsible for adverse fetal effects linked to smoking. These products cause decreased availability of oxygen to maternal tissues and to the fetus.

It is estimated that 70% of women who discontinue tobacco use during pregnancy will relapse within 1 year of childbirth (40). Relapse prevention strategies for former smokers are most effective if begun in the third trimester of pregnancy and continued throughout the postpartum period (41). Postpartum relapse prevention strategies include close monitoring of smoking status, providing opportunities to congratulate abstinence and support success, reinforcing steps taken towards quitting, and advising those still considering a cessation attempt. In addition, cessation resources may be directed to include domestic partners who smoke because environmental tobacco smoke affects the child's health and increases the risk of relapse in the postpartum patient. Tobacco cessation telephone counseling offered nationally and by many states also may prove helpful to prevent relapse during this vulnerable period (see "Resources"). An important predictor of abstinence from tobacco use following pregnancy is continued breastfeeding. (See ACOG Educational Bulletin No. 260 "Smoking Cessation During Pregnancy" for additional information on tobacco use and cessation during pregnancy and the "Resources" section at the end of this chapter.)

Effects on Children

The smoke from cigarettes of women who smoke in the presence of their infants and children contributes to many health issues. Infants exposed to secondhand smoke are more susceptible to respiratory diseases, otitis media, asthma, and SIDS (4). Among children with established asthma, secondhand smoke exposure may cause additional episodes and increase its severity (42).

Smoking Cessation

Tobacco users experience multiple interactions with clinical providers. Seventy percent of adult smokers reported at least one visit to a physician in the preceding 12 months, with more than two thirds reporting more than one visit (43). Additionally, more than 75% of women want to quit smoking, and 47% of female smokers have made an attempt to quit within the past year (4). According to a recent study, patients welcomed counseling about smoking cessation from their primary care physicians and are more satisfied with physicians who provide counseling (44). Yet observations of health care providers indicate that clinicians often fail to assess and treat tobacco dependence. Approximately one half of patients report never having been asked about their smoking status (4). When smoking is recognized, very few tobacco users are offered assistance to quit.

Many barriers exist to smoking cessation counseling and therapy. Only 21% of practicing physicians indicate that they have received adequate training to help their patients stop smoking (43). In addition, practitioners may feel that current time constraints in clinical practice limit the possibility of a smoking cessation intervention. However, effective smoking cessation interventions can be brief; studies have shown that as little as 3 minutes of counseling enhances cessation rates (45). All health care professionals can be effective in their efforts to address smoking prevention and smoking cessation within the context of routine care.

Specific Issues on Cessation for Women

Women experience more difficulty than men with smoking cessation, especially in the initial cessation period, and are more prone to relapse (46). In addition to concerns about weight control and possibility of depression, women may experience variability in mood and withdrawal as a function of the menstrual cycle phase (4). Some studies show that women may require greater social support to achieve abstinence (4). Smoking-associated environmental cues appear to influence smoking behavior more in women than in men. Therefore, social support to modify the environment assumes greater importance. Women also may fear discord in relationships because of smoking cessation. A woman may feel her tobacco-using partner would be threatened by her quit attempt. In addition, she may fear isolation from friends with whom she shares smoking breaks. Once voiced, the woman often is able to strategize how she might best cope with envisioned relational issues brought about by her smoking cessation.

Guidelines for Intervention

The Agency for Health Care Research and Quality has published specific recommendations for clinicians providing smoking cessation therapy (Fig. 9). Effective

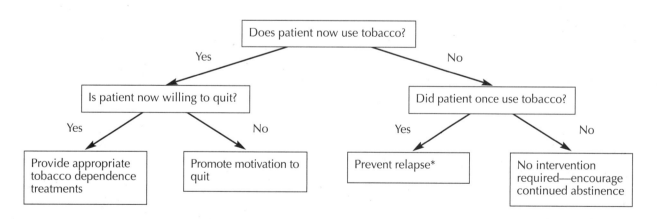

*Relapse prevention interventions are not necessary in the case of the adult who has not used tobacco for many years.

Fig. 9. Algorithm for treating tobacco use. (Fiore MC, Bailey WC, Cohen SJ, Dorfman SF, Goldstein MG, Gritz ER, et al. Treating tobacco use and dependence. Clinical practice guideline. Rockville [MD]: U.S. Department of Health and Human Services. Public Health Service; 2000.)

interventions begin with screening all patients for tobacco use on a regular basis and offering them treatment. The Agency for Health Care Research and Quality recommends a brief smoking cessation intervention known as the 5 A's (Box 15) for screening and treating tobacco dependence. The 5 A's are applicable to outpatient office visits. This intervention is not only clinically effective, but it also is extremely cost-effective relative to other commonly used disease prevention interventions and medical treatments (47). After assessing smokers for their willingness to quit smoking, physicians and office staff can encourage smoking cessation by ensuring that all smokers are identified, monitored, and counseled appropriately at every office visit. Smoking cessation interventions delivered by health and social care providers (eg, physicians, dentists, nurses, psychologists, social workers) markedly increase cessation rates compared with interventions with no health care provider involvement (eg, self-administered interventions) (47).

In those individuals unwilling to consider smoking cessation, providers can enhance the motivation to quit by reviewing the multiple health risks associated with smoking and the numerous benefits of living smoke free. Follow-up that reinforces counseling on the health risks of smoking and provides appropriate referrals for additional cessation counseling and medical therapy is an important component of intervening with women who smoke.

For patients who have recently quit, relapse prevention is especially important because of the chronic relapsing nature of tobacco dependence (43). Clinicians can provide brief effective relapse prevention treatment by reinforcing the patient's decision to quit, reviewing the benefits of quitting, and assisting the patient in resolving any residual problems they have encountered from quitting (43). The clinician also can recommend that the patient avoid situations in which women typically smoke, such as drinking coffee or alcohol.

Counseling and Behavioral Therapy

Counseling in multiple forms has been shown to enhance smoking cessation rates. Social support from partners, family, friends, coworkers, or service providers and general problem solving counseling both produced abstinence rates of 16% compared with 11% in patients with no counseling or behavioral therapy (43). Patients who do not receive social support have more difficulty quitting smoking and are more prone to relapse.

Box 15   Smoking Cessation Guidelines for Clinicians

The 5 A's Approach

Ask about tobacco use

Identify and document tobacco use status for every patient at every visit.

Advise to quit

In a clear, strong, and personalized manner, urge every tobacco user to quit.

Assess willingness to make a quit attempt

Is the tobacco user willing to make a quit attempt at this time?

Assist in quit attempt

For the patient willing to make a quit attempt, use counseling and pharmacotherapy to help her quit:

1. Suggest and encourage the use of problem-solving methods and skills for smoking cessation (eg, identify "trigger" situations).

2. Provide social support as part of the treatment (eg, "we can help you quit").

3. Arrange social support in the smoker's environment (eg, identify "quit buddy" and smoke-free space).

4. Provide self-help smoking cessation materials.

Arrange follow-up

Schedule follow-up contact, preferably within the first week after the quit date.

U.S. Department Health and Human Services. Treating tobacco use and dependence: a systems approach. A guide for health care administrators, insurers, managed organizations, and purchasers. US PHS, Washington, DC: US DHHS; 2000.

In smoking cessation treatment, the following types of counseling can be incorporated into patient interactions:

- Practical counseling and problem solving skills: educate patients on the importance of total abstinence from smoking; anticipate and avoid triggers; remove all tobacco from their environment; identify and avoid risk factors for relapse, such as alcohol, exposure to other smokers, and time pressure; and address fears about weight gain and stress management.

- Social support as a part of treatment: communicate caring and encouragement.

- Social support outside of treatment: encourage a smoke-free home; provide information on community resources; and reinforce the useful role of supportive family and friends (43).

- Telephone and web-based tobacco counseling: encourage patients to use the counsel and support of the telephone tobacco quit line offered by many states as well as the interactive tobacco cessation web sites (see "Resources" for details).

Many smokers benefit from self-help smoking materials and community-based peer support programs, such as Nicotine Anonymous, as an adjunct to other strategies, including health care provider advice and counseling (43). (See "Resources" for a list of some available smoking cessation materials.)

Pharmacotherapy

Numerous effective medications for smoking cessation currently are available. In most cases, it is inappropriate to reserve pharmacotherapy until patients have made an attempt to quit on their own because 90–95% of unaided quit attempts end in failure (43). All smokers trying to quit should be offered pharmacotherapy, except those who are pregnant, breastfeeding, those with medical contraindications, and those smoking fewer than 10 cigarettes daily (43).

Nicotine replacement therapy and bupropion sustained release are considered first-line therapy by the U.S. Food and Drug Administration (FDA). Each has been documented to increase significantly the rate of long-term smoking abstinence and are proved to be cost effective to treat tobacco dependence as compared with advice or counseling alone (48). In fact, both bupropion and nicotine replacement therapy are considered to be among the most cost effective of all health care interventions (49). In the event that these agents alone or in combination are ineffective, clonidine and nortriptyline are second-line agents that may be considered. Table 13 presents a summary of currently available pharmacotherapies for smoking cessation and the estimated abstinence rates for each treatment option.

First-Line Medications

The FDA has approved first-line pharmacotherapies for tobacco dependence as safe and effective (4). These drugs are in nicotine replacement products: nicotine patch, gum, nasal spray, inhaler, sublingual tablets and lozenges, and bupropion sustained release. First-line medications have shown to be efficacious and should be recommended as an initial approach to tobacco cessation, except when contraindicated. The effectiveness of pharmacologic treatments is enhanced when coupled with advice and counseling (43). Few studies have followed-up for longer than 1 year on the rate of abstinence from tobacco after using pharmacotherapies.

Nicotine Therapy. All of the commercially available forms of nicotine replacement therapy are effective as part of a strategy to promote smoking cessation. These products increase quit rates 1.5-fold to 2-fold regardless of the treatment setting (50). Nicotine replacement therapy provides a controlled amount of nicotine in a form that does not contain the other 4,000 harmful components of tobacco smoke (51). Nicotine-containing medications can provide relief of withdrawal symptoms while smokers adapt to life without cigarettes. In active cigarette smoking, nicotine is absorbed rapidly with large variability in plasma concentrations. By contrast, nicotine replacement therapy administration results in slower, lower, and less variable plasma concen-trations. Nicotine replacement therapy should be recommended for smokers who are likely to be nicotine dependent except when contraindicated. Special consideration about the degree of the patient's nicotine dependence needs to be given those who smoke fewer than 10 cigarettes per day, are pregnant or breastfeeding, or are adolescents (see section on adolescent smokers) (43, 52). Most often, nicotine dependence is found in those who smoke greater than one pack of cigarettes per day, smoke within 30 minutes of getting up in the morning, or who have experienced nicotine withdrawal symptoms with prior attempts at cessation (43).

Nicotine replacement therapy is contraindicated for patients with hypersensitivity or allergies to nicotine, recent MI, worsening angina, or life-threatening arrhythmia. Continued smoking while using nicotine replacement therapy has not been proved to cause an increase in cardiovascular events (53). All nicotine replacement therapy products should be used with caution, however, in those with existing myocardial disease (43).

Nicotine gum and patches are the most studied forms of nicotine replacement therapy. Nicotine gum

Table 13. Medications for Smoking Cessation and Estimated Abstinence Rates

Pharmacotherapy	Contraindications	Adverse Effects	Dosage	Duration	Estimated Abstinence Rates*
First-Line Medications					
Bupropion sustained release	History of seizures, eating disorder, breastfeeding, children and adolescents, concurrent use of Wellbrutrin or monoamine oxidase inhibitors, or during detoxification from sedatives or alcohol. Pregnancy category B	Insomnia, dry mouth	150 mg every morning for 3 days then 150 mg twice daily	7–12 weeks; maintenance up to 6 months	30.5%
Nicotine gum	Allergies to nicotine, recent myocardial infarction, worsening angina, or serious arrhythmia. Pregnancy category C	Mouth soreness, dyspepsia	1–24 cigarettes per day, use 2-mg gum (up to 24 pieces per day) 25 or more cigarettes per day use 4-mg gum (up to 24 pieces per day)	Up to 12 weeks	23.7%
Nicotine patch	See Nicotine gum Pregnancy category D	Local skin reaction, insomnia	—	—	17.1%
Nicoderm CQ	—	—	21 mg/24 h 14 mg/24h 7 mg/24h	Dosage is determined by nicotine dependence and tapered during 6–8 week period	
Nicotrol	See Nicotine Gum.		15mg/16h	8 weeks	
Nicotine inhaler	Pregnancy category D	Local irritation of mouth and throat	6–16 cartridges per day	Up to 6 months	22.8%
Nicotine nasal spray	See Nicotine Gum. Pregnancy category D	Nasal irritation	8–40 doses per day	3–6 months	30.5%
Nicotine lozenge†	See Nicotine Gum. Pregnancy category D	Not known	2 mg and 4 mg according to individual program starting with 9 to 24 per day.	12 weeks	Not determined
Second-Line Medications					
Clonidine	Rebound hypertension when abruptly discontinued. Multiple drug interactions. Pregnancy category C	Dry mouth, drowsiness, dizziness, sedation	0.15–0.75 mg/d	3–10 weeks	25.6%
Nortriptyline	Risk of arrhythmias, recent myocardial infarction. Interacts with monoamine oxidase inhibitors. Pregnancy category C	Sedation, dry mouth	25 mg/d increasing to 75–100 mg/d	12 weeks	30.1%

*Estimated abstinence rates: percentage of smokers in a group or treatment condition who were abstinent at a follow-up point that occurred at least 5 months after treatment. Few studies followed participants for more than 1 year.

†For more information on the nicotine lozenge, go to http://commitlozenge.quit.com/how/default.aspx?id=26.

Note: the information in this table is a summary; see package inserts for complete information and specific prescribing instructions.
Fiore MC, Bailey WC, Cohen SJ, Dorfman SF, Goldstein MG, Gritz ER, et al. Treating tobacco use and dependence. Clinical practice guideline. Rockville (MD): U.S. Department of Health and Human Services. Public Health Service; 2000.

is available exclusively over-the-counter and works to promote smoking cessation when used alone, but counseling enhances proper use and technique (4). It is helpful to remind women to read the package insert regarding how to "chew and park" the gum. In the most highly nicotine-dependent smokers, 4 mg of gum seems to be the most effective form of nicotine replacement therapy at present. In less dependent smokers, the transdermal patch may be more convenient. The patch offers a consistent level of nicotine release over a 16–24 hour period (depending on brand). Nicotine patches can be purchased over-the-counter as well as by prescription. The patch is available in 7- to 21-mg strengths and for either 15- or 24-hour use in accordance with a nicotine dependence algorithm on the package. The dosage may be tapered over a 6–8 week period. Local skin irritation resulting from patch use can be greatly decreased if patch sites are rotated. Removal at bedtime may relieve the insomnia some women experience while using the patch.

Nicotine inhalers and nasal sprays are available by prescription only and are efficacious smoking cessation treatments (43). The nicotine lozenge has recently been approved for over-the-counter sale by the FDA and is available in 4-mg and 2-mg strength (54). The inhaler, nasal spray, and lozenge deliver nicotine rapidly to the bloodstream, resembling the effect of cigarette smoking. For smokers with intense cravings and for whom monotherapy nicotine replacement therapy is not effective, the nicotine replacement therapy patch may be combined with another form of nicotine replacement therapy, such as gum or nasal spray, and ad libitum (43). Nicotine replacement therapy may not be equally effective in all patients, and some studies report a reduced efficacy of nicotine replacement therapy in women; however, nicotine replacement therapy has a prominent role to play in tobacco cessation for women and is likely to be safer and more readily available than nonnicotine replacement therapy medications (51).

Bupropion Sustained Release. Bupropion sustained release is available only by prescription. Initially marketed as Wellbrutrin, a treatment for depression, bupropion sustained release has both dopaminergic or adrenergic agonist activity (55). Bupropion sustained release has been shown to decrease nicotine withdrawal symptoms and postpone postcessation weight gain. In a recent review of published data on bupropion sustained release, the medication significantly enhanced cessation rates. Treatment must begin at least 1 week before cessation and may be taken for up to 12 weeks (56). In one trial, bupropion sustained release used with the nicotine patch was found to be significantly more effective than the patch alone (56). Bupropion sustained release may benefit all smokers attempting cessation, including those with no history of depression. This medication also may be helpful in those patients who have not been successful using nicotine replacement therapy in quitting. Reported side effects of bupropion sustained release include seizures, insomnia, dry mouth, and nausea. However, side effects occur infrequently. Bupropion sustained release has not been tested for use during lactation. It is contraindicated in patients with seizure disorders, those with a current or prior diagnosis of bulimia or anorexia nervosa, and in those undergoing abrupt discontinuation of alcohol or sedatives. Concurrent use of a monoamine oxidase inhibitor also is contraindicated (55).

Second-Line Medications

Second-line medications are those for which there is evidence for treating tobacco dependence but have not been approved by the FDA for tobacco treatment and have more potential side effects than first-line medications. Second-line treatments may be considered for use on a case-by-case basis after first-line treatments have been used or considered (43).

Clonidine. Clonidine is a prescription drug originally used as an antihypertensive. It has been studied extensively as a medication for smoking cessation. It acts on the central nervous system and may reduce withdrawal symptoms in various addictive behaviors, including tobacco use. Several trials have shown effective smoking cessation in women, but not in men, after the use of clonidine (51). Because of a high incidence of side effects, such as dry mouth and sedation, clonidine may be considered a second-line therapy for most patients. Severe rebound hypertension may occur if the drug is discontinued rapidly. Clonidine interacts with calcium channel blockers, β-blockers, digitalis, sedatives, and tricyclic antidepressants. It may be targeted to a subgroup of smokers who also may benefit from its sedative effects, as in those expected to experience high levels of agitation and anxiety at the time of nicotine abstinence (57).

Nortriptyline. Nortriptyline, a tricyclic antidepressant, can aid smoking cessation. Trials of nortriptyline show increased quit rates under physician supervision, with the efficacy of the drug independent of its antidepressant effects (58). Nortriptyline use may be associated with arrhythmias. It is contraindicated following a recent MI or with concurrent use of monoamine oxidase inhibitors. Other antidepressants, including tricyclic and selective serotonin reuptake inhibitors, have not had documented effects as successful aids in smoking cessation (43).

Other Pharmacologic Treatments. Other pharmacologic treatments that have been used for nicotine dependence include naltrexone (an opiod receptor antagonist), lobeline (a partial nicotine agonist), fluoxetine (an antidepressant), and anxiolytic agents. There is insufficient evidence to support the use of these medications for smoking cessation at the present time (43).

Other Therapies

Patients may present with requests for advice about nontraditional therapies for smoking cessation. Acupuncture has been suggested as an adjuvant therapy in achieving nicotine abstinence. A recent review of 18 publications revealed no clear evidence that acupuncture is effective for smoking cessation (59).

Aversion therapy pairs the pleasurable stimulus of smoking a cigarette with some unpleasant stimulus. The objective is to extinguish the urge to smoke. Rapid smoking is the most commonly used technique. Aversion smoking interventions appear to increase abstinence rates and may be used with smokers who desire such therapy or for those unsuccessful with other methods (43).

The effect of exercise on smoking cessation outcome requires further study. A meta-analysis of available literature demonstrates a positive effect of exercise on quit rates, but research on larger study populations would be helpful (60).

Special Considerations

Weight Gain

Many women are deterred from quitting smoking because of the fear of weight gain. Smoking cessation among women typically is associated with a weight gain of approximately 6–12 lb in the year after they quit smoking (4). The personal experience of another woman's weight gain during cessation may reinforce the fear of uncontrollable eating. However, actual weight gain during cessation does not predict relapse to smoking (4). Weight gain is not caused by a change in chronic resting metabolic rates after smoking cessa-

tion; tobacco smoke is not an anorectic or a thermogenic agent (51). Weight gain with smoking cessation seems to be caused by a transient increase in oral intake without any change in physical activity. In the Nurses' Health Study, middle-aged women who quit smoking and simultaneously increased their exercise levels minimized weight gain associated with smoking cessation (61). A nutritious diet of low-fat foods, drinking large amounts of non- or low-caloric liquids, and regular exercise can help smokers cope with withdrawal symptoms and minimize weight gain. Several medications prescribed for smoking cessation (particularly nicotine replacement therapy gum and bupropion) may help delay weight gain; however, once the medications are discontinued, most women will experience weight gain (43).

Depression

A history of depression and current depressive symptoms are both independently associated with failure to quit smoking. Some individuals use nicotine to self-treat depression. As a result, smoking cessation may trigger clinical depression in susceptible individuals (62). Antidepressants may be useful aids to smoking cessation in individuals with a past history of depression. Most studies found that those with depression who used bupropion sustained release had significantly higher smoking cessation rates (4).

Adolescents

Each day more than 4,000 children and adolescents try their first cigarette, and more than 2,000 other children and adolescents become daily smokers (5). Smoking among adolescents is a critical issue because most smoking initiation begins before age 18 years, and 82% of adult smokers said they first tried a cigarette before age 18 years (4). This has contributed to the epidemic of long-term nicotine dependence because data suggests that the earlier the onset of smoking, the more severe the addiction is likely to be (63).

A review of predictors of smoking for male and female adolescents suggests that girls who smoke are more self-confident, rebellious, socially advanced, and sexually experienced than their nonsmoking peers (64). Adolescents also begin smoking because of advertising, social and parental norms, peer influence, parental smoking, weight control, and curiosity (65). Adolescent girls who smoke reported continued use because it was "really hard" to quit smoking. One study showed that adolescent females were more likely than adolescent males to report having difficulty going 1 day without smoking and report relying on cigarettes to improve daily functioning (4). Smoking during adolescence produces significant health problems, including cough, phlegm production, increased number and severity of respiratory illness, decreased physical fitness, and reduced lung function (65).

Adolescent Tobacco Prevention

Because tobacco use often begins during pre-adolescence (66), clinicians should routinely assess for tobacco use and intervene with their adolescent patients. Nearly all tobacco use begins before high school, suggesting that if adolescents are kept tobacco free, many will never begin smoking later in adulthood. Tobacco, alcohol, and other drug use counseling is a component of comprehensive anticipatory guidance discussions with adolescent patients. Adolescents who smoke or use any tobacco products should be assessed further to determine their pattern of use. Opportunities to discuss tobacco and other substance abuse may be identified at the time of routine health care as well as when patients are seen for treatment of injuries or episodic illness. It is ideal to interview adolescents privately during each office visit with the reassurance of confidentiality and a discussion of its limits (67, 68). Because of an adolescent's preoccupation with body image, the provider may find it valuable to discuss the effects of smoking and other tobacco products on the adolescent's hair, skin, and breath (68). Adolescents also are open to messages emphasizing the deceptive marketing practices of tobacco companies, which include the placement of smoking in popular teen movies and television shows (69). Counseling also should include a discussion of long-term health consequences, including the possible effect on a female's reproductive potential (68). The clinician's guidance for the parent and other adult caregivers of the early and middle adolescent may include ways to monitor and council the adolescent on tobacco use (68). The clinician also can become involved in supporting effective strategies to curtail adolescent tobacco use at the state and local levels that include supporting excise taxes on tobacco products and restrictive public area and school smoking policies (69).

Oral Contraceptive Use

For most adolescents, OCs can be used regardless of smoking status. Although adolescents, as well as all women, should be encouraged not to smoke, cigarette smoking does not contraindicate use of combination OCs by adolescents as it does for women older than 35 years who smoke. This is because of the low risk of cardiovascular disease among adolescents. The risk that OCs would precipitate hypertension is remote for adolescents (68).

Adolescent Smoking Cessation

Adolescents vastly underestimate the addictiveness of nicotine (69). Because regular smoking typically begins in the adolescent years, smoking cessation messages and methods are essential for adolescents (43). A recent study shows that adolescents' smoking status was identified in 72.4% of office visits, but smoking cessation counseling was provided to adolescent smokers in only 16.95% of office visits (4). Yet, surveys show that 71–83% of adolescent smokers had already experienced an unsuccessful attempt at cessation (69). Clinicians should screen for smoking annually as part of an effort to reduce smoking in adolescents (68, 70, 71).

Another study concluded that clinicians who make an effort to prepare adolescents to quit smoking through motivational interventions, such as brief interventions provided in the office using the 5 A's, adolescent-focused cessation pamphlets, and encouragement, produce higher quit rates than naturally occurring quit rates (43). (See "Resources" for adolescent-specific information.)

Pharmacotherapy for Adolescents

Clinicians may consider the use of nicotine replacement therapy for adolescents when other behavioral treatments have failed and when tobacco dependence is obvious. Confidence of the patient's tobacco dependence and intention to quit can be determined by a thorough assessment of dependence, number of cigarettes smoked per day, and body weight before instituting pharmacotherapy. There is no evidence that nicotine replacement therapy is harmful for children and adolescents (72). Because there may be instances when minors may not be able to purchase over-the-counter nicotine replacement therapy products, some adolescents will need prescription nicotine replacement therapy. Bupropion sustained release is not recommended for use with children and adolescents because its safety and efficacy have not been established (55).

Coding for Smoking Interventions

Health plans do not universally reimburse for either brief or intensive smoking interventions. Some plans may cover medications but not counseling, whereas others may cover counseling but not over-the-counter drugs. If smoking cessation counseling is a covered benefit, providers can code for insurance billing by using the International Classification of Diseases, Ninth Revision, Clinical Modification code 305.1 (tobacco use disorder, tobacco dependence from the Mental Health section) or other diagnoses as appropriate. Many smokers have smoking-related medical diagnoses. For example, the clinician might report smoker's bronchitis or cough (491.0), smoker's throat (472.1), or smoker's tongue (528.6). The Current Procedural Terminology* (CPT®) code reported will vary according to circumstances.

- If the physician counsels the patient at a separate encounter (eg, not as a component of a preventive or problem-oriented visit), he can report a CPT procedure code from the series 99401–99404 (preventive medicine counseling). The correct code depends on the documented time spent counseling the patient. These services are often not covered by insurers.

- If the physician counsels the patient as part of a problem-oriented visit, the procedure coding will vary. If the patient has symptoms, these should also be reported with an appropriate diagnosis code such as those listed previously.

- If more than 50% of the total time spent with the patient was face-to-face counseling, the clinician can report a CPT code according to the typical time listed in the code. Requirements for a complete history, physical examination, and medical decision-making do not apply. For example: An established patient is seen for a problem. The physician performs a problem-focused history and examination and straightforward medical decision-making (the levels of service required for code 99212, which has a typical time of 10 minutes). He also counsels the patient face-to-face for 15 minutes. The total time spent with the patient is 25 minutes. The physician reports code 99214 (which has

typical time of 25 minutes). If the physician spent only 8 minutes in face-to-face counseling with this patient, he reports 99212, using the levels of service to determine the correct code. He cannot report a code according to time spent with the patient because he did not spend more than 50% of the time counseling the patient.

- If the physician counsels the patient as part of a preventive medicine service, then the counseling cannot be reported separately. Preventive medicine services (codes 99281–99397) include counseling/anticipatory guidance/risk factor reduction interventions as part of the service.

- If the physician counsels a pregnant patient as part of a routine antepartum visit, it may be possible to report the service separately. Report a preventive counseling code (99401–99404) with a –25 modifier (significant, separately identifiable E/M service on the same day as another service). It is essential that this service be documented as a separate, significant E/M service in the patient's record. Although it is appropriate to report these services separately, insurers may not reimburse for them.

- If the physician sees a pregnant patient who has symptoms or whose smoking is affecting management of the pregnancy, report diagnosis code 648.43 (mental condition in mother complicating pregnancy) or other diagnoses to indicate symptoms, plus 305.1 (tobacco use disorder). Report a problem-oriented E/M code according to face-to-face time spent with the patient. If the counseling is performed during a routine antepartum visit, add a modifier –25 to the E/M code. If she is seen for a separate visit, no modifier is needed. Many payers will not reimburse for this counseling.

- If a nurse counsels the patient, and if nurses are recognized by the insurance company as "qualified" providers of the service, then code 99211 (established patient office visit) is reported. If the nurse is not recognized as a caregiver, the services will not be covered.

References

1. Bergen AW, Caporaso N. Cigarette smoking. J Natl Cancer Inst 1999;91:1365–75.

2. Centers for Disease Control. Mothers who smoked cigarettes during pregnancy, according to mother's detailed race, Hispanic origin, age, and education: Selected States, 1989–2001. National Center for Health Statistics, Hyattsville (MD); 2003. Available at: http://www.cdc.gov/nchs/data/hus/tables/2003/03hus011.pdf. Retrieved September 22, 2004.

3. Centers for Disease Control. Cigarette smoking-related mortality. Atlanta (GA); 2001. Available at: http://www.cdc.gov/tobacco/research_data/health_consequences/mortali.htm. Retrieved December 30, 2003.

4. U.S. Department of Health and Human Services. Women and smoking: a report of the Surgeon General. Washington, DC: U.S. Government Printing Office; 2001. Available at: http://www.hhs.gov/surgeongeneral/library/womenandtobacco/. Retrieved September 24, 2004.

5. Substance Abuse and Mental Health Services Administration. Tobacco use in America: findings from the 1999 NHSDA. Rockville (MD): SAMHSA; 2003. Available at: http://www.samhsa.gov/OAS/NHSDA/tobacco/highlights.htm. Retrieved December 30, 2003.

6. Everett SA, Husten CG, Kann L, Warren CW, Sharp D, Crossett L. Smoking initiation and smoking patterns among US college students. J Am Coll Health 1999;48:55–60.

7. Trends in cigarette smoking among high school students— United States, 1991–2001. MMWR Morb Mortal Wkly Rep 2002;51:409–12.

8. U.S. Public Health Service. Treating tobacco use and dependence: fact sheet. Washington, DC: USPHS; 2000.

9. Mueller L, Ciervo CA. Smoking in women. J Am Osteopath Assoc 1998;98 suppl:S7–10.

10. Pidoplichko VI, DeBiasi M, Williams JT, Dani JA. Nicotine activates and desensitizes midbrain dopamine neurons. Nature 1997;390:401–4.

11. Prokopczyk B, Cox JE, Hoffman D, Waggoner SE. Identification of tobacco-specific carcinogen in the cervical mucus of smokers and nonsmokers. J Natl Cancer Inst 1997;89:868–73.

12. Hoffmann D, Hoffman I. The changing cigarette. 1950–1995. J Toxicol Environ Health 1997;50:307–64.

13. Nordlund LA, Cartensen JM, Pershagen G. Cancer incidence in female smokers: a 26-year follow-up. Int J Cancer 1997;73:625–8.

14. Augudo A, Ahrens W, Benhamou E, Benhamou S, Boffeta P, Darby SC, et al. Lung cancer and cigarette smoking in women: a multicenter case-control study in Europe. Int J Cancer 2000;88:820–7.

15. U.S. Department of Health and Human Services. The health consequences of smoking: a report of the Surgeon General. Washington, DC: U.S. Government Printing Office; 2004. Available at: http://www.surgeongeneral.gov/library. Retrieved September 22, 2004.

16. Kjellberg L, Hallmans G, Ahren AM, Johansson R, Bergman F, Wadell G, et al. Smoking, diet, pregnancy, and oral contraceptive use as risk factors for cervical intraepithelial neoplasia in relation to human papillomavirus infection. Br J Cancer 2000;82:1332–8.

17. Castle PE, Wacholder S, Lorincz AT, Scott DR, Sherman ME, Glass AG, et al. A prospective study of high-grade cervical neoplasia risk among human papillomavirus-infected women. J Natl Cancer Inst 2002;94:1406–14.

18. American College of Obstetricians and Gynecologists. Cervical cytology screening. ACOG Practice Bulletin No. 45. Obstet Gynecol 2003;102:417–27.

19. Modugno F, Ness RB, Cottreau CM. Cigarette smoking and the risk of mucinous and nonmucinous epithelial ovarian cancer. Epidemiology 2002;13:467–71.

20. Spangler JG. Smoking and hormone-related disorders. Prim Care 1999;26:499–511.

21. Friedman GD, Tekawa I, Sadler M, Sidney S. Smoking and mortality, the Kaiser Permanente experience. In: National Cancer Institute. Changes in cigarette-related disease risks and their implication for prevention and control. Smoking and Tobacco Control Monograph 8. Bethesda (MD): NCI; 1997. p. 477–99. NIH Pub No. 97–4213.

22. Willett WC, Green A, Stampfer MJ, Speizer FE, Colditz GA, Rosner B, et al. Relative and absolute excess risks of coronary heart disease among women who smoke cigarettes. N Engl J Med 1987;317:1303–9.

23. Al-Delaimy WK, Manson JE, Solomon CG, Kawachi I, Stampfer MJ, Willett WC, et al. Smoking and risk of coronary heart disease among women with type 2 diabetes mellitus. Arch Intern Med 2002;162:273–9.

24. Vriz O, Nesbitt S, Krause L, Majahalme S, Lu H, Julius S. Smoking is associated with higher cardiovascular risk in young women than in men. The Tecumseh Blood Pressure Study. J Hypertens 1997;15:127–34.

25. Prescott E, Hippe M, Schnohr P, Hein HO, Vestbo J. Smoking and risk of myocardial infarction in women and men: longitudinal population study. BMJ 1998;316:1043–7.

26. Njolstad I, Arnesen E, Lund-Larsen PG. Smoking, serum lipids, blood pressure and sex differences in myocardial infarction: a 12-year follow-up of the Finnmark Study. Circulation 1996;93:450–6.

27. Hankey GJ. Smoking and risk of stroke. J Cardiovasc Risk 1999;6:207–11.

28. Tanis BC, van den Bosch MA, Kemmeren JM, Cats VM, Helmerhorst FM, Algra A, et al. Oral contraceptives and the risk of myocardial infarction. N Engl J Med 2001;345:1787–93.

29. Vessey M, Painter R, Yeates D. Mortality in relation to oral contraceptive use and cigarette smoking. Lancet 2003;362:185–91.

30. Rosenberg L, Palmer JR, Shapiro S. Decline in the risk of myocardial infarction among women who stop smoking. N Eng J Med 1990;322:213–7.

31. Wainer R. Smoking and ovarian fertility [French]. Gynecol Obstet Fertil 2001;29:881–7.

32. Jensen J. Smoking and postmenopausal hormone replacement therapy. Br J Clin Pract Suppl 1996;86:6–8.

33. Law MR, Hackshaw AK. A meta-analysis of cigarette smoking, bone mineral density and risk of hip fracture: recognition of a major effect. BMJ 1997;315:841–6.

34. Krall EA, Dawson-Hughes B. Smoking increases bone loss and decreases intestinal calcium absorption. J Bone Miner Res 1999;14:215–20.

35. Augood C, Duckitt K, Templeton AA. Smoking and female infertility: a systematic review and meta-analysis. Hum Reprod 1998;13:1532–9.

36. Cramer DW. Smoking and female fertility. In: Shields W, Kennedy C, editors. ARHP clinical proceedings: current issues in smoking and reproductive health. 1996 October; Washington, DC: Association of Reproductive Health Professionals; 1996. p. 5–6.

37. Hughes EG, Brennan BG. Does cigarette smoking impair natural or assisted fecundity? Fertil Steril 1996;66:679–89.

38. Andres RL, Day MC. Perinatal complications associated with maternal tobacco use. Semin Neonatol 2000;5:231–41.

39. American Academy of Pediatrics, American College of Obstetricians and Gynecologists. Guidelines for perinatal care, 5th ed. Elk Grove Village (IL); AAP; Washington, DC: ACOG; 2002.

40. Fingerhut LA, Kleinman JC, Kendrick JS. Smoking before, during, and after pregnancy. Am J Public Health 1990:80:541–4.

41. Lando HA, Valanis BG, Lichtenstein E, Curry SJ, McBride CM, Pirie PL, et al. Promoting smoking abstinence in pregnant and postpartum patients: a comparison of 2 approaches. Am J Manag Care 2001:7:685–93.

42. US Environmental Protection Agency. Asthma and indoor environments—asthma triggers—secondhand smoke. Available at: http://www.epa.gov/iaq/asthma/triggers/shs.html. Retrieved February 6, 2004.

43. Fiore MC, Bailey WC, Cohen SJ, Dorfman SF, Goldstein MG, Gritz ER, et al. Treating tobacco use and dependence. Clinical practice guideline. Rockville (MD): U.S. Department of Health and Human Services, Public Health Service; 2000.

44. Barzilai DA, Goodwin MA, Zyzanski SJ, Stange KC. Does health habit counseling affect patient satisfaction? Prev Med 2001; 33:595–9.

45. National Cancer Institute. How to help your patients stop smoking: a National Cancer Institute manual for physicians. Bethesda (MD): NCI; 1995. NIH Publication No. 95–3064.

46. Pomerleau CS. Smoking and nicotine replacement treatment issues specific to women. Am J Health Behav 1996;20:291–9.

47. U.S. Department of Health and Human Services. Treating tobacco use and dependence: a systems approach. A guide for health care administrators, insurers, managed organizations, and purchasers. US PHS. Washington, DC: US DHHS; 2000.

48. National Institute for Clinical Excellence. Guidance on the use of nicotine replacement therapy (NRT) and bupropion for smoking cessation. Technology Appraisal Guidance No. 39. London: NICE; 2002.

49. Song F, Raftery J, Aveyard P, Hyde C, Barton P, Woolacott N. Cost-effectiveness of pharmacological interventions for smoking cessation: a literature review and decision analytic analysis. Med Decis Making 2002;22:S26–37.

50. Silagy C, Lancaster T, Stead L, Mant D, Fowler G. Nicotine replacement therapy for smoking cessation (Cochrane Review) In: The Cochrane Library, Issue 1, 2004. Chichester, UK: John Wiley & Sons, Ltd.

51. Perkins KA. Metabolic effects of cigarette smoking. J Appl Physiol 1992;72:401–9.

52. American College of Obstetricians and Gynecologists. Smoking cessation during pregnancy. ACOG Educational Bulletin 260. Washington, DC: ACOG; 2000.

53. Zevin S, Jacob P 3rd, Benowitz NL. Dose-related cardiovascular and endocrine effects of transdermal nicotine. Clin Pharmacol Ther 1998;64:87–95.

54. GlaxoSmithKline. US Food and Drug Administration approves effective new tool to help smokers quit. Available at: http://www.gsk.com/press_archive/press_10312002.htm. Retrieved January 8, 2004.

55. GlaxoSmithKline. Zyban (bupropion hydrochloride) sustained-release tablets. In: Physicians' desk reference. 58th ed. Montvale (NJ): Thomson PDR; 2004. p. 1687–92.

56. Hughes JR, Goldstein MG, Hurt RD, Shiffman S. Recent advances in the pharmacotherapy of smoking. JAMA 1999;281:72–6.

57. Gourlay SG, Stead LF, Benowitz NL. Clonidine for smoking cessation (Cochrane Review). In: The Cochrane Library, Issue 4, 2003. Chichester, UK: John Wiley & Sons, Ltd.

58. Benowitz NL, Dempsey DA, Goldenberg RL, Hughes JR, Dolan-Mullen P, Ogburn PL, et al. The use of pharmacotherapies for smoking cessation during pregnancy. Tob Control 2000;9: iii91–iii94.

59. White AR, Rampes H, Ernst E. Acupuncture for smoking cessation (Cochrane Review). In: The Cochrane Library, Issue 1, 2004. Chichester, UK: John Wiley & Sons, Ltd.

60. Nishi N, Jenicek M, Tatara K. A meta-analytic review of the effect of exercise on smoking cessation. J Epidemiol 1998; 8:79–84.

61. Kawachi I, Troisi RJ, Rotnitzky AG, Coakley EH, Colditz GA. Can physical activity minimize weight gain in women after smoking cessation? Am J Pub Health 1996;86:999–1004.

62. Bock BC, Goldstein MG, Marcus BH. Depression following smoking cessation in women. J Subst Abuse 1996;8:137–44.

63. Breslau N, Peterson EL. Smoking cessation in young adults: age at initiation of cigarette smoking and other suspected influences. Am J Public Health 1996;86:214–20.

64. Clayton S. Gender differences in psychosocial determinants of adolescent smoking. J Sch Health 1991;61:115–20.

65. U.S. Department of Health and Human Services. Preventing tobacco use among young people: a report of the Surgeon General. Washington, DC: U.S. Government Printing Office; 1994. Available at: http://www.cdc.gov/tobacco/sgr/sgr_1994/index.htm. Retrieved October 19, 2004.

66. DiFranza JR, Savageau JA, Fletcher K, Ockene JK, Rigotti NA, McNeill AD, et al. Measuring the loss of autonomy over nicotine use in adolescents. The DANDY (Development and Assessment of Nicotine Dependence in Youths) study. Arch Pediatr Adolesc Med 2002;156:397–403.

67. Tobacco, alcohol, and other drugs; the role of the pediatrician in prevention and management of substance abuse. AAP Policy Statement. American Academy of Pediatrics. Pediatrics 1998; 101:125–8.

68. American College of Obstetricians and Gynecologists. Health care for adolescents. Washington, DC: ACOG; 2003.

69. Sargent JD, DiFranza JR. Tobacco control for clinicians who treat adolescents. [published erratum appears in CA Cancer J Clin 2003;53:316.] CA Cancer J Clin 2003;53:102–23.

70. Thorndike AN, Ferris TG, Stafford RS, Rigotti NA. Rates of U.S. physicians counseling adolescents about smoking. J Nat Cancer Inst 1999;91:1857–62.

71. Elster AB, Kuzhets NJ. AMA guidelines for adolescent preventive services (GAPS): recommendations and rationale. Baltimore (MD): Williams & Wilkins; 1994.

72. Hurt RD, Croghan GA, Beede SD, Wolter TD, Croghan IT, Patten CA. Nicotine patch therapy in 101 adolescent smokers: efficacy, withdrawal symptom relief, and carbon monoxide and plasma cotinine levels. Arch Pediatr Adolesc Med 2000;154: 31–37.

Resources

ACOG Resources

A Clinician's Guide to Helping Pregnant Women Quit Smoking: Includes a free CME-accredited guide that outlines how to integrate the "5 A's" and a slide presentation with lecture notes. To order, e-mail smoking@acog.org.

American College of Obstetricians and Gynecologists. Good health before pregnancy: preconceptional care. ACOG Patient Education Pamphlet AP056. Washington, DC: ACOG; 1999.

American College of Obstetricians and Gynecologists. It's time to quit smoking. ACOG Patient Education Pamphlet AP065. Washington, DC: ACOG; 2000.

American College of Obstetricians and Gynecologists. Smoking cessation during pregnancy. ACOG Educational Bulletin 260. Washington, DC: ACOG; 2000.

American College of Obstetricians and Gynecologists. Tobacco use and adolescent girls. Tool Kit For Teen Care Fact Sheet AA415. Washington, DC: ACOG; 2003.

"Ask About Tobacco Use" chart stickers (AA268)

Patient Workbook: Need Help Putting Out That Cigarette (AP424)

Poster: Be Good to Yourself, Smoking Hurts You. We Can Help You Quit

Virtual Clinic. Smoking Cessation for Pregnancy and Beyond. CD ROM includes lectures and case discussion, interactive patient simulations for case-based learning, real-life patient interviews and web resources. Can be ordered through the ACOG distribution center or downloaded at http://www.iml.dartmouth.edu/edu/education/cme/smoking (high-speed internet access required).

Other Resources

The resources listed as follows are for information purposes only. Referral to these sources and web sites does not imply the endorsement of ACOG. This list is not meant to be comprehensive. The exclusion of a source or web site does not reflect the quality of that source or web site. Please note that web sites are subject to change without notice.

Smoking Cessation Programs and Self-help Materials

Many states offer free or low cost smoking cessation counseling services consisting of telephone quitlines, group or individual counseling programs, as well as materials to help the smoker quit and prevent relapse. To access, check with the state or local public health office or tobacco control program.

Agency for Health Care Quality and Research
540 Gaither Road
Rockville, MD 20850
Tel: 800-358-9295
E-mail: ahrqpubs@ahrq.gov
Web: www.ahrq.gov/path/tobacco.htm

The Agency for Health Care Quality and Research offers free and low-cost materials for consumers in English and Spanish, including "easy to read" consumer booklets on tobacco cessation for all smokers and pregnant women. Its web site has consumer materials, posters, and provider guidelines that can be downloaded.

American Academy of Family Physicians
11400 Tomahawk Creek Parkway
Leawood, KS 66211-2672
Tel: 800-944-0000
Web: www.aafp.org

The American Academy of Family Physicians developed *Patient Education in Your Practice: A Handbook for the Office Setting* in 2000. This is a handbook on clinician patient education techniques. CME credit is available.

American Cancer Society
2200 Century Parkway, Suite 950
Atlanta, GA 30345
Tel: 800-227-2345
Web: www.acs.org

The American Cancer Society (ACS) collects and disseminates data, supports anti-tobacco legislation, undertakes advocacy and media initiatives; and supports the Great American Smokeout each November. Programs and self-help material are available for smokers. Fresh Start is the society's group smoking-cessation program run at the local chapter level. A local ACS chapter can be contacted for information. Make This a Fresh-Start Family is a curriculum for health care providers who give personal counseling to pregnant women and mothers of young children to stop smoking.

American Legacy Foundation
2030 M Street, NW, 6th Floor
Washington, DC 20036
Tel: (202) 454-5555
Fax: (202) 454-5599
E-mail: info@americanlegacy.org
Web: www.americanlegacy.org

The American Legacy Foundation is a national independent foundation created by the tobacco master settlement agreement to prevent tobacco use in children and eliminate the disparities in access to tobacco prevention and cessation services. This foundation provides grants and technical assistance and training to support innovative tobacco control efforts and offers free information to help women stop smoking at 800/4-A-Legacy or online at http://women.americanlegacy.org. The Legacy Great Start Campaign is a 24/7 quitline specifically for pregnant smokers offering telephone counseling and materials at 866-66-START.

American Lung Association
61 Broadway, 6th Floor
New York, NY 10006
Tel: (212) 315-8700
Web: www.lungusa.org

The American Lung Association provides anti-tobacco advocacy and support for smoking cessation. Local chapters run smoking cessation clinics. The national organization has a web-based smoking cessation counseling program called "Freedom From Smoking."

Asthma and Allergy Foundation
1233 20th Street, NW, Suite 402
Washington, DC 20036
Tel: (202) 466-7643; 800-7-ASTHMA
Fax: (202) 466-8940
E-mail: info@aafa.org
Web: www.aafa.org

The Asthma and Allergy Foundation provides information and advocacy on the issue of environmental tobacco smoke for clinicians, educators, and consumers.

Campaign for Tobacco-Free Kids
National Center for Tobacco-Free Kids
1400 Eye Street, NW, Suite 1200
Washington, DC 20005
Tel: (202) 296-5469
Web: www.tobaccofreekids.org

The Campaign for Tobacco-Free Kids provides state specific data, particularly on child and adolescent tobacco use and the direct and indirect cost of use and environmental tobacco smoke. It works to change public policy on tobacco at the federal, state, and community level.

Centers for Disease Control and Prevention
Office on Smoking and Health
Mail Stop K-50
4770 Buford Highway, NE
Atlanta, GA 30341-3717
Web: www.cdc.gov/tobacco/index.htm

The Office on Smoking and Health in the Centers for Disease Control and Prevention leads and coordinates efforts at preventing tobacco use among youth, promotes smoking cessation among youth and adults, protects nonsmokers from environmental tobacco smoke, and works to eliminate tobacco-related health disparities. The office provides data and educational materials for consumers, clinicians, and legislators; funds research and demonstration projects; and provides online cessation and advocacy information. It produced *Women and Tobacco: Seven Deadly Myths*, which is an educational video for young women exploring the myths about smoking and encouraging women to become smoke-free. The video and workbook can be downloaded from the web site at http://www.cdc.gov/tobacco/christy/myths.htm.

The Chest Foundation
Tel: 800-343-ACCP (2227)
Web: www.chestnet.org/education/physician/tobacco/index.php

The Chest Foundation produced a Tobacco Cessation Tool Kit. This kit is based on the clinical practice guidelines and provides screening forms, check lists, chart stickers, pharmacotherapy information, and resources for patients and clinicians.

Dental Tobacco Cessation Consultants, Inc.
Indiana University School of Dentistry
1121 W Michigan Street
Indianapolis, IN 46202
Tel: (317) 274-3859
Fax: (317) 274-2419
Web: www.iusd.iupui.edu/depts/ob/tobaccoeduc_control.htm

Joan and Arden Christen of Dental Tobacco Cessation Consultants, Inc. developed *The Female Smoker: From Addiction to Recovery: A Professional Teaching Monograph*. This book provides strategies for clinical and community support for women's smoking cessation.

Environmental Protection Agency
Indoor Environments Division
1200 Pennsylvania Avenue, NW
Mail Code 6609J
Washington, DC 20460
Tel: (202) 343-9370
Fax: (202) 343-2392
Web: www.epa.gov/smokefree

The Environmental Protection Agency has programs and information to reduce child, employee, and public exposure to environmental tobacco smoke. This includes the "Smokefree Homes" program, environmental tobacco smoke speaker's kits, and brochures and facts sheets for consumers and professionals.

International Network of Women Against Tobacco
PO Box 224
Metuchen, NJ 08840
Tel: (732) 549-9054
Fax: (732) 549-9056
Web: www.inwat.org

The International Network of Women Against Tobacco collects and distributes information regarding global women and tobacco issues, supports the development of women-centered tobacco use prevention and cessation programs, and assists in the organization and planning of conferences on tobacco control.

Joe Chemo
Web: www.joechemo.org

The Joe Chemo Interactive web site allows visitors to test their "Tobacco IQ," get a personalized "Smoke-o-Scope," and send free Joe Chemo E-Cards. It has information for teachers, health care providers, and smokers who want to quit.

Join Together
1 Appleton Street, 4th floor
Boston, MA 02116-5223
Tel: (617) 437-1500
Fax: (617) 437-9394
E-mail: info@jointogether.org
Web: www.jointogether.org

Join Together provides advocacy and information for professionals and consumers on issues of tobacco, substance abuse, and gun violence. It has daily and weekly journal scans as well as weekly updates on funding opportunities.

March of Dimes
1275 Mamaroneck Avenue
White Plains, NY 10605
Tel: 888-MODIMES (888-663-4637)
Web: www.modimes.org

The March of Dimes supports research through the national office and community projects and grand rounds presentations through local chapters. It has informational materials for consumers and providers. The national office can be contacted for local contact information.

National Conference on State Legislatures
444 North Capitol Street, NW, Suite 515
Washington, DC 20001
Tel: (202) 624-5400
Fax: (202) 737-1069
Web: www.ncsl.org

The National Conference on State Legislatures is a source for research, publications, consulting assistance, meetings, and seminars to inform state legislators on policy issues, such as tobacco use. It tracks state-by-state legislation on key tobacco issues.

National Latino Council on Alcohol and Tobacco Prevention
1616 P Street NW, Suite 430
Washington, DC 20009
Tel: (202) 265-8054
E-mail: lcat@nlcatp.org
Web: www.nlcatp.org

The National Latino Council on Alcohol and Tobacco Prevention works through policy analysis, community education, training, and information dissemination by way of a network of community councils.

Nicotine Anonymous World Services
419 Main Street, PMB #370
Huntington Beach, CA 92648
Tel: (415) 750-0328
Web: www.nicotine-anonymous.org

Nicotine Anonymous World Services is a nonprofit fellowship of men and women who help each other to lead nicotine-free lives. It offers meetings and literature for individuals.

QuitNet
1 Appleton Street, 4th Floor
Boston, MA 02116
Tel: (617) 437-1500
Fax: (617) 437-9394
Web: www.quitnet.com

QuitNet provides online smoking cessation counseling and information in English and Spanish.

Quit Smoking Internet Discussion Groups
Web: www.geocities.com/HotSprings/Spa/8122/

Quit Smoking Internet Discussion Groups provide active links to forums, pen pals, chat rooms, and newsgroups for those interested in stopping smoking.

Smoke-Free Families National Dissemination Office
Cecil G. Sheps Center for Health Services Research
CB #7590, 725 Airport Road
University of North Carolina at Chapel Hill
Chapel Hill, NC 27599-7590
Tel: (919) 843-7663
Fax: (919) 966-9764
E-mail: smokefreefamilies@unc.edu
Web: www.smokefreefamilies.org

Smoke-Free Families is a program funded through the Robert Wood Johnson Foundation that is dedicated to finding innovative evidence-based treatment for pregnant smokers. It provides professional resources, funds research and demonstration projects, advocates for tobacco legislation, and provides direct assistance to smokers.

Society for Women's Health Research
1828 L St, NW, Ste 625
Washington, DC 20036
866-HERCANCER
http://www.hercancer.com

The Society for Women's Health Research web site provides information about differences between men and women in lung cancer and tobacco addiction, with links to resources for finding clinical trials and medical research processes.

Women's Tobacco Prevention Network
Employee and Family Resources, Inc.
505 Fifth Ave, Ste 930
Des Moines, IA 50309
888-251-4507
Fax: (515) 288-4534
http://www.efr.org/wtpn

Women's Tobacco Prevention Network works primarily with national associations serving women to focus on tobacco issues and to assist women and organizations in preventing and eliminating tobacco use, especially among underrepresented populations.

Intimate Partner Violence and Domestic Violence

Key Points

- Intimate partner violence and domestic violence cross all racial, ethnic, religious, educational, age, and socioeconomic lines and have tremendous social, economic, and public health implications.

- The medical community can play a vital role in identifying intimate partner violence and domestic violence cases and halting the cycle of abuse.

- Although obstetrician–gynecologists may be called to see patients with acute injuries to the genitalia or reproductive system, they are more likely to see nonacute presentations of abuse.

- Being female is a significant enough risk factor for intimate partner violence and domestic violence to warrant screening every patient at periodic intervals, such as annual examinations and new patient visits.

- With disclosure of ongoing intimate partner violence and domestic violence, the physician's responsibility is to acknowledge the abuse, implement the support system for immediate referrals, assess safety, assist with reporting as necessary, document appropriately, and provide ongoing clinical care. For disclosure of past violence, the responsibilities are similar but generally do not require immediate intervention for safety and reporting.

- Pregnancy is an especially risky time for an abused woman. Screening for intimate partner violence and domestic violence should, therefore, occur at the first prenatal visit, at least once per trimester, and at the postpartum visit.

- Adolescents are at risk for intimate partner violence and domestic violence. Screening adolescents and providing information about intimate partner violence and domestic violence to adolescents is important.

- It is useful to have a specific protocol for responding to intimate partner violence and domestic violence that can be easily implemented and uses available resources.

- A basic understanding of legal measures and considerations can enhance a physician's ability to counsel and assist women in violent relationships.

Intimate partner violence is a worldwide problem . . . . It crosses all ethnic, religious, educational, and socioeconomic lines . . .

169

Intimate partner violence is a worldwide problem that affects women disproportionately. It crosses all racial, ethnic, religious, educational, and socioeconomic lines and has tremendous social, economic, and public health implications (1–3). Intimate partner violence is not a new phenomenon but rather is rooted in a deep history throughout the world. It often is referred to as gender-based violence and has been declared a violation of human rights (4).

Although there is no single definition of intimate partner violence that satisfies all medical, social, and criminal justice purposes, the term "intimate partner violence" typically refers to violence perpetrated against adolescent and adult women within the context of past or current intimate relationships. The term "domestic" violence also is used by many to describe intimate partner violence. This term, however, encompasses other forms of violence, including abuse of older individuals and children.

Although victims of intimate partner violence may be male or female, cases overwhelmingly involve female victims (5). The violence can involve actual or threatened physical, sexual, psychologic, financial, or emotional trauma against another individual. It is best understood on the basis of the relationship context in which the violence occurs, the behaviors of the abuser, and the function and expectations that these behaviors serve (6). The violence is meted out in a deliberate, repetitive, and ongoing, but unpredictable, process that also uses harassment, intimidation, and threats of additional violence to achieve control over the victim (Fig. 10) (6, 7).

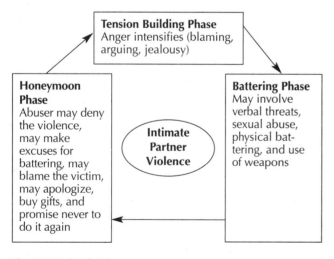

Fig. 10. Cycle of violence.

Physical violence can include throwing objects, pushing, kicking, biting, slapping, hitting, beating, threatening with any form of weapon, or using a weapon. Sexual violence takes many forms, including rape and other nonconsensual sexual activities. It can include sabotaging the use of birth control or refusal to follow safer sex practices. The focus of psychologic or emotional abuse is harassment and includes verbal abuse (name calling, denigration, degradation, blaming); threats; social isolation (from family, friends, and work); and deprivation of food, money, transportation, medications, and access to health care (8). It also can include destruction of personal property and pet abuse. Financial abuse or the rationing or control of medications or resources frequently is involved when elderly victims are concerned. Stalking is a severe form of harassment and is considered a significant risk factor for major harm (9).

Intimate partner violence often occurs within a larger framework of family violence that can include physical or sexual abuse of a child, elder mistreatment, and abuse of adults who are disabled. Victims of all ages share certain fundamental elements of abuse and victimization, but the mechanisms and short- and long-term sequelae are different for child, adolescent, reproductive-aged, and elderly victims (3).

Attention to the effects of intimate partner violence and domestic violence first appeared in the literature in the 1970s. During the succeeding decades, intimate partner violence and domestic violence became recognized as both a criminal act and a major public health problem. As a result, guidelines and templates for screening, diagnosis, and treatment have been developed and disseminated by numerous medical professional organizations, including the American College of Obstetricians and Gynecologists (ACOG) (8, 10–12), and incorporated into licensing and credentialing criteria (13). Since the mid-1980s, ACOG has been advocating against intimate partner violence and domestic violence and for the improvement of women's health through active involvement of its fellowship (14). Obstetrician–gynecologists are in the unique position to provide assistance because of the special nature of the patient–physician relationship and the many opportunities that are available during the course of pregnancy, annual examinations, and follow-up visits for ongoing care.

Epidemiology

The true prevalence of intimate partner violence and domestic violence is difficult to ascertain. Recent efforts to standardize definitions have produced more generalizable and consistent data within the United States. These estimates of prevalence, however, are most likely still understated because many victims fear disclosing their personal experiences of violence.

It is estimated that 2 million women are abused every year by someone they know (15). Surveys suggest that 25% of women in the United States have reported partner violence at some time during their lives, creating a one in four lifetime chance for experiencing family violence (16). Approximately one third of female victims experienced violence more than once during the preceding 6 months.

According to the Department of Justice, intimate partner violence accounts for 22% of all violent crimes against women (17). The Centers for Disease Control and Prevention reports that approximately one in three female homicides is caused by intimate partner violence, whereas only 5% of male homicides are caused by this kind of violence (18). Two thirds of all rapes are committed by an intimate partner (19).

All age groups are affected by intimate partner violence and domestic violence. Four percent of intimate partner homicide cases occur in adolescents and are reported as early as age 12 years. Peak rates occur among those aged between 20–39 years. Six percent of partner homicides occur in women older than 65 years (18). Among all pregnant women, 0.9–21% experience domestic violence (20).

Health Effects

Thirty percent of female intimate partner violence victims have injuries that require significant medical attention (16). Thirty-seven percent of women seen in hospital emergency departments are thought to be victims of intimate partner violence or domestic violence, although it is well established that only a fraction of the cases seen there are recognized or documented as such (21). Injuries often are severe and most commonly involve the head, face, breasts, or abdomen (8). Other symptoms associated with intimate partner violence include general symptoms of pain (headache, backache, body ache), abdominal discomfort and digestive problems, and sleep and eating disorders (22, 23). These are likely to be clinical manifestations of internalized stress (ie, somatization). The cyclic repetition of intimate partner violence and the constant threat of violence juxtaposed with kindness eventually lead to psychologic weakness and helplessness that can manifest as posttraumatic stress disorder and battered woman syndrome (24).

Posttraumatic Stress Disorder

In victims of abuse, posttraumatic stress disorder often is associated with depression, anxiety disorders, substance abuse, somatization, and suicide. Research confirms the long-term physical and psychologic consequences of ongoing or past violence (25). The stress of living in a ongoing abusive relationship contributes to chronic headaches; chronic pelvic pain; sleep and appetite disturbances; sexual dysfunction; abdominal problems; palpitations; chronic vaginitis; and mental health problems, such as feelings of inadequacy and self-blame, depression, mood and anxiety disorders, suicidal ideation, and suicide (25, 26).

Battered Woman Syndrome

Battered woman syndrome is based on the ongoing failure to identify the etiology of acute injuries and coexisting emotional distress (27, 28). Over time this leads to somatization with the development of medically unexplained symptoms. On a repetitive basis, the inability to eradicate the symptoms leads to progressive and significant frustration for both victim/patient and physician. As these patients continue to seek care for recurring injuries or long-term problems, they develop thick medical records with multiple physician visits; see many consultants; and have multiple prescriptions, especially for analgesics and psychotropic medications.

A national cross-sectional survey of 1,800 women showed that those who are victims of lifetime physical or sexual abuse have poorer health status, some form of disability or a chronic condition, are more depressed and anxious, and report more difficulty in receiving needed medical care when compared with never-abused women (29). Mental health symptoms associated with intimate partner violence include feelings of inadequacy and self-blame, substance abuse, and suicide attempts (25, 26).

Obstetric and Gynecologic Presentations

Although obstetrician–gynecologists may be called to see patients with acute injuries to the genitalia or reproductive system, they are more likely to see nonacute presentations of abuse. These include chronic and unexplained pelvic pain; urinary frequency, urgency, and dysuria; sexual dysfunction (as dyspareunia, vaginismus, libido changes, and anxiety related to sexuality); irritable bowel syndrome; recurrent vaginitis; irregular menstrual patterns; specific trauma to the genitalia and breasts from sexual assaults, including bite marks; and sexually transmitted diseases (STDs) from partner infidelity. Persistent, recurrent, or resistant vaginitis and STDs can be associated with physical and sexual abuse (30). The association of partner violence with STDs can occur through rape and coitus without a condom. A woman's request to use a condom or disclosing to her partner that she has an STD, especially human immunodeficiency virus (HIV), can trigger violence (30–33). Awareness of these presentations can help in addressing a particular clinical issue that has been difficult to resolve or in working with a "difficult" patient (Box 16).

Women who present with an unintended pregnancy may be victims of abuse. Unintended pregnancies account for approximately 40% of all pregnancies but may account for as many as 70% of pregnancies in abused women. The national rape-related pregnancy rate is 5% per rape among victims of reproductive age (age 12–45 years), accounting for approximately 32,000 pregnancies per year. Most of these pregnancies involved a known perpetrator (29.4% boyfriend, 17.6% husband, 11.8% relative, 5.9% father-stepfather) (34). In addition, women who have been physically or psychologically abused as children or adolescents are at increased risk for unintended pregnancy. (See discussions on child and adolescent abuse under "Special Populations" in this chapter and the chapter on "Adult Manifestations of Childhood Sexual Abuse.")

Many victims of intimate partner violence will not disrobe completely for a pelvic examination when asked to do so. In spite of a clear intellectual understanding of what is necessary for a successful examination, victims of physical and sexual assault may have difficulty assuming the lithotomy position, may withdraw rapidly even before the perineum is touched,

---

Box 16   Clinical Manifestations That Alert the Physician to Possible Intimate Partner Violence and Domestic Violence

No single presentation confirms intimate partner violence or domestic violence. Clinical judgment is imperative.

- Delayed presentation and inadequate explanations of physical injuries (eg, unexplained bruises or abrasions)
- Unusual difficulty during the gynecologic examination:
  —Excessive distress or discomfort out of proportion to the clinical situation
  —Avoidance behavior (eg, excessive sensitivity in the perineal area, clenching buttocks; keeping knees together, flattened affect or "zoning out"
- Chronic and unexplained pelvic pain, urinary symptoms, sexual dysfunction, or irritable bowel syndrome
- Persistent/recurrent/resistant vaginitis or sexually transmitted disease in spite of adequate treatment
- Vague, repetitive, and elusive somatic symptoms such as headache, backache, palpitations, abdominal and digestive problems, or sleep and eating disorders
- Unintended pregnancy
- Symptoms of posttraumatic stress disorder: depression, anxiety, phobias, panic attacks, feelings of shame, inadequacy, and worthlessness, suicidal ideation

---

and manifest other forms of avoidance behavior such as clenching the buttocks and keeping their knees together, even when repeatedly asked to permit the examination. During examinations, they may appear to "zone out," demonstrate excessive distress or discomfort out of proportion to the clinical symptoms, or deny actual pain on examination. Some will cry and not be able to offer an explanation for this behavior. These are all suggestive of posttraumatic stress disorder and are clues that a woman may have been or currently is being physically or sexually abused.

Social and Economic Effects

The societal and economic effects of intimate partner violence are profound. The costs of intimate partner violence against women exceed an estimated $5.8 billion. These costs include nearly $4.1 billion in the direct costs of medical care and mental health care (35). These considerable expenses result in significantly higher costs to health insurance plans for intimate partner violence victims than for the general female enrollee (36).

Services for victims of intimate partner violence are lacking. More than 30% of women requesting refuge in battered women's shelters are turned away for lack of space, and many have little to no economic resources for independent living. These women, especially those with children, often are left homeless or return to their violent homes (37). This also is true for adolescents, elderly victims, or women with substance abuse issues. A system that is prepared to assist and advocate for both the victim and the physician is needed.

Physicians' Responsibilities in Responding to Intimate Partner Violence

The medical community can play a vital role in identifying intimate partner violence and domestic violence cases and halting the cycle of abuse. A summary of the physician's responsibilities in addressing intimate partner violence and domestic violence is shown in Box 17. Regardless of the types of victimization a woman has experienced, providing a safe and private setting in which she can discuss the problem and receive support is paramount to her recovery. Fulfilling these responsibilities may be daunting, time consuming, and confusing in terms of balancing patient safety and autonomy, legal requirements for reporting, and treating medical concerns (38–41). Often, physicians are inadequately trained, have insufficient support, are constrained for time, fear offending the client, and feel powerless in treating or ending the abuse cycle (40, 42). Approximately 90% of female patients in a primary care population, however, believe that physicians can help with problems related to abuse (39).

Simply asking about violence and abuse in a compassionate way can be a significant first step. A simple inquiry can demonstrate caring and sensitivity and signal that violence is not acceptable. Characteristically, abused women will not disclose their abuse voluntarily for numerous reasons (Box 18). However, many women will respond if they are asked directly. Even if victims do not reveal themselves to their physicians, hearing validating messages and knowing that options and resources may be available has prompted many victims to seek help on their own (43, 44).

Screening and Identification

Screening all patients, not just those in whom abuse is suspected, is the key to improving the overall health status of women. More than 70% of abused women have never discussed abuse with their physicians. For those who have, physicians initiated the discussion only 25% of the time (45). Because of the prevalence of violence, being female is a significant enough risk factor to warrant universal screening of all women for intimate partner violence and domestic violence at periodic intervals, such as annual examinations and new patient visits. The goals of identifying an abused woman are to prevent further abuse and improve her health status by expanding the focus of partner violence and abuse from crisis intervention to crisis prevention, managing long-term health issues, and,

---

Box 17

The Physician's Responsibility in Addressing Intimate Partner Violence and Domestic Violence

- Implement universal screening
- Acknowledge the trauma
- Assess immediate safety of patient and children
- Help establish a safety plan
- Review options
- Offer educational materials and a list of community and local resources (including toll-free hotline)
- Provide referrals
- Document interactions
- Provide ongoing support at subsequent visits

Box 18   Reasons for Lack of Disclosure

- Fear of retaliation from the partner
- Fear of police and court involvement
- Embarrassment and shame
- Not trusting the health care provider
- Fear of deportation among immigrant women
- Concerns for confidentiality
- Belief that physicians lack interest or time to discuss abuse

ultimately, preventing abuse (46). Discussing partner violence and providing universal screening establishes that the problem of intimate partner violence is medically relevant. If the patient is a victim or subsequently experiences some form of interpersonal violence, she may be more likely to report it and receive medical attention (43, 44). Regular and consistent use of abuse assessment questions on standard medical records can increase the success of screening (47). Actively asking each patient directly increases the likelihood of disclosure, more so than passively asking with a questionnaire (48). Furthermore, the probability of success is improved when screening is done privately by a concerned and sincere questioner.

Abuse victims often are accompanied to health care appointments by the perpetrator, who may appear overprotective or overbearing. Because partner control is a key factor in violence and abuse, it is essential to discuss abuse in private, apart from the partner and apart from children, family, or friends. It also is important to avoid using a family member or friend as an interpreter when asking someone with limited English proficiency questions about violence. A prefacing statement suggests the physician's concern and that screening for abuse is something the physician does with all patients. A simple phrase, such as "I would like to ask you a few questions about physical, sexual, and emotional trauma because we know that these are common issues that affect women's health," demonstrates awareness and sensitivity and provides context for the inquiry. Disclosure rates will be higher if the questions use behaviorally specific descriptions rather than the terms "abuse," "domestic violence," or "rape." Some examples of behaviorally specific phras-

ing are shown in Box 19. Screening recommendations for specific populations are discussed in the "Special Populations" section.

Most perpetrators do not lash out at others, even at those they believe can jeopardize their control over their victims. However, infrequently the physician and clinical staff may become targets of verbal attacks or threats by an enraged perpetrator. Law enforcement officials increasingly recognize the need for prompt response should this be necessary. Also, they may be helpful in devising security plans for physicians' offices and staff.

Intervention: Responding to "YES"

Positive responses will be encountered if universal screening is used. Within a busy office setting, it is therefore, imperative that action plans be outlined in advance. The most important and effective strategy in

Box 19   Behaviorally Specific Phrasing for Screening Questions

- Has anyone close to you ever threatened to hurt you?
- Has anyone ever hit, kicked, choked, or hurt you physically?
- Has anyone, including your partner or a family member, ever forced you to do something sexually that you did not want to do?
- Are you ever afraid of your partner or anyone at home?

For teens:
- Has anyone touched you in a way that made you feel uncomfortable?
- Has anyone ever forced you to have sex?
- Has anyone ever hurt you physically or emotionally?

For pregnant women:
- Since you became pregnant, have you been physically hurt by anyone?

For elderly individuals:
- Has anyone ever taken anything of yours without asking?

an office setting is to acknowledge the trauma to the patient by providing education and support and assuring the victim that she is not responsible for the abuse. Often, victims blame themselves for the actions that were taken against them. The physician must be prepared to discuss the abuse and establish a plan to address the presenting medical and psychosocial issues. It also is very important to offer referrals to community support services. Most agencies for victims of abuse and rape crisis centers have expertise in dealing with all forms of violence against women. A list of resources should be readily available in medical offices and hospital emergency departments. The list should include the national 24-hour toll-free hotline (800-799-SAFE [7233] and 800-787-3224 [TDD]), telephone numbers for police departments, emergency departments, shelters for victims of abuse, counseling services, and advocacy agencies that can provide legal, financial, and emotional support. The ACOG web site (www.acog.org) lists state and local resources. Additional information often can be found in the telephone book.

Once intimate partner violence or domestic violence has been identified and acknowledged, the next step is to assess the safety of the patient and that of any children. If the woman believes that her safety is endangered if she returns to her home, shelter should be offered by contacting or referring her to social services, homeless shelters, or community services for battered women. If the patient is afraid for her safety and shelter space is not immediately available, sometimes special arrangements can be made to admit the patient into a hospital until other arrangements can be made. This can be difficult to arrange. If the patient is not in need of immediate shelter, she should be provided with information on community resources and referred for continued assistance and support. In particularly distressed women, an assessment for suicide risk may be indicated. In acute crisis situations that involve serious risks to the life of the victim, her children, or others, crisis intervention resources should be used. These instances are rare in the office setting, occurring more commonly in emergency settings. Marital counseling is contraindicated, and, for the safety of the patient, abuse issues should never be discussed with the abuser.

Establishing a safety plan is an important step in the intervention process; ACOG distributes pocket cards with suggested steps that can be very helpful

(see Box 20 for suggested steps for patients to take when ready to leave the abusive situation). These cards or other resource materials can be handed directly to the patient or left in patient restrooms where they can be retrieved without being seen by an accompanying partner. Displaying and providing educational materials on intimate partner violence and domestic violence and its consequences is a part of the intervention process. It sends a message to women that their physicians' offices are both a resource and a safe place should they encounter abuse or choose to disclose victimization. It reinforces validating messages and can help motivate victims to take action toward ending the violence.

Success in caring for abused women requires an appreciation of the reasons women remain in abusive and dangerous relationships. Patients have the right to decide whether to remain in or leave a relationship. Many physicians think in terms of abused

---

Box 20   Making an Exit Plan

Making a decision to leave an abusive relationship can be very difficult. It may take time for you to feel ready. Call a woman's shelter; someone there can help with a safety plan—you don't have to give anyone your name. If you are ready to leave:

- Pack a bag in advance and leave it at a neighbor's or friend's house. Include cash or credit cards and extra clothes for you and your children. Take a favorite toy or plaything.

- Hide an extra set of car and house keys outside of your house in case you have to leave quickly.

- Take important papers, such as:

  —Birth certificates for you and your children

  —Health insurance cards and medicine

  —Deed or lease to your house or apartment

  —Checkbook and extra checks

  —Social security number or green card/work permit

  —Court papers or orders

  —Driver's license or photo identification

  —Pay stubs

patients' denial or that they are frustrating and difficult patients (49). Others may try to rescue a patient from her relationship (50, 51). Abused women, however, think in terms of their safety and their children's safety. Many are terrorized into helplessness. They fear that they will be beaten again or even killed or that their children or older family members will be attacked. Therefore, they may feel that it may be safer not to leave. Some are pressured by well meaning, but uninformed, friends and family to remain in the relationship. Most, however, are isolated from family and friends, have no social support, and find that there is inadequate space in battered women's shelters. They think in practical terms of lack of income, housing, health insurance, and other factors necessary to establish independent living. Others will not want to leave; rather, they simply want the abuse to stop (50, 51).

The decision to take action can be a long and difficult process and can include many attempts to leave a violent relationship before it is left permanently. Therefore, to assume that a patient can leave without consequences suggests that the woman has more control than is apparent and implies that she is part of the problem. It ignores the possibility of long-term psychologic sequelae from childhood or adolescent abuse and the cumulative effects that past or present abuse can have on a woman. It ignores the dynamics of violence, the true perpetrator, and the criminal nature of partner and family abuse.

Documentation

Documentation should be done following any screening, even if the response is "no." Accurate documentation following a positive response to intimate partner violence and domestic violence screening is no different than any other recording of patient interactions. Precise and accurate recording of findings, especially for repeated episodes of care, however, has special significance in intimate partner violence and domestic violence cases (15, 52, 53). Over time, specific documentation can lead to identification of intimate partner violence or domestic violence as the underlying issue and common denominator for a variety of symptoms, such as persistent unresolved chronic conditions or repetitive injuries and emergency visits. Documentation is forensic evidence. It provides concrete evidence of violence and abuse and may prove to be

crucial to the outcome of any legal case. It substantiates the occurrence of violence when a victim requests reimbursement for advocacy services related to intimate partner violence and domestic violence (53) as, for example, under the Victims of Violent Crimes Act.

When documenting positive responses to screening questions, it is advantageous to use direct and specific quotations of the patient's explanation of her injuries and a body map to locate and describe the appearance of injuries. Photographs are desirable and of great value in legal proceedings, but the patient's consent should be obtained and noted in the patient's medical record (8). Photographs should be identified with the patient's name, the date and time, and the photographer's name. Cameras with instant imaging are ideal tools, although 35 mm film may be preferred in some jurisdictions. Use of computerized online photography may pose a risk to preservation of evidence because a case could be made for computerized alteration of images. Additional documentation needed includes a full history and review of symptoms; psychologic, social, and sexual histories; findings from laboratory and other diagnostic procedures; and management plans, including follow-up and referrals and, if required, law enforcement notification. Some states specifically define what must be documented as part of their intimate partner violence and domestic violence reporting laws.

Proper documentation using assigned International Classification of Diseases, Ninth Revision, Clinical Modification (ICD-9-CM), and Current Procedural Technology (CPT) coding* is necessary for reimbursement. Specifically dedicated ICD-9-CM codes for partner violence in the 995.8 series are a validation that intimate partner violence and domestic violence has serious health consequences. However, CPT codes are not specifically directed to intimate partner violence and domestic violence, but do describe the level of care, such as codes for complex evaluation and management; preventive medicine services; and preventive medicine counseling (eg, as with developing safety plans, providing referrals). Documentation with coding permits more accurate data acquisition

---

*CPT codes, descriptions, and material only are copyright 2004 American Medical Association. All Rights Reserved. No fee schedules, basic units, relative values, or related listings are included in CPT. The AMA assumes no liability for the data contained herein. Applicable FARS/DFARS restrictions apply to government use.

and analysis to assess effectiveness of care for victims and develop more effective clinical strategies, guidelines, and policies. It also helps to improve the health care response to intimate partner violence and domestic violence and to develop risk management policies. Lastly, documentation with coding serves as an aid to justify coverage by insurance carriers and health maintenance organizations for services such as reconstructive facial and dental surgery or other therapies to address the chronic effects of certain injuries (53).

Special Populations

Child Abuse and Children of Violent Families

Violence between intimate partners may be the most important risk factor for child abuse. Child abuse occurs in 33–77% of families in which there is abuse of adults and at a rate that is 15 times higher than in families without intimate partner violence (11, 54). There is a 60% overlap between violence against children and violence against women in the same family, and as the frequency of violence against the woman increases, the odds of her child being abused also increases (55, 56).

Children and adolescents from violent homes demonstrate more psychologic morbidity compared with children in nonviolent homes. This is manifested as behavioral, emotional, social, and cognitive problems and expressed as aggression, anxiety, depression, and poor social interactions and school performance (57). Sleep disturbances, enuresis, and separation anxiety are seen in younger children. Eating disorders, manipulative behavior, problems with abandonment and control, pregnancy, suicidal or homicidal thoughts, and drug and alcohol abuse are seen in older children and adolescents who have witnessed abuse (58). Female children who are exposed to violence in the home are at increased risk for becoming future victims; male children are at increased risk of becoming perpetrators of interpersonal violence. Each of these responses are a function of role-modeling and learned behavior (59, 60). A detailed description of the effects of childhood abuse on adult women's health is provided in the chapter on "Adult Manifestations of Childhood Sexual Abuse."

Children in violent homes need as much care and attention as the abused woman. Once an abused woman with children is identified, the role of the obstetrician–gynecologist is to bring this to the attention of those who will provide family case management. Actively making referrals to such resources is essential, because the abused woman may not be willing or able to do so on her own, especially if she fears retaliation or loss of child custody. Conversely, some battered women seek help through their children.

Adolescents

Adolescents are at high risk for intimate partner violence and domestic violence. Adolescents are at risk for physical and sexual abuse from parents, family members, and dating partners. More than 30% of female adolescents report partner violence in their heterosexual relationships (61). Adolescents are vulnerable to dating violence because of identity issues, neediness, insecurity, and naiveté. Many adolescents lack skills to help them recognize and avoid violent dating situations; some even believe that violence in a dating relationship is justifiable in certain situations (62).

Both adolescent abuse and adolescent pregnancy are associated with childhood physical and sexual abuse, earlier onset of sexual activity, and unwanted sexual experiences (63). Sexually abused adolescents are more likely to have been pregnant than those without histories of abuse (64).

As with child abuse, adolescent violence is associated with partner violence in adult life (65). It is important to identify and address dating and family violence and to provide prevention efforts and education to assist the adolescent in recognizing and avoiding future violence (66). Prevention efforts and education are important for both female and male adolescent populations.

Abuse During Pregnancy

Pregnancy is considered an especially risky time for an abused woman. Abuse during pregnancy affects both maternal and fetal well-being (67). A 1996 review of the prevalence of violence during pregnancy reported a range of 1% to 20%, with many studies identifying rates between 4% and 8% (20). Higher rates are identified when screening occurs more than once during the pregnancy (eg, at each visit or at least once during each trimester) (68, 69). Evidence suggests that the severity and frequency of violence can escalate during pregnancy (70–72) and become even more prevalent in the postpartum period (20, 71, 72). Violence may occur more frequently in pregnancy than other conditions for which routine screening is done, such as gestational diabetes and preeclampsia (20). In other cases, violence may subside during the pregnancy and resume in the postpartum period (74).

In pregnant adolescents, the prevalence of abuse, particularly sexual abuse, may be greater than for adult pregnant women (69). This is because an adolescent can face abuse by either a parent or other family members as well as her partner. As with pregnant adults, abuse may begin long before conception occurs (64).

The dynamics of intimate partner violence on the woman, fetus, and neonate range from direct physical attacks that create serious injuries with potentially fatal outcomes to tactics of intimidation that lead to deprivation and secondary physical, physiologic, and psychologic stress effects on the woman and fetus. The latter tactics include restricted nutrition and prescriptions and limited access to prenatal care (late prenatal care, missed office visits) by the controlling partner.

Pregnancy complications, such as poor maternal weight gain, infection, anemia, and second- and third-trimester bleeding, occur more commonly among pregnant women who are battered than among those who are not battered (47, 69). Injuries in pregnancy commonly involve the abdomen, uterus, and breasts. These may be directed attacks intended to harm the pregnancy (75). Severe maternal complications include injuries to the uterus, liver, and spleen; pelvic fracture with retroperitoneal hemorrhage; placental abruption; preterm labor; and preterm rupture of the membranes (76). Injuries to other parts of the body also are seen in pregnancy.

Fetal complications include pregnancy loss, stillbirth, neonatal death, preterm delivery, low birth weight, and direct injuries (eg, fetal fractures) (30, 76, 77). The severity and extent of injuries to the uterus and the fetus in late pregnancy may be related to increasing vulnerability to trauma because of extrapelvic expansion of the body and reduced amniotic fluid volume as pregnancy advances.

Regular contact with medical providers increases the likelihood of disclosure; therefore, pregnancy offers a unique opportunity to screen and identify partner and family violence. Screening all patients at various times during the pregnancy is important because some women do not disclose abuse the first time they are asked. Screening should occur at the first prenatal visit, at least once per trimester, and at the postpartum checkup.

Women With Disabilities

Women with disabilities can experience physical, sexual, or emotional abuse and are vulnerable to neglect or exploitation. This abuse can include withholding of necessary assistive devices, care, or treatment. Most often the abuse is by a male known to the victim, particularly in sexual abuse. The risk for experiencing abuse is the same between women with physical disabilities and those without physical disabilities. Underreporting is likely caused by fear and dependency on the abuser. Women with physical disabilities are more at risk for abuse by attendants or health care providers and more likely to experience a longer duration of abuse (78). It has been estimated that more than 30% of women with developmental disabilities have been sexually abused in their lifetimes. Women with Down syndrome are particularly vulnerable because of their passive, obedient, and affectionate behavior (79). Intimate partner violence and domestic violence should be considered in these populations. For additional information on this population, including a screening tool specifically designed for women with disabilities, refer to the "Access to Reproductive Health Care for Women With Disabilities" chapter.

Immigrant Women

Intimate partner violence is disproportionately common in women of ethnic and cultural minorities (80). Immigrant and refugee women are susceptible to violence and abuse because of isolation and manipulation by their partners, language and cultural differences, and lack of awareness of their rights and legal and social resources (81). Immigrants often do not trust advocates from outside their communities and may fear the police and deportation based on experiences in their countries of origin. These women are under great pressure to maintain cohesive family structures, no matter what the cost, and comply with their abusers' demands and behaviors. Furthermore, in some ethnic groups, traditional practices of abuse and violence are cultural norms (eg, wife beating, honor killing). Thus, the prevalence of abuse in these populations may be greater than 50% (82).

Because of the increasing number of women of many cultures who appear for care, it is important for physicians to maintain cultural sensitivity and awareness (see "Cultural Competency, Sensitivity, and Awareness in the Delivery of Health Care" chapter). It is important to note that even if not yet approved for U.S. residency, abused immigrant women can be protected under the Violence Against Women Act. They are able to seek shelter, health care, and advocacy, as well as apply for residency without the batterer's sponsorship. State benefits are available under various aid programs, including those for children. Many immigrant women are unaware of these opportunities. Provision of this information by physicians to this population can be invaluable.

Lesbian, Gay, Bisexual, and Transgender Communities

In 2000, there were approximately 4,400 documented cases of lesbian, gay, bisexual, and transgender partner abuse, with a prevalence rate of between 20% and 35%, similar to that among heterosexual couples (83). The processes of power and control; the cyclicity; and the severity of physical, sexual, and emotional violence in the lesbian, gay, bisexual, and transgender communities are the same as in partner abuse in all other populations.

Abused lesbian, gay, bisexual, and transgendered individuals may stay in their relationships longer because there is a greater tendency for denial and failure to acknowledge intimate partner violence within these communities. Often, lesbian, gay, bisexual, and transgendered individuals are manipulated by their partners into remaining in their relationships through fear of being "outed" to family and friends or at work. Being outed carries the risk of losing social and financial support and losing one's job (83).

Often, lesbian, gay, bisexual, and transgendered individuals are stigmatized and isolated from mainstream society by their sexual orientation or gender identity. Myths in mainstream society contribute to a lack of both understanding and acknowledgment of intimate partner violence in these communities. The legal, law enforcement, and advocacy response systems can be insensitive to abuse of lesbian, gay, bisexual, and transgendered individuals, incorrectly assuming that intimate partner violence does not occur in these populations. Thus, these women may have limited access to violence prevention and advocacy programs or to protective services that are otherwise provided by the law. Several states define

domestic violence in ways that exclude individuals in same-sex relationships from access to protective orders (84). In some states, the definition allowed for access to protective orders by individuals in same-sex relationships, but sodomy laws were a deterrent to their use. The U.S. Supreme Court ruling in *Lawrence v. Texas* invalidated sodomy laws, thereby enhancing access to protective orders (83). Protecting privacy and confidentiality is critical because of the risk of public discrimination and insensitivity.

Given these complex factors, in clinical encounters it is preferable that the physician not assume the sexual orientation of any patient, the sex of the batterer, or that the patient is "out." It is best that gender-neutral terms be used with respect to partners and expressions of sexuality when conducting universal screening for abuse. (For more detailed information, refer to the "Primary Care of Lesbians and Bisexual Women in Obstetric and Gynecologic Practice" and "Health Care for Transgendered Individuals" chapters.)

Domestic Elder Abuse

The general term "elder mistreatment" refers to: 1) intentional actions that result in harm or create a serious risk of harm (whether or not the harm is intended) to a vulnerable elder by a caregiver or other person who stands in a trust relationship to the elder; or 2) failure by a caregiver to satisfy the elder's basic needs or to protect the elder from harm (85). Domestic elder abuse is distinguished from self-neglect (failure of an older individual to satisfy his or her own basic needs and to protect himself or herself from harm) and abuse perpetrated by non-family caregivers in the home and institutional settings. The National Elder Abuse Incidence Study estimates that approximately 450,000 older individuals in domestic settings are abused or neglected annually. Women make up 58% of victims of elder abuse (86).

It generally is acknowledged that these findings detect only the most overt cases of abuse and, thus, significantly underestimate the incidence of domestic elder abuse (85). It is estimated that only 1 out of 14 elder abuse cases is reported to a public agency (87). Underreporting of elder family abuse may be related to the setting in which the abuse occurs and the relationship between the victim and the abuser. In almost 90% of incidents with a known perpetrator, the abuser is a family member, usually an adult child or spouse (86, 88).

Abuse can be physical, sexual, and psychologic and also includes neglect (refusal or failure to fulfill care giving obligations), abandonment (desertion), and financial exploitation (illegal or improper exploitation of funds or other assets through undue influence or misuse of power of attorney). Generally, neglect is the most common form of elder abuse (55%), followed by physical abuse (15%), exploitation (12%), and emotional abuse (8%) (89). Abused elders have poorer health and higher mortality from injuries compared with nonabused elders (90). There is an increasing proportion of emergency room visits by abused elderly individuals related to both injuries and the exacerbation of chronic diseases (91). As with younger adult victims, the clinical presentations are injuries or symptoms that may not coincide with the stated history (see Box 21 for signs of neglect and financial exploitation).

For the obstetrician–gynecologist, the importance of elder domestic violence relates to the increasing number of older women in the population (92). Currently, 60% of the population aged 65 years and older is female (93). Older women seek care for pelvic floor relaxation, sexual dysfunction, breast and reproductive tract cancer, and other problems. Identification of abuse in this population may be difficult because few physicians are fully aware of domestic violence in the elderly or the extent of the problem. They may ignore signs and symptoms of elder mistreatment, assuming that somatic symptoms are related to aging. They also may be uncomfortable with the responsibility of further assessment and action (87, 94). A victim's fear, intimidation, and lack of opportunity also may retard the disclosure of the problem.

Physicians or other health care workers who provide acute or chronic medical care to older adults may see these individuals on a regular basis and have unique opportunities for screening and assessment. Additionally, an opportunity for screening and recognition exists during all health-related encounters with older individuals, such as routine gynecologic examinations. Incorporating screening related to elder abuse and neglect into these encounters will increase identification of abuse. Physicians should assess patients for elder abuse and respond to

---

Box 21   Signs of Neglect and Financial Exploitation in Older Women

Neglect

- Malnutrition
- Dehydration
- Hypothermia or hyperthermia
- Decubitus ulcers
- General health deterioration
- Excessive dirt or body odor
- Lack of necessary prosthetic devices (dentures, glasses, hearing aids, etc.)
- Evidence of under- or over-use of medications

Financial exploitation

- Woman appears reluctant to seek necessary medical care
- Sudden inability to pay bills or purchase medicines or personal items
- Fear or anxiety when discussing finances
- Extraordinary interest by family member in the older individual's assets

---

patients who are victims of elder abuse as they would to domestic violence in general (95).

Legal Issues

A basic understanding of legal measures and considerations can enhance a physician's ability to counsel and assist women in violent relationships. Because there is significant variation among state laws in terms of the requirements for health care providers, familiarity with local laws and policies is critical. Health care providers can contact their state medical society for up-to-date information about these laws.

Reporting

All states require physicians to report suspected child abuse. Almost all states require physicians to report injuries sustained by a gun, knife, or other deadly weapon. A number of states also require the reporting of injuries resulting from acts of violence or nonaccidental acts. In many instances, these laws may require the reporting of injuries resulting from intimate partner violence and domestic violence. The general intent of these laws is to detect and prosecute criminal activity. Several states explicitly direct health care providers to report acts of domestic violence and abuse or neglect of incompetent elderly or vulnerable adults. However, no uniform approach to reporting intimate partner violence and domestic violence exists among these states.

Reporting of current abuse, particularly mandatory reporting, is controversial among victims, physicians, the law enforcement and legal communities (Table 14). The intent of mandatory domestic abuse reporting laws is to identify and protect victims before the next act of violence. Opponents of mandatory reporting repeatedly raise concerns for the victims' safety and confidentiality subsequent to reporting (96–99), the inadequate infrastructure of services for victims of violence (96, 100), and the lack of data to support the assumed benefits of mandatory reporting. This suggests that mandatory reporting is not yet justified and should not be implemented without provisions that allow women to override or veto reporting requirements. Before supporting further implementation of mandatory reporting laws by states, a comprehensive evaluation of the effect of existing mandatory reporting laws is needed. Particular attention should be given to analyzing their effect on the use and availability of support services, the frequency of physician screening, and the incidence of intimate partner violence and domestic violence.

Physicians should be familiar with laws pertaining to the reporting of intimate partner violence and domestic violence, including elder abuse, and should contact state officials to learn under what conditions, to whom, and how these reports should be made. Resources include state and local medical societies, state attorneys general offices, domestic violence agencies, area agencies on aging, and hospital policy and procedure manuals. State laws generally provide physicians with immunity from civil or criminal liability if good faith is used when filing a report of suspected or confirmed domestic abuse (96).

Preserving Privacy and Confidentiality

Breaches in privacy and confidentiality expose a victim to further physical and emotional consequences and various forms of social discrimination. Violence

Table 14. Mandatory Reporting of Intimate Partner Violence and Domestic Violence

Support	Opposition
■ Underscores that intimate partner violence and domestic violence are crimes.	■ No data to support the benefits of enactment of these laws.
■ Acknowledges that the power imbalance endemic to many abusive relationships often prevents or deters the abused individual from seeking available legal remedies.	■ Laws may place a woman at greater risk of retaliation from the perpetrator. ■ Most state laws do not include provisions that permit the victim to "veto" the filing of a report of intimate partner violence and domestic violence by someone other than the victim. ■ A court order of protection or restraining order is not a guarantee against reprisal by the abusive partner.
■ Can help to identify battered women so that services and protection can be provided before violence recurs.	■ Mandatory reporting laws can diminish the woman's right to autonomy and self-determination and can render the victim as incompetent. ■ Reporting requirements presuppose the availability of resources to help an abused woman establish a new life for herself and her children.
■ May prompt physicians and others to implement universal screening in part to avoid penalties and liability issues.	■ They may compromise the essential tenet of physician–patient confidentiality and trust. This can deter victims from confiding in their physicians or from seeking health care, thus affecting victims' health status. ■ Laws may inhibit providers from screening patients for abuse. ■ Reporting may impair a woman's ability to plan and negotiate a safe exit for herself and her children and may lead to an inability to establish economic independence; loss of child custody; and, for some women, deportation.

may escalate if the perpetrator learns that a report has been filed and retaliates, especially if the woman leaves her relationship. Inappropriate access to confidential health information has led to insurance discrimination against victims of intimate partner violence and domestic violence. As recently as 1995, more than one half of health insurers were using intimate partner violence and domestic violence documentation to make insurance coverage decisions, resulting in denial of insurance or higher premiums for a "pre-existing" condition (101). Since that time, model state legislation has been developed and promoted to end this problem. Some states have enacted domestic violence insurance discrimination protections. Experts are concerned, however, that many of these laws do not protect the woman adequately (102).

Other forms of inappropriate access to information have led to discrimination by employers in hiring, firing, and promotions; community stigma, with public harassment and humiliation; and discrimination in the courts, including loss of child custody (103, 105). These discriminatory practices have led to avoidance behavior by women (eg, withholding information, lying, paying out of pocket, not filing insurance claims, physician-shopping to minimize accumulation of information and to keep records separate, and avoiding care completely). The result is inadequate or no care and poorer health (103). The fundamental issues in privacy and confidentiality center around preserving a woman's right to choose if, how, when, and to whom her information about abuse is disclosed, and allowing, as much as possible, the patient to control or limit the release and distribution of information among different users who have different needs for that information. Types of disclosure that can expose domestic abuse inadvertently include access by the perpetrator to information from a child's medical record; release of a patient's name, birth date, social security number, and address in billing and benefits explanations that are sent to the perpetrator; inappropriate distribution of health information by health plans and health information clearinghouses; electronic transmission of claims; and phone calls and release of information to family. The possibility of retaliation or discrimination should not deter physicians from documenting abuse in the medical record.

Recommendations have been made for the use and disclosure of health information for victims of intimate partner violence and domestic violence based on respecting autonomy and confidentiality to assure victims' safety and quality of care and to protect their rights to social programs. These include limiting information to what is requested or necessary for a specific need; specifically advising patients before release on how information will be used and to whom it will be disclosed, including mandatory reporting; giving patients the right to authorize release of information, to limit what information is released, and to refuse the release of information when their need for privacy outweighs the user's need for information; and enforcing safeguards and penalties for unauthorized access to information (103). The Health Insurance Portability and Accountability Act provides important new protections that address some of these recommendations (105).

The confidentiality of the patient who is a victim of intimate partner violence or domestic violence needs to be protected by not making phone calls, sending bills, or having other types of contact with the patient where her abuser can discover that she has revealed her situation or locate the woman if she has left the relationship. All office staff should be oriented thoroughly to the extreme sensitivity of this issue, and appropriate arrangements should be made for sharing information with or about the patient. Similar care should be taken with releasing data to outside agencies seeking information.

References

1. Benson ML, Fox GL. When violence hits home: how economics and neighborhood play a role. Research in Brief. Washington, DC: U.S. Department of Justice, Office of Justice Programs; 2004. NCJ 205004. Available at: http://www.ncjrs.org/pdffiles1/nij/205004.pdf. Retrieved November 5, 2004.

2. Heise L, Ellsberg M, Gottemoeller M. Ending violence against women. Population reports; Series L, No 11. Baltimore (MD): Johns Hopkins University; 1999. Available at: http://www.infoforhealth.org/pr/l11/violence.pdf. Retrieved June 4, 2004.

3. Sushma K. Domestic violence against women and girls. United Nations Children's Fund (UNICEF). Innocenti Digest 2000; 6:1–30.

4. United Nations. Declaration on the elimination of violence against women. United Nations Resolution A/Res/48/104. New York (NY): UN; 1993. Available at: http://www.un.org/documents/ga/res/48/a48r104.htm. Retrieved June 8, 2004.

5. Rennison CM. Intimate partner violence, 1993–2001. Bureau of Justice Statistics Crime Data Brief. Washington, DC: U.S. Department of Justice, Office of Justice Programs; 2003. NCJ

197838. Available at: http://www.ojp.usdoj.gov/bjs/pub/pdf/ ipv01.pdf. Retrieved June 8, 2004.

6. Ganley AL. The health impact of domestic violence. In: Warshaw C, Ganley AL. Improving the health care response to domestic violence: a resource manual for health care providers. 2nd ed. San Francisco (CA): Family Violence Prevention Fund; 1996. p. 15-6.

7. Saltzman LE, Fanslow JL, McMahon PM, Shelley GA. Intimate partner violence surveillance: uniform definitions and recommended data elements. Version 1.0. Atlanta (GA): Centers for Disease Control and Prevention, National Center for Injury Prevention and Control; 2000. Available at: http://www.cdc.gov/ncipc/pub-res/Intimate partner violence_surveillance/Intimate%20partner%20violence.pdf. Retrieved June 8, 2004.

8. American Medical Association. Diagnostic and treatment guidelines on domestic violence. Chicago (IL): AMA; 1992.

9. Tjaden P, Thoennes N. Stalking in America: findings from the national violence against women survey. Research in Brief. Washington, DC: U.S. Department of Justice, Office of Justice Programs; 1998. Available at http://www.ncjrs.org/pdffiles/ 169592.pdf. Retrieved June 8, 2004.

10. Adolescent assault victim needs: a review of issues and a model protocol. American Academy of Pediatrics Task Force on Adolescent Assault Victim Needs. Pediatrics 1996;98:991-1001.

11. The role of the pediatrician in recognizing and intervening on behalf of abused women. American Academy of Pediatrics Committee on Child Abuse and Neglect. Pediatrics 1998; 101:1091-2.

12. American Academy of Family Physicians. Violence (position paper). Leawood (KS): AAFP; 2004. Available at: http://www.aafp.org/x7132.xml. Retrieved June 2, 2004.

13. Joint Commission on Accreditation of Health Care Organizations. 2004 hospital accreditation standards (HAS). Oakbrook Terrace (IL): JCAHO; 2004.

14. Jones RF 3rd, Horan DL. The American College of Obstetricians and Gynecologists: a decade of responding to violence against women. Int J Gynaecol Obstet 1997;58:43-50.

15. Isaac NE, Enos VP. Documenting domestic violence: how health care providers can help victims. Research in brief. Washington, DC: U.S. Department of Justice, Office of Justice Programs; 2001. NCJ 188564. Available at: http://www.ncjrs.org/pdffiles1/nij/188564.pdf. Retrieved July 16, 2004.

16. Tjaden P, Thoennes N. Prevalence, incidence, and consequences of violence against women: findings from the National Violence Against Women Survey. Research in Brief. Washington, DC: U.S. Department of Justice, Office of Justice Programs; 1998. NCJ 172837. Available at: http://www.ncjrs.org/pdffiles/172837.pdf. Retrieved June 8, 2004.

17. Rennison CM, Welchans S. Intimate partner violence. Bureau of Justice Statistics Special Report. Washington, DC: U.S. Department of Justice; 2000. NCJ 178247. Available at:

http://www.ojp.usdoj.gov/bjs/pub/pdf/ipv.pdf. Retrieved June 8, 2004.

18. Paulozzi LJ, Saltzman LE, Thompson MP, Holmgreen PH. Surveillance for homicide among intimate partners—United States, 1981-1998. MMWR CDC Surveill Summ 2001;50(3): 1-15.

19. Tjaden P, Thoennes N. Full report of the prevalence, incidence, and consequences of violence against women: findings from the National Violence Against Women Survey. Washington, DC: U.S. Department of Justice, National Institute of Justice; 2000. NCJ 183781. Available at: http://www.ncjrs.org/pdffiles1/nij/ 183781.pdf. Retrieved June 8, 2004.

20. Gazmararian J, Lazorick S, Spitz AM, Ballarad TJ, Saltzman LE, Marks JS. Prevalence of violence against women [published erratum appears in JAMA 1997;277:1125]. JAMA 1996;275:1915-20.

21. Rand MR. Violence-related injuries treated in hospital emergency departments. Bureau of Justice Statistics Special Report. Washington, DC: U.S. Department of Justice; 1997. NCJ-156921. Available at: http://www.ojp.usdoj.gov/bjs/ pub/pdf/vrithed.pdf. Retrieved June 8, 2004.

22. Coker AL, Smith PH, Bethea L, King MR, McKeown RE. Physical health consequences of physical and psychological intimate partner violence. Arch Fam Med 2000;9:451-7.

23. Coker AL, Smith PH, McKeown RE, King MR. Frequency and correlates of intimate partner violence by type: physical, sexual, and psychological battering. Am J Public Health 2000;90:553-9.

24. Silva C, McFarlane J, Soeken K, Parker B, Reel S. Symptoms of post traumatic stress disorder among abused women in a primary care setting. J Womens Health 1997;6:543-52.

25. Commonwealth Fund. Addressing domestic violence and its consequences: policy report of the Commonwealth Fund Commission on Women's Health. New York (NY): CF; 1998.

26. Wilt S, Olson S. Prevalence of domestic violence in the United States. J Am Med Womens Assoc 1996;51:77-82.

27. Walker LE. The battered woman syndrome. 2nd ed. New York (NY): Springer; 2000.

28. Chez RA, Jones RF 3rd. The battered woman. Am J Obstet Gynecol 1995;173:677-9.

29. Gerbert B, Johnston K, Caspers N, Bleecker T, Woods A, Rosenbaum A. Experiences of battered women in health care settings: a qualitative study. Women Health 1996;24:1-17.

30. Eby K, Campbell JC, Sullivan CM, Davidson WS 2nd. Health effects of experiences of sexual violence for women with abusive partners. Health Care Women Int 1995;16:563-76.

31. Gielen AC, O'Campo P, Faden RR, Eke A. Women's disclosure of HIV status: experiences of mistreatment and violence in an urban setting. Women Health 1997;25:19-31.

32. Zierler S, Cunningham WE, Andersen R, Shapiro MF, Nakazono T, Morton S, et al. Violence victimization after HIV infection in a US probability sample of adult patients in primary care [published erratum appears in Am J Public Health 2000;90:447]. Am J Public Health 2000;90:208-15.

33. Gielen AC, McDonnell KA, Burke JG, O'Campo P. Women's lives after an HIV-positive diagnosis: disclosure and violence. Matern Child Health J 2000;4:111–20.

34. Holmes MM, Resnick HS, Kilpatrick DG, Best CL. Rape-related pregnancy: estimates and descriptive characteristics from a national sample of women. Am J Obstet Gynecol 1996;175: 320–4; discussion 324–5.

35. Costs of intimate partner violence against women in the United States. Centers for Disease Control and Prevention, National Center for Injury Prevention and Control. Atlanta (GA): CDC; 2003. Available at: http://www.cdc.gov/ncipc/pub-res/Intimate partner violence_cost/intimate partner violenceBook–Final–Feb18.pdf. Retrieved June 8, 2004.

36. Wisner CL, Gilmer TP, Saltzman LE, Zink TM. Intimate partner violence against women: do victims cost health plans more? J Fam Pract 1999;48:439–43.

37. National Coalition for the Homeless. Domestic violence and homelessness. NCH Fact Sheet #8. Washington, DC: NCH; 1999. Available at: http://www.nationalhomeless.org/domestic.html. Retrieved July 14, 2004.

38. Chambliss LR, Bay RC, Jones RF 3rd. Domestic violence: an educational imperative? Am J Obstet Gynecol 1995;172:1035–8.

39. Friedman LS, Samet JH, Roberts MS, Hudlin M, Hans P. Inquiry about victimization experiences. A survey of patient preferences and physician practices. Arch Intern Med 1992; 152:1186–90.

40. Gerbert B, Caspers N, Bronstone A, Moe J, Abercrombie P. A qualitative analysis of how physicians with expertise in domestic violence approach the identification of victims. Ann Intern Med 1999:131;578–84.

41. Horan DL, Chapin J, Klein L, Schmidt LA, Schulkin J. Domestic violence screening practices of obstetrician–gynecologists. Obstet Gynecol 1998;92:785–9.

42. Sugg N, Inui T. Primary care physicians' response to domestic violence. Opening Pandora's box. JAMA 1992;267:3157–60.

43. Parsons LH, Zaccaro D, Wells B, Stovall TG. Methods of and attitudes toward screening obstetrics and gynecology patients for domestic violence. Am J Obstet Gynecol 1995;173:381–6; discussion 386–7.

44. McFarlane J, Parker B, Soeken K, Silva C, Reel S. Safety behaviors of abused women after an intervention during pregnancy. J Obstet Gynecol Neonatal Nurs 1998;27;64–9.

45. Plichta SB, Falik M. Prevalence of violence and its implications for women's health. Womens Health Issues 2001;11:244–58.

46. Hyman I, Guruge S, Stewart DE, Ahmad F. Primary prevention of violence against women. Womens Health Issues 2000;10: 288–93.

47. McFarlane J, Wiist WH. Documentation of abuse to pregnant women: a medical chart audit in public health clinics. J Womens Health 1996;5:137–42.

48. McFarlane J, Christoffel K, Bateman L, Miller V, Bullock L. Assessing for abuse: self-report versus nurse interview. Public Health Nurs 1991;8:245–50.

49. Walker EA. Medically unexplained physical symptoms. Clin Obstet Gynecol 1997;40:589–600.

50. Gerbert B, Abercrombie P, Caspers N, Love C, Bronstone A. How health care providers help battered women: the survivor's perspective. Women Health 1999;29:115–35.

51. Rodriguez MA, Craig AM, Mooney DR, Bauer HM. Patient attitudes about mandatory reporting of domestic violence. Implications for health care professionals. West J Med 1998: 169;337–41.

52. Rudman WJ, Davey D. Identifying domestic violence within inpatient hospital admissions using medical records. Women Health 2000;30:1–13.

53. Rudman WJ. Coding and documentation of domestic violence. San Francisco (CA): Family Violence Prevention Fund; 2000. Available at: http://endabuse.org/programs/healthcare/files/codingpaper.pdf. Retrieved June 8, 2004.

54. Osofsky JD. The impact of violence on children. Future Child 1999;9:33–49.

55. McKibben L, De Vos E, Newberger EH. Victimization of mothers of abused children: a controlled study. Pediatrics 1989; 84:531–5.

56. Ross SM. Risk of physical abuse to children of spouse abusing parents. Child Abuse Negl 1996;20:589–98.

57. Kolbo JR. Risk and resilience among children exposed to family violence. Violence Vict 1996;11:113–28.

58. Sinclair D. Understanding wife assault: a training manual for counsellors and advocates. Toronto (ON): Ontario Government Bookstore, Publications Services Section; 1985.

59. Singer MI, Anglin TM, Song LY, Lunghofer L. Adolescents' exposure to violence and associated symptoms of psychological trauma. JAMA 1995;273:477–82.

60. Hurley DJ, Jaffe P. Children's observations of violence: II. Clinical implications for children's mental health professionals. Can J Psychiatry 1990;35:471–6.

61. Halpern CT, Oslak SG, Young ML, Martin SL, Kupper LL. Partner violence among adolescents in opposite-sex romantic relationships: findings from the National Longitudinal Study of Adolescent Health. Am J Public Health 2001;91:1679–85.

62. Parrot A. Acquaintance rape among adolescents: identifying risk groups and intervention strategies. J Soc Work Hum Sex 1989;8:47–61.

63. Adams JA, East PL. Past physical abuse is significantly correlated with pregnancy as an adolescent. J Pediatr Adolesc Gynecol 1999;12:133–8.

64. Elders MJ, Albert AE. Adolescent pregnancy and sexual abuse. JAMA 1998;280:648–9.

65. Henton J, Cate R, Koval J, Lloyd S, Christopher S. Romance and violence in dating relationships. J Fam Issues 1983;4:467–82.

66. American College of Obstetricians and Gynecologists. Health care for adolescents. Washington, DC: ACOG; 2003.

67. Campbell JC. Abuse during pregnancy: progress, policy, and potential. Am J Public Health 1998;88:185–7.

68. McFarlane J, Parker B, Soeken K, Bullock L. Assessing for abuse during pregnancy. Severity and frequency of injuries and associated entry into prenatal care. JAMA 1992;267:3176–8.

69. Parker B, McFarlane J, Soeken K. Abuse during pregnancy: effects on maternal complications and birth weight in adult and teenage women. Obstet Gynecol 1994;84:323–8.

70. Berenson AB, San Miguel VV, Wilkinson GS. Prevalence of physical and sexual assault in pregnant adolescents. J Adolesc Health 1992;13:466–9.

71. Helton AS, McFarlane J, Anderson ET. Battered and pregnant: a prevalence study. Am J Public Health 1987;77:1337–9.

72. Stewart DE, Cecutti A. Physical abuse in pregnancy. CMAJ 1993;149:1257–63.

73. Gazmararian JA, Adams MM, Saltzman LE, Johnson CH, Bruce FC, Marks JS, et al. The relationship between pregnancy intendedness and physical violence in mothers of newborns. The PRAMS Working Group. Obstet Gynecol 1995;85:1031–8.

74. Gazmararian JA, Petersen R, Spitz AM, Goodwin MM, Saltzman LE, Marks JS. Violence and reproductive health: current knowledge and future research directions. Matern Child Health J 2000;4:79–84.

75. Campbell JC, Oliver C, Bullock L. Why battering during pregnancy? AWHONNS Clin Issues in Perinat Women's Health Nurs 1993;4:343–9.

76. Newberger EH, Barkan SE, Lieberman ES, McCormick MC, Yilo K, Gary LT, et al. Abuse of pregnant women and adverse birth outcome. Current knowledge and implications for practice. JAMA 1992;267:2370–2.

77. Covington DL, Hage M, Hall T, Mathis M. Preterm delivery and the severity of violence during pregnancy. J Reprod Med 2001; 46:1031–9.

78. Young ME, Nosek MA, Howland C, Chanpong G, Rintala DH. Prevalence of abuse of women with physical disabilities. Arch Phys Med Rehabil 1997;78 (suppl 5):S34–8.

79. Bradshaw KD, Elkins TE, Quint EH. The patient with mental retardation: issues in gynecologic care. Dallas (TX): UT Southestern Medical Center at Dallas; Raritan (NJ): Ortho–McNeil Pharmaceutical; 1996.

80. Lee RK, Thompson VL, Mechanic MB. Intimate partner violence and women of color: a call for innovations. Am J Public Health 2002;92:530–4.

81. Haile-Mariam T, Smith J. Domestic violence against women in the international community. Emerg Med Clin North Am 1999;17:617–30, vi.

82. Davis RC, Erez E. Immigrant populations as victims: toward a multicultural justice system. Research in Brief. Washington, DC: U.S. Department of Justice, Office of Justice Programs; 1998. NCJ 167571. Available at: http://www.ncjrs.org/pdffiles/167571.pdf. Retrieved June 4, 2004.

83. Lesbian, gay, bisexual and transgender domestic violence in 2002. A report of the National Coalition of Anti-Violence Programs. New York (NY): NCAVP; 2003. Available at: http://www.avp.org/publications/reports/2002ncavpdvrpt.pdf. Retrieved June 8, 2004.

84. Lesbian, gay, bisexual and transgender domestic violence in 2001. A report of the National Coalition of Anti-Violence Programs. New York (NY): NCAVP; 2002. Available at: http://www.avp.org/publications/reports/2001ncavpdvrpt.pdf. Retrieved August 11, 2004.

85. National Research Council. Elder mistreatment: abuse, neglect, and exploitation in an aging America. Washington, DC: The National Academies Press; 2003.

86. National Center on Elder Abuse. The national elder abuse incidence study. Final report. Washington, DC: Administration for Children and Families and the Administration on Aging; 1998. Available at: http://www.aoa.gov/eldfam/Elder_Rights/Elder_Abuse/AbuseReport_full.pdf. Retrieved June 4, 2004.

87. American Medical Association. Diagnostic and treatment guidelines on elder abuse and neglect. Chicago (IL): AMA; 1994.

88. Pillemer K, Finkelhor D. The prevalence of elder abuse: a random sample survey. Gerontologist 1988;28:51–7.

89. National Center for Elder Abuse. Reporting of elder abuse in domestic settings. Elder Abuse Information Series, No. 3. Washington, DC: NCEA; 1997. Available at http:///www.elderabusecenter.org/pdf/basics/fact3.pdf. Retrieved June 8, 2004.

90. Lachs MS, Williams CS, O'Brien S, Pillemer KA, Charlson ME. The mortality of elderly mistreatment. JAMA 1998;280:428–32.

91. Lachs MS, Williams CS, O'Brien S, Hurst L, Kossack A, Siegal A, et al. ED use by older victims of family violence. Ann Emerg Med 1997;30:448–54.

92. Aging in the United States—past, present, and future. Washington, DC: U.S. Census Bureau; 1997. Available at: http://www.census.gov/ipc/prod/97agewc.pdf. Retrieved June 8, 2004.

93. Hetzel L, Smith A. The 65 years and over population: 2000. Census 2000 Brief. Washington, DC: U.S. Census Bureau; 2001. Available at: http://www.census.gov/prod/2001pubs/c2kbr01-10.pdf. Retrieved June 8, 2004.

94. Wisconsin Coalition Against Domestic Violence. Elder abuse, neglect and family violence: a guide for health care professionals. Madison (WI): WCADV; 1999.

95. American College of Obstetricians and Gynecologists. Violence against women. In: Precis: an update in obstetrics and gynecology. Primary and preventive care. 3rd ed. Washington, DC: ACOG; 2004. p. 116–33.

96. Hyman A, Schillinger D, Lo B. Laws mandating reporting of domestic violence. Do they promote patient well-being? JAMA 1995;273:1781–7.

97. AMA opposes mandatory medical reporting. Domest Violence Report 1997;3(1):1, 7.

98. Chez RA, Jones RF 3rd. Treating battered women: the medicolegal aspects. OBG Manage 1996;8(6):29–30.

99. Hyman A, Chez RA. Mandatory reporting of domestic violence by health care providers: a misguided approach. Womens Health Issues 1995;5:208–13.

100. Rodriguez MA, Quiroga SS, Bauer HM. Breaking the silence. Battered women's perspectives on medical care. Arch Fam Med 1996;5:153–8.

101. Pennsylvania Coalition Against Domestic Violence, Women's Law Project. Insurance discrimination against victims of domestic violence. Harrisburg (PA): PCADV; Philadelphia (PA): WLP, 1998.

102. Family Violence Prevention Fund. State-by-state legislative report card on health care laws and domestic violence. San Francisco (CA): FVPF; 2001. Available at: http://www.endabuse.org/statereport/list.php3. Retrieved June 2, 2004.

103. Family Violence Prevention Fund. Health privacy principles for protecting victims of domestic violence. San Francisco (CA): FVPA; 2000. Available at: http://www.healthprivacy.org/usr_doc/37713%2E.pdf. Retrieved June 2, 2004.

104. Miccio GK. A reasonable battered mother? Redefining, reconstructing, and recreating the battered mother in child protective proceedings. Harv Womens Law J 1999;22:89–121.

105. Family Violence Prevention Fund. Summary of new federal medical privacy protections for victims of domestic violence. San Francisco (CA): FVPF; 2003. Available at: http://endabuse.org/programs/healthcare/files/hipaa/HIPAAsummary.pdf. Retrieved June 3, 2004.

106. Rodriguez MA, Sheldon WR, Bauer HM, Perez-Stable EJ. The factors associated with disclosure of intimate partner abuse to clinicians. J Fam Pract 2001;50:338–44.

Resources

ACOG Resources

American College of Obstetricians and Gynecologists. Clinical aspects of domestic violence for the obstetrician–gynecologist. Washington, DC: ACOG; 2002.

American College of Obstetricians and Gynecologists. Domestic elder abuse: practical tools for providers of women's health care. Washington, DC: ACOG; 2003.

American College of Obstetricians and Gynecologists. Domestic violence. ACOG Patient Education Pamphlet AP083. Washington, DC: ACOG; 2002.

American College of Obstetricians and Gynecologists. Domestic violence: the role of the physician in identification, intervention, and prevention. Washington, DC: ACOG; 1995.

American College of Obstetricians and Gynecologists. Precis: primary and preventive care. Washington, DC: ACOG; 2004.

American College of Obstetricians and Gynecologists Violence Against Women Home Page (www.acog.org, click on "Women's Issues" and then "Violence Against Women")—contains contact information for state domestic violence and sexual assault coalitions, screening tools, bibliographies, and fact sheets.

Limited quantities of the materials listed as follows can be obtained for free by e-mailing violence@acog.org.

American College of Obstetricians and Gynecologists. Domestic violence cards: no matter how you say it, it's all abuse. Washington, DC; ACOG. (Larger quantities can be purchased through the ACOG bookstore at: http://sales.acog.org.)

General information packet includes fact sheet, national domestic violence organizations list, commonly asked questions, and a bibliography on intimate partner violence/domestic violence.

Rolodex Cards:
- "No matter how you say it, it's all abuse" rolodex cards with national hotline phone numbers and information about screening.

- Sexual assault rolodex cards include tools for screening teens and information on sexual assault.

American College of Obstetricians and Gynecologists. Stay Alert! Stay Safe! Pocket Card Washington, DC; ACOG.

Other Resources

The resources listed as follows are for information purposes only. Referral to these sources and web sites does not imply the endorsement of ACOG. This list is not meant to be comprehensive. The exclusion of a source or web site does not reflect the quality of that source or web site. Please note that web sites are subject to change without notice.

American Academy of Family Physicians
11400 Tomahawk Creek Parkway
Leawood, KS 66211-2672
Tel: 800-274-2237; (913) 906-6000
Web: www.aafp.org

The American Academy of Family Physicians works to decrease violence through activities such as developing teaching modules for members to present to medical students, residents, hospital staff, and community groups; creating an ongoing education program for members on screening, recognition, and treatment of violence; supporting or developing university-, hospital, or office-based protocols and policies about family violence; publicizing to members the hotline numbers for organizations that help physicians and patients deal with abuse; offering continuing medical education for members to increase their skills in screening for, identifying, and treating cases of intimate partner violence/domestic violence; participating in public policy initiatives and legislative reform to protect victims and rehabilitate batterers; partnering with other organizations committed to decreasing family violence; and promoting reasonable and responsible control of firearms and other weapons.

The American Academy of Pediatrics
141 Northwest Point Boulevard
Elk Grove Village, IL 60007-1098
Tel: (847) 434-4000
Fax: (847) 434-8000
Web: www.aap.org

The American Academy of Pediatrics has a Committee on Injury, Violence and Poison Prevention that develops recommendations designed to assist health care providers from the pediatric and family health settings address adult domestic violence victimization and childhood exposure to domestic violence through screening, assessment, documentation, intervention, and referrals.

American Bar Association
Commission on Domestic Violence
740 15th Street, NW, 9th Floor
Washington, DC 20005-1022
Tel: (202) 662-1000
Web: www.abanet.org/domviol/home.html; www.abanet.org/aging

The American Bar Association (ABA) houses a Commission on Domestic Violence, which provides information about a wide-range of domestic violence issues. The web site for this commission includes listings of ABA policies, training materials, legal briefs, and sample legal forms relevant to domestic violence issues and proceedings. The web site also provides information about upcoming events and training opportunities. The ABA also has a Commission on Law and Aging that works to strengthen and secure the legal rights, dignity, autonomy, quality of life, and quality of care of elders. With this in mind, the commission examines a wide range of law-related issues including health and long-term care and elder abuse.

American Medical Association
515 N State Street
Chicago, IL 60610
Tel: 800-621-8335
Web: www.ama-assn.org

The American Medical Association (AMA) works on advocacy efforts at the state and federal levels of government and in concert with state medical associations and national medical specialty societies to advocate on behalf of patients and the medical profession. The AMA established the National Advisory Council on Violence and Abuse to offer advice on effective strategies and programs to eliminate family violence in our society.

American Medical Women's Association
801 N Fairfax Street, Suite 400
Alexandria, VA 22314
Tel: (703) 838-0500
Fax: (703) 549-3864
Web: www.amwa-doc.org

The American Medical Women's Association (AMWA) is an organization of women physicians and medical students that functions at the local, national, and international level to advance women in medicine and improve women's health. The AMWA seeks to provide and develop leadership, advocacy, education, expertise, mentoring, and strategic alliances. Violence against women is one of the women's health issues AMWA works to address.

Family Violence Prevention Fund
383 Rhode Island Street, Suite 304
San Francisco, CA 94103-5133
Tel: (415) 252-8900
Fax: (415) 252-8991
Web: endabuse.org

The Family Violence Prevention Fund is a nonprofit organization that works to prevent violence within the home and in the community to help those whose lives are affected by violence. It has programs addressing issues including public education, health care, children, public policy, and immigrant women. It also provides information on how to become active in the fight against family violence by providing e-mail alerts upon request and information on how to contact Congress. Its web site includes an extensive list of violence prevention resources.

National Center on Elder Abuse
1201 15th Street, NW, Suite 350
Washington, DC 20005-2842
Tel: (202) 898-2586
Fax: (202) 898-2583
Web: www.elderabusecenter.org

The National Center on Elder Abuse is a national resource for elder rights, law enforcement and legal professionals, public policy leaders, researchers, and the public. The center's mission is to promote understanding, knowledge sharing, and action on elder abuse, neglect, and exploitation. The center makes available news and resources; collaborates on research; provides consultation, education, and training; identifies and provides information about promising practices and interventions; answers inquiries and requests for information; operates a listserv forum for professionals; and advises on program and policy development.

National Coalition Against Domestic Violence
PO Box 18749
Denver, CO 80218-0749
Tel: (303) 839-1852
Fax: (303) 831-9251

Public Policy Office
1633 Q Street, NW, Suite 210
Washington DC 20009
Tel: (202) 745-1211
Fax: (202) 745-0088
Web: www.ncadv.org

The National Coalition Against Domestic Violence (NCADV) is a grassroots, nonprofit membership organization working since 1978 to end violence in the lives of women and children. Its work includes the provision of a national network for state coalitions and local programs serving battered women and their children, public policy at the national level, technical assistance, community awareness campaigns, general information and referrals, and publications on the issue of domestic violence. In addition, NCADV sponsors a national conference every 2 years to further advocacy efforts for battered women.

National Youth Violence Prevention Resource Center
PO Box 6003
Rockville, MD 20849-6003
Tel: 866-SAFEYOUTH (866-723-3968); 800-243-7012 (TTY)
Fax: (301) 562-1001
Web: www.safeyouth.org

Developed by the Centers for Disease Control and Prevention with 10 other Federal partners, the National Youth Violence Prevention Resource Center provides current information developed by federal agencies and the private sector pertaining to youth violence. A gateway for professionals, parents, youth, and other interested individuals, the Resource Center is designed for those looking for the latest tools to help talk to children, to provide alternatives to violent resolutions to conflicts and problems, to stop bullying, to prevent teen suicide, and to end violence committed by and against young people.

The Sidran Institute
200 E Joppa Road, Suite 207
Towson, MD 21286
Tel: (410) 825-8888
Fax: (410) 337-0747
Web: www.sidran.org

The Sidran Institute is a nationally focused nonprofit organization devoted to helping people who have experienced traumatic life events, including family violence. Its education and advocacy efforts seek to promote greater understanding of the early recognition and treatment of trauma-related stress in children, the understanding of trauma and its long-term effect on adults, and the strategies leading to greatest success in self-help recovery for trauma survivors.

U.S. Department of Justice
Office for Victims of Crime
810 7th Street, NW
Washington, DC 20531
Tel: 800-851-3420
Web: www.ojp.usdoj.gov/ovc

The Office for Victims of Crime (OVC) was established by the 1984 Victims of Crime Act to oversee diverse programs that benefit victims of crime. The OVC provides funding to state victims' assistance and compensation programs. The agency supports trainings designed to educate criminal justice and allied professionals regarding the rights and needs of crime victims. The OVC is one of five bureaus and four offices with grant-making authority within the Office of Justice Programs, U.S. Department of Justice.

U.S. Department of Justice
Office on Violence Against Women
810 7th Street, NW
Washington, DC 20531
Tel: (202) 307-6026; (202) 307-2277 (TTY)
Fax: (202) 307-3911
Web: www.ojp.usdoj.gov/vawo

The Office on Violence Against Women handles the U.S. Department of Justice's legal and policy issues regarding violence against women, coordinates departmental efforts, provides national and international leadership, and responds to requests for information regarding violence against women.

YWCA of the U.S.A.
1015 18th Street, NW, Suite 1100
Washington, DC 20036
Tel: (202) 467-0801 or 800-YWCA US1
Fax: (202) 467-0802
Web: www.ywca.org

The YWCA of the U.S.A. is a national leader in violence prevention, offering programs and services to more than 700,000 women and children annually. The YWCAs across the country help women escape, recover from, and prevent violence in their lives and the lives of their families. The YWCA supports anti-violence policies that seek to eliminate violence and identifies and supports alternatives to violence at home, school, at work, and in neighborhoods.

Sexual Assault

Key Points

- The legal definition of criminal sexual assault is any genital, oral, or anal penetration by a part of the accused's body or by an object using force or without the victim's consent.

- Many victims of a sexual assault do not identify the event as a rape; therefore, behavior-specific questions are recommended to increase case findings.

- Rape-related pregnancy contributes substantially to unintended pregnancy in the United States.

- The most common sexually transmitted diseases (STDs) reported in sexual assault victims also are those most common in the general community and include trichomoniasis, gonorrhea, and *Chlamydia trachomatis* infection.

- Victims of physical and sexual assault are at a great risk of developing posttraumatic stress disorder. Clusters of symptoms may not appear for months or even years after the traumatic experience.

- If a history of sexual abuse has been obtained, the clinician needs to be aware that various health care procedures can be triggers for panic and anxiety reactions. Pelvic, rectal, endovaginal ultrasound, and breast examinations may be traumatic.

- Physicians should be aware of the existence of local protocols, including the use of specially trained sexual assault nurse examiners (SANEs) or sexual assault forensic examiners (SAFEs).

- The physician conducting an evidentiary evaluation of a victim of sexual assault has a number of responsibilities, both medical and legal, and should be aware of state and local statutory or policy requirements that may involve the use of assessment kits for gathering evidence.

Physicians who make screening for a history of sexual assault a routine part of clinical practice provide tertiary prevention of long-term and persistent physical and mental health consequences of sexual assault.

- For adolescents, there are several special concerns, including pregnancy and drug-facilitated sexual assault. Embarrassment, fear of retribution, feelings of guilt, and lack of knowledge of their rights frequently are cited reasons for adolescents not disclosing victimization.

- Alcohol and drug use influences date and acquaintance rape.

Definitions

The legal term rape traditionally has referred to forced vaginal penetration of a woman by a male assailant. Many jurisdictions have now abandoned this terminology in favor of the gender-neutral term sexual assault. The legal definition of criminal sexual assault is any genital, oral, or anal penetration by a part of the accused's body or by an object using force or without the victim's consent (1). Criminal sexual assault, or rape, often is further characterized to include acquaintance rape, date rape, "statutory rape," child sexual abuse, and incest. These terms generally relate to the age of the victim and her relationship to the abuser.

Acquaintance and date rape refer to sexual assaults committed by someone known to the victim. Instances in which the perpetrator is related to the victim generally are defined as incest. Although incest refers to sexual intercourse among family members, or those legally barred from marriage (2), this definition has been broadened conceptually to include step-relatives and parental figures living in the home. "Statutory rape" refers to consensual sexual intercourse with a female younger than a specified age. The age at which an adolescent may consent to sexual intercourse varies by state and ranges from 14 to 18 years. Sexual assault occurring in childhood also is defined by most states as child abuse. The National Center on Child Abuse and Neglect defines childhood sexual abuse as "contact or interaction between a child and an adult when the child is being used for the sexual stimulation of that adult or another person." Childhood sexual abuse is further defined such that abuse may be committed by another minor when that individual is either significantly older than the victim (often defined as more than 5 years) or when the abuser is in a position of power or control over the child (3).

Incidence and Prevalence

Reliable information on national rates of sexual assault requires assembling information from a variety of sources. The method of obtaining data influences the estimates of the incidence and prevalence of rape and sexual assault. Data that rely on reporting to law enforcement officials will always underestimate the incidence of sexual assault, and most population surveys are limited to individuals aged 18 years and older. Interviews or surveys that query on lifetime expe-

riences with sexual assault yield extraordinary rates of sexual assault in childhood and adolescence and are the basis for a component of prevalence data.

Many victims of a sexual assault do not identify the event as a rape; therefore, behavior-specific questions are recommended to increase case findings (4). Gateway or general questions produce more conservative estimates of incidence or prevalence (5).

Key findings of the National Violence Against Women (NVAW) survey, which was conducted from 1995 to 1996, are summarized as follows (6):

- A total of 17.6% of all women surveyed reported that they had been the victim of a completed or attempted rape during their lifetime. Most experiences were of completed rapes (14.8% of women surveyed).

- More than one half (54%) of the women who reported an attempted or completed rape were younger than 18 years when victimized; 21.6% were younger than 12 years when they were first raped, and 32.4% were aged 12–17 years.

- Of the women who reported a rape before age 18 years, only 14.3% were assaulted by a stranger.

- When data on women of color are combined, there is no significant difference in sexual assault rates compared with white women: 19.8% of women of color and 17.7% of white women had experienced a completed or attempted rape in their lifetime. American Indian and Alaska Native women were significantly more likely than Caucasian, African-American, or mixed-race women to report that they had been raped, and Hispanic women were significantly less likely than other women to report a lifetime experience of rape. Data are inadequate to characterize the experiences of Asian and Pacific Islander women.

- A total of 41.4% of women who were raped since age 18 years were physically assaulted during their most recent rape.

- Fewer than one half, only 35.6%, of women injured during their most recent rape received medical treatment.

The National College Women Sexual Victimization Survey (NCWSV) assessed a range of sexual victimization incidents in a national sample of women attending 2- or 4-year colleges in fall 1996. The rate of completed and attempted rape incidents during 1 academic year was 35.3 per 1,000 female students (7). It was estimated that 20–25% of women attending colleges might become victims of sexual assault over the course of college enrollment, which currently lasts an average of 5 years (7). Incidence and prevalence data support the conclusion that sexual assault most commonly occurs among young women aged 16–24 years (8).

Medical Consequences of Sexual Assault

The medical consequences of sexual assault can be considered as acute and chronic phenomena. Both categories can be characterized further as those of general medical significance and those of specific reproductive health consequence.

The NVAW survey estimated that there are more than 300,000 rape-related physical assaults against women annually (6). Acute, traumatic injuries reported can be relatively minor, including scratches, bruises and welts, but some women will sustain fractures, head and facial trauma, lacerations, or bullet wounds. The risk of injury was increased for adult female rape victims if the perpetrator was a current or former intimate partner; if the rape occurred in the victim's or perpetrator's home; if the rape was completed; if harm to the victim or another was threatened by the perpetrator; if a gun, knife, or other weapon was used during the assault; or if the perpetrator was using drugs or alcohol at the time of the assault. No relationship was found between the risk of injury and the victim's race or age.

Genital injury patterns have been described primarily in studies of emergency room populations. An analysis of 1,076 cases of sexual assault in an urban level 1 trauma center found that 52.7% of women had documented genital trauma; vaginal assault was the most common (9). A series that used colposcopy to evaluate genital trauma compared findings in women with nonconsensual and consensual intercourse. Multiple site trauma was more common in nonconsenting women. Trauma types varied by vulvar site: tears were most often detected on the posterior fourchette and fossa, abrasions on the labia, and ecchymoses on the hymen (10).

Sexual assault is associated with a risk of exposure to pregnancy and STDs. Rape-related pregnancy contributes substantially to unintended pregnancy in the United States. A national sample assessed the prevalence and incidence of rape and pregnancy among other physical and mental health outcomes over a 3-year period (11). The national rape-related pregnancy rate was calculated to be 5% per rape among women aged 12–45 years (11). This would be equivalent to approximately 32,000 pregnancies as a result of rape each year. Fifty percent of women who became pregnant as a result of rape opted for pregnancy termination (11). Almost one half of victims received no medical attention in immediate temporal proximity to the assault (11). Women who might become pregnant should be offered emergency contraception. Table 15 lists emergency contraception options.

Rape-related STD infection is a major concern for victims and health care providers. At the time of a clinical examination, however, it often is not possible to distinguish readily in adult women between a preexisting infection and one that was acquired as a result of the assault. In addition, sexual assault victims often do not complete follow-up visits to obtain the additional cultures or other tests necessary to document a change from the baseline. Often sexual assault victims may delay presentation for medical care, and thus, experience intercurrent circumstances such as interval acts of consensual intercourse that make differentiation of new infections or pregnancy more difficult. Although most sexual assaults are committed by an individual known to the victim, it is not common for evaluation and testing for STDs to be performed on the alleged perpetrator.

The most common STDs reported in sexual assault victims also are those most common in the general community and include trichomoniasis, gonorrhea, and *Chlamydia trachomatis* infection (12). Prophylaxis for STDs are summarized in Table 16. Sexually transmitted diseases in children known or suspected of being abused also include these common diseases. Two additional conditions related to sexual abuse should be considered in children: 1) bacterial vaginosis and 2) human papillomavirus infection. When screening for multiple genital infections is carried out, bacterial vaginosis is most commonly reported, and the presence of condylomata may represent fondling even in the absence of evidence for other genital contact (13). (For more information on sexual assault in this population, refer to the "General Management of Pediatric Gynecology Patients" chapter.)

Table 15. Prescriptive Equivalents of Dedicated Products and Common Oral Contraceptives for Use as Emergency Contraception*

Brand	Manufacturer	Pills Per Dose	Ethinyl Estradiol Per Dose (µg)	Levonorgestrel Per Dose (mg)†
Plan B®‡	Barr	1 white pill	0	0.75
Alesse®	Wyeth-Ayerst	5 pink pills	100	0.5
Aviane™	Barr	5 orange pills	100	0.5
Cryselle®	Barr	4 white pills	120	0.6
Enpresse™	Barr	4 orange pills	120	0.5
Lessina®	Barr	5 pink pills	100	0.5
Levlen®	Berlex	4 light orange pills	120	0.6
Levlite™	Berlex	5 pink pills	100	0.5
Levora®	Watson	4 white pills	120	0.6
Lo/Ovral®	Wyeth-Ayerst	4 white pills	120	0.6
Lutera™	Watson	5 white pills	100	0.5
Low-Ogestrel®	Watson	4 white pills	120	0.6
Nordette®	Wyeth-Ayerst	4 light orange pills	120	0.6
Ogestrel®	Watson	2 white pills	100	0.5
Ovral®	Wyeth-Ayerst	2 white pills	100	0.5
Ovrette®	Wyeth-Ayerst	20 yellow pills	0	0.75
Portia®	Barr	4 pink pills	120	0.6
Seasonale®	Barr	4 pink pills	120	0.6
Tri-Levlen®	Berlex	4 yellow pills	120	0.5
Triphasil®	Wyeth-Ayerst	4 yellow pills	120	0.5
Trivora®	Watson	4 pink pills	120	0.5

*Treatment consists of two doses taken 12 hours apart; first dose to be taken within 72 hours of unprotected sex. Women who take combined emergency contraceptive pills may experience nausea or vomiting. Antinausea medicine is, therefore, recommended. The risk of nausea and vomiting with progestin-only emergency contraceptive pills is far lower than the risk with combined emergency contraceptive pills. The hormonal content of the Yuzpe regimen includes 100 µg of ethinyl estradiol and 1 mg of norgestrel or 0.5 mg of levonorgestrel in each of the two doses. There may be other oral contraceptive pills that are not listed here that provide the proper hormonal content to meet the Yuzpe regimen.
†The progestin in Ovral, Ogestrel, Lo/Ovral, Low-Ogestrel, and Ovrette is norgestrel, which contains two isomers, only one of which (levonorgestrel) is bioactive; the amount of norgestrel in each tablet is twice the amount of levonorgestrel.
‡Plan B is the only dedicated product specifically marketed for emergency contraception in the United States. Preven, a combined emergency contraceptive, is no longer available in the U.S. market.

Adapted with permission from Trussell J, Koenig J, Ellertson C, Stewart F. Preventing unintended pregnancy: the cost-effectiveness of three methods of emergency contraception. Am J Public Health 1997;87:932–7.

Note: to include your name in a directory of providers of emergency contraception, go to http://www.not-2-late.com or http://ec.princeton.edu/. For updates to this table, go to http://ec.princeton.edu/questions/dose.html. For other information, go to http://www.arhp.org and www.plannedparenthood.org/ec.

The human immunodeficiency virus (HIV) status of the assailant in a sexual assault is often unknown or unavailable. The U.S. Department of Health and Human Services now recommends that an individual seeking care within 72 hours after nonoccupational exposure to blood, genital secretions, or other potentially infective body fluids of an individual known to have HIV receive a 28-day course of highly active antiretroviral therapy (HAART), initiated as soon as possible after exposure. For an individual seeking care within 72 hours of such an exposure to an individual of unknown HIV status, clinicians should evaluate the risks and benefits of nonoccupational postexposure prophylaxis (nPEP) on a case-by-case basis. For individuals initiating care more than 72 hours after exposure, the clinician might consider prescribing nonoccupational postexposure prophylaxis for exposures conferring a serious risk for transmission if in their judgment the diminished potential benefit of treatment outweighs the potential risks for adverse events from antiretroviral medications (14). Sexual assault typically has multiple characteristics that increase the risk of HIV transmission if the perpetrator is infected, including genital or rectal trauma leading to bleeding RJ, multiple traumatic sites involving lacerations or deep abrasions, and the presence of preexisting genital infection in the victim (15). Threatening to infect an individual with HIV infection has been

reported as an intimidation factor. The victim may have some awareness of the likelihood of risk factors for infection in the perpetrator, such as intravenous drug use, based on the location of the assault or other observations. These same factors represent potential risk for exposure to hepatitis B and hepatitis C.

Various general health effects have been associated with female sexual violence experiences. Increases in patient-reported symptoms, diminished levels of functional capacity, alterations in health perceptions, and decreased positivity of overall quality of life have all been reported as sequelae of childhood and adult sexual abuse (16, 17). Most women with a history of sexual assault will not have reported it to a nonpsychiatric physician. Yet, women with a history of sexual assault are more likely to present with chronic pelvic pain, dysmenorrhea, menstrual cycle disturbances, and sexual dysfunction than those without such a his-

Table 16. Testing and Medical Prophylaxis for Sexual Assault Victims

Sexually Transmitted Disease Infections	Prophylaxis
Gonococcal infection	Ceftriaxone, 125 mg intramuscularly in a single dose PLUS
Chlamydia trachomatis infection	Metronidazole, 2 g orally in a single dose, PLUS azithromycin, 1 g orally single dose;
	OR
Trichomoniasis	Doxycycline, 100 mg twice daily orally for 7 days
Bacterial vaginosis	(Testing for gonorrhea, chlamydia, and *Trichomonas vaginalis* should be done at initial examination. If vaginal discharge, malodor, and itching are present, examination for bacterial vaginosis and candidiasis should be conducted.)
Syphilis	Routine prophylaxis is not currently recommended. (Serologic tests should be conducted at initial evaluation, and repeated 6, 12, and 24 weeks after the assault.)
Hepatitis B	Postexposure hepatitis B vaccination (without hepatitis B immune globulin) administered at time of initial examination if not previously vaccinated. Follow-up doses should be administered at 1–2 months and 4–6 months after first dose. (Serologic tests should be conducted at initial evaluation.)
Human immunodeficiency virus infection (HIV)	≤72 hours postexposure with an individual known to have HIV, 28 day course of highly active retroviral therapy (HAART). Consultation with an HIV specialist is recommended. (Serologic tests should be conducted at initial evaluation, and repeated 6, 12, and 24 weeks after the assault.) ≤72 hours postexposure to an individual of unknown HIV status, or >72 hours postexposure, individualized assessment
Herpes simplex virus infection	Routine prophylaxis is not currently recommended but should be individualized if there is a report of a genital lesion on assailant. A 7–10 day course of acyclovir, famcyclovir, or valacyclovir may be offered. However, there are no data on the efficacy of this treatment.
Human papillomavirus infection	There is no preventive treatment recommended at this time.
Pregnancy	Emergency contraception. First dose should be given within 72 hours of the assault.
Injuries	Tetanus toxoid booster, 0.5 mL intramuscularly, if more than 10 years since last immunization.

Adapted from Sexually transmitted diseases treatment guidelines 2002. Centers for Disease Control and Prevention. MMWR 2002;51(RR-6):1–8; Smith OK, Grohskopf LA, BLack RJ, Auerbach JD, Veronese F, Struble KA, et al. Antiretroviral postexposure prophylaxis after sexual, injection-drug use, or other nonoccupational exposure to HIV in the United States: recommendations from the U.S. Department of Health and Human Services. MMWR Recomm Rep 2005;54(RR-2):1–20; and Holmes M. Sexually transmitted infections in female rape victims. AIDS Patient Care STDS 1999;13:703–8.

tory (18). The frequency with which these conditions are encountered in clinical practice and the prevalence of lifetime sexual assault predicates a significant likelihood that the victimization experience will be alluded to during an element of routine evaluation and treatment approaches. It is important to recognize these signs. (For a detailed discussion of physical and biomedical effects seen in adulthood as manifestations of childhood sexual abuse, see the "Adult Manifestations of Childhood Sexual Abuse" chapter.)

Psychologic and Mental Health Consequences of Sexual Assault

A woman who is sexually assaulted loses control over her life during the period of the assault. Her integrity, and sometimes her life, are threatened. She may experience intense anxiety, anger, or fear. After the assault, a "rape-trauma" syndrome often occurs. The acute phase (immediate response) may last for hours or days and is characterized by distortion or paralysis of the individual's coping mechanisms. The outward responses vary from complete loss of emotional control to an apparently well-controlled behavior pattern. The signs may include generalized pain throughout the body; headache; eating and sleep disturbances; and emotional symptoms, such as depression, anxiety, and mood swings. The next phase, the delayed (or organization) phase, is characterized by flashbacks, nightmares, and phobias as well as somatic and gynecologic symptoms. This phase often occurs months or years after the event and may involve major life adjustments (19, 20).

This rape-trauma syndrome is similar to a grief reaction in many respects. As such, it can only be resolved when the victim has emotionally worked through the trauma and personal loss related to the event and replaced it with other life experiences. The counseling offered to the victim for her current phase of the syndrome can help her to understand her psychologic and physical responses, thereby diminishing the symptoms. The additional, longer-term mental health sequelae of sexual assault can be quite varied and significant. Preliminary work in a group of women with a current diagnosis of major depression and a history of childhood sexual or physical abuse

demonstrated a six-fold increase in adrenocorticotropic hormone response to stress as compared with controls (21). This response was interpreted as hyperreactivity of the hypothalamic–pituitary–adrenal axis and autonomic nervous system because of corticotropin-releasing factor hypersecretion being a persistent consequence of childhood abuse and contributing to certain aspects of psychopathology.

Posttraumatic stress disorder may be one type of such psychopathology. It is a complex disorder associated with exposure to extreme trauma (usually an event that was perceived as life threatening). Although first described in combat veterans, victims of physical and sexual assault also are at great risk of developing posttraumatic stress disorder. Clusters of symptoms may not appear for months or even years after a traumatic experience. These clusters are typical symptom categories associated with posttraumatic stress disorder, such as re-living the event. Here, affected individuals experience flashbacks, recurring nightmares, and, more specifically, intrusive images that appear at any time. Extreme emotional or physical reactions, including shaking, chills, palpitations, or panic reactions, often accompany vivid recollections of the attack. Avoiding reminders of the event constitutes another symptom cluster in posttraumatic stress disorder. In so doing, individuals with posttraumatic stress disorder become emotionally numb, withdrawing from friends and family and losing interest in every day activities. There may be an even deeper reaction of denial of awareness that the event actually happened. Symptoms such as easy startling, being hypervigilant, irritability, sleep disturbances, and lack of concentration are part of a third symptom cluster known as hyper-arousal. Individuals with posttraumatic stress disorder often will have a number of co-occurring conditions, such as depression, dissociative disorders (losing conscious awareness of the present or "zoning out"), addictive disorders, and many physical symptoms (22). When these behaviors are seen in clinical practice, it is important to consider a connection with more remote events rather than the immediate practice situation. If a history of sexual abuse has been obtained, the clinician needs to be aware that various health care procedures can be triggers for panic and anxiety reactions. Pelvic, rectal, breast, and endovaginal ultrasound examinations may be traumatic.

The medical and psychologic implications of sexual assault have a subsequent association with tobacco, alcohol, and illicit drug use and abuse. Cigarette use has been linked to problems in psychologic functioning, including posttraumatic stress disorder in Vietnam War veterans (23). It is interpreted as a coping mechanism, and there is evidence for a neurotransmitter-mediated effect of nicotine on mood. The negative health consequences of tobacco use in women are well established. (See "Smoking and Women's Health" chapter for more information.)

Alcohol abuse, including binge drinking, and illicit drug use and dependence, have a longer-term association with sexual assault. In a study of female twins discordant for self-reported childhood sexual abuse, the risks of bulimia and alcohol and other drug dependence were significantly higher in the exposed twin (24). A survey of women seeking substance abuse treatment found that prevalence rates of completed rape or other type of sexual assault for women were 64.2% and 44.8%, respectively (25). The prevalence rates for lifetime and current crime-related (inclusive of other types of physical assaults) posttraumatic stress disorder were 61.2% and 40.3%, respectively, for the women in the study (25).

The literature now contains multiple reports on the association between sexual assault in adolescents and maladaptive weight control techniques and eating disorders (26). Laxative use or vomiting to lose weight were significantly associated with dating sexual violence in the 1999 Massachusetts Youth Risk Behavioral Survey (27). In an adult population-based survey, regression analysis controlling for multiple demographic factors demonstrated that men and women with sexual assault histories were more likely than those not assaulted to report thinking they were too fat, losing 15 lb or more, admitting to one or more eating disorder symptoms, and experiencing sudden weight changes (28). Analysis of a survey of girls in grades 9–12 indicated an elevated probability (by 6–13%) that girls who experienced dating violence and unwanted sexual contact would report purging and diet pill consumption (29). In a study of female weight lifters, 13% of the group reported adolescent or adult rape. A subset of this group reported the use of anabolic steroids to gain muscle mass and had a pattern of activity suggestive of compulsive weight lifting interpreted to be a psychologic response to the abuse (30).

Roles and Responsibilities of Physicians

Physicians can practice primary prevention by being involved in advocacy in professional, community, and educational spheres. In addition, the American College of Obstetricians and Gynecologists recommends that physicians routinely screen all patients for sexual assault (31). The likelihood of disclosure increases with successive inquiries. Physicians who make screening for a history of sexual assault a routine part of clinical practice provide tertiary prevention of long-term and persistent physical and mental health consequences of sexual assault. Additionally, physicians should be aware of the existence of local protocols including the use of specially trained sexual assault nurse examiners or sexual assault forensic examiners. In recent years, there has been a trend toward the implementation of hospital-based programs to provide acute medical and evidentiary examinations by sexual assault nurse examiners or sexual assault forensic examiners. Physicians play a role in the policy and procedure development and implementation of these programs, and serve as sources for referral, consultation, and follow-up. In some parts of the country, however, obstetrician–gynecologists will still be the first point of contact for evaluation and care in the acute aftermath of a sexual assault. In addition, virtually all obstetrician–gynecologists will be called on to perform evaluations and, if conducting screening for history of sexual assault, will realize the utility of this information to the conduct of primary care and specialty care practice.

The physician conducting an evidentiary evaluation of a victim of sexual assault has a number of responsibilities, both medical and legal, and should be aware of state and local statutory or policy requirements that may involve the use of assessment kits for gathering evidence. Local law enforcement guidelines may not carry the weight of law; instead, they may be set forth by what cases are prosecuted. Specific responsibilities are determined by the patient's needs and by state law. Physicians' roles in evaluation of sexual assault victims are summarized in Box 22. Should a victim communicate with the physician's office, emergency room, or clinic before presenting for evaluation, she

---

Box 22   Physician's Role in Evaluation of Sexual Assault Victims

Medical issues

- Ensure informed consent is obtained from patient

- Assess and treat physical injuries or triage and refer

- Obtain pertinent past gynecologic history

- Perform physical examination, including pelvic examination (with appropriate chaperone or support person present)

- Obtain appropriate specimens for sexually transmitted disease testing

- Obtain baseline serologic tests for hepatitis B, human immunodeficiency virus, and syphilis

- Provide appropriate infectious diseases prophylaxis as indicated

- Provide or arrange for provision of emergency contraception as indicated

- Provide counseling regarding findings, recommendations, and prognosis

- Arrange follow-up medical care and referrals for psychosocial needs

Legal issues*

- Provide accurate recording of events

- Document injuries

- Collect samples (pubic hair, fingernail scrapings, vaginal secretion and discharge samples, saliva, blood-stained clothing or other personal articles) as indicated by local protocol or regulation

- Identify the presence or absence of sperm in the vaginal fluids and make appropriate slides

- Report to authorities as required

- Ensure security of chain of evidence

*Many jurisdictions have prepackaged "rape kits" for the initial forensic examination that provide specific containers and instructions for the collection of physical evidence and for written and pictorial documentation of the victim's subjective and objective findings. Hospital emergency rooms or the police themselves may supply the kits when called to respond or when bringing a patient to the hospital. Most often the emergency physician or specially trained nurse response team will perform the examination, but all physicians should be familiar with the forensic examination procedure. If called to perform this examination and the physician has no or limited experience, it may be judicious to call for assistance because any break in the technique in collecting evidence, or break in the chain of custody of evidence, including improper handling of samples or mislabeling, will virtually eliminate any effort to prosecute in the future.

---

should be encouraged to come immediately to a medical facility and be advised not to bathe, douche, urinate, defecate, wash out her mouth, clean her fingernails, smoke, eat, or drink.

In addition to fulfilling legal requirements, the informed consent process helps the victim participate in regaining control of her body and her circumstances. After acute injuries have been determined and stabilized, a careful history and physical examination should be performed. A clinical chaperone and possibly a support individual or victim advocate should be present during the history taking and physical examination. The physician should ask the victim to state in her own words what happened. The patient may be asked to identify her assailant or provide a description if unknown to her. Although this information also may be recorded with the police, it may be facilitated by discussion with the physician and may be pertinent to the conduct of the examination and assessment of risks. The patient also should be asked to provide

details of the sexual acts imposed to allow appropriate examination and specimen collection.

A history of previous obstetric and gynecologic conditions should be recorded, and it is necessary to determine whether the patient may have a preexisting pregnancy or be at risk for pregnancy. Women who might become pregnant should be offered emergency contraception. A careful physical examination of the entire body should be performed and photographs or drawings made of injuries. Rape and sexual assault are legal terms that should not be used in medical records. Rather, the physician should report findings as "consistent with . . ." whatever aspect of the reported assault is being evaluated.

The physician should document the emotional condition of the patient as judged by direct observation and examination. If the victim is a minor, the physician should report the incident to the appropriate authorities as required by law. An effort should be made to have a parent or parental figure become involved unless such an individual represents a security threat to the victim. When the physical and medical–legal needs of the patient have been addressed, the physician should discuss with the patient the degree of injury and the probability of infection or pregnancy. The physician should describe the general course that the patient may be expected to follow and how follow-up is to be arranged and carried out. Patients may be less likely to develop posttraumatic stress disorder if they understand what constitutes a normal reaction to such trauma. Other health personnel, particularly those trained to respond to rape-trauma victims, should be consulted to provide immediate intervention if necessary and to facilitate counseling and follow-up. Physicians are urged to assemble and maintain a list of these individuals and other resources for referral of the patient (see "Resources").

Because of the emotional intensity of the acute experience, a woman may not remember all of what is said. Therefore, it is helpful to provide all instructions and plans in writing. Generally, a visit for clinical and psychologic follow-up should take place within 1–2 weeks and scheduled thereafter as indicated by results and assessments at that time.

Special Concerns and Considerations

Childhood Sexual Abuse

Childhood sexual abuse is associated with adult revictimization, including rape, domestic violence, physical assault, and alcohol and drug abuse (32). Special consideration must be given to avoid retraumatization in pre-and peripubertal girls. The assailant almost always has some form of acquaintanceship to the victim; therefore, there are immediate and longer-term security issues. Referrals to a health care facility or provider specializing in child sexual abuse may be appropriate. The objectives of the physical examination are to identify for legal purposes any signs of sexual contact; to identify and treat adverse consequences of assault, such as injuries or STDs; and to reassure the child and caregiver about the child's physical well being. The external genitalia should be inspected and when possible, photographed. A colposcope with a camera attachment or hand-held camera with a macro-lens may be used. A speculum examination rarely should

be performed in a prepubertal patient (33). Forcible restraint is never appropriate and sedation is rarely indicated for adequate examination for injuries, treatment, or procurement of evidence. The physician must learn what reports to authorities need to be initiated or already have taken place, depending on when they become involved in evaluation and treatment (see "General Management of Pediatric Gynecology Patients" chapter).

Adolescents

For adolescents, there are several additional special concerns, including pregnancy and drug-facilitated sexual assault. Embarrassment, fear of retribution, feelings of guilt, and lack of knowledge of their rights frequently are cited reasons for adolescents not disclosing victimization. The adolescent victim also may feel that she in some way contributed to her rape because her experience does not fit popular concepts of rape involving an assailant unknown to the victim (34). The risk of rape-related pregnancy is increased among adolescents because they are more likely to be repeatedly assaulted because of the predominance of an incestuous relationship with the perpetrator and their relatively low use of ongoing contraception.

All 50 states and the District of Columbia have laws that specify when sexual activity with a minor is illegal. The age at which an adolescent may consent to sexual intercourse varies by state and ranges from age 14 years to 18 years; an adolescent younger than this age is defined as being incapable of consenting. Most adolescent girls have a partner who is within their age range. However, sexual abuse is a greater risk with the presence of an older partner. A California cohort of adolescent mothers was studied to discern characteristics of paternity. Adult males were the fathers of 24.3% of the infants born to mothers aged 11–12 years, with a mean paternal age of 22.7 years (range 20–36 years). Adult males fathered 26.8% of infants born to mothers aged 13–14 years, with a mean paternal age of 22.5 years (range 20 to 58 years). The mean age difference between mothers aged 15–17 years and the fathers was approximately 6 years and it was 4 years for women aged 18–19 years (35).

Sexual victimization has been linked to subsequent high-risk behaviors in adolescents, including early initiation of consensual intercourse and unplanned pregnancy, lack of initiation and continuation of contraception, and involvement in physically assaultive relationships (36–38). Delayed onset of prenatal care in an adolescent pregnancy and lack of adherence are not uncommon in pregnancies associated with sexual abuse. The young women themselves have psychosocial trauma, understandable rejection or denial of the pregnancy, and may be further victimized by the perpetrator. Management of adolescent pregnancy under these circumstances requires patience, insight, compassion, and collaboration with the entire health services team.

Date rape is a subcategory of acquaintance rape wherein nonconsensual sex occurs between two individuals who are in a romantic or developing romantic relationship. This discussion focuses on young individuals and adolescents in heterosexual relationships. For a discussion of issues related to lesbian relationships, see the "Primary Care of Lesbians and Bisexual Women in Obstetric and Gynecologic Practice" chapter. The concept of date rape was first reported in the 1950s as a phenomenon involving college students, but the considerations are broader at this time (39). Adolescents are more likely to subscribe to "rape myths," such as rapists are more likely to be strangers. Many adolescents have not yet developed the necessary skills to recognize and avoid potentially dangerous dating or social situations. Adolescent males and females may bring different expectations to dating situations and attribute different meanings to the same behaviors. Prevention of sexual assault of adolescents, which primarily occurs between acquaintances, requires education at the individual and community level.

Substance Use and Sexual Assault

Reports are conflicting on the influence of alcohol and other drug use by the victim or the perpetrator at the time of a sexual assault. There is evidence, however, that alcohol and other intoxicants play a role in increasing risk for sexual assault among adolescents and college students. In one study assessing self-reported substance use by the victim, substance use was reported by 51% of victims, with alcohol alone in 40% and in combination with drugs in 7% (40). Alcohol and marijuana are the most commonly used drugs among adolescents and young adults; therefore, they appear most consistently in screens for drug use in association with sexual assault (41). Recently, a

group of drugs known as "club drugs" have appeared on the youth social scene. Several of these have been implicated in what is known as drug-facilitated sexual assault. The presence of multiple other psychoactive drugs, including potent sedatives, has been reported in drug-facilitated sexual assault. A list of drugs that have been used are listed in Table 17. The rapid acting benzodiazepine, flunitrazepam (Rohypnol), and the banned euphoriant γ-hydroxybutyrate (GHB), have received the widest attention. There are controversies as to how commonly these drugs have been used, with one screening survey reporting less than 3% of samples being positive for flunitrazepam or GHB (41). Such surveys use a variety of different sample procurement protocols and rely on samples obtained in reported cases of sexual assault; therefore, there are credible opinions that the use of these drugs is considerably greater.

Substance use by the victim in the immediate pre-assault period was associated with decreased memory for key aspects of the assault because of the significant anterograde amnesic effect of the drugs (42). This type of impairment is a contributor to the low rates of reporting to law enforcement as well as presentation for medical evaluation and care. In addition to amnesia, these drugs act rapidly to produce sedation, disinhibition, muscle relaxation, and loss of consciousness; alcohol potentiates these effects.

Flunitrazepam is not marketed legally in the United States but is available in Europe and Mexico. Street

Table 17. Drugs Used to Facilitate Sexual Assault

Most commonly used:	Alcohol* Marijuana (Cannabis)*
Associated with increased incidence of sexual assault:	Flunitrazepam (Rohypnol)* γ-hydroxybutyrate (GHB)* γ-butyrolactone (GBL)* 1, 4, butanediol (BD) Ketamine*
Reported in various series:	Alprazolam Chloral hydrate Clonazepam Diazepam Meprobamate Midazolam Phencylcidine* Temazepam Triazolam Zolpidem

*For more information, go to http://www.clubdrugs.org.

Adapted with permission from: Schwartz RH, Milteer R, LeBeau MA. Drug-facilitated sexual assault ("Date Rape"). South Med J 2000;93:558–61. © Lippincott Williams & Wilkins.

names for flunitrazepam include "roofies," "ruffies," "R-2," "roche," "Mexican Valium," and "forget-me pill." It is odorless and tasteless but does discolor or cloud liquids to which it is added. Even though it has been banned in the United States since 1990, GHB, an anabolic agent that is easily synthesized, can be obtained in bars, clubs, and gyms. Street names include "Grievous Body Harm," "Easy Lay," "Georgia Home Boy," "G," and "liquid ecstasy." In liquid or powder form, GHB is colorless and odorless when added to a drink. It is reported to have a salty taste. Fruit-flavored and dark colored beverages may be more likely to be adulterated intentionally. There are two pro-drugs that are metabolized by alcohol and aldehyde dehydrogenases to euphoriant GHB. Gamma-butyrolactone ("Blue Nitro") and 1,4, butanediol are industrial solvents that are sold as dietary supplements with claims for increased libido and improved sexual functioning. They are highly toxic, with deaths having been reported in association with their use (43). Adolescents should be provided with prevention messages about opened beverages and drinks served at group social events in addition to advice regarding under-age and excessive alcohol use.

Other Populations

There are a variety of additional circumstances in which physicians need to be aware of an increased likelihood that a particular patient may have experienced sexual assault or be at increased risk of sexual assault. Many women in prison and jail are victims of sexual abuse by the male custodial staff. The abuse includes provocative and offensive language, groping of breasts and genitalia during searches, and undressing the women, in addition to rape. Physicians, along with other health care professionals who provide health services to incarcerated women, must be aware of custodial assault. In addition, after women are released or paroled, they may seek health care in the community health care setting with physical and psychologic sequelae. (See "Health and Health Care for Incarcerated Adult and Adolescent Females" chapter).

Sexual assault and rape have been widely reported as occurring in areas experiencing civil war and social disruption. Rape of women of all ages often is a strategically perpetrated act of war, particularly in those conflicts based on racial or ethnic divisions. Many women who have relocated to the United States are asylum seekers, refugees who may have spent extended time in camps and transition facilities, or former residents of countries with repressive human rights records. These women have an increased risk of history of sexual assault (44, 45). Medical care of these women should include screening for a history of sexual assault. Members of the same community of origin who are already settled in the United States may be able to assist in culturally appropriate support services.

Expanded insurance coverage and guidelines for preventive care now foster more gynecologic care for the elderly, including women who are residents of nursing homes and long-term care facilities. During routine screening evaluations or indicated care for this population, physicians may become aware of the possibility that these patients have been recent victims of sexual abuse. The differential diagnosis of unexplained vaginal or rectal bleeding, vaginal discharge, and vaginal foreign bodies should include sexual abuse. (Special considerations for women with mental and physical disabilities, lesbians, bisexual women, and transgendered individuals are reviewed in corresponding chapters of this book.)

The population prevalence of sexual assault is such that there will be victims as well as perpetrators among health care professionals. Health care training and experience do not provide victims with immunity from the medical and psychologic sequelae described in this chapter. The experience of sexual assault also may limit the ability of a health care professional to screen for sexual assault or to respond effectively in acute care situations. These individuals may need peer support, counseling support, and other appropriate interventions. Health care professionals who are regularly exposed to sexual assault victims or who encounter particularly violent or traumatic cases may need debriefing interventions to process the feelings precipitated by the experiences.

References

1. American Medical Association. Strategies for the treatment and prevention of sexual assault. Chicago (IL): AMA; 1995.

2. Hibbard RA, Orr DP. Incest and sexual abuse. Semin Adolesc Med 1985;1:153–64.

3. National Center on Child Abuse and Neglect. Child sexual abuse: incest, assault and sexual exploitation. Washington, DC: US Department of Health and Human Services; 1981.

4. Basile KC, Saltzman LE. Sexual violence surveillance: uniform definitions and recommended data elements. Atlanta (GA): National Center for Injury Prevention and Control, Centers for Disease Control and Prevention; 2002. Available at: http://www.cdc.gov/ncipc/pub–res/sv_surveillance/SexViolSurv.pdf. Retrieved September 20, 2004.

5. Acierno R, Resnick HS, Kilpatrick DG. Health impact of interpersonal violence. 1: Prevalence rates, case identification, and risk factors for sexual assault, physical assault, and domestic violence in men and women. Behav Med 1997;23:53–64.

6. Tjaden P, Thoennes N. Full report of the prevalence, incidence, and consequences of violence against women. Findings from the National Violence Against Women Survey. Washington, DC: US Department of Justice, National Institute of Justice; 2000. Publication No. NCJ183781.

7. Fisher BS, Cullen FT, Turner MG. The sexual victimization of college women. Washington, DC: US Department of Justice, National Institute of Justice; 2000. Publication No. NCJ182369.

8. Riggs N, Houry D, Long G, Markovchick V, Feldhaus KM. Analysis of 1,076 cases of sexual assault. Ann Emerg Med 2000;35:358–62.

9. Catalano SM. Criminal victimization, 2003. Bureau of Justice Statistics National Crime Victimization Survey. Washington, DC: U.S. Department of Justice, Office of Justice Programs; 2004. NCJ 205455. Available at: http://www.ojp.usdoj.gov/bjs/pub/pdf/cv03.pdf. Retrieved November 4, 2004.

10. Slaughter L, Brown CR, Crowley S, Peck R. Patterns of genital injury in female sexual assault victims. Am J Obstet Gynecol 1997;176:609–16.

11. Holmes MM, Resnick HS, Kilpatrick DG, Best CL. Rape-related pregnancy: estimates and descriptive characteristics from a national sample of women. Am J Obstet Gynecol 1996;175:320–5.

12. Lamba H, Murphy SM. Sexual assault and sexually transmitted infections: an updated review. Int J of STD AIDS 2000;11:487–91.

13. Beck-Sague CM, Solomon F. Sexually transmitted diseases in abused children and adolescent and adult victims of rape: review of selected literature. Clin Infect Dis 1999;28(suppl 1):S74–83.

14. Smith OK, Grohskopf LA, Black RJ, Auerbach JO, Veronese F, Struble KA, et al. Antiretoviral postexposure prophylaxis after sexual, injection-drug use, or other nonoccupational exposure to HIV in the United States: recommendations from the U.S. Department of Health and Human Services. MMWR Recomm Rep 2005;54 (RR-2):1–20.

15. Fong C. Post-exposure prophylaxis for HIV infection after sexual assault: when is it indicated? Emerg Med J 2001;18:242–5.

16. Plichta SB, Falik M. Prevalence of violence and its implications for women's health. Womens Health Issues 2001;11:244–58.

17. Dickinson LM, deGruy FV 3rd, Dickinson WP, Candib LM. Health-related quality of life and symptom profiles of female survivors of sexual abuse. Arch Fam Med 1999;8:35–43.

18. Golding JM, Wilsnack SC, Learman LA. Prevalence of sexual assault history among women with common gynecologic symptoms. Am J Obstet Gynecol 1998;179:1013–9.

19. Burgess AW, Holmstrom LL. Rape trauma syndrome. In: Rape: victims of crisis. Bowie (MD): Brady; 1974. p. 37–50.

20. van der Kolk BA. The body keeps the score: memory and the evolving psychobiology of posttraumatic stress. Harv Rev Psychiatry 1994;1:253–65.

21. Heim C, Newport DJ, Heit S, Graham YP, Wilcox M, Bonsall R, et al. Pituitary–adrenal and autonomic responses to stress in women after sexual and physical abuse in childhood. JAMA 2000;284:592–7.

22. PTSD Alliance. Posttraumatic stress disorder: a guide for the frontline. New York (NY): PTSD Alliance; 2000.

23. Acierno RA, Kilpatrick DG, Resnick HS, Saunders BE, Best CL. Violent assault, posttraumatic stress disorder, and depression. Risk factors for cigarette use among adult women. Behav Modif 1996;20:363–84.

24. Kendler KS, Bulik CM, Silberg J, Hettema JM, Myers J, Prescott CA. Childhood sexual abuse and adult psychiatric and substance use disorders in women: an epidemiological and cotwin control analysis. Arch Gen Psychiatry 2000;57:953–9.

25. Dansky BS, Saladin ME, Coffey SF, Brady KT. Use of self-report measures of crime-related posttraumatic stress disorder with substance use disordered patients. J Subst Abuse Treat 1997;14:431–7.

26. Ackard DM, Neumark–Sztainer D, Hannan PJ, French S, Story M. Binge and purge behavior among adolescents: associations with sexual and physical abuse in a nationally representative sample: the Commonwealth Fund Survey. Child Abuse Neglect 2001;6:771–85.

27. Silverman JG, Raj A, Mucci LA, Hathaway JE. Dating violence against adolescent girls and associated substance use, unhealthy weight control, sexual risk behavior, pregnancy, and suicidality. JAMA 2001;286:572–9.

28. Laws A, Golding JM. Sexual assault history and eating disorder symptoms among White, Hispanic, and African-American women and men. Am J Public Health 1996;86:579–82.

29. Thompson KM, Wonderlich SA, Crosby RD, Mitchell JE. Sexual violence and weight control techniques among adolescent girls. Int J Eat Disord 2001;29:166–76.

30. Gruber AJ, Pope HG Jr. Compulsive weight lifting and anabolic drug abuse among women rape victims. Compr Psychiatry 1999;40:273–7.

31. American College of Obstetricians and Gynecologists. Guidelines for women's health care. 2nd ed. Washington, DC: ACOG; 2002.

32. Coid JW, Petruckevitch A, Feder G, Chung W, Richardson J, Moorey S. Relation between childhood sexual and physical abuse and risk of revictimisation in women: a cross-sectional survey. Lancet 2001;358:450–4.

33. Guidelines for the evaluation of sexual abuse of children: subject review. American Academy of Pediatrics Committee on Child Abuse and Neglect. Pediatrics 1999;103:186–91.

34. The Commonwealth Fund. In their own words: adolescent girls discuss health and health care issues. New York: Louis Harris and Associates; 1997.

35. Taylor DJ, Chavez GF, Adams EJ, Chabra A, Shah RS. Demographic characteristics in adult paternity for first births to adolescents under 15 years of age. J Adolesc Health 1999; 24:251–8.

36. Elders MJ, Albert AE. Adolescent pregnancy and sexual abuse. JAMA 1998;280:648–9.

37. Boyer D, Fine D. Sexual abuse as a factor in adolescent pregnancy and child maltreatment. Fam Plann Perspect 1992;24: 4–11, 19.

38. Stock JL, Bell MA, Boyer DK, Connell FA. Adolescent pregnancy and sexual risk–taking among sexually abused girls. Fam Plann Perspect 1997;29:200–3, 227.

39. Rickert VI, Wiemann CM. Date rape among adolescents and young adults. J Pediatr Adolesc Gynecol 1998;11:167–75.

40. Slaughter L. Involvement of drugs in sexual assault. J Reprod Med 2000;45:425–30.

41. Mullins ME. Laboratory confirmation of flunitrazepam in alleged cases of date rape. Acad Emerg Med 1999;6:966–8.

42. Seifert SA. Substance use and sexual assault. Subst Use Misuse 1999;34:935–45.

43. Zvosec DL, Smith SW, McCutcheon JR, Spillane J, Hall BJ, Peacock EA. Adverse events, including death, associated with the use of 1,4, butanediol. N Engl J Med 2001;344:87–94.

44. Malhotra N, Sood M. Sexual assault—a neglected public health problem in the developing world. Int J Gynaecol Obstet 2000; 71:257–8.

45. Amnesty International. Broken bodies, shattered minds. Torture and ill-treatment of women. London: AI; 2001.

Resources

ACOG Resources

American College of Obstetricians and Gynecologists. Acquaintance and date rape. ACOG Tool Kit For Teen Care Fact Sheet FS002. Washington, DC: ACOG; 2003.

American College of Obstetricians and Gynecologists. Acquaintance and date rape. Tool Kit for Teen Care Fact Sheet AA415. Washington, DC: ACOG:2003.

American College of Obstetricians and Gynecologists Violence Against Women Home Page (www.acog.org, click on "Women's Issues" and then "Violence Against Women")—contains contact information for state sexual assault coalitions, screening tools, bibliographies, and fact sheets.

Limited quantities of the materials listed as follows can be obtained for free by contacting violence@acog.org:

- American College of Obstetricians and Gynecologists. Stay Alert! Stay Safe! Pocket Card. Washington, DC; ACOG.

- Sexual Assault rolodex cards include tools for screening teens and information on sexual assault.

Other Resources

The resources listed as follows are for information purposes only. Referral to these sources and web sites does not imply the endorsement of ACOG. This list is not meant to be comprehensive. The exclusion of a source or web site does not reflect the quality of that source or web site. Please note that web sites are subject to change without notice.

American College of Emergency Physicians
1125 Executive Circle
Irving, TX 75038-2522
Tel: 800-798-1822; (972) 550-0911
Fax: (972) 580-2816
Web: www.acep.org

The American College of Emergency Physicians (ACEP) exists to support quality emergency medical care and to promote the interests of emergency physicians. The ACEP's web site provides visitors with fact sheets on topics including domestic violence, current policy regarding domestic violence, help for victims, and the role of emergency personnel. The ACEP web site also has an extensive list of injury prevention resources.

American Medical Association
515 N State Street
Chicago, IL 60610
Tel: 800-621-8335
Web: www.ama-assn.org

The American Medical Association (AMA) works to improve the health of communities and strengthen the patient–physician relationship. Its web site provides links to AMA publications on sexual assault. The newest publication, Intimate Partner Violence, was designed to raise physician's awareness of intimate partner violence and provide information to help treat those patients who are victims.

The Feminist Majority Foundation
1600 Wilson Boulevard, Suite 801
Arlington, VA 22209
Tel: (703) 522-2214
Fax: (703) 522-2219
Web: www.feminist.org/911/resources_af.html

The Feminist Majority Foundation (FMF), which was founded in 1987, is an organization dedicated to women's equality, reproductive health, and nonviolence. In all spheres, FMF utilizes research and action to empower women economically, socially, and politically. *911 for Women: Sexual Assault and Rape Crisis Resources* provides state-specific contact information for victims of rape and sexual assault.

Llamanos
Tel: 800-223-5001; 800-688-4889 (TTY)
Web: www.llamanos.org

Llamanos is a 24-hour, statewide hotline in Massachusetts for Spanish-speaking women and men who have been raped or sexually assaulted and need support or counseling. It also is available for the family members or friends who might be affected. This service is free and confidential. There is always someone available to provide counseling over the phone in times of crisis and to refer people to their nearest rape crisis center for more comprehensive services.

National Coalition Against Domestic Violence
PO Box 18749
Denver, CO 80218
Tel: (303) 839-1852
Fax: (303) 831-9251
Web: www.ncadv.org

The National Coalition Against Domestic Violence is dedicated to the empowerment of battered women and their children and therefore is committed to the elimination of personal and societal violence in the lives of battered women and their children. It works for major societal changes necessary to eliminate both personal and societal violence against all women and children.

National Institute on Alcohol and Alcohol Abuse
5635 Fishers Lane, MSC 9304
Bethesda, MD 20892-9304
Web: www.niaaa.nih.gov

The National Institute on Alcohol and Alcohol Abuse supports and conducts biomedical and behavioral research on the causes, consequences, treatment, and prevention of alcoholism and alcohol-related problems. It also provides leadership in the national effort to reduce the severe and often fatal consequences of these problems and is one of 19 institutes that comprise the National Institutes of Health. Its web site provides publications in English and Spanish discussing the intersection of alcohol abuse and sexual assault.

National Institute of Justice
810 Seventh Street, NW
Washington, DC 20531
Tel: (202) 307-2942
Fax: (202) 307-6394
Web: www.ojp.usdoj.gov/nij

The National Institute of Justice (NIJ) is the research, development, and evaluation agency of the U.S. Department of Justice and is solely dedicated to researching crime control and justice issues. It provides objective, independent, nonpartisan, evidence-based knowledge, and tools to meet the challenges of crime and justice, particularly at the state and local levels. Under the Office of Research and Evaluation, NIJ houses the Violence and Victimization Research Division and the Crime Control and Prevention Research Division, where the public can obtain information about sexual assault.

Posttraumatic Stress Disorder Alliance
Tel: 877-507-PTSD
Web: www.ptsdalliance.org

The Posttraumatic Stress Disorder Alliance is a group of professional and advocacy organizations, including ACOG, that have joined forces to provide educational resources to individuals diagnosed with posttraumatic stress disorder and their loved ones; those at risk for developing posttraumatic stress disorder; and medical, health care, and other frontline professionals.

Promote Truth
Women's Center of Jacksonville
5644 Colcord Avenue
Jacksonville, FL 32211
Tel: (904) 722-3000
Fax: (904) 722-3100
Web: www.promotetruth.org

The mission of the Promote Truth web site is to empower teens through safe, anonymous support and information about sexual violence issues. Promote Truth was created by the Rape Recovery Team at the Women's Center of Jacksonville, Florida.

Rape, Abuse and Incest National Network
635-B Pennsylvania Avenue, SE
Washington, DC 20003
Tel: (202) 544-1034; Hotline: 800-656-HOPE (4673)
Fax: (202) 544-3556
Web: www.rainn.org

Founded by singer-songwriter Tori Amos, the Rape, Abuse and Incest National Network (RAINN) is a 24-hour resource that routes callers to the closest rape crisis center by reading the area code and prefix of the caller's telephone number. However, not every local rape crisis center participates in RAINN. If there is no center in RAINN located near the victim, it is suggested that the victim contact state or local rape crisis centers directly by referring to ACOG's web site or the local government section of the phonebook.

Sexual Assault Resource Service
Web: www.sane-sart.com

The Sexual Assault Resource Service web site, which runs the Sexual Assault Nurse Examiner-Sexual Assault Response Team (SANE-SART) program, contains a guide designed for nursing professionals involved in providing evaluations of sexually abused victims. It is the goal of this web site to provide information and technical assistance to individuals and institutions interested in developing new SANE-SART programs or improving existing ones.

Sidran Institute
200 E Joppa Road, Suite 207
Towson, MD 21286
Tel: (410) 825-8888
Fax: (410) 337-0747
Web: www.sidran.org

The Sidran Institute is a nationally focused nonprofit organization devoted to education, advocacy, and research to benefit people who are suffering from injuries of traumatic stress.

United States Department of Justice
Office on Violence Against Women
810 7th Street, NW
Washington, DC 20531
Tel: (202) 307-6026; (202) 307-2277 (TTY)
Fax: (202) 307-3911
Web: www.usdoj.gov/vawo

The Office on Violence Against Women, housed in the Office of Justice Programs, was created in 1995 to implement the 1994 Violence Against Women Act and to lead the national effort to stop domestic violence, sexual assault, and stalking of women. The Office on Violence Against Women administers grants to help states, tribes, and local communities transform the way in which criminal justice systems respond to violent crimes against women.

Adult Manifestations of Childhood Sexual Abuse

Key Points

- Obstetrician–gynecologists will regularly provide care for women who are survivors of childhood sexual abuse. To ensure that patients receive appropriate care, obstetricians and gynecologists should screen women for such histories.

- Childhood sexual abuse may be defined as any exposure to sexual acts imposed on children, who inherently lack the emotional, maturational, and cognitive development to understand or to consent to such acts. These acts do not always involve sexual intercourse or physical force; rather, they involve manipulation and trickery.

- The long-term effects of childhood sexual abuse are varied, complex, and often devastating for survivors. Symptoms that once served as effective survival strategies eventually may result in significant physical or mental health problems. An understanding of and appreciation for the long-term effects of abuse are essential in developing a differential diagnosis, formulating treatment strategies, and providing patient care.

- Depression, anxiety, and anger are the most reported emotional responses to childhood sexual abuse. Adults with a history of sexual abuse may have as much as a four-time greater lifetime risk for major depression than individuals not abused as children.

- Once it is known that a patient is a survivor of childhood sexual abuse, there are a number of ways that the obstetrician–gynecologist can offer support, including the use of empowering messages and counseling referrals.

- Obstetrician–gynecologists must be sensitive to the possibility of re-traumatizing adult survivors of childhood sexual abuse during health care procedures. Pelvic and rectal examinations, vaginal ultrasounography, and breast examinations may be particularly traumatic for sexual abuse survivors, and it is important for providers to give survivors as much control as possible.

> *Adult childhood sexual abuse survivors have disproportionately high rates of use of health care services, more severe symptoms with more complex patterns of presentation, and often have somatic symptoms that do not respond to routine treatment.*

Obstetricians and gynecologists encounter patients with a wide array of symptoms that may be associated with a history of childhood sexual abuse. Frequently, the underlying cause of these symptoms is not recognized by the physician and, in many cases, by the patient. For some survivors of childhood sexual abuse, there is minimal compromise to their adult functioning. Others will have myriad psychologic, physical, and behavioral symptoms as a result of their abuse (1). Adult childhood sexual abuse survivors have disproportionately high rates of use of health care services, more severe symptoms with more complex patterns of presentation, and often have somatic symptoms that do not respond to routine treatment (2–4). These issues can create frustration for women and treatment challenges for their physicians. An understanding of the magnitude and effects of childhood sexual abuse, along with knowledge about screening and intervention methods, can help obstetricians and gynecologists offer appropriate care and support to patients with such histories.

Definitions

Childhood sexual abuse can be defined as any exposure to sexual acts imposed on children who inherently lack the emotional, maturational, and cognitive development to understand or to consent to such acts. These acts do not always involve sexual intercourse or physical force; rather, they involve manipulation and trickery. Authority and power enable the perpetrator to coerce the child into compliance. Characteristics and motivations of perpetrators of childhood sexual abuse vary: some may act out sexually to exert dominance over another individual; others may initiate the abuse for their own sexual gratification (5, 6).

Although specific legal definitions may vary among states, there is widespread agreement that abusive sexual contact can include breast and genital fondling, oral and anal sex, and vaginal intercourse. Definitions have been expanded to include noncontact events, such as coercion to watch sexual acts or posing in child pornography (7).

Prevalence

The prevalence of childhood sexual abuse in the United States is unknown. Because of the shame and stigma associated with abuse, many victims never disclose such experiences. Incest was once thought to be so rare that its occurrence was inconsequential. In the past 25 years, however, there has been increased recognition that incest and other forms of childhood sexual abuse occur with alarming frequency (8). Researchers have found that victims come from all cultural, racial, and economic groups (9).

Current estimates of incest and other childhood sexual abuse range from 12% to 40%, depending on settings and population. Most studies have found that among women, approximately 20%—or one in five— have experienced childhood sexual abuse (9). Consistent with this range, studies have revealed that:

- Among girls who had sex before age 13 years, 22% reported that first sex was nonvoluntary (10).

- Twelve percent of girls in grades 9 through 12 reported they had been sexually abused; 7% of girls in grades 5 through 8 also reported sexual abuse. Of all the girls who experienced sexual abuse, 65% reported the abuse occurred more than once, 57% reported the abuser was a family member, and 53% reported the abuse occurred at home (11).

- Approximately 40% of the women surveyed in a primary care setting had experienced some form of childhood sexual contact; of those, one in six had been raped as a child (12).

- A national telephone survey on violence against women conducted by the National Institute of Justice and the Centers for Disease Control and Prevention found that 18% of 8,000 women surveyed had experienced a completed or attempted rape at some time in their lives. Of this number, 22% were younger than 12 years and 32% were aged between 12 and 17 years when they were first raped (9).

Sequelae

Although there is no single syndrome that is present universally in adult survivors of childhood sexual abuse, there is an extensive body of research that documents adverse short- and long-term effects of such abuse. To treat and manage survivors of childhood sexual abuse appropriately, it is useful to understand that survivors' symptoms or behavioral sequelae often represent coping strategies used in response to abnormal, traumatic events. These coping mechanisms are used for protection during the abuse or later to guard against feelings of overwhelming helplessness and terror. Although some of these coping strategies may eventually lead to health problems, survivors may be misdiagnosed or mislabeled if symptoms are evaluated outside their original context (Box 23) (5).

In addition to the psychologic distress that may potentiate survivors' symptoms, there is evidence that abuse may result in biophysical changes. For example, one study found that after controlling for history of psychiatric disturbance, adult survivors had lowered thresholds for pain (13). It also has been suggested that chronic or traumatic stimulation (especially in the pelvic or abdominal region) heightens sensitivity, resulting in persistent pain, such as abdominal and pelvic pain, or other bowel symptoms (14, 15).

Although responses to sexual abuse vary, there is remarkable consistency in mental health symptoms, especially depression and anxiety. These mental health symptoms may be found alone or more often in tandem with physical and behavioral symptoms. More extreme symptoms are associated with abuse onset at an early age, extended or frequent abuse, incest by a parent, or use of force (4). Responses may be mitigated by such factors as inherent resiliency or supportive responses from individuals who are important to the victim (4). Even without therapeutic intervention, some survivors maintain the outward appearance of being unaffected by the abuse. Most, however, experience pervasive and deleterious consequences (4).

The primary aftereffects of childhood sexual abuse have been divided into seven distinct but overlapping categories (16):

1. Emotional reactions
2. Symptoms of posttraumatic stress disorder
3. Self-perceptions
4. Physical and biomedical effects
5. Sexual effects
6. Interpersonal effects
7. Social functioning

Responses can be greatly variable and idiosyncratic within the seven categories. Also, survivors may fluc-

---

Box 23   Common Symptoms in Adult Survivors of Childhood Sexual Abuse

Physical presentations

- Chronic pelvic pain
- Gastrointestinal symptoms/distress
- Musculoskeletal symptoms
- Obesity, eating disorders
- Insomnia, sleep disorders
- Pseudocyesis
- Sexual dysfunction
- Asthma, respiratory ailments
- Addiction
- Chronic headache
- Chronic back pain

Psychologic and behavioral presentations

- Depression and anxiety
- Posttraumatic stress disorder symptoms
- Dissociative states
- Repeated self-injury
- Suicide attempts
- Lying, stealing, truancy, running away
- Poor contraceptive practices
- Compulsive sexual behaviors
- Sexual dysfunction
- Somatizing disorders
- Eating disorders
- Poor adherence to medical recommendations
- Intolerance of or constant search for intimacy
- Expectation of early death

---

tuate between being highly symptomatic and relatively symptom free. Health care providers should be aware that such variability is normal. Some common life events that may trigger the return of physical or psychologic symptoms for a childhood sexual abuse survivor who, until such time, functions well are listed in Box 24 (4).

> **Box 24   Common Life Event Symptom Triggers for Childhood Sexual Abuse Survivors**
>
> - Pregnancy or birth of a child
> - Illness or death of parent or perpetrator
> - Divorce of parents
> - Age of survivor's child the same as onset of abuse
> - Key "anniversary" dates or holidays
> - Family reunions
> - Illness or injury of a child
> - Hospitalization or medical workup
> - Workplace situation that mirrors a relationship with abuser
> - Home relocation, especially to geographic area where abuse occurred
> - Viewing movies or television shows with abuse content

Emotional Reactions

Emotional sequelae are the aftereffects most frequently reported by adult survivors. Depression, anxiety, and anger are the most reported emotional responses to childhood sexual abuse. Adults with a history of sexual abuse may have as much as a four-fold greater lifetime risk for major depression than individuals not abused as children (17). A recent study found that 46% of abused girls had depressive symptoms; 54% of the abused girls reported suicidal ideation (11). Anxiety disorder is 10 times more likely to be diagnosed among abuse survivors than among nonabused individuals (18). The anxiety may be especially pronounced in intimate or close relationships or when interacting with authority figures. Fear, shame, humiliation, guilt and self-blame, grief, and urges to hurt herself often are mentioned. All these emotions may have behavioral, somatic, and relational manifestations (5, 17).

Symptoms of Posttraumatic Stress

Adult survivors of childhood sexual abuse frequently have symptoms of posttraumatic stress disorder. Responses tend to fall into two categories that may alternate or parallel each other: 1) intrusive or re-expe-riencing symptoms and 2) numbing or denial symptoms (16). Especially prominent are the intrusive posttrau-matic stress disorder-related nightmares or flashbacks—sudden, intrusive sensory experiences, which often involve visual, auditory, olfactory, and tactile sensations reminiscent of the original assault. These nightmares or flashbacks are experienced as though they were occurring in the present rather than as a memory of a past event. Triggers of flashbacks may include sexual stimuli or interactions, gynecologic or pelvic examinations, abusive behavior by other adults, disclosure of the abuse experiences to others, or reading or viewing sexual or violent media content (17).

Dissociative disorders have been linked to sexual abuse and are believed to be complex posttraumatic conditions used to numb or deny the incident(s). Survivors may experience amnesia, the partial or total loss of memory. Derealization or depersonalization may result in a survivor separating her mind from her body and her emotions. The survivor may experience the sensation of floating in space while observing her physical body. No emotional pain is connected with this observation. Physicians may observe a patient "zoning out." Dissociative identity disorder allows an individual to separate a group of related psychologic activities or memories into autonomously functioning units, as in the generation of multiple personalities (16, 19). Although dissociative defenses may effectively numb the memory or help the patient deny the experience of the abuse, they also may interfere with self-protection. Such patients may seek care for conditions related to secondary interpersonal violence, such as rape (18).

Self-Perceptions

The development of a sense of self is thought to be one of the earliest developmental tasks of young children. It typically unfolds in the context of early relationships (16, 17). The development of a positive self-perception is adversely affected by the following traumatic factors of abuse (16):

- Traumatic sexualization or the introduction of premature and coerced sexual involvement with an adult
- Powerlessness or the exploitation of a child's vulnerability to those in authority
- Betrayal by an adult who breaks the trust of the relationship, especially if the abuse was committed by a parent

- Stigmatization or the sense of shame and belief that the individual is fundamentally defective, which is internalized by the child and often carried throughout life

In an attempt to make sense of sexual abuse, most children develop the belief that something about them caused the abuse to happen or that they somehow deserved to be abused (16). As adults, survivors of childhood sexual abuse may maintain the image of the abuser as good, whereas they view themselves as bad. These images, therefore, perpetuate the notion that they were deserving of the abuse and are not entitled to assistance and rescue. Such beliefs frequently result in high-risk or self-destructive behaviors and in engaging in abusive relationships.

The closer the relationship between the child and the perpetrator, the greater the extent of the trauma caused by childhood sexual abuse (16, 17). If the trust and protection ascribed to primary caregivers, such as parents or guardians is violated by mistreatment, a child's sense of self is badly damaged and the world becomes viewed as unsafe. Without basic trust, individuals lack the ability to cope, causing them to overreact to stress or painful events (17). The establishment of personal boundaries is essential for psychologic stability, allowing an individual to interact with another individual without sacrificing his or her own identity, values, or preferences. Individuals with a history of sexual violence may not have had the opportunity to establish a secure sense of self. Adults molested early in life have more problems in understanding or relating to others independent of their experiences or needs, and they may not be able to perceive or experience their own internal states independent of the reactions or demands of others (20). Many such individuals may exhibit "loose boundaries," where they are overly compliant. Conversely, they may have excessively "rigid boundaries," where they are hostile or threatened.

Physical and Biomedical Effects

One review of the literature on the sequelae of adult survivors of childhood sexual abuse summarized the biomedical sequelae of childhood sexual abuse as having the following manifestations (21):

- Chronic or diffuse pain, either the result of trauma or conversion symptoms representative of the abuse

- Symptoms of anxiety or depression
- Eating and substance abuse disorders
- Self-neglect

It is common for survivors of childhood sexual abuse to exhibit physical symptoms in areas that were sexually traumatized (16). Some examples of chronic and diffuse pain in sexual abuse survivors are listed in Box 25.

Eating disorders, especially obesity and bulimia, have been linked to a past history of sexual abuse. A

Box 25   Examples of Chronic and Diffuse Pain in Sexual Abuse Survivors*

Headaches
- Migraine
- Temporomandibular joint syndrome
- Muscle tension

Genitourinary symptoms
- Chronic pain
- Rectal discomfort
- Hemorrhoids
- Constipation
- Diarrhea
- Irritable bowel syndrome
- Spastic colon

Gastrointestinal problems
- Gagging
- Nausea, vomiting
- Choking

Conversion symptoms
- Fainting
- Vertigo
- Seizures
- Muscle tension/spasms
- Joint pain
- Tinnitus
- Respiratory problems
- Asthma
- Shortness of breath

*May be suggestive of the abuse or somatic signs of depression.

recent survey found that girls reporting physical or sexual abuse were almost three times as likely to binge and purge as those who said they had not been abused (32% versus 12%) (11). The abused girls also were likely to binge and purge frequently. One in six abused girls reported such behavior more than once per week, and 13% of the abused girls said they did so daily.

Substance abuse often is the result of the survivor's attempt to either self-medicate the symptoms of sexual abuse or to avoid memories about the abuse. Self-neglect, including neglect of basic needs such as sleep, rest, and food, can result in exacerbation of existing medical problems as well as predisposition to medical problems. The survivor can have dental problems as a result of dental phobia related to trauma involving the oral cavity and often will avoid preventive health examinations out of fear of physicians (21).

In addition to physical problems that develop from the abuse, adverse health consequences frequently are associated with many of the behaviors commonly used, consciously or unconsciously, as coping devises. Furthermore, risky coping behaviors, such as smoking and alcohol or drug use, may be used chronically because they are perceived to be effective in relieving symptoms. According to a 1998 study, adults abused as children are (22):

- Twice as likely to smoke
- Nearly twice as likely to be severely obese
- Nearly twice as likely to be physically inactive
- Nearly five times more likely to have a history of alcohol abuse
- Nearly four times as likely to abuse illicit drugs
- Seven times more likely to have injected drugs
- Three times more likely to have had 50 or more intercourse partners
- Nearly twice as likely to have had a sexually transmitted disease (STD)

Sexual Effects

Disturbances in sexual identity and sexual functioning are prominent in studies of incest survivors (23). Women sexually abused in childhood may develop gender and sexual identities that emphasize self-worth based on sexuality. Moreover, they may unconsciously attempt to re-create sexual situations to control and change the outcome. Attempts at this "trauma mastery," coupled with inadequate personal boundaries and low self-esteem, may help to explain childhood sexual abuse survivors' increased risk for engaging in unsafe sexual behaviors that have negative health consequences, such as STDs and unintended pregnancy. One study found that compared with their nonabused pregnant counterparts, sexually abused adolescents began intercourse earlier, were more likely to have used drugs and alcohol, and were less likely to use contraception (24).

The pronounced sexual dysfunction in adult survivors of incest has been described as "the most obvious example of conditioned, abuse-related fear" (17). Because of the association between sexual stimuli and invasion or pain, many adults abused as children report fear or anxiety-related difficulties during sexual contact.

For adult survivors, the most frequently reported chronic sexual problems include fear of intimate relationships, feelings of repulsion or lack of enjoyment, flashbacks during sexual activity, dysfunctions of desire and arousal, and primary or secondary anorgasmia. Compulsive promiscuity and prostitution also may be present because survivors often confuse sexuality with nurturing behavior (21). There is no evidence that a history of childhood sexual abuse is related to sexual orientation.

Interpersonal Effects

For incest survivors, the ability to have emotionally healthy relationships with others may be damaged profoundly. Many survivors have relationships that are unstable and include patterns of excessive self-sufficiency, withdrawal, and hostility. Others may assume the caretaking of others, extreme dependence, overcompliance, learned helplessness, and nonassertion (16).

The inability of childhood sexual abuse survivors to separate themselves from others may manifest as problems with defining their boundaries and individual rights when faced with the needs and demands of others. Such problems are frequently associated with great difficulties in interpersonal relationships, including gullibility, inadequate self-protectiveness, and likelihood of being victimized or abused by others (17).

Deleterious and troubling sequelae to childhood sexual abuse include the apparent vulnerability of women with such histories to be repeatedly victimized later in life, often on multiple occasions, by individuals who may or may not be known to them. This tendency to be victimized repeatedly may be the result of a general vulnerability in dangerous situations and to exploitation by untrustworthy people. Childhood abuse seems to have the effect of making adult women less skilled at self-protection and more apt to accept being victimized by others (25).

Social Functioning

The social functioning of childhood sexual abuse survivors varies considerably. Survivors' social functioning can range from exceptional and overfunctioning to greatly deficient and deviant, exhibiting such behaviors as delinquency, prostitution, dangerous sexual practices (including sadomasochism, indiscriminate sexual activity, and sexual abuse of others), and substance abuse. Overfunctioning often is an attempt to palliate the profound low self-esteem that survivors have and to channel their anxiety. Conversely, researchers suggest that some of the most marginally functional and disenfranchised members of society, such as the chronically mentally ill and the homeless, may have histories of sexual abuse at the core of their problems (16).

As previously discussed, not all survivors will have the same symptoms or symptoms of equal severity. A literature review of factors that moderate and mediate the effects of childhood sexual abuse found that heightened adult distress results from:

- Molestation at an especially early age
- Extended and frequent abuse
- Incest by a biologic parent
- The presence of force
- A greater number of perpetrators

The most pronounced psychologic problems also are predicted by the presence of other concomitant forms of child maltreatment, including physical and psychologic abuse or neglect, and subsequent victimization in adulthood (17).

For most survivors, childhood sexual abuse frequently occurs in conjunction with other forms of child abuse or household dysfunction. For example, a survey was administered to members of a large health maintenance organization to determine exposure to several categories of adverse childhood experiences, including physical or sexual abuse, violence against the mother, or living with household members who

were substance abusers. The risk of long-term adverse consequences increased dramatically as the number of adverse experiences increased for an individual. The study revealed that 65% of the individuals reporting childhood sexual abuse also reported one other type of adverse experience; 41% reported two additional adverse experiences (22).

Effects on Reproductive Health and Pregnancy

Gynecologic problems, including chronic pelvic pain, dyspareunia, vaginismus, and nonspecific vaginitis, are common symptoms of adult survivors of childhood sexual abuse (6, 21, 26–28). Disturbances in sexual interest and sexual functioning are widely reported and range from sexual inhibition to compulsive sexuality (6, 21, 29, 30).

Disturbances of desire, arousal, and orgasm are among the inhibitory aftereffects of childhood sexual abuse and likely result from the association between sexual activity, violation, and pain. Conversely, compulsive sexuality, promiscuity, and prostitution also may occur (21). Childhood sexual abuse is significantly associated with prostitution (30, 31). Early adolescent or unintended pregnancy also is suggestive of a history of sexual abuse (31). This may be the direct result of incest or a result of promiscuity without the use of contraceptives, a sign of impaired self-care (21, 24). The incidence of STDs also is higher in childhood sexual abuse survivors, and adolescent and adult survivors of childhood sexual abuse are at greater risk of human immunodeficiency virus (HIV) infection than those without such histories (12, 32). Survivors may be less likely to have regular Pap tests and may seek little or no prenatal care (33, 34).

Vaginal examinations may be associated with terror and pain for abuse survivors. Additionally, feelings of vulnerability in the lithotomy position, being connected to intravenous lines and labor monitors, and being examined by relative strangers in the delivery room may leave the survivor vulnerable to re-experiencing past feelings of powerlessness, violation, and fear. The physical pain of labor and delivery also may trigger memories of past abuse with or without conscious memory of or connection to the earlier abuse (4, 5, 35–37).

Pregnancy and childbirth may be an especially difficult time for survivors for a variety of reasons.

Pregnancy may trigger memories of abuse. In some cases, women with no prior conscious memories of their abuse may begin to experience emotions, dreams, or partial memories that are troubling. With all of the attendant changes in a woman's body and her lifestyle, coping mechanisms that had previously kept the abusive history from her memory may now fail, and what she had once repressed comes to the surface (36, 37). Pregnant women reporting a history of childhood sexual abuse are significantly more likely than those without such history to report suicidal ideation and depression (13, 19, 38). Pregnant adolescents also have been found to be more likely to report substance abuse during pregnancy and to give birth to significantly smaller and less mature infants (39). Smoking was common among pregnant survivors of childhood sexual abuse (40). There are no consistent data regarding adverse pregnancy outcome for women with histories of childhood sexual abuse.

Issues Affecting Memory

Controversy continues over the issue of delayed recall of childhood sexual abuse. Although most emotionally laden events are stored in memory along with their accompanying effects, traumatic memory is different (4). Proponents of "false memory syndrome" contend that experiments and studies on memory prove that "false memories" can be implanted readily. Currently, research results are divided on this issue. It is not incumbent on the obstetrician–gynecologist to make a determination of the veracity of "recovered memories." Rather, a prudent obstetrician–gynecologist should be a supportive ally for all patients and should consult with a mental health practitioner with experience working with sexual abuse issues. Not every mental health practitioner has such expertise.

Screening

With recognition of the extent of family violence, medical groups have issued recommendations for screening all patients (especially women) for histories of abuse (4). Patients overwhelmingly favor universal inquiry about sexual assault (41). At the same time, they report a reluctance to initiate a discussion of this subject. Following are some basic guidelines:

- Make the question "natural." As physicians ask patients about possible sexual abuse, they will develop increased comfort with the process. They should be aware of their body language and avoid a guarded or closed posture. Over time, they will ask about sexual abuse as routinely as they ask about menstrual cycles.

- Normalize the experience. As physicians learn to ask questions in a natural way, they may want to offer explanatory statements, such as: "About one woman in five was sexually abused as a child. Because these experiences can affect health and well-being, I ask all of my patients about unwanted touching or sexual experiences in childhood."

- Give the patient control over disclosure. Ask every patient about childhood abuse and rape trauma, but let her control what she says and when she says it. She will be the best judge of how to keep her emotional defenses intact.

- If the physician suspects abuse, but the patient chooses not to disclose it, she can be assured that the physician is a resource for her if she ever needs to discuss such issues. Patients very commonly bring up the subject three to four visits later, especially if they have developed trust and want assistance.

- If the patient says "yes," it is important to ask whether she has ever talked with anyone about the abuse or rape. Many women will have dealt with the issues in another forum. Questions about whether any parts of the breast or pelvic examination cause her emotional discomfort should be posed at this time.

- If the patient has never talked with anyone about her abuse or rape, this is likely to be a very emotional time for her. Revelations often are accompanied by much anguish. Sitting quietly through this period can be difficult but is very important. Excessive reassurance negates the pain of her experience. Detached self-protection or anger directed toward the perpetrator limit her ability to work through her emotional pain. If the physical portion of the examination has not yet been done, it should be postponed until another visit. If she is in an examination gown, allowing her to compose and dress herself may help her to regain some control. This is a good time to ask if she wishes to see a therapist. If the patient appears overtly depressed, the physician should ask about suicidal ideas, intentions, or attempts in the past.

Even when questions are carefully phrased and the assessment has been conducted in a caring and sensitive manner, some patients with histories of abuse will not disclose their experiences. Survivors may need to test the physician's trustworthiness with such information. In other instances, repression does not allow survivors access to such memories at the time of the physician's questioning. Despite the possibility that survivors will not be able to respond positively to the physician's questions, they will be made aware that the physician is someone who considers such information essential to comprehensive health care (8). It has been suggested that not inquiring about sexual abuse gives tacit support to the survivor's belief that abuse does not matter, that it does not have long-term effects, and that it is a subject that is not to be discussed (42).

If screening does not occur and the patient appears to tolerate pelvic examinations or other procedures, the obstetrician–gynecologist may mistakenly assume that the patient does not have a history of abuse. Instead, many survivors may not be able to express discomfort or fear and may silently experience a great deal of distress (42). Given the frequency of childhood sexual abuse and its many deleterious sequelae across the life span, patients should be screened for such histories periodically. Evaluating only those women who have symptoms that create a high index of suspicion will likely result in many abuse survivors being undetected (43).

Intervention

Once it is known that a patient is a survivor of childhood sexual abuse, there are a number of ways that the obstetrician–gynecologist can offer support. This includes the use of empowering messages and counseling referrals.

Positive Messages

Some positive and healing responses to the disclosure of abuse include letting the patient know that (21, 42, 44):

- She is the victim of abuse. She is in no way to blame. The perpetrator is always at fault.

- It took a great deal of courage for her to disclose the abuse.

- She has been heard and believed.

- Her symptoms "make sense" given what she has experienced.

- She has the right to say "no" or "stop" during any examination or procedure. She can and should set limits for herself. She has the right to control who touches her body and when and how. Physicians should ask permission to begin an examination.

- She also has the right to maintain her silence on the issue.

Counseling Referrals

Traumatized patients generally benefit from mental health care. Survivors who have disclosed abuse should be asked if they have ever talked to anyone about their experiences. For patients who have not sought such care, the obstetrician–gynecologist can be a powerful ally in the patient's healing by offering support and referral. Not every mental health professional is experienced in working with childhood sexual abuse survivors. Every effort should be made to refer them to professionals with significant experience in abuse-related issues.

Physicians may begin compiling a list of experts with experience in abuse. Contacting state boards of psychology or medicine often can be beneficial in locating therapists who are skilled in treating victims of such trauma. Veterans' centers, battered women's shelters, and rape crisis centers often are familiar with therapists and programs that treat various types of trauma, as are many university-based counseling programs. Because of the relationship between trauma histories and alcohol and drug abuse, therapists should be skilled in working with individuals who have dual diagnoses (43). Obstetrician–gynecologists should become familiar with appropriate crisis hotlines that may operate in their communities.

When referring patients to other professionals, it is especially helpful to identify a specific purpose. For example, saying, "I would like Dr. Hill to assess you to determine if your past abuse is contributing to your current health problems" is more effective than telling the survivor that her symptoms are all "psychologic" and that she should see a therapist (44). It is important to secure the patient's express authorization before speaking to the therapist when collaborative practice between the obstetrician–gynecologist and therapist is warranted.

It is important to help the patient not feel abandoned or rejected when a counseling referral is made. If it is appropriate, the physician should emphasize his or her ongoing involvement in the patient's case. If the therapist or agency that the patient is being referred to is known personally by the physician, the patient will feel more confident about the referral. The obstetrician–gynecologist also should reassure the survivor that she is reacting in normal, predictable ways for someone who has survived such abuse (44).

Avoiding Retraumatization

Obstetrician–gynecologists must be sensitive to the possibility of retraumatizing adult survivors of childhood sexual abuse during health care procedures. The risk for retraumatization is present during such care because many procedures involve touch, are invasive, and are performed by authority figures in positions of control or power. All procedures need to be thoroughly explained in advance, and whenever possible the patient should be allowed to suggest ways that the procedure can be done to lessen her fear. This may mean allowing the patient to invite friends or family members to be present (16).

Pelvic, rectal, vaginal ultrasound, and breast examinations may be particularly traumatic for sexual abuse survivors, and it is important for providers to give survivors as much control as possible. Techniques to increase the patient's comfort include talking her through the steps, maintaining eye contact, allowing her to control the pace, allowing her to see more (eg, use of a mirror in pelvic examinations), or having her assist during her examination (ie, putting her hand over the physician's to guide the examination) (4, 42). It is always important to ask permission to touch the patient, especially during the examinations previously mentioned.

References

1. McCauley J, Kern DE, Kolodner K, Dill L, Schroeder AF, DeChant HK, et al. Clinical characteristics of women with a history of childhood abuse: unhealed wounds. JAMA 1997;277:1362-8.

2. Koss MP, Koss PG, Woodruff WJ. Deleterious effects of criminal victimization on women's health and medical utilization. Arch Intern Med 1991;151:342-7.

3. Drossman DA, Leserman J, Nachman G, Li ZM, Gluck H, Toomey TC, et al. Sexual and physical abuse in women with functional or organic gastrointestinal disorders. Ann Intern Med 1990;113:828-33.

4. American Medical Association. Diagnostic and treatment guidelines on mental health effects of family violence. Chicago (IL): AMA; 1995.

5. Hendricks-Matthews M. Long-term consequences of childhood sexual abuse. In: Rosenfeld JA, Alley N, Acheson LS, Admire JB, editors. Women's health in primary care. Baltimore (MD): Williams and Wilkins; 1997. p. 267-76.

6. Britton H, Hansen K. Sexual abuse. Clin Obstet Gynecol 1997;40:226-40.

7. Maltz W. Adult survivors of incest: how to help them overcome the trauma. Med Aspects Hum Sex 1990;24:42-7.

8. Hendricks-Matthews M. Caring for victims of childhood sexual abuse. J Fam Pract 1992;35:501-2.

9. Tjaden P, Thoennes N. Prevalence, incidence, and consequences of violence against women: findings from the national violence against women survey. Research in brief. Washington, DC: U.S. Dept of Justice, Office of Justice Programs; 1998. NCJ 172837.

10. Moore KA, Driscoll A. Partners, predators, peers, protectors: males and teen pregnancy. New data analyses of the 1995 National Survey of Family Growth. In: Not just for girls: the roles of boys and men in teen pregnancy prevention. Washington, DC: National Campaign to Prevent Teen Pregnancy; 1997. p. 7-12.

11. Schoen C, Davis K, Collins KS, Greenberg L, Des Roches C, Abrams M. The Commonwealth Fund survey of the health of adolescent girls. New York (NY): The Commonwealth Fund; 1997.

12. Walker EA, Torkelson N, Katon WJ, Koss MP. The prevalence rate of sexual trauma in a primary care clinic. J Am Board Fam Pract 1993;6:465-71.

13. Scarinci IC, McDonald-Haile J, Bradley LA, Richter JE. Altered pain perception and psychosocial features among women with gastrointestinal disorders and history of abuse: a preliminary model. Am J Med 1994;97:108-18.

14. Cervero F, Janig W. Visceral nociceptors: a new world order? Trends Neurosci 1992;15:374-8.

15. Drossman DA. Physical and sexual abuse and gastrointestinal illness: what is the link? Am J Med 1994;97:105-7.

16. Courtois CA. Adult survivors of sexual abuse. Prim Care 1993;20:433-46.

17. Briere JN, Elliott DM. Immediate and long-term impacts of child sexual abuse. Future Child 1994;4(2):54-69.

18. Kaplan SJ. Family violence: a clinical and legal guide. Washington, DC: American Psychiatric Press; 1996.

19. Anderson G, Yasenik L, Ross CA. Dissociative experiences and disorders among women who identify themselves as sexual abuse survivors. Child Abuse Negl 1993;17:677-86.

20. Cole PM, Putnam FW. Effect of incest on self and social functioning: a developmental psychopathology perspective. J Consult Clin Psychol 1992;60:174-84.

21. Wahlen SD. Adult survivors of childhood sexual abuse. In: Hendricks-Matthews M, editor. Violence education: toward a solution. Kansas City (MO): Society of Teachers of Family Medicine; 1992. p. 89–102.

22. Felitti VJ, Anda RF, Nordenberg D, Williamson DF, Spitz AM, Edwards V, et al. Relationship of childhood abuse and household dysfunction to many of the leading causes of death in adults. The Adverse Childhood Experiences (ACE) Study. Am J Prev Med 1998;14:245–58.

23. Putnam FW. Disturbances of "self" in victims of childhood sexual abuse. In: Kluft RP, editor. Incest-related syndromes of adult psychopathology, Washington, DC: American Psychiatric Press; 1990. p. 113–31.

24. Boyer D, Fine D. Sexual abuse as a factor in adolescent pregnancy and child maltreatment. Fam Plann Perspect 1992; 24:4–11, 19.

25. Rieker PP, Carmen EH. The victim-to-patient process: the disconfirmation and transformation of abuse. Am J Orthopsychiatry 1986;56:360–70.

26. Harrop-Griffiths J, Katon W, Walker E, Holm L, Russo J, Hickok L. The association between chronic pelvic pain, psychiatric diagnosis, and childhood sexual abuse. Obstet Gynecol 1988;71:589–94.

27. Reiter RC, Shakerin LR, Gambone JC, Milburn AK. Correlation between sexual abuse and somatization in women with somatic and nonsomatic chronic pelvic pain. Am J Obstet Gynecol 1991;165:104–9.

28. Toomey TC, Hernandez JT, Gittelman DF, Hulka JF. Relationship of sexual and physical abuse to pain and psychological assessment variables in chronic pelvic pain patients. Pain 1993;53:105–9.

29. Luster T, Small SA. Sexual abuse history and number of sex partners among female adolescents. Fam Plann Perspect 1997;29:204–11.

30. Widom CS, Kuhns JB. Childhood victimization and subsequent risk for promiscuity, prostitution, and teenage pregnancy: a prospective study. Am J Public Health 1996;86:1607–12.

31. Bachmann GA, Moeller TP, Benett J. Childhood sexual abuse and the consequence in adult women. Obstet Gynecol 1988; 71:631–42.

32. Lodico MA, DiClemente RJ. The association between childhood sexual abuse and prevalence of HIV-related risk behaviors. Clin Pediatr (Phila) 1994;33:498–502.

33. Springs FE, Friedrich WN. Health risk behaviors and medical sequelae of childhood sexual abuse. Mayo Clin Proc 1992; 67:527–32.

34. Burian J. Helping survivors of sexual abuse through labor. MCN Am J Matern Child Nurs 1995;20:252–6.

35. Grant LJ. Effects of childhood sexual abuse: issues for obstetric caregivers. Birth 1992;19:220–1.

36. Waymire V. A triggering time. Childbirth may recall sexual abuse memories. Awhonn Lifelines 1997;1(2):47–50.

37. Rhodes N, Hutchinson S. Labor experiences of childhood sexual abuse survivors. Birth 1994;21:213–20.

38. Farber EW, Herbert SE, Reviere SL. Childhood abuse and suicidality in obstetrics patients in a hospital-based urban prenatal clinic. Gen Hosp Psychiatry 1996;18:56–60.

39. Stevens-Simon C, McAnarney ER. Childhood victimization: relationship to adolescent pregnancy outcome. Child Abuse & Neglect 1994;18:569–75.

40. Grimstad H, Schei B. Pregnancy and delivery for women with a history of child sexual abuse. Child Abuse Negl 1999;23:81–90.

41. Friedman LS, Samet JH, Roberts MS, Hudlin M, Hans P. Inquiry about victimization experiences. A survey of patient preferences and physician practices. Arch Intern Med 1992; 152:1186–90.

42. Holz KA. A practical approach to clients who are survivors of childhood sexual abuse. J Nurse Midwifery 1994;39:13–8.

43. Hendricks-Matthews M. Recognition of sexual abuse. J Am Board Fam Pract 1993;6:511–3.

44. Laws A. Sexual abuse history and women's medical problems. J Gen Intern Med 1993;8:441–3.

Resources

ACOG Resources

ACOG Violence Against Women Home Page (www.acog.org, click on "Women's Issues" and then "Violence Against Women")

Other Resources

The resources listed as follows are for information purposes only. Referral to these sources and web sites does not imply the endorsement of ACOG. This list is not meant to be comprehensive. The exclusion of a source or web site does not reflect the quality of that source or web site. Please note that web sites are subject to change without notice.

Adult Survivors of Child Abuse
PO Box 14477
San Francisco, CA 94114
Tel: (415) 928-4576
Web: www.ascasupport.org

Adult Survivors of Child Abuse (ASCA) is a support program designed by the Morris Center for Healing from Child Abuse specifically for adult survivors of physical, sexual, or emotional child abuse or neglect. Both an individual component and a group component comprise ASCA's support structure. The Morris Center is a nonprofit organization whose mission is to provide recovery options for adult survivors of childhood abuse.

Communities Against Violence Network
2711 Ordway Street NW, #111
Washington, DC 20008
Tel: (202) 255-0202
E-mail: cavent@pobox.com
Web: www.cavnet2.org

Through an international network of professionals, the Communities Against Violence Network works to enhance collaboration among rape crisis centers, law enforcement, prosecutors, advocates, and others. It also addresses sexual assault, rape, incest, domestic violence, youth violence, and victimization of people with disabilities.

Family Violence & Sexual Assault Institute
6160 Cornerstone Court East
San Diego, CA 92121
Tel: (858) 623-2777 ext. 416
Fax: (858) 646-0761
Web: www.fvsai.org

The mission of the Family Violence & Sexual Assault Institute (FVSAI) is to improve the quality of life for individuals on an international level by sharing and disseminating vital information, improving networking among professionals, and assisting with program evaluation, consultation, and training that promotes violence-free living. In addition, FVSAI works to develop and provide treatment programs with the highest quality program consultation and evaluation; increase research in the areas of family violence, child maltreatment, sexual assault, and spouse/partner abuse; disseminate information on an international level to those working in the family violence and sexual assault fields; bring together professionals to network, share, and explore ways to end violence and abuse; and conduct conferences, workshops, and professional training on all aspects of family violence.

National Sexual Violence Resource Center
123 North Enola Drive
Enola, PA 17025
Tel: 877-739-3895; (717) 909-0710
Fax: (717) 909-0714
Web: www.nsvrc.org

Serving as a central clearinghouse for the voluminous resources and research, the National Sexual Violence Resource Center (NSVRC) provides a place to turn to for information, help, and support. The NSVRC works to influence policy, practice, and research pertaining to sexual violence by providing greater interaction, investigation, and review and by promoting awareness within the anti-sexual violence movement.

National Training Center on Domestic and Sexual Violence
7800 Shoal Creek Boulevard, Suite 120N
Austin, TX 78757
Tel: (512) 407-9020
Fax: (512) 407-9022
Web: www.ntcdsv.org

The National Training Center on Domestic and Sexual Violence develops and conducts training and consultation, works to influence policy, and promotes collaboration and diversity in working to end domestic and sexual violence.

Posttraumatic Stress Disorder Alliance
Resource Center
Tel: 877-507-PTSD
E-mail: info@ptsdalliance.org
Web: www.ptsdalliance.org

The Posttraumatic Stress Disorder Alliance is a group of professional and advocacy organizations that have joined forces to provide educational resources to individuals diagnosed with posttraumatic stress disorder and their loved ones; those at risk for developing posttraumatic stress disorder; and medical, health care, and other frontline professionals. The College is a member of this alliance.

Rape, Abuse and Incest National Network
635-B Pennsylvania Avenue, SE
Washington, DC 20003
Tel: 800-656-HOPE
Fax: (202) 544-3556
Web: www.rainn.org

The Rape, Abuse and Incest National Network (RAINN) is the nation's largest anti-sexual assault organization and operates the National Sexual Assault Hotline at 800-656-HOPE. With a national perspective and broad reach, RAINN is a resource for media, policymakers, and the public. Extensive outreach programs and partnerships with television, radio, and print media allow RAINN to maximize public education while minimizing costs.

Stop It Now!
PO Box 495
Haydenville, MA 01039
Tel: (413) 268-3096
E-mail: info@stopitnow.org
Web: www.stopitnow.com

Stop It Now! is a national, public health-based organization working to prevent and ultimately eradicate child sexual abuse. Through public education, policy advocacy, and research and evaluation, Stop It Now! calls on abusers and potential abusers to stop their abusive behavior and get help.

Speaking Out About Rape
69 East Pine Street
Orlando, FL 32801
Tel: (407) 836-9692
Fax: (407) 836-9693
E-mail: soar99@worldnet.att.net
Web: www.soar99.org

Speaking Out About Rape is a nonprofit organization dedicated to educating society about rape and its impact, protecting victim's rights, making certain the medical and judicial systems are victim-friendly, and helping survivors speak out.

Violence Against Women Electronic Network
6400 Flank Drive, Suite 1300
Harrisburg, PA 17112-2778
Tel: 800-537-2238
Fax: (717) 545-9456
Web: www.vawnet.org

The Violence Against Women Electronic Network (VAWnet) supports development, implementation, and maintenance of effective violence against women intervention and prevention efforts at national, state, and local levels through electronic communication and information dissemination. Participants in VAWnet—including state domestic violence and sexual assault coalitions, allied organizations, and individuals—can access online database resources and engage in information sharing, problem-solving, and issue analysis via e-mail and a series of issue-specific forums facilitated by nationally recognized experts in the field of violence against women. It also operates an extensive searchable, electronic library that is available to the general public. It provides links to external sources, an "In the News" section, and access to articles and audio and video resources focused on intimate partner and sexual violence and related issues.

Appendixes

Appendix A

ACOG *Statement of Policy*
As issued by the ACOG Executive Board

ACCESS TO WOMEN'S HEALTH CARE

Excellence in women's health care is an essential element of the long-term physical, intellectual, social and economic well-being of any society. It is a basic determinant of the health of future generations.

The American College of Obstetricians and Gynecologists is the representative organization of physicians who are qualified specialists in providing health services unique to women. ACOG calls for quality health care appropriate to every woman's needs throughout her life and for assuring that a full array of clinical services be available to women without costly delays or the imposition of geographic, financial, attitudinal or legal barriers.

The College and its membership are committed to facilitating both access to and quality of women's health care. Fellows should exercise their responsibility to improve the health status of women and their offspring both in the traditional patient-physician relationships and by working within their community and at the state and national levels to assure access to high-quality programs meeting the health needs of all women.

In addition, it is critical that all Americans be provided with adequate and affordable health coverage. There remains a considerable and increasing portion of the American population that does not have health insurance coverage. As a result, those individuals often defer obtaining preventive and medical services, jeopardizing the health and well-being of themselves and their families. The College supports universal coverage that is designed to improve the individual and collective health of society. Expanding health coverage to all Americans must become a high priority.

Approved by the Executive Board July 1988
Amended September 1999
Amended and Reaffirmed July 2003

The American College of Obstetricians and Gynecologists
409 12th Street, SW, PO Box 96920 • Washington, DC 20090-6920 Telephone 202-638-5577

Appendix B

ACOG *Statement of Policy*
As issued by the ACOG Executive Board

TOBACCO ADVERTISING AIMED AT WOMEN AND ADOLESCENTS

The American College of Obstetricians and Gynecologists opposes the unconscionable targeting of women of all ages by the tobacco industry.

The health risks of tobacco use to women are well documented. It also is well known that smoking by a pregnant woman may be harmful to her fetus. It is unnecessary to catalogue all of these risks here. Because of these well-known dangers, it is irresponsible for tobacco companies to single out women, especially those who are young, educationally or otherwise disadvantaged women, and encourage them to smoke.

Specifically, tobacco companies must stop targeting their advertising to encourage adolescent women to smoke cigarettes. The health of all women and future generations demands that consideration.

Approved by the Executive Board July 1990
Reaffirmed July 2000
Revised and approved July 2004

The American College of Obstetricians and Gynecologists
409 12th Street, SW, PO Box 96920 • Washington, DC 20090-6920 Telephone 202-638-5577

Index

Note: Page numbers followed by the letters *b, f, n,* and *t* indicate boxes, figures, footnotes, and tables, respectively.

A

Abuse
  of adolescents, 95, 177
  child, 177, 190, 191
  confidentiality and, 181–182
  drug (substance). *See* Substance abuse
  elder, 179–180, 180*b*
  of incarcerated females, 95
  by intimate partner, 170, 171, 178. *See also* Violence, intimate partner
  in pregnancy, 120, 177–178
  privacy and, 181–182
  sexual. *See* Sexual abuse
  of substances. *See* Substance abuse
  of women with disabilities, 44, 178
Abuse assessment screen–disability, 44, 45*b*
Acquaintance rape, 190, 198. *See also* Date rape
Acquired immunodeficiency syndrome. *See* Human immunodeficiency virus (HIV)
Acupuncture, for smoking cessation, 160
Acyclovir, for pediatric patients, 30
Addiction, 106–107. *See also* Substance abuse
Adolescent(s)
  age of consent for sexual intercourse, 197
  and date rape, 198
  with disabilities, reproductive health care for, 53
  incarcerated, abuse of, 95
  and intimate partner violence, 171
  lesbian or bisexual, issues faced by, 66
  lung growth in, smoking and, 153
  misuse of over-the-counter drugs, 110–111

Adolescent(s) *(continued)*
  pregnancy in
    abuse and, 177, 178
    rape-related, 197–198
    sexual assault and, 197–198
    smoking cessation for, 161–163
    smoking in, 160–161
      and oral contraceptive use, 161
      prevalence of, 160
      prevention of, 161
    substance abuse in
      CRAFFT test for, 116, 116*t*
      detection and treatment of, confidentiality of, 117
      screening test for, 116, 116*t*
    violence against, 177
Adoption rights, of same-sex partners, 67
Aging women, lesbian or bisexual, 66. *See also* Elder abuse
Alcohol
  abuse of
    costs of, 107
    diagnosis of, 110
    effects of, 121–123, 132*t*–133*t*
    gender differences in, 107
    in pregnancy, 119, 120–121, 122–123
    risk reduction in, 113
    screening questionnaires for, 113–116, 114*t*–116*t*
    in sexual assault victim, 195
    signs and symptoms of, 110
    in survivors of childhood sexual abuse, 208
    treatment of, 118
  and sexual assault, 130, 198, 199
  use in pregnancy
    epidemiology of, 108, 108*t*, 109, 109*f*
    prevention of, 112–113, 113*f*
    screening questionnaires for, 115*t*, 116
Alcohol abstinence syndrome, neonatal, 122
Alcohol-related birth defect (ARBD), 123

Alcohol-related neurodevelopmental disorder (ARND), 123
Alprazolam, 129
Ambiguous genitalia, 24–25
American College of Obstetricians and Gynecologists
  "At-Risk Drinking and Illicit Drug Use: Ethical Issues in Obstetric and Gynecologic Practice," 120
  statement of policy
    on access to women's health care, 217
    on tobacco advertising aimed at women and adolescents, 152, 219
Amphetamine, abuse of, 127, 134*t*–135*t*
Androgen therapy, for transsexual patients, 80–81, 81*b*
Androgynes, 76
Anesthesia, for examination, in women with developmental disabilities, 49–50
Anger, childhood sexual abuse and, 206
Anxiety, childhood sexual abuse and, 205, 206
Anxiolytics, for smoking cessation, 160
Aphasia, 51–52
ARBD. *See* Alcohol-related birth defect
ARND. *See* Alcohol-related neurodevelopmental disorder
Atopic dermatitis, in pediatric patients, 31
AUDIT questionnaire, 114*t*, 116
Autism, 42
Autonomic hyperreflexia, 45–46
Aversion therapy, for smoking cessation, 160

B

Bacterial vaginosis
  in children, 191
  in lesbians and bisexual women, 64
  sexual assault and, 191, 193*t*
Barbiturates, abuse of, 129–130, 132*t*–133*t*